Copyright and Collective Authorship

As technology makes it easier for people to work together, large-scale collaboration is becoming increasingly prevalent. In this context, the question of how to determine authorship – and hence ownership – of copyright in collaborative works is an important question to which current copyright law fails to provide a coherent or consistent answer. In Copyright and Collective Authorship, Daniela Simone engages with the problem of how to determine the authorship of highly collaborative works. Employing insights from the ways in which collaborators understand and regulate issues of authorship, the book argues that a recalibration of copyright law is necessary, proposing an inclusive and contextual approach to joint authorship that is true to the legal concept of authorship but is also more aligned with creative reality.

Dr. Daniela Simone is a Lecturer in Law at University College London, where she is also a Co-Director of the Institute of Brand and Innovation Law. Dr Simone holds BCL, MPhil and DPhil degrees from the University of Oxford. Prior to moving to the UK, she was awarded a BA/LLB (Hons I) degree from the University of Sydney, Australia, was admitted to the Supreme Court of New South Wales and worked as a lawyer for a global commercial law firm in Sydney.

Cambridge Intellectual Property and Information Law

As its economic potential has rapidly expanded, intellectual property has become a subject of front-rank legal importance. Cambridge Intellectual Property and Information Law is a series of monograph studies of major current issues in intellectual property. Each volume contains a mix of international, European, comparative and national law, making this a highly significant series for practitioners, judges and academic researchers in many countries.

Series Editors

Lionel Bently
Herchel Smith Professor of Intellectual Property Law, University of Cambridge

Graeme Dinwoodie
Professor of Intellectual Property and Information Technology Law, University of Oxford

Advisory Editors

William R. Cornish, *Emeritus Herchel Smith Professor of Intellectual Property Law, University of Cambridge*

François Dessemontet, *Professor of Law, University of Lausanne*

Jane C. Ginsburg, *Morton L. Janklow Professor of Literary and Artistic Property Law, Columbia Law School*

Paul Goldstein, *Professor of Law, Stanford University*

The Rt Hon. Sir Robin Jacob, *Hugh Laddie Professor of Intellectual Property, University College London*

Ansgar Ohly, *Professor of Intellectual Property Law, Ludwig-Maximilian University of Munich*

A list of books in the series can be found at the end of this volume.

Copyright and Collective Authorship

Locating the Authors of Collaborative Work

Daniela Simone

University College London

CAMBRIDGE
UNIVERSITY PRESS

University Printing House, Cambridge CB2 8BS, United Kingdom

One Liberty Plaza, 20th Floor, New York, NY 10006, USA

477 Williamstown Road, Port Melbourne, VIC 3207, Australia

314–321, 3rd Floor, Plot 3, Splendor Forum, Jasola District Centre, New Delhi – 110025, India

79 Anson Road, #06–04/06, Singapore 079906

Cambridge University Press is part of the University of Cambridge.

It furthers the University's mission by disseminating knowledge in the pursuit of education, learning, and research at the highest international levels of excellence.

www.cambridge.org
Information on this title: www.cambridge.org/9781107199958
DOI: 10.1017/9781108186070

© Daniela Simone 2019

The author asserts her moral rights, including the right to be identified as the author of this work.

This publication is in copyright. Subject to statutory exception and to the provisions of relevant collective licensing agreements, no reproduction of any part may take place without the written permission of Cambridge University Press.

First published 2019

Printed and bound in Great Britain by Clays Ltd, Elcograf S.p.A.

A catalogue record for this publication is available from the British Library.

Library of Congress Cataloging-in-Publication Data
Names: Simone, Daniela, 1983– author.
Title: Copyright and collective authorship : locating the authors of collaborative work / Daniela Simone , University College London.
Description: Cambridge [UK] ; new York, NY : Cambridge University Press, 2019. | Series: Cambridge intellectual property and information law | Includes bibliographical references.
Identifiers: LCCN 2018048870 | ISBN 9781107199958
Subjects: LCSH: Copyright. | Authorship. | Copyright – Art. | Wikipedia. | User-generated content – Law and legislation. | Electronic encyclopedias.
Classification: LCC K1440 .S56 2019 | DDC 346.04/82–dc23
LC record available at https://lccn.loc.gov/2018048870

ISBN 978-1-107-19995-8 Hardback

Cambridge University Press has no responsibility for the persistence or accuracy of URLs for external or third-party internet websites referred to in this publication and does not guarantee that any content on such websites is, or will remain, accurate or appropriate.

Contents

Acknowledgements	*page* viii
Abbreviations	x
Table of Cases	xii
Table of Statutes	xx

1	**Copyright Law and Collective Authorship**	**1**
	1.1 Introduction	1
	1.2 Methodological Approach	6
	1.3 A Roadmap	8
2	**Authorship and Joint Authorship**	**15**
	2.1 The Concept of Authorship in the CDPA	17
	2.2 The Joint Authorship Test	29
	2.2.1 A Contribution That Is Not Distinct	30
	2.2.2 Collaboration or Common Design	31
	2.2.3 A Significant Contribution of the Right Kind	35
	2.3 A Critique of the Application of the Joint Authorship Test	42
	2.3.1 Factual Specificity	43
	2.3.2 The Pragmatic Instrumental Approach	43
	2.3.3 A Preoccupation with Aesthetic Neutrality	50
	2.4 The Factual and the Normative Dimensions of the Joint Authorship Test	53
	2.5 Copyright Scholarship: Theories of Authorship	58
	2.5.1 The Romantic Author	59
	2.5.2 Ginsburg's Search for Copyright's Author	62
	2.5.3 Nimmer v Goldstein (and Beyond)	63
	2.5.4 The Value of Social and Cultural Conceptions of Authorship	67
	2.6 Conclusion	70
3	**Wikipedia**	**72**
	3.1 Authorship Dynamics: Promoting Sharing	73
	3.2 Copyright Subsistence on Wikipedia	78
	3.2.1 Is Wikipedia (or Parts Thereof) an Original Literary Work?	78
	3.2.2 Are Wikipedia Contributors Copyright Authors?	86
	3.3 Copyleft Licences and the Ambivalent Role of Copyright Law	90
	3.4 Insights for Copyright Law	95

v

4 Australian Indigenous Art — 100
- 4.1 Indigenous Art — 102
  - 4.1.1 Authorship Dynamics: Building and Sustaining Cultural Identity — 102
  - 4.1.2 Background to the Issue of Protecting Indigenous Cultural Expressions — 105
- 4.2 Protecting Indigenous Art with Copyright — 109
  - 4.2.1 Cases Prior to *Bulun Bulun* — 110
  - 4.2.2 Bulun Bulun — 112
  - 4.2.3 *Bulun Bulun*'s Limited Legacy — 115
- 4.3 Other Solutions for the Protection of Indigenous Cultural Expressions — 122
  - 4.3.1 Protocols and Codes of Conduct — 123
  - 4.3.2 Collective/Certification Trade Marks — 124
  - 4.3.3 Contract — 125
  - 4.3.4 Sui Generis Legislation — 126
- 4.4 Insights for Copyright Law — 127

5 Scientific Collaborations — 131
- 5.1 Authorship Dynamics: Constructing Authority — 132
- 5.2 Regulating Scientific Authorship with Private Ordering — 139
  - 5.2.1 Biomedical Science Collaborations: An Authorship Crisis — 139
  - 5.2.2 Particle Physics Collaborations: The Bureaucratisation of Authorship — 145
- 5.3 The Application of Copyright Law — 148
- 5.4 Insights for Copyright Law — 154

6 Film — 159
- 6.1 Authorship Dynamics: The Pragmatic Value of Authorship — 161
- 6.2 The Subsistence of Copyright — 169
  - 6.2.1 A Brief Historical Note — 170
  - 6.2.2 Explaining the Complexity of Film Copyright — 171
  - 6.2.3 Film as a First Fixation — 176
  - 6.2.4 Film as a Dramatic Work — 180
  - 6.2.5 The Pitfalls of Pragmatic Reasoning — 187
- 6.3 Private Ordering — 192
- 6.4 Insights for Copyright Law — 196

7 Characteristics of Collective Authorship and the Role of Copyright Law — 201
- 7.1 The Nature of Collective Authorship — 201
- 7.2 The Meaning of Authorship for Each Collective Authorship Group — 204
  - 7.2.1 Different Meanings of Authorship — 205
  - 7.2.2 Authorship Signifies Responsibility for the Work — 206
  - 7.2.3 Authorship Signals Status within a Particular Community — 208
  - 7.2.4 Power Dynamics Affect the Attribution of Authorship — 209
- 7.3 The Gap between Copyright Law's Assumptions about Authorship and Creative Reality — 210
- 7.4 Bridging the Gap between Copyright Law and Creative Reality with Private Ordering — 213
  - 7.4.1 Successful Examples — 213

	7.4.2 Less Successful Examples	215
	7.4.3 The Benefits and Limitations of Relying upon Private Ordering	216
7.5	The Role of Copyright Law and Its Concepts	224
7.6	Summary	229

8 **An Inclusive, Contextual Approach to the Joint Authorship Test**   231

    8.1 The Relevance of Social Norms   233
    8.2 The Dangers of Deferring to Social Norms   238
    8.3 A Framework for Considering Social Norms   241
    8.4 Revisiting the Critique of the Joint Authorship Test   246
        8.4.1 Factual Specificity   246
        8.4.2 The Preoccupation with Aesthetic Neutrality   246
        8.4.3 The Pragmatic Instrumental Approach   247
    8.5 An Inclusive and Contextual Approach to the Joint Authorship Test   250
    8.6 Alternative Approaches to Joint Ownership   256
        8.6.1 The Current Approach to Joint Ownership   257
        8.6.2 A View from the United States   262
        8.6.3 A Proposal for a Modest Legislative Amendment   266
    8.7 Final Note   269

Bibliography   273
Index   294

Acknowledgements

This book would not have been possible without the support of many people. I owe a great debt of gratitude to Graeme Dinwoodie, who supervised my DPhil thesis, for his formidable expertise, great generosity, unwavering support and dynamism. Also to Mireille van Eechoud and Dev Gangjee who made the viva voce examination a thought-provoking and enjoyable experience, which has been a great resource in shaping this book.

I have been fortunate to be able to develop my ideas as a result of lively discussions with many scholars and friends. I am grateful for feedback from participants at the Intellectual Property Scholars Conference (DePaul University, 2011); the Authorship Dynamics and the Dynamic Work HERA Workshop (University of Cambridge, 2012); the Oxford Intellectual Property Discussion Group (2014) and graduate conferences at Queen Mary, King's College London and Oxford. Observations great and small from a number of intellectual property scholars have helped enormously in the development of this book, in particular, the anonymous reviewers of the manuscript, Isabella Alexander, Tanya Aplin, Barton Beebe, Lionel Bently, Laura Biron, Catherine Bond, Kathy Bowrey, Christopher Buccafusco, Robert Burrell, Pascale Chapdelaine, Elena Cooper, Giuseppina D'Agostino, Richard Danbury, Séverine Dusollier, Ilanah Fhima, Matt Fisher, Michael Fraser, Robert Gomulkiewicz, Jonathan Griffiths, Michael Handler, Emily Hudson, Marta Iljadica, Sir Robin Jacob, Phillip Johnson, Barbara Lauriat, Yin Harn Lee, Brigitte Lindner, Luke McDonagh, Poorna Mysoor, Justine Pila, Graham Reynolds, Mark Rose, Uma Suthersanen, Dilan Thampapillai, David Vaver and Kimberlee Weatherall.

I would be remiss not to thank the members of the Oxford Intellectual Property Research Centre, the fantastic group of intellectual property doctoral students at the University of Oxford and members of the Oxford Law Faculty for many conversations on fine points of copyright law as well as broader philosophical issues. Whilst at Oxford, I also benefited from the support and assistance of many scholars, administrators and librarians at the Faculty of Law, Worcester College and the International Office.

I am particularly grateful to the University of Sydney for a visiting period in March–April 2017, which allowed me to make useful progress on this book and to discuss my work with some of Sydney's vibrant intellectual property community. I am thankful to the Arts Law Centre of Australia, especially Robyn Ayres and Alida Stanley, for useful discussions about the protection of Indigenous art in the early stages of this project.

The difficult task of turning a thesis into a book was made immeasurably easier by research assistance and attentive proof-reading from the wonderful Lynne Chave, as well as the support and guidance of many colleagues and friends at University College London.

I would like to express my gratitude to the many extraordinary teachers who have encouraged and inspired me over the years, particularly, Deirdre Coleman, Elaine Moore, Mary Crock, Peter Gerangelos, Hilary Astor, and Patricia Loughlan.

To Mum and Dad, your selfless love created the many opportunities with which my life has been blessed. Thank you for being a constant source of strength and support. Mike and Tonia (Leo and Olivia); Nick and Steph; Cath – thank you so much for your love, support and encouragement at every difficult turn. Thanks to my grandparents; to Juliet, Peter, Chris; and Sr Teresita for their thoughtfulness and kind prayers. To Alicia, Amanda, Annie, Bipana, Chloe, Erie, Jen, Laura, Leo, Maria, Megan, Nahal, Natasa, Rani, Sam, Sarah, Tania and Vasiliki - a big thank you for sharing the ups and downs of this project with me. I very much appreciate the kindness and hospitality of Cristina, Luciano, Alessandro and friends in Genoa. Finally, words cannot adequately express my gratitude to Andrea, who has been there on every step of this journey, rigorously challenging my ideas and always believing in me.

***

Some of the research this book draws upon has been published in an earlier form: 'Copyright or Copyleft? Wikipedia as a Turning Point for Authorship' (2014) 25(1) King's LJ 102, 'Dreaming Authorship: Copyright Law and the Protection of Indigenous Cultural Expressions' (2015) 37(4) EIPR 240 and 'Recalibrating the Joint Authorship Test: Insights from Scientific Collaborations' (2013) 26(1) IPJ 111.

The law is stated as at 1 September 2018.

Abbreviations

1911 Act	Copyright Act 1911
1956 Act	Copyright Act 1956
Bently et al.	L Bently, B Sherman, D Gangjee and P Johnson, *Intellectual Property Law* (OUP 2018)
Berne	Berne Convention for the Protection of Literary and Artistic Works of 9 September 1886
Copinger et al.	KM Garnett, G Davies, G Harbottle, WA Copinger and EP Skone James, *Copinger and Skone James on Copyright* (16th edn, Sweet & Maxwell 2011)
Cornish et al.	W Cornish, D Llewelyn and T Aplin, *Intellectual Property: Patents, Copyright, Trade Marks and Allied Rights* (8th edn, Sweet & Maxwell 2013)
CDPA	Copyright Designs and Patents Act 1988
Database Directive	Directive 96/9/EC of the European Parliament and of the Council of 11 March 1996 on the Legal Protection of Databases
Gregory Report	'Report of the Board of Trade Copyright Committee' (Her Majesty's Stationery Company October 1952) Cmd 8662
InfoSoc Directive	Directive 2001/29/EC of the European Parliament and of the Council of 22 May 2001 on the harmonisation of certain aspects of copyright and related rights in the information society
IPQ	Intellectual Property Quarterly
JIPLP	Journal of Intellectual Property Law and Practice
Laddie et al.	H Laddie, P Prescott and M Vitoria, *The Modern Law of Copyright and Designs* (4th edn, LexisNexis 2011)

Rental and Related Rights Directive	Directive 2006/115/EC of the European Parliament and of the Council of 12 December 2006 on rental right and lending right and on certain rights related to copyright in the field of intellectual property (codified version) (replacing Council Directive 92/100/EEC of 19 November 1992 on rental and lending right and on certain rights relating to copyright in the field of intellectual property)
Senate Report	Australian Senate Standing Committee on Environment, Communications, Information Technology and the Arts, *Indigenous Art – Securing the Future: Australia's Indigenous Visual Arts and Craft Sector* (June 2007)
Term Directive	Directive 2006/116/EC of the European Parliament and of the Council of 12 December 2006 on the term of protection of copyright and related rights (codified version) (repealing and replacing Council Directive 93/98/EEC of 29 October 1993 harmonizing the term of protection of copyright and certain related rights)
TRIPS	Agreement on Trade-Related Aspects of Intellectual Property Rights 1994

Table of Cases

Note: Locators followed by 'n' denote a reference in the footnotes to the text.

United Kingdom

Abraham Moon v Thornber [2012] EWPCC 37, [2013] FSR 17, 24n49, 25n51, 26n70
Adventure Film Productions v Tully [1993] EMLR 376 (Ch), 177n123
Anacon v Environmental Research [1994] FSR 359 (Ch), 175n109
Anya v Wu [2004] EWCA Civ 755, 148n95, 150n105, 154n126, 155n127, 222n86
Baigent v Random House Group [2006] EWHC 719, [2006] EMLR 16, 81n55
Baigent v Random House Group [2007] EWCA Civ 247, [2008] EMLR 7, 81n55
Bamgboye v Reed [2002] EWHC 2922, [2004] 5 EMLR 61, 25n54, 27n78, 28n83, 32n102, 33n106, 33n107, 37n131, 37n134, 40, 40n152, 44n172, 48n193, 56n242, 87n85, 138n49, 156n130, 209n25, 258n158
Beckingham v Hodgens [2002] EWHC 2143 (Ch), [2002] EMLR 45, 30, 30n90, 31n95, 33, 33n106, 35n118, 35n119, 37, 37n128, 37n132, 44n171, 47n187, 47n189, 52, 56n243, 88, 89, 156n130, 183n165, 185n176, 257n154, 258n157, 260n173
Beckingham v Hodgens [2003] EWCA Civ 143, [2003] EMLR 18, 30n90, 32, 32–33n104, 33, 33n106, 88, 89, 150n102, 156n130, 182n164, 251n121
Beechwood House Publishing t/a Binley's v Guardian Products [2010] EWPCC 1200, 85n73
Beggars Banquet Records v Carlton Television [1993] EMLR 349 (Ch), 177n124
Biotrading and Financing Oy v Biohit [1996] FSR 393 (Ch), 80n45, 80n46
Biotrading and Financing Oy v Biohit [1998] FSR 109 (CA), 80n45, 80n46

Table of Cases

Blacklock v Peterson [1915] 2 Ch 376, 22n33

BP Refinery (Westernport) Pty Ltd v President, Councillors and Ratepayers of the Shire of Hastings (1977) 52 ALJR 20, (1977) 180 CLR 266 (PC), 114n66, 261n174

Brighton v Jones [2004] EWHC 1157, [2005] FSR 288, 26n63, 31n96, 32, 32n99, 32n101, 38n141, 39n144, 40, 41, 41n153, 43n164, 45, 46n184, 46–47n185, 47, 47n186, 47n187, 48n192, 79n40, 117n82, 148n96, 158n138, 182n163, 183n168, 183n169, 185n178, 260n173, 262n182

Brown v Mcasso [2005] FSR 846 (EWPCC), 30n92, 32n102, 33n106, 35n117, 37, 37n131, 37n133, 43n164, 52, 56n242, 56n244, 87n85, 209n25

Brown v Mcasso [2005] EWCA Civ 1546, [2006] FSR 480, 35n117

Brutus v Cozens [1973] AC 854 (HL), 57n247

Cala Homes v Alfred McAlpine Homes [1995] EWHC 7, [1995] FSR 818, 20n22, 30n92, 36n127, 39n147, 40n151, 41, 41n154, 41n155, 42, 50n205, 62, 63, 80n44, 86n78, 118, 118n85, 119n86, 119n89, 148n97, 157, 157n132, 157n135, 207, 207n19, 255, 258n161

Cescinsky v Routledge [1916] 2 KB 325, 258n162, 259n167, 259n169, 263n192

Century Communications v Mayfair Entertainment [1993] EMLR 335, 177n124

Chapman v Smith (1754) 2 Ves Sen 506, 28 ER 324 (Ch), 244n84

Chappell v Redwood Music [1980] 2 All ER 817, [1981] RPC 337 (HL), 184n172

Coffey v Warner/Chappell Music [2005] EWHC 449 (Ch), [2005] FSR 34, 57n248, 84n65, 176n111, 252n127

Confetti Records v Warner Music UK Ltd [2003] EWHC 1274 (Ch), 262n183

Creation Records v News Group Newspapers [1997] EMLR 444 (Ch), 109n38, 172, 173n93

Cummins v Bond (1926) 1 Ch 167, 20, 248n104

Designers Guild Ltd v Russell Williams (Textiles) Ltd [2001] 1 WLR 2416, [2001] FSR 11, 36n126

Donoghue v Allied Newspapers [1938] 1 Ch 106 (Ch), 26n61, 32n99, 41n153, 41n158, 48n196, 86n77, 117n82, 148n96, 148n98, 157n135, 184n175

Dramatico Entertainment v British Sky Broadcasting [2012] EWHC 268, [2012] RPC 27, 180n150

Elanco Products v Mandops (Agrochemical Specialists) [1980] RPC 213 (CA), 22n33, 80n49

Electronic Techniques v Critchley [1997] FSR 401 (Ch), 175n109

Express Newspapers Plc v News (UK) Ltd [1991] FSR 36 (Ch), 261n175
Exxon v Exxon Insurance [1982] Ch 119 (CA), 22n34, 52n220, 78–79n37
Fisher v Brooker and Onward Music [2006] EWHC 3239, [2007] FSR (12) 255, 32n102, 35, 37n133, 56, 56n244, 87, 209n25
Fisher v Brooker [2009] UKHL 41, [2009] 1 WLR 1764, 44n172, 138n49, 183n166, 258n158, 260n173
Football Association Premier League v Panini UK [2004] FSR 1 (CA), 173n93
Football Association Premier League v QC Leisure (No 2) [2008] EWHC 1411 (Ch), 177n120
Football League v Littlewoods Pools [1959] Ch 637, 22n33
Francis Day and Hunter v 20th Century Fox [1940] AC 112 (PC), 78–79n37
Fylde Microsystems v Key Radio Systems [1998] FSR 449 (Ch), 26n64, 32n99, 35n119, 39n145, 40n149, 46–47n185, 52n221, 86, 113n61, 148n96, 157n137, 185
George Hensher v Restawile Upholstery [1976] AC 64 (HL), 51n210, 51n211
Godfrey v Lees [1995] EMLR 307 (Ch), 29n89, 35n116, 35n118, 46n184, 50n205, 81n53, 86n76, 87n85, 138n48, 260n173, 262n181
Green v Broadcasting Corp New Zealand [1989] 2 All ER 1056, 80n46, 180n146
Griggs v Evans [2003] EWHC 2914 (Ch), [2004] FSR 31, 192n222, 261n178
Hadley v Kemp [1999] EMLR 589 (Ch), 26n63, 29n89, 30n90, 32n99, 32n100, 32n101, 36n127, 37, 37n132, 38n140, 39n143, 39n148, 40, 45, 45n179, 46n184, 46–47n185, 47, 47n186, 48n191, 48n192, 52n223, 56n243, 86n76, 86n79, 121n98, 156n130, 157n136, 158n138, 182n163, 185n176, 235n22
Hatton v Kean (1859) 7 CB NS 268, 141 ER 819, 40n149, 40n151, 45n178, 248n104
Hayes v Phonogram [2002] EWHC 2062 (Ch), [2003] ECDR 11, 35n118, 42n161, 47n187
Hollinrake v Truswell [1894] 3 Ch 420 (CA), 52, 78–79n37
Hughes v Paxman [2007] RPC 2, 267n214
Interlego v Tyco Industries [1989] AC 217 (PC), 26n67, 79n39, 80n46, 81n51, 118n85, 217n52, 235n21
IPC Media v Highbury-Leisure Publishing [2004] EWHC 2985, [2005] FSR 20, 57n248, 80n46, 81n53, 84n65, 176n111
Kelly v Cinema Houses Ltd [1928–35] MCC 362, 172n83
Kenrick v Lawrence (1890) 25 QBD 99, 113n61, 119n86
King Features Syndicate v O and M Kleeman [1941] AC 417 (HL), 172n84
LA Gear v Hi-Tec Sports [1992] FSR 121 (CA), 79

Ladbroke v William Hill [1964] 1 WLR 273, [1964] 1 All ER 465 (HL), 22n33, 24n48, 78n36

Lauri v Renad [1892] 3 Ch 402, 44n170, 257, 257n154, 258n156, 258n161

Levy v Rutley (1871) LR 6 CP 523, (1871) 24 LT 621, 31, 31n95, 32, 32n103, 45, 45n178, 80n47, 88n86, 149n100

L'Oréal v Bellure [2007] EWCA Civ 968, 22n34, 25n58

Lucasfilm v Ainsworth [2008] EWHC 1878, [2009] FSR 103, 26n67, 51, 51n218, 171n82, 172, 173, 173n92, 174, 174n99, 175n105, 182n159, 184, 190n209

Lucasfilm v Ainsworth [2009] EWCA Civ 1328, [2010] Ch 503, 173n92, 173n96, 253n130, 261n177

Lucasfilm v Ainsworth [2011] UKSC 39, [2012] 1 AC 208, 173, 173n96, 253n130

MacMillan v Cooper (1924) 40 TLR 186 (PC), 81, 81n52

MacMillan Publishers v Thomas Reed Publications [1993] FSR 455 (Ch), 82, 89, 97n132, 243n75

Mail Newspapers v Express Newspapers [1987] FSR 90 (Ch), 44n170, 257n155

Martin v Kogan [2017] EWHC 2927 (IPEC), 25n52, 31n96, 32n99, 35n117, 36, 37n136, 38n139, 39, 39n147, 40, 42, 42n161, 47n186, 48n193, 56, 67n299, 87n81, 88, 150n103, 157n133, 182n164, 183n168

Massine v de Basil [1936–45] MCC 223 (CA), 261n177

Mei Fields Designs v Saffron Cards and Gifts [2018] EWHC 1332, 25n53

Merchandising Corporation of America v Harpbond [1983] FSR 32 (CA), 109n38, 172n85

Millar v Taylor (1769) 4 Burr 2303, 98 ER 201 (Ct of KB), 244n82

Minder Music v Sharples [2015] EWHC 1454, 35n119, 42n161

Mirage Studios v Counter-Feat Clothing [1991] FSR 145 (Ch), 172n84

Moyna v Secretary of State for Work and Pensions [2003] UKHL 44, [2003] 1 WLR 1929, 57n247

Newspaper Licensing Agency v Meltwater [2011] EWCA 890, 23n43, 24n48, 78–79n37

Noah v Shuba [1991] FSR 14 (Ch), 150n105, 151n107, 155n127, 222n86, 250n118

Norowzian v Arks (No 1) [1998] FSR 394 (Ch), 51, 51n217, 176n114, 177n120, 181, 184

Norowzian v Arks (No 2) [2000] FSR 363 (CA), 160n7, 175n105, 180, 180n145, 181, 181n152, 198

Nova Productions Limited v Mazooma Games [2006] EWHC24, 180n147

Nova Productions Limited v Mazooma Games [2007] EWCA Civ 219, [2007] RPC 25, 180n147

O'Neill v Paramount [1983] CAT 235, 172n83
Powell v Head (1879) 12 Ch D 686, 44n173, 257n154, 258n161, 258n162, 259n168, 263n191
R v Higgs [2008] EWCA 1324, [2009] 1 WLR 73, 177n120
Redwood Music v Chappell (1982) RPC 109 (QB), 30–31n94, 80n48
Rexnold v Ancon [1983] FSR 245 (HC), 80n46
Robin Ray v Classic FM [1998] FSR 622 (Ch), 20n22, 29n89, 39n147, 41, 41n156, 48n196, 79n40, 86n76, 86n78, 117n82, 119n89, 148, 156n131, 157n132, 157n133, 192n222, 261n174, 261n178
Samuelson v Producers Distributing [1932] 1 Ch 201, (1932) 48 RPC 580, 55n240, 221n79
SAS Institute Inc v World Programming Ltd [2013] EWHC 69 (Ch), 26n70
SAS Institute v World Programming [2013] EWCA Civ 1482, [2014] RPC 8, 17n5, 24, 24n50, 36n126
Sandman v Panasonic [1998] FSR 651 (Ch), 175n109
Sawkins v Hyperion Records [2005] EWCA 565, [2005] 1 WLR 3281, 26n66, 50n207, 51, 81n51, 81n54, 117n80, 118n85, 121n98, 217n52, 235n21
Shelley Films v Rex Features [1994] EMLR 134, 172
Slater v Wimmer [2012] EWPCC 7, 177n125, 177n126, 178, 179n135, 198, 198n262, 198n264, 199n265, 254n138, 258
Spelling Goldberg Productions v BPC Publishing [1981] RPC 283 (CA), 176, 177n120
Springfield v Thame (1903) 89 LT 242 (Ch), 31
Stuart v Barrett [1994] EMLR 448 (Ch), 35n118, 37n135, 42n161, 44n171, 48n191, 50n205, 86n79, 87n83, 87n85, 257n154, 258n157
Sweeney v Macmillan Publishers [2002] RPC 35 (Ch), 80n43, 80n44
Tate v Fullbrook [1908] 1 KB 821 (CA), 41n159, 184n175, 185n178
Tate v Thomas [1921] 1 Ch 503, 41n159, 185n178
Taylor v Maguire [2013] EWHC 3804, [2014] ECDR 4, 24n49, 25n51
Taylor v Rive Droite Music [2004] EWHC 1605, [2004] All ER 88, 79n41
Temple Island Collections v New English Teas [2012] EWPCC 1, [2012] All ER 49, 24n49, 25n51, 185n181
The Reject Shop v Manners [1995] FSR 870 (DC), 79n39
Ultra Marketing v Universal Components [2004] EWHC 468, [2004] All ER 229, 80n45
University of London Press v University Tutorial Press [1916] 2 Ch 601 (Ch), 20, 22n33, 24n48, 78n36
Walter v Lane [1900] AC 539 (HL), 20n23, 20n24, 26n62, 62n271
Waterlow Directories v Reed Information Services [1992] FSR 409 (Ch), 22n33
Wiseman v George Weidenfeld & Nicolson Ltd [1985] FSR 525 (Ch), 46–47n185, 52n222, 55n240, 149n100, 221n79

Table of Cases   xvii

European Union

C-203/02 *British Horseracing Board v William Hill* [2004] ECR I-10415, [2005] RPC 260, 85, 85n73
C-444/02 *Fixtures Marketing Ltd v Organismos Prognostikon Agonon Podosfairou AE* [2004] ECR I-10549, 84n68, 84n69, 85n72
C-545/07 *Apis-Hirstovich EOOD v Ladorka AD* [2009] ECR I-1627, 84n68
C-5/08 *Infopaq International v Danske Dagblades Forening* [2009] ECR I-6569, 5n25, 17n5, 19, 22-25, 22n35, 22n36, 23n42, 24n47, 26n68, 36, 36n126, 39n142, 57, 57n249, 78n36, 78–79n37, 81, 81n56, 83, 83n63, 144n80, 173n93, 175, 217n52
C-403/08 and C-429/08 *Football Association Premier League v QC Leisure* [2012] 1 CMLR 29, [2012] ECDR 8, 23n40, 24n47, 26, 26n65, 177n120, 180n149
C-393/09 *Bezpecnostn'ı softwarová asociace v Ministerstvo Kultury (BSA)* [2011] ECDR 3, [2011] FSR 18, 23n39, 23n42, 24n47, 25n56, 26, 26n65
C-145/10 *Painer v Standard Verlags* [2012] ECDR 6, 23n42, 25n51, 25n56, 27n71, 63n274, 81n56, 185n181
C-277/10 *Luksan v Van der Let* [2013] ECDR 5, 19n15
C-604/10 *Football Dataco v Yahoo! UK* [2012] ECDR 10, 23, 23n41, 23n42, 23n43, 24n50, 85n74
C-310/17 *Levola Hengelo BV v Smilde Foods BV* EU:C:2018:899, 5n25, 24n47, 176n110

Australia

Aboriginal Sacred Sites Protection Authority v Maurice; Re the Warumbingu Land Claim [1986] FCA 90, (1986) 10 FCR 104 (Fed. Ct. of Australia), 122n104
Acohs v Ucorp [2010] FCA 57 (Fed. Ct. of Australia); [2012] FCAFC 16 (Full Fed. Ct. of Australia), 30n90, 34n114, 100–101n1
Aristocrat Leisure Industries v Pacific Gaming [2000] FCA 1273 (Fed. Ct. of Australia), 121n97
Australian Competition and Consumer Commission v Australian Dreamtime Creations [2009] FCA 1545 (Fed. Ct. of Australia), 122n108
Australian Competition and Consumer Commission v Nooravi [2008] FCA 2021 (Fed. Ct. of Australia), 122n108
BP Refinery (Westernport) Pty Ltd v Hastings Shire Council (1977) 180 CLR 266 (PC), 114n66, 261n174
Bulun Bulun v Nejlam Investments (unreported, Fed. Ct. of Australia, Darwin 1989), 103n12, 110n42

Bulun Bulun v R & T Textiles (1998) 86 FCR 244 (Fed. Ct. of Australia), 43n165, 101, 109, 112-122, 128-130, 207, 207n19, 228, 255, 255n144
Burge v Swarbrick [2007] HCA 17 (High Court of Australia), 50n208
Foster v Mountford [1976] 29 FLR 233 (NT SC), 122n100, 122n104
IceTV Pty Ltd v Nine Network Australia Pty Ltd [2009] HCA 14, (2009) 239 CLR 458 (High Court of Australia), 5n23, 100–101n1, 117n83
Kalamazoo v Compact Business Systems (1983) 5 IPR 213 (Qld SC), 120n96
Milpurrurru v Indofurn Pty Ltd (1994) 54 FCR 240 (Fed. Ct. of Australia), 104n14, 109n35, 110–112, 111n50, 113, 116n78, 122n102, 128, 202n4
Milwell v Olympic Amusement (1999) 85 FCR 436 (Full Fed. Ct. of Australia), 34n114, 119n86, 121n97
Neowarra v Western Australia [2003] FCA 1402 (Fed. Ct. of Australia), 114n63
Primary Healthcare v Federal Commissioner of Taxation [2010] FCA 419 (Fed. Ct. of Australia), 30n90, 100–101n1
Prior v Lansdowne Press [1977] RPC 511, [1977] FLR 59 (Vic SC), 44n171, 149n100, 258n157, 258n161
Sega Enterprises v Galaxy Electronics (1996) 35 IPR 161, (1997) 37 IPR 462 (Fed. Ct. of Australia), 120–121, 120n96, 121n97
Stevens v Kabushiki Kaisha Sony Computer Entertainment [2005] HCA 54, 224 CLR 193 (High Court of Australia), 121n97
Telstra v Phone Directories [2010] FCA 44 (Fed. Ct. of Australia), [2010] FCAFC 149 (Full Fed. Ct. of Australia), 2n12, 5n23, 34n114, 43n165, 82n61, 100–101n1, 117n83, 122n100
Western Australia v Ward [2002] HCA 28, (2002) 213 CLR 1 (High Court of Australia), 114n63
Victoria Park Racing & Recreation Grounds Co Ltd v Taylor [1937] HCA 45, (1937) 58 CLR 479 (High Court of Australia), 22n34
Yumbulul v Reserve Bank of Australia [1991] FCA 332, 21 IPR 481 (Fed. Ct. of Australia), 109n35, 110, 110n43, 112, 126n132, 129n142, 220n70, 249n111

United States

16 Casa Duse v Merkin 791 F3d 247 (2d Cir, 2015), 64n282, 66, 66n294, 190–191, 191n215
Aalmuhammed v Lee 202 F3d 1227 (9th Cir, 2000), 5n23, 34n111, 45n175, 64n280, 64n282, 65, 65n290, 187–191, 198, 199, 199n265, 262n189
Bridgeman Art Library v Corel 36 F Supp 2d 191 (SDNY, 1999), 117n80

Carter v Bailey 64 Me 458 (SC of Maine, 1874), 34n111, 262n184, 262n188, 263n190
Childress v Taylor 945 F2d 500 (US CA 2nd Cir, 1991), 32–33n104, 33n109, 38n138, 64n282
Chou v University of Chicago 254 F3d 1347 (Fed Cir, 2001), 143n77, 150n105
Erickson v Trinity Theatre 13 F3d 1061 (7th Cir, 1994), 38n138, 64n282
Feist Publications Inc v Rural Telephone Service (1991) 499 US 340 (USSC), 144n80
Gaiman v McFarlane 360 F3d 644 (7th Cir, 2004), 38n138, 65n292
Garcia v Google 743 F3d 1258 (9th Cir, 2014), 786 F3d 733 (9th Cir, 2015), 5n23, 117n82, 189-191, 189n198, 191n214, 192n220, 198
Jacobsen v Katzer 535 F 3d 1373 (US CA Fed Cir, 2008), 91–92
Johnson v Schmitz 119 FSupp 2d 90 (D Conn, 2000), 143n77, 150n105
Nichols v Universal Pictures 45 F2d 119 (2nd Cir, 1930), 172n83
Pullman-Standard v Swint (1982) 456 US 273 (USSC), 53n229
Thomson v Larson 147 F3d 195 (2d Cir, 1998), 33n110, 34n111, 38n138, 65
Weissmann v Freeman 684 FSupp 1248 (SDNY, 1988), 868 F2d 1313 (2nd Cir, 1989), 151–153, 154n126, 155, 155n127, 209, 222n86

Other Jurisdictions

Carlos RL v Javier AA and Maria Cruz DA [2002] ECDR 23 (Madrid CA 12th Section, Spain), 149n101
Case II CSK 527/10, 22 June 2010 (Polish SC), 255n141
Elisha Qimron v Hershel Shanks [1993] 7 EIPR D-157 (Israeli SC), 81n54
Fabrikant c. Swamy (2011) QCCS 1385 (Superior Court of Quebec, Canada), 151n107
Heptulla v Orient Longman [1989] 1 FSR 598 (Indian High Court), 40n151, 41n158, 50n205, 157n135
Land Transport Safety Authority of New Zealand v Glogau [1999] 1 NZLR 261 (Wellington CA, New Zealand), 34n114
Neudorf (Darryl) v Nettwerk Productions [2000] RPC 935 (British Columbia SC, Canada), 32–33n104

Table of Statutes

UK
Copyright Act 1911, 100, 170, 170n71, 185
Copyright Act 1956, 27, 30, 30n92, 30–31n94, 100–101n1, 170, 170n73, 170n75, 171n80, 180n143, 183n167
Copyright Designs and Patents Act 1988, 2n11, 9, 13, 14, 15–19, 24n47, 25n57, 26, 26n70, 27–29, 42, 44, 48, 49n197, 49n202, 51, 51n216, 52, 54, 55, 61n261, 62, 63n276, 70, 73, 78, 84, 84n68, 85n70, 86, 86n76, 89, 92, 96, 100, 100–101n1, 148, 159, 160, 164, 169, 170, 172n87, 173, 173n93, 175, 175n109, 179, 181, 185n176, 186, 197, 204n12, 207n20, 208, 211, 217, 218, 221, 223, 228, 238n43, 240, 247, 248, 251, 254, 257–259, 259n167, 266, 267n214, 268n221, 269, 271, 272n231
Dramatic Copyright Act 1833, 41n159, 170n71, 185n178
Fine Arts Copyright Act 1862, 170n71
Interpretation Act 1978, 259n167
Law of Property Act 1925, 264n202, 265n203, 265n204
Patents Act 1977, 259n165, 267n214
Trustee Act 1925, 264n202, 265n205
Trustee Act 2000, 265n205
Trusts of Land and Trustees Appointment Act 1997, 265n205

Europe
92/100/EEC Rental and Related Rights Directive 1992, 19n15, 27n76, 176n113
93/98/EEC Term Directive 1993, 19n15, 23n38, 27n76, 170n76, 176n113, 179n141
96/9/EC Database Directive 1996, 19n15, 23n38, 25n57, 84, 84n66, 85n70
2001/29/EC Information Society Directive 2001, 22, 24n50
2009/24/EC Computer Programs Directive 2009, 19n15

Australia

Competition and Consumer Amendment (Exploitation of Indigenous Culture) Bill 2017 (Cth), 123
Copyright Amendment (Indigenous Communal Moral Rights) Bill (Draft) 2003 (Cth), 108n30, 123, 123n110
Copyright Act 1968 (Cth), 100, 111n51, 113, 117n83, 119
Native Title Act 1993 (Cth), 112n57, 113n62
Resale Royalty Right for Visual Artists Act 2009 (Cth), 123n109
Trade Marks Act 1995 (Cth), 124n117

Other Jurisdictions

Agreement on Trade-Related Aspects of Intellectual Property Rights 1994, 18n13
Berne Convention for the Protection of Literary and Artistic Works of 9 September 1886, 18, 18n11, 18n12, 23, 26n70, 28n81, 181, 272
Copyright Act 1976 (US) (United States Code, Title 17), 28n82, 30n93, 33, 63n276, 65n283, 88n91, 189n199, 190n206, 262n185, 263n192
Pacific Model Law (Model for the Protection of Traditional Knowledge and Expressions of Culture 2002), 127n139

1 Copyright Law and Collective Authorship

1.1 Introduction

Large-scale collaboration is becoming increasingly widespread and is now a prominent feature of the economic and cultural landscape.[1] This is due, in large part, to advances in digital and communications technology which have made it easier than ever before for people to work together. The most iconic symbol of modern collaboration, Wikipedia, averages 515 new articles per day.[2] Thousands of contributors collaborate in adding to, editing and contesting Wikipedia's content – in June 2018, for example, each article on Wikipedia had been edited, on average, 98 times.[3] Contemporary examples of large-scale collaboration are numerous[4] (consider: open source software, 'citizen science' projects, and the crowdsourcing of architectural designs,[5] films,[6] books,[7]

---

[1] D Tapscott and A Williams, *Wikinomics: How Mass Collaboration Changes Everything* (Atlantic Books 2008); K Sawyer, *Group Genius: The Creative Power of Collaboration* (Basic Books 2007) 15; K Sawyer, *Explaining Creativity: The Science of Human Innovation* (OUP 2nd ed 2012) 231–233; MM Biro, 'Smart Leaders and the Power of Collaboration', *Forbes* (3 March 2013) <www.forbes.com/sites/meghanbiro/2013/03/03/smart-leaders-and-the-power-of-collaboration>; 'The Collaborative Economy: Impact and Potential of Collaborative Internet and Additive Manufacturing' (Science and Technology Options Assessment Panel Study, European Parliament, PE 547.425, Dec 2015) <www.europarl.europa.eu/thinktank/fr/ document.html?reference=EPRS_S TU(2015)547425>. All websites referred to in this book were last accessed on 17 August 2018 unless otherwise stated.

[2] <en.wikipedia.org/wiki/Wikipedia:Statistics> (considering only the English language version of Wikipedia).

[3] <stats.wikimedia.org/EN/TablesWikipediaEN.htm>. At the time of writing, 120,446 contributors had performed an edit within the previous 30 days: <en.wikipedia.org/wiki/Wikipedia:Wikipedians>.

[4] There are countless tools that facilitate such collaboration, from the wiki software that Wikipedia uses to a more a generic tool, such as Amazon's Mechanical Turk, which provides a platform for the distribution of small tasks to many workers at low prices: <www.mturk.com/mturk/welcome>.

[5] For example: <www.arcbazar.com>. [6] For example: <www.userfarm.com/en>.

[7] Such as the cookbook <www.gooseberrypatch.com> or the novel 'One Million Penguins' described at <fanfiction.wikia.com/wiki/A_Million_Penguins>.

advertising,[8] and 3D printer product designs, to name just a few). Indeed, some suggest that collaborative efforts may now have become the paradigmatic form of creativity.[9] Although collaborative creativity is by no means new, large-scale collaboration, or collective authorship, creates unique challenges (as well as opportunities).[10] This book is concerned with the challenges that collective authorship poses to copyright law.[11]

In today's information economy, intellectual property law is of fundamental importance. It provides the main set of rules governing the allocation of property-style rights in a broad array of intellectual products. In this context, the question of how to determine the authorship, and hence the first ownership of copyright, in works created by groups of people requires urgent attention. Yet, copyright law does not provide a coherent or consistent answer to this question. In the UK there have been no cases explicitly considering the authorship of works created by large numbers of potential authors.[12] The copyright case law on joint authorship is confined to situations involving disputes between only a few contributors, and scholars have observed that the reasoning adopted in many such cases lacks the analytical clarity necessary to provide general guidance.[13] This is the first book to engage with the problem of determining the authorship of works of collective authorship from a copyright law point of view.

---

[8] For example: <www.victorsandspoils.com>.
[9] A Bell and G Parchomovsky, 'Copyright Trust' (2015) 100 Cornell LRev 1015.
[10] In their best-selling book, *Wikinomics*, Tapscott and Williams (n1) 31–33 make the bold claim that 'mass collaboration changes everything'. They identify a fundamental shift in the way that work and innovation are conducted, which they foresee will ultimately transform the current economic system – arguing that businesses must 'collaborate or perish'.
[11] Throughout the book, a work of 'collective authorship' refers to any work that is created by many contributors. It is not intended to be confined by the meaning of 'collective work' in s178 of the Copyright Designs and Patents Act 1988 ('CDPA'), although most works of collective authorship are likely to fall within this definition. 'Collective' is preferred to 'collaborative' to avoid confusion when considering which contributors might be joint authors of such a work for copyright law's purposes (given that collaboration is a requirement for joint authorship). The term 'group authorship' has been avoided, as it might seem to imply cohesion between contributors, which is unnecessarily under-inclusive.
[12] There have been a number of cases considering the joint authorship of film in the USA: 2.5.3, 6.2.5. The question has also arisen in Australia, for example, *Telstra v Phone Directories* [2010] FCA 44, [2010] FCAFC 149 (joint authorship of a telephone directory, largely compiled using computer software with some human input not established).
[13] L Zemer, 'Contribution and Collaborations in Joint Authorship: Too Many Misconceptions' (2006) 1(4) JIPLP 283; A Stokes, 'Authorship, Collaboration and Copyright a View from the UK' (2002) Entertainment LRev 121.

The book offers a comprehensive analysis of copyright law's concept of authorship and, in particular, joint authorship. This analysis provides the doctrinal foundation upon which the book's general argument – that copyright law's joint authorship test needs to be recalibrated for the digital age – is constructed. In addressing the question of how copyright law ought to determine the authorship of collaborative work, the book primarily follows an inductive approach. Four cases studies, broadly representative of the phenomenon of collective authorship, are considered in detail. Each of these cases studies break new ground in exploring the significance for copyright law of the mismatch between creative norms in environments in which collaboration flourishes (Science, Film, Indigenous art, Wikipedia) and copyright law's rules on authorship. The book, thus, employs insights from the ways in which collaborators understand and regulate issues of authorship themselves to assess copyright law's approach to joint authorship critically.

This book is written during a period when copyright law appears to be suffering from a crisis of legitimacy.[14] In recent decades, the successful lobbying of rights holders and the internationalisation of copyright law has led to the expansion of copyright protection.[15] This has resulted in a copyright regime which has often been accused of being geared more towards protecting the corporations involved in producing and distributing creative works, than it is towards rewarding and incentivising authors.[16] At the same time, non-compliance with copyright law is becoming increasingly widespread, and in some quarters, normalised (viz. the anti-copyright law platform of the Pirate Party, the 'Guerrilla

---

[14] E.g. S Dusollier, 'Open Source and Copyleft: Authorship Reconsidered?' (2003) 26 Columbia J of L and Arts 281: 'The institution of copyright is in ill repute these days'; N Elkin-Koren, 'Tailoring Copyright to Social Production' (2011) 12(1) Theoretical Inquiries in L 309, 310: ' ... a regime in crisis'.

[15] The entertainment, software and database industries have been particularly important drivers of copyright expansionism. Acknowledging the influence of 'lobbynomics' on UK copyright policy: I Hargreaves, 'Digital Opportunity: A Review of Intellectual Property and Growth for HMG' (2011) available at: <www.gov.uk/government/publications/digital-opportunity-review-of-intellectual-property-and-growth> p 18.

[16] Whilst the subject-matter and scope of exclusive rights has been broadened, there appears to have been relatively little corresponding effort to ensure that actual creators benefit. Creators, dependent on intermediaries to fund/disseminate their work, often make little money from their creations and any control which they might exercise over them is likely to be short-lived. Despite the enormous value that copyright industries add to the economy, most creators cannot earn a living from their creative work: J Litman, 'Real Copyright Reform' (2010) 96(1) Iowa LRev 1; J Ginsburg, 'How Copyright Got a Bad Name For Itself' (2002) 26(1) Columbia J of L and the Arts 61; R Giblin and K Weatherall, 'A Collection of Impossible Ideas' in R Giblin and K Weatherall (eds) *What if We could Reimagine Copyright?* (ANU Press, 2017), 316.

open access movement',[17] etc.). The Creative Commons and the Free Software movements, which cast themselves as an 'ethical alternative' to copyright, have also been gaining popularity. As copyright law is frequently accused of being out of touch with modern creative realities, non-compliance may appear unsurprising.[18] Indeed, psychologists have demonstrated that people are more likely to obey laws they consider to be legitimate and fair.[19] In light of this legitimacy crisis, a search for the best way to apply the joint authorship test ought to begin with the reality of creativity.[20] As Jane Ginsburg argued over a decade ago, refocusing on authors and the act of creating may help restore a proper perspective on copyright law.[21] In this spirit, this book focuses on the dynamics of creativity in four instances of collective authorship.

The figure of the author is at the heart of copyright's sense of its own identity and purpose.[22] Although 'authorship' bears significant doctrinal and normative weight, as a concept, it remains extremely vague and open-textured. Despite increasing interest in legal scholarly

---

[17] B Bodó, 'Pirates in the Library – An Inquiry into the Guerrilla Open Access Movement' (8th Annual Workshop of the International Society for the History and Theory of Intellectual Property, CREATe, University of Glasgow, UK, 6–8 July 2016) available at <ssrn.com/abstract=2816925>.

[18] T Tyler, 'Compliance with Intellectual Property Law: A Psychological Perspective' (1996) 29 International L and Politics 219, 227 arguing that people are more likely to obey a law that reflects public morality. On the link between the perceived lack of transparency with respect to the beneficiaries of intellectual property protection and this crisis of legitimacy: C Geiger, 'The Social Function of Intellectual Property Rights' in GB Dinwoodie (ed) *Intellectual Property Law: Methods and Perspectives* (Edward Elgar 2013) 153, 155.

[19] For example, the important work of T Tyler, *Why People Obey the Law* (Princeton UP 2006) and ibid. Of course the allocation of copyright is only one part of this complex question. The scope of copyright protection and its limitations also affect perceptions of its fairness; and there is no doubt that the ease of infringement coupled with the challenges of enforcement greatly facilitate non-compliance.

[20] RR Kwall, *The Soul of Creativity: Forging a Moral Rights Law for the US* (Stanford UP 2009) 5 draws upon Tyler's work to argue that laws governing authors' rights are likely to be ignored if they fail to embrace widely shared norms regarding authorship. Similarly, J Ginsburg, 'The Author's Place in the Future of Copyright' in R Okediji (ed) *Copyright in an Age of Exceptions and Limitations* (CUP, 2015) 60, 62: 'The disappearance of the author moreover justifies disrespect for copyright—after all, those downloading teenagers aren't ripping off the authors and performers, the major record companies have already done that'.

[21] J Ginsburg, 'The Concept of Authorship in Comparative Copyright Law' (2003) 52 De Paul L Rev 1063, 1071; also L Bently, 'R v Author: From Death Penalty to Community Service' (2008) 32(1) Columbia J of L & the Arts 1.

[22] The protection, reward and incentivisation of creators has always been at the heart of copyright law, notwithstanding the fact that sometimes it has been used to protect against unfair competition (2.1, n 34) or has been seen to work to the benefit of distributors and publishers more than creators.

literature in recent times, authorship remains very under-theorised.[23] In the case law its meaning is often treated as self-evident. Such vagueness may have been thought a rhetorical asset, as strategic ambiguity permits copyright law to serve competing regulatory purposes simultaneously.[24] Since the birth of copyright law, authorship has been a hotly contested issue, as stake holders battle to define the beneficiaries and reach of copyright protection.[25] (The so-called 'monkey selfie' dispute is a recent example that has received media attention.[26]) Legal scholarship's relative historical neglect of the bounds of authorship might be attributed to a reluctance to open this 'can of worms'.[27]

Now is the right time to start prising the can of worms open for at least two reasons. First, part of the response to copyright's crisis of legitimacy ought to be realignment with its *raison d'être:* the encouragement of authorship and the protection of authors. Second, changes to the creative landscape facilitated by digital technology mean that courts are increasingly likely to be faced with disputes that require definition of the outer

---

[23] Much theoretical scholarship has focused upon the philosophical underpinnings of copyright law, assigning authorship an instrumental role according to the scholars' preferred view. Ginsburg (n 21) provides a notable exception. Recently, there has been more interest in authorship. In Europe, for example: M van Eechoud (ed) *The Work of Authorship* (Amsterdam UP, 2014); Bently (n21). In the USA following *Aalmuhammed v Lee* 202 F3d 1227 (9th Cir, 2000) and *Garcia v Google* 743 F3d 1258 (9th Cir, 2014), 786 F3d 733 (9th Cir, 2015), for example: C Buccafusco, 'A Theory of Copyright Authorship' (2016) 102 Virginia LRev 1229; J Tehranian 'Sex, Drones & Videotape: Rethinking Copyright's Authorship-Fixation Conflation in the Age of Performance' (2017) 68 Hastings LJ 1319; S Balganesh, 'Causing Copyright' (2017) 117(1) Columbia LRev 1, 5 n17 referring to much of this scholarship. In Australia, following *IceTV Pty Ltd v Nine Network Australia Pty Ltd* [2009] HCA 14, (2009) 239 CLR 458 and *Telstra v Phone Directories* [2010] FCA 44, [2010] FCAFC 149, for example: E Adeney, 'Authorship and Fixation in Copyright Law: A Comparative Comment' (2011) 35 Melbourne University LRev 677; J McCutcheon, 'The Vanishing Author in Computer-Generated Works: A Critical Analysis of Recent Australian Case Law' (2013) 36(3) Melbourne LRev 915.

[24] M Spence, *Intellectual Property* (OUP 2007), ch 2.

[25] The contours of the concepts of authorship, originality and the copyright work together outline the boundaries of copyright entitlement. Although the CJEU in Case C-5/08 *Infopaq v Danske Dagblades Forening* [2009] ECR I-6569 seems to suggest the primacy of originality in determining copyright subsistence, there are some restrictions on what might be considered a protectable 'work' at the EU level: C-310/17 *Levola Hengelo* EU: C:2018:899 [40]-[41] (it must be capable of being expressed in a precise and objective manner).

[26] The dispute concerned the subsistence and ownership of copyright in a 'selfie' photograph taken by a macaque monkey. See further: Tehranian (n23) 1352–1355.

[27] As authorship is necessarily bound up with the rationale for copyright protection, to the extent that a coherent normative underpinning for copyright law remains elusive, scholarly caution may be warranted. W Fisher 'Theories of Intellectual Property' in S Munzer (ed) *New Essays in the Legal and Political Theory of Property* (2001) <www.tfisher.org/publications.htm> demonstrates that each of the common justifications for copyright protection contain flaws concluding that the explanatory power of these theories is limited.

limits of the concept of authorship.[28] Although a complete theory of authorship is beyond the scope of this book, its more modest aim is to take us a step further down the path to defining the copyright law's concept of authorship. It tests copyright law's ability to meet the two challenges of legitimacy in, and suitability for, the digital age by probing one particularly difficult scenario: collective authorship.

Although scholars broadly agree that current copyright law is ill-equipped to meet the challenges of determining the authorship of highly collaborative works, they proffer different explanations. Some suggest that the influence of the 'romantic author', a literary trope which presents the author as a solitary creative genius, has left copyright law ill-adapted to collaborative creativity.[29] Others offer a more fundamental critique of copyright law, suggesting that it simply lacks the conceptual tools to deal with the forms of creativity that flourish in the modern digital world (many of which are highly collaborative).[30] This book does not ask *why* copyright might be ill-suited to collaborative creativity. Instead, it tackles the underlying assumption that copyright law *is* unable to deal with collective authorship. I argue there are appropriate tools to determine the authorship of works of collective authorship, provided that when applying the joint authorship test, judges make better use of their conceptual tool box.

1.2 Methodological Approach

In his report for the UK government on the reform of copyright law, Ian Hargreaves stressed the importance of evidence-based policy making.[31] Such policy-making is not possible unless scholarly work to helps to join the dots between legal concepts and creative reality. In recent times there has been a significant growth in interest amongst intellectual property law scholars in empirical projects and economic analysis. Yet these methodologies are not always the best equipped to capture some of the less

---

[28] US courts have already confronted some of these challenges: Tehranian (n23); Buccafusco (n23) 1233–1234. Collective authorship is only one such challenge. New media and artificial intelligence provide new avenues for creativity and with the ready availability of smart phones and other technological tools anyone can be a creator.

[29] See M Woodmansee and P Jaszi (eds), *The Construction of Authorship: Textual Appropriation in Law and Literature* (Duke UP, 1994); M Rose, *Authors and Owners: The Invention of Copyright* (Harvard UP 1993); D Saunders *Authorship and Copyright* (Routledge 1992); J Boyle, *Shamans, Software and Spleens: Law and the Construction of the Information Society* (Harvard UP 1996). Others suggest that there are better explanations of the current state of copyright law, e.g. Bently (n21).

[30] JP Barlow, 'The Economy of Ideas: Selling Wine Without Bottles on the Global Net' <www.eff.org/pages/selling-wine-without-bottles-economy-mind-global-net>.

[31] Hargreaves (n15).

quantifiable aspects of copyright law. This book takes a broad, interdisciplinary approach, drawing on the expertise of a wide range of scholars from the Humanities and Social Sciences who have thought deeply on issues relating to collaborative authorship from different perspectives and in a variety of contexts. The book seeks to embrace complexity in order to develop a richer, more nuanced understanding of the role of copyright law within creative communities, with the view that such an approach is more likely to generate realistic workable solutions.

Compelling arguments have been made that the relationship between copyright law and creativity needs to be rethought.[32] This book takes up this challenge. In so doing it forms part of a growing body of work which reacts to the abstract approach of previous copyright scholarship.[33] Indeed, the book adopts a primarily practical, inductive approach by evaluating the dynamics of creativity and the regulation of the incidents of authorship in cases of collective authorship. This research is also situated within the ongoing debate on the distance between social norms and copyright law.[34] By taking creative practice as its starting point, the book proposes ways in which copyright law might use social practices to bridge this gap, and thereby reclaim some of its lost credibility.

The four case studies considered in this book have been chosen because they provide complementary pieces of the jigsaw of 'real-world' collective authorship. They concern the creation of different types of copyright works (literary, artistic, dramatic, film) in very different economic sectors. They are fairly representative of the range of collaborative practices, encompassing both a new form of creativity (Wikipedia) and one with an ancient origin (Australian Indigenous art). They embrace hi-tech (Science, Film) as well as amateur (Wikipedia) examples. In each case, authorship is driven by different impulses, from largely commercial motivations (Film), to religious and spiritual motivations (Indigenous art), to reputation and knowledge creation motivations (Science) and even as a recreational pursuit (Wikipedia). They also provide examples of a range of different ways in which issues of authorship might be self-regulated by creators.

---

[32] J Cohen, 'Creativity and Culture in Copyright Theory' (2007) 40 University of California Davis LRev 1151.

[33] Ibid; RK Walker and B Depoorter, 'Unavoidable Aesthetic Judgments in Copyright Law: A Community of Practice Standard' (2015) 109(2) Northwestern University LRev 343.

[34] For example: L Bently and L Biron, 'Discontinuities between legal conceptions of authorship and social practices: What, if anything, is to be done?' in van Eechoud (n23) 237; LJ Murray, S Tina Piper and K Robertson, *Putting Intellectual Property in Its Place: Rights Discourses, Creative Labor, and the Everyday* (OUP 2014); M Schultz, 'Fear and Norms and Rock & Roll: What Jambands Can Teach Us About Persuading People to Obey Copyright Law' (2006) 21 Berkeley Technology LJ 651, 654; J Tehranian, 'Infringement Nation: Copyright Reform and the Law/Norm Gap' (2007) Utah LRev 537.

Adopting the interdisciplinary, inductive method just discussed, this book asks how the joint authorship test ought to be applied to yield a suitable mechanism for determining the authorship of collective authorship works. For these purposes, *suitable* is taken to mean:
- a test that serves copyright law's purposes to incentivise and reward creativity;[35] and
- a test that is credible to creators and the creative community concerned (because of the importance of some congruency between law and social norms, both in enhancing the law's perceived legitimacy and in promoting compliance).[36]

This book primarily focuses upon the interpretation of the joint authorship test in UK copyright law, as influenced by European law. The fruits of this analysis will, however, be of interest to scholars and practitioners in other jurisdictions which face similar issues. Indeed, the analysis in Chapter 4 considers Australian law, while Chapters 2, 6 and 8 refer to the law of the United States. These different national approaches to questions of authorship, joint authorship and joint ownership provide an interesting counterpoint to UK law.

1.3 A Roadmap

In order to provide a solid foundation for the argument, the book begins with a doctrinal and theoretical analysis of the concepts of authorship and joint authorship in UK copyright law (Chapter 2). I consider the impact of recent jurisprudence of the Court of Justice of the European Union ('CJEU'), since its strides towards harmonisation of the originality requirement feeds directly into copyright law's conception of authorship. Although the contours of the concept of authorship are uncertain, I identify its stable core: a more than de minimis contribution of creative choices or intellectual input to the protected expression.[37]

---

[35] Although these are most commonly cited by commentators, there are a number of other possible purposes of copyright law. For example, encouraging the distribution of creative works, promoting individual flourishing or fostering the achievement of a just and attractive culture. See Fisher (n28) for an overview of the many different views on the theoretical underpinnings of copyright law. In Chapter 2 I argue that the concept of authorship might be affected by one's view of copyright law's purpose and offer a definition of the minimum core of authorship, similar to a 'mid-level principle' of the sort discussed by R Merges, *Justifying Intellectual Property* (Harvard UP, 2011), see further ch 2, n88.

[36] Tyler (n18); K Burleson, 'Learning from Copyright's Failure to Build its Future' (2014) 89(3) Indiana LJ 1299; also Q4, FAQs on Copyright <euipo.europa.eu/ohimportal/en/web/observatory/faqs-on-copyright-hr>; GN Mandel, 'The Public Perception of Intellectual Property' (2014) 66 Florida LRev 261. See further 8.1.

[37] 2.1.

Then, I turn to the joint authorship test found in the Copyright, Designs and Patents Act 1988 ('CDPA').[38] I argue that the definition of a work of joint authorship implies that it is the result of creators working together to create something that is *greater* than the sum of its parts.[39] I argue that this conception serves as useful guide in the application of the test. An analysis of the case law reveals that it is difficult to assess whether, or not, the current statutory test provides a suitable mechanism for determining the authorship of works of collective authorship because the case law is limited, and the test is rarely applied in an analytical manner. Three themes are discussed: (i) the factual specificity of the joint authorship test; (ii) the pragmatic instrumental approach to the implementation of the test; and (iii) the preoccupation with aesthetic neutrality.[40] Although factual specificity results in an uncertain jurisprudential picture, ultimately it is a strength of the test allowing it the flexibility to adapt to different creative contexts.[41] The second and third themes are more problematic, as they lead to lack of analytical clarity in judicial reasoning, which hampers predictability and risks a chilling effect on collaborative creativity.

A trend, evident in copyright scholarship and the case law, is associated with the second theme that favours a restrictive approach to the application of the joint authorship test.[42] I refer to this as the *pragmatic instrumental approach*. Its proponents have been persuaded, primarily for pragmatic reasons, that authorship should be concentrated in the hands of one or a few dominant creators. The worry is that a work's exploitation will be impeded if it has too many joint owners who are unable to agree.[43] The pragmatic instrumental approach is undesirable for a number of reasons. Most notably, it tends to conflate the (importantly separate) concepts of authorship and ownership, and it seems to impose a higher standard of authorship for joint works than is justified by the wording of the CDPA and the case law on authorship more generally.

---

[38] Unless otherwise indicated, throughout this book statutory provisions refer to sections of the CDPA.
[39] 2.2. [40] 2.3. [41] 2.3.1.
[42] 2.3.2. In the US context, the debate between restrictive and inclusive approaches to joint authorship has been explicitly played out between two eminent copyright scholars: Melville Nimmer and Paul Goldstein, see: M LaFrance, 'Authorship, Dominance, and the Captive Collaborator: Preserving the Rights of Joint Authors' (2001) 50 Emory LJ 193, 196–197, 259–261; PS Fox, 'Preserving the Collaborative Spirit of American Theatre: The Need for a "Joint Authorship Default Rule" in Light of the Rent Decision's Unanswered Question' (2001) 19 Cardozo Arts & Entertainment LJ 497, 507–509. The restrictive view is currently favoured by most US courts, although not without criticism: J Dougherty, 'Not a Spike Lee Joint? Issues in the Authorship of Motion Pictures under US Copyright Law' (2001) 49 UCLA LRev 225.
[43] On this view, the more owners there are the greater the possibility of hold-ups occurring. On joint ownership of copyright: 8.6.1.

The third theme is a preoccupation with aesthetic neutrality. I argue that judicial concern about passing judgement on the aesthetic merits of a work has led to a reticence to explicitly engage with aesthetic criteria in the application of the joint authorship test.[44] Yet, as the case law demonstrates, it is difficult, if not impossible to apply the joint authorship test without resort to aesthetic criteria.

I conclude the discussion of the case law on joint authorship by laying groundwork for a more analytical approach to the application of the test in distinguishing the questions of fact from the question of law at its heart (what constitutes protectable authorial input?).[45] The final sections of Chapter 2 seek insights from the scholarly literature on authorship to further enrich this doctrinal analysis.[46]

Then, I look outward at the realities of collective authorship. I consider the regulation of the attribution of authorship and the social incidents of authorship (benefits, responsibilities, etc.) in four case studies of collective authorship:

(i) Wikipedia (Chapter 3);
(ii) Australian Indigenous art (Chapter 4);
(iii) Scientific collaborations (Chapter 5); and
(iv) Film (Chapter 6).

Each case study has been approached with similar questions in mind and the chapters follow a common structure. Each chapter includes four parts: an analysis of the dynamics of creativity and the social norms which operate to regulate the attribution and social incidents of authorship in that particular context; an attempt to apply copyright's subsistence rules to the case study subject matter, thereby identifying any gaps or uncertainties; an assessment of any private ordering measures adopted to address these gaps; and identification of the insights which the case study may provide for copyright law. The four parts are ordered in the sequence which best aids a clear presentation of the relevant issues.

Chapter 7 draws together the many disparate insights from the case studies to develop five broad themes which elucidate the role of copyright law in regulating collective authorship. These might be summarised, in broad-brush terms, as follows:

1. **The nature of collective authorship**[47] Collective authorship tends to involve: a division of labour; the sharing of responsibility for the creative or intellectual content of the work among many contributors; and social norms that regulate the creative process, often also

---

[44] 2.3.3.
[45] 2.4. I argue that the questions of fact relate to the existence of 'collaboration' and a 'significant' contribution which is 'not distinct'.
[46] 2.5.   [47] 7.1.

determining the rights and responsibilities of contributors. In this light, it is obvious that the search for one or two 'controlling minds' to be identified as the authors of a work of collective authorship misses the mark because it fails to reflect how large groups work together to create.

2. **The different meanings of authorship**[48] Although authorship dynamics differ in each collective authorship context, authorship is usually understood as signifying responsibility for what is considered valuable about the content of the work (according to community-specific criteria). Authorship often signals a special status within a particular creative community with power dynamics in that community sometimes affecting who receives authorial credit.

3. **There is a gap between copyright law's assumptions about authorship and creative reality**[49] In particular, copyright law's assumptions regarding the incentives which motivate authors to create often fails to tally with the primary motivations for works of collective authorship, which are frequently non-economic in nature. Furthermore, the attribution and regulation of authorship is often nuanced and varies greatly in different creative contexts. This contrasts to copyright law's standard one-size-fits-all approach.

4. **Bridging the gap between copyright law and creative reality with private ordering**[50] In general, collective authorship groups are fairly successful in self-managing the incidents of authorship. This is achieved by drawing upon a variety of private ordering mechanisms which can offer flexible, tailored and context-specific solutions. Private ordering, however, proves less successful where a power imbalance exists within the authorship group. In this context, legal standards have the potential to play an important role in enabling collective action and improving the quality of private ordering.

5. **The role of copyright law and its concepts**[51] Copyright law rules about authorship establish a standard having both legal *and* expressive value, but the manner in which the law influences creative communities is sometimes complex or indirect.

Chapter 8 applies the case study lessons to the previous theoretical and doctrinal analysis of joint authorship. I explain why the working premise originally proposed in Chapter 2 – that a work of joint authorship is one which is greater than the sum of its parts – is a good fit for collective authorship. Adopting this view, Chapter 8 proffers an *inclusive, contextual approach* to the joint authorship test, which reflects the concept of authorship at the heart of UK copyright law and better aligns with the reality of collective authorship. I outline a few key elements of my reasoning here.[52]

---

[48] 7.2.   [49] 7.3.   [50] 7.4.   [51] 7.5.   [52] See, further, 8.6.

An *inclusive* approach, i.e., one which is more open to the possibility of a work having multiple authors, best reflects the way in which collective authorship groups work together to create copyright works.
- An inclusive approach sets an 'authorship' threshold for a joint work which is on par with that already established for a work of individual authorship, not one which is more demanding.[53]
- The case studies reveal that the fears underlying the pragmatic instrumental approach are ill-founded or over-stated. Rather than facing exploitation hold-ups, collective authorship groups seem generally adept at managing ownership issues supported by social norms or other private ordering mechanisms such as contracts.[54]
- Even where private ordering proves less satisfactory, the case studies still support an inclusive approach to joint authorship because receiving the title of 'author' may prove to be a valuable bargaining chip in any negotiations with more powerful players.[55]
- Finally, a restrictive approach to copyright authorship restricts access to moral rights too. The case studies reveal that collaborators may be more concerned about attribution, and other, non-economic consequences of authorship, than they are about, e.g., royalties or control.

A *contextual* approach to joint authorship might be achieved by taking direct account of the social norms which govern authorial groups when determining questions of fact which arise in the joint authorship test.[56] This calls for a rebalancing in the way the joint authorship test is applied, with more emphasis on the collaboration limb of the test.
- One of the strengths of the current joint authorship test is that it is flexible enough to adapt to different creative contexts. The case studies reveal that there is no single dynamic for collective creativity. Thus, flexibility is an essential feature of any joint authorship test if it is to remain in touch with the creative realities of collective authorship.
- The principle that judges ought not to adjudicate the subsistence of copyright based upon their view of the aesthetic *merits* of the work is consistent with the use of aesthetic criteria.[57] However, it is vital that judicial reasoning refers to such criteria explicitly, rather than being obscured behind a cloak of aesthetic neutrality.
- The social norms that govern creativity within a particular authorship group are an independent source of information that is likely to be helpful in answering questions of fact.[58]

---

[53] p 48.   [54] 7.4.   [55] 6.3, 7.4.3, 7.5.
[56] 2.4 (identifying the questions of fact in the joint authorship test); 8.5 (setting out an inclusive, contextual approach to the application of the test).
[57] 2.3.3, 8.4.2.   [58] 2.2.4, 8.1.

Yet, as well as potential benefits, there are also dangers inherent in incorporating social norms in legal decision-making.[59] Therefore, I suggest a framework for assessing the usefulness of social norms based on their (i) certainty, (ii) representativeness and (iii) policy implications.[60] In the CDPA, authorship is also ultimately and importantly, a legal question.[61] In the joint authorship test, the requirement for authorship is expressed as a requirement that the contribution be of the 'right kind' in the copyright sense. This requirement provides an additional filter when it comes to the incorporation of social norms in copyright decisions.

It is hoped that the approach proposed in this book would not only bring the joint authorship test closer in line with the reality of collective authorship, but also provide a useful analytical framework to promote greater clarity in judicial decision-making. This solution draws upon the natural strengths of the UK's common-law legal system and the flexible, incremental and problem-based approach to law-making that it allows. Although this book is primarily about authorship and joint authorship, there are inevitable implications of this analysis for the law of joint ownership. These are considered in 8.6, which sets out the current approach to joint ownership, considers some alternatives and proposes modest legislative amendment.

Chapter 8 concludes with some more general food for thought which arises from the analysis of collective authorship in the book.[62] In particular, this research supports the view that it is time to review the influence which instrumental, economic incentives-based reasoning wields in shaping the ongoing development of copyright law and policy.[63] Previous scholarship exploring non-economic motivations for authorship and the role of social norms in regulating creativity has called this 'incentive story' of copyright protection into question.[64] Yet most of this of this literature has focused on 'negative spaces' – domains in which creativity thrives despite little, or no, copyright protection being

---

[59] 8.1, 8.2. [60] 8.3. [61] 2.4. [62] 8.7.
[63] A valuable resource in this debate is: J Silbey, *The Eureka Myth: Creators, Innovators, and Everyday Intellectual Property* (Stanford Press, 2014). See also: JC Fromer, 'Expressive Incentives in Intellectual Property' (2012) 98 Virginia LRev 1745; O Bracha and T Syed, 'Beyond Efficiency: Consequence-Sensitive Theories of Copyright' (2014) 29 Berkeley Tech LJ 229. The importance of the non-economic incidents of authorship in motivating creators suggests a need to take a broader approach to implementing moral rights than the UK has been comfortable with to date: I Stamatoudi, 'Moral Rights of Authors in England: The Missing Emphasis on the Role of Creators' (1997) 4 IPQ 478; J Ginsburg, 'Moral Rights in the Common Law System' (1990) 1(4) Entertainment LRev 121.
[64] Elkin-Koren (n14); Silbey ibid.

available.[65] It is open to debate whether such activities ought to be regulated by copyright law. The case studies considered here, however, provide a more serious challenge to the incentive story *because* they fall squarely within copyright law's recognised domain. The case studies demonstrate that authorship is a more complex and multi-dimensional phenomenon that current copyright law appears to give it credit for.

This book also underlines the important role which copyright law serves as a touchstone for good authorship standards. At its best, copyright law can provide a valuable bulwark against unhealthy power dynamics within creative communities which cause authorship to gravitate to dominant players at the expense of other creators. At its worst, copyright law might end up bolstering the positions of such dominant players (typically, orchestrators and investors) at the expense of the real creators, simply because of a misplaced desire to simplify rights and ensure efficient exploitation. The latter scenario would seem to support the view that copyright law's ideal is out-of-touch with creators' experiences. Thus, this book urges an approach that would allow copyright law to reconnect both with creative realities and also with its own *raison d'être:* rewarding and incentivising creators. Although the CDPA may seem to offer little guidance on the definition of authorship, as the next chapter will show, in fact, its description of the author as the one who *creates* a work clearly reveals the heart of this concept.

[65] For example, the work of comedians, chefs and magicians. E Rosenblatt, 'A Theory of IP's Negative Space' (2011) 34(3) Columbia J of L and the Arts 317 provides an overview of this literature. See also: K Raustiala and C Sprigman, 'The Piracy Paradox: Innovation and Intellectual Property in Fashion Design' (2006) 92 Virginia LRev 1687; D Oliar and C Sprigman, 'There's No Free Laugh (Anymore): The Emergence of Intellectual Property Norms and the Transformation of Stand-up Comedy' (2008) 94 Virginia LRev 1787; E Fauchart and EA von Hippel, 'Norm-Based Intellectual Property Systems: The Case of French Chefs' (2008) 19(2) Organization Science 187; CJ Buccafusco, 'On the Legal Consequences of Sauces: Should Thomas Keller's Recipes Be Per Se Copyrightable?' (2007) 24 Cardozo Arts & Entertainment LJ 1121; J Loshin, 'Secrets Revealed: How Magicians Protect Intellectual Property without Law' in C Corcos, *Law and Magic: A Collection of Essays* (Carolina Academic Press 2008) 123.

2 Authorship and Joint Authorship

This chapter provides the legal and conceptual background for the analysis of the case studies in the following four chapters. Its purpose is to provide an overview and critique of the provisions on authorship and joint authorship in the CDPA. Although the contours of copyright law's concept of authorship are uncertain, it has a stable core in that it refers to the creator of the protected expression. I argue that the best view is that authorship requires at least a de minimis contribution of creative choices or intellectual input to the protected expression. This provides a baseline that is coherent with the underlying purposes of copyright law and consistent with recent case law.[1]

The body of cases applying the joint authorship test is relatively limited. Together these cases paint an uncertain jurisprudential picture, which makes it difficult to predict the outcome were the test to be applied to a work of collective authorship. Part of this uncertainty is associated with the factually specific nature of joint authorship cases. Factual specificity is unavoidable. Indeed, it is desirable because it allows for a single test to apply sensibly in a variety of different creative contexts. A more serious weakness in the existing jurisprudence, however, is a lack of analytical clarity when the joint authorship test is applied to the facts, making clear legal advice difficult and hampering predictability. There is also a concerning tendency in some of the cases to adopt an unnecessarily restrictive interpretation, which would tend to concentrate authorship in the hands of one or more dominant or controlling contributors.

I argue that the lack of analytical clarity in the case law on joint authorship arises for one of two reasons. First, in applying the joint authorship test, judges are sometimes concerned about practical

---

[1] A stronger conception of authorship is possible and may even be desirable, but any such a conception would entail highly contestable normative choices which are unnecessary for the argument in this book. The purpose of this book is to uncover and evaluate the existing principles as they apply to cases of collective authorship, not to advocate any particular theory of authorship. In this way, it is hoped that the analysis will be useful irrespective of the normative view of copyright law which one might prefer.

difficulties that may arise where there are many owners of a single copyright interest. Pragmatic, instrumental reasons thus may persuade judges to adopt a more demanding requirement for authorship in the case of a joint work than for works of individual authorship. This is likely to make it particularly difficult for non-dominant authors to establish joint authorship. This approach is problematic from a doctrinal point of view as it tends to conflate the separate concept of 'authorship' with 'ownership'; and reads stricter requirements into the joint authorship test than is justified by both the wording of the test and its legislative context.

Secondly, judicial commitment to aesthetic neutrality can obscure the important role of aesthetic considerations in decisions involving joint authorship. Aesthetic considerations are inescapably relevant to the question of whether, or not, a particular contribution to a collaborative work amounts of authorship, notwithstanding the overriding importance of legal considerations to any such determination. A reticence to engage openly with such matters can lead to brief, superficial or opaque reasoning. Although authorship is ultimately a legal question that may be influenced by one's view of the purpose of copyright law, it is also inevitably linked to creative practice. Judges are necessarily influenced by pervasive social and cultural views about creators and the creative process in the application of copyright law's rules of subsistence. Indeed, a great strength of copyright's concept of authorship is its inbuilt flexibility, which allows it to adapt to changes in creative practices over time and in different creative sectors. This book argues that a restrained but principled process is needed for incorporating aesthetic considerations.

This chapter begins by outlining UK copyright law's concept of authorship (as influenced by EU law); and then, the provisions of the joint authorship test in the CDPA. In the third section, I consider how the joint authorship test has been applied in the case law, discussing three themes which explain the difficulty of predicting how it might apply to works of collective authorship. The legal analysis is concluded in the fourth section, which distinguishes the factual and normative dimensions of the joint authorship test. The penultimate section seeks to enrich the doctrinal analysis with insights from the scholarly literature on authorship in copyright law. Valuable understanding is gleaned from US scholarship critiquing the restrictive approach that US courts taken to film authorship in recent times. The chapter ends by suggesting that the authorship practices of creative communities might provide some insight on the question of how best to apply the joint authorship test to works of collective authorship.

2.1 The Concept of Authorship in the CDPA

Although authorship is an important organising concept for copyright law, it has not yet been translated into any clear test.[2] Section 9(1) of the CDPA simply provides that the author of a work is the person who creates it. In determining authorship courts often take into account factual matters, such as the context within which creativity occurs. But ultimately, authorship is a question of law which is understood by reference to matters that lie outside of a dictionary definition of the word, such as the policy aims of copyright law.[3] In this section, I explain the two aspects of the concept of authorship: its factual/causative dimension and its normative dimension. I argue that a requirement for a modicum of creativity or intellectual contribution is actually hard-wired into the provisions of the CDPA on authorship. Thus, authorship ought to require a more than de minimis contribution of creative choices or intellectual input to the protected expression. Although this view of authorship has not always prevailed in the case law,[4] it may be more likely to do so in the future as a result of the Court of Justice of European Union's application of a new harmonised standard for originality, the intellectual creation test.[5]

---

[2] One might contend that a clear test is not possible, on the basis that authorship must be formulated with a certain degree of vagueness in order to adapt to a variety of different creative contexts. Yet, as a linchpin of the scheme embodied the CDPA, the coherence and legitimacy of the law requires authorship to be constituted of legal principles with relatively stable core content. The fact that current copyright jurisprudence on authorship is under-developed, lacking a fully-elaborated normative account of authorship to serve as a guide, does not mean that one is not possible. Indeed, as advances in technology create more situations which stretch the limits of copyright's notion of authorship, this jurisprudence is likely to mature and over time, a clearer test may emerge. As to the challenges technology poses to authorship (discussed in the US context): J Tehranian, 'Sex, Drones & Videotape: Rethinking Copyright's Authorship-Fixation Conflation in the Age of Performance' (2017) 68 Hastings LJ 1319; C Buccafusco, 'A Theory of Copyright Authorship' (2016) 102 Virginia LRev 1229, 1233–1234.
[3] L Bently, B Sherman, D Gangjee and P Johnson, *Intellectual Property Law* (OUP 2018) 126 considering the concept of the 'author' to operate as a legal fiction.
[4] Historically, copyright law has sometimes been used as protection against unfair competition or free-riding. In such cases investment, effort or routine labour has sometimes been considered relevant authorial input. See n34.
[5] Following Case C-5/08 *Infopaq v Danske Dagblades Forening* [2009] ECR I-6569 [45] (*Infopaq*), discussed below at p 22–25. The intellectual creation test is likely to continue to have influence in the UK, as the UK will adopt EU law as at the date of Brexit; and the test has now been incorporated into UK law in a number of cases (e.g., *SAS Institute v World Programming* [2013] EWCA Civ 1482, [2014] RPC 8 [82] (*SAS*)). However, as will be discussed, the precise effect of this test on UK law remains unclear. R Arnold, L Bently, E Derclaye and G Dinwoodie, 'IP Law Post-Brexit' (2017) 101 (2) Judicature 65 note that Canadian and Australian courts have adopted similar approaches when departing from the UK test. This may offer a persuasive point of reference for UK courts in developing the test post-Brexit. For an analysis of the impact of Brexit, also: G Dinwoodie and RC

Authorship is the linchpin of the scheme embodied in the CDPA. Thus, jurisdictional connection with the author of a work is one of the bases for qualification for copyright protection.[6] The author is also a point of reference for the duration of copyright and moral rights protection.[7] The author is usually the first owner of copyright subsisting in a work[8] and is entitled to various moral rights in respect of the work, namely, the attribution right and the right to object to derogatory treatment.[9] Despite the importance of the concept of authorship, it is relatively under-theorised at all jurisdictional levels (international, regional and national).[10]

There is no definition of 'author' at the international level, despite the pervasiveness of this term in important legal sources.[11] Ricketson and Ginsburg argue that one might deduce some characteristics of authorship from the description of 'literary and artistic works' that must be protected under the Berne Convention.[12] In particular, they suggest that Article 2 could be read as providing that such works are protected insofar as they constitute intellectual creations.[13] Ricketson and Ginsburg take a broad view of the meaning of 'intellectual creation' that would include common law iterations of the threshold originality standard for copyright protection which have tended to put more emphasis on labour and skill, than creativity.[14] Given the open-textured nature of the term 'intellectual creation' and the absence of any more complete articulation of authorship in subsequent international agreements, it should be no surprise that

---

Dreyfuss, 'Brexit and IP: The Great Unravelling?' (2017) 39 Cardozo L Rev 967; A Ramalho and M Gracia, 'Copyright after Brexit' (2017) 12(8) JIPLP 669.

[6] s153, s154.   [7] s12, s13A, s13B.   [8] s11.   [9] s77, s80.

[10] J Ginsburg, 'The Concept of Authorship in Comparative Copyright Law' (2003) 52 De Paul LRev 1063, 1066 observes that the concept has not been very well articulated in the case law. Recently, a number of cases concerning issues of authorship have sparked more interest in this concept in the US and Australia (see ch 1, n23).

[11] S Ricketson and J Ginsburg, *International Copyright and Neighbouring Rights: The Berne Convention and Beyond* (2nd ed, OUP 2006), Vol 1, 358–359 suggest two possible explanations for the failure to include a definition of authorship in the Berne Convention: (i) a fairly general consensus among the nations represented at the early conferences on the question of who was an author; (ii) diverging standards among nations as to the level of creativity required for authorship.

[12] The conception of authorship mandated by the Berne Convention is also affected by Art 15 (rebuttable presumption that the person whose name appears on the work in the usual manner is the author and hence entitled to institute infringement proceedings).

[13] Art 2(5): 'Collections of literary or artistic works such as encyclopaedias and anthologies which, by reason of the selection and arrangement of their contents, *constitute intellectual creations* shall be protected as such, without prejudice to the copyright in each of the works forming part of such collections' (emphasis added). The term intellectual creation can also be found in the TRIPS Agreement, Art 10(2).

[14] Ricketson and Ginsburg (n11) 359 thus deduce that intellectual creation does not require a novel or inventive contribution.

there has been significant national variation when it comes to designating authorship.

Although the figure of the author is ubiquitous in European Union copyright law, only small fragments of a definition might be found in the relevant EU Directives.[15] Recent CJEU decisions are beginning to fill in the picture. *Infopaq* and subsequent cases indirectly harmonise aspects of authorship by harmonising the standard for protection (originality) and the scope of protection of the copyright work. The full impact of this jurisprudence remains to be seen, but it is a point to which I will return. First, I begin by considering the UK approach to authorship prior to the CJEU's foray into this area.

Authorship is the cornerstone of copyright law, however, when it comes to providing a definition of this concept the UK statute is brief. At first, the CDPA's definition of an author as someone who 'creates' a work may not seem particularly illuminating,[16] but I argue that this description does, in fact, imply certain characteristics of authorship. These inherent characteristics can be inferred from provisions deeming certain persons be 'taken to be' the author of particular works (i.e., persons who would not otherwise fit within the definition of an 'author').[17]

The Oxford English Dictionary defines 'create' as follows:

... to make, form, set up or bring into existence (something which has not existed before); to produce (a work of imagination or invention; an artefact).[18]

This definition captures two senses in which authorship might operate in copyright law. The first sense, which is the predominant understanding, is of creator as *originator/source*. Here the focus is on the causal connection between the creator and what is created. In this sense, a creator is a person who produces an artefact/work in that they cause it to come into existence.[19] The second sense is of creator as *innovator* and focuses on the act of creation, that is, the production of something that has an inventive, imaginative or creative quality. It is this second sense of create

---

[15] The Database Directive (Art 4) and Computer Programs Directive (Art 2.1) assume that an author is a natural person. It is also clear that the principal director is one of the authors of a film: Case C-277/10 *Luksan v van der Let* [2013] ECDR 5 (considering the Satellite and Cable Directive, Rental and Related Rights Directive and Term Directive). See further, Ricketson and Ginsburg (n11) ch 7.
[16] s9(1): 'In this Part "author", in relation to a work, means the person who creates it'.
[17] See p 27–28.
[18] The most pertinent definition (i.e., 'Of a human agent') on the online version of the *Oxford English Dictionary* <www.oed.com>.
[19] The use of the word 'artefact', defined as 'an object made or modified by human workmanship...' *Oxford English Dictionary*, ibid, is also telling. The concept of authorship in copyright similarly seems to require a human creator (see n81).

which primarily distinguishes this word from other words that denote origination such as 'make' or 'produce'.

In the case law, authorship consists of least two dimensions: a factual, causative dimension and a normative dimension.[20] The former is the most evident. The factual, causative dimension corresponds to the first meaning of 'create'. According to this view an author is conceived of as the originator of the work. Thus, in *Cummins v Bond*, a medium was held to be the author of the 'automatic writing' she produced during a séance because she had written every word of it.[21] Although this might seem to imply the need for writing, in fact, what is required is 'something approximating penmanship' – that is – responsibility for the *expression* of the work.[22] The expression is the intangible property that copyright protects (for example, a 'literary work' or a 'musical work'). It is abstract and ought to be distinguished from the 'fixation', or physical object, in which that expression is embodied or recorded. So, where a clerk takes dictation of a letter, the author of the resulting literary work is the person who composed the letter (not the clerk who has merely 'fixed' that expression to paper).[23]

The normative dimension of authorship is more nebulous. It serves to demarcate the boundaries of copyright protection in terms of the matter which the law *ought to* protect. In order to understand the normative dimension of authorship it is helpful to consider another closely related concept: originality. Authorship and originality are like two sides of the same coin.[24] It is an original contribution that makes a contributor an author.[25] In the classic formulation of the originality test from *University of London Press v University Tutorial Press*, the word 'original' is distanced from the ordinary meaning which denotes novelty or inventiveness.[26]

---

[20] S Balganesh, 'Causing Copyright' (2017) 117(1) Columbia LRev 1 makes a similar observation in relation to US copyright law.

[21] (1926) 1 Ch 167, 175. The medium was the originator of the words, as they had not been copied. Their supposed 'spiritual origin' was irrelevant in this regard.

[22] *Cala Homes v Alfred McAlpine Homes* [1995] EWHC 7, [1995] FSR 818; *Robin Ray v Classic FM* [1998] FSR 622 (Ch).

[23] *Walter v Lane* [1900] AC 539 (HL), 554 (Lord Justice James). On the complex relationship of copyright to the material fixation of its subject matter, see: YH Lee, 'The Persistence of the Text: The Concept of the Work in Copyright Law – Part 1' (2018) 1 IPQ 22 and Part 2 (2018) 2 IPQ 107.

[24] Existing understandings of originality developed (prior to any express requirement for originality in copyright legislation) from judicial interpretation of the notion of authorship: *Walter v Lane*, ibid.

[25] This is particularly evident in the case law on derivative works and joint authorship. Discussion of the emphasis on the 'authorship' limb in the application of the joint authorship test follows at 2.2.3.

[26] [1916] 2 Ch 601, 608–609 (Peterson J): '... the act does not require that the expression must be in an original or novel form, but that the work must not be copied from another work – that it should originate from the author'.

Instead, originality requires the work to originate from the author in that it is not copied. Yet more often in subsequent copyright jurisprudence, 'original' seems to imply that which merits copyright protection. As such, the originality test appears to contain additional, more specific requirements, which are unstated and potentially shifting because the case law rarely identifies the underlying normative justification which the outcome relies upon.[27]

As the originality requirement sets the threshold for copyright protection, it is necessarily affected by one's view of the purpose of copyright law, which shapes one's perspective of the kind of creative activities that ought to benefit from copyright protection. The lack of a consensus on the best theoretical justification for copyright protection may explain why the case law sometimes appears to offer conflicting guidance.[28] In common law jurisdictions, the predominant justification for copyright law assumes that legal rights incentivise authors to create because protection enables authors to control their work, for example, by extracting royalties for reproductions. Yet, the economic incentive story has limited explanatory power, which leads some to prefer justifications based on natural rights (e.g., arising from the labour invested by the author in the creative process or the fact their personality is imbued in the resulting work) or 'social planning' arguments linked to the promotion of cultural flourishing. Because an original contribution is required from an author, any uncertainty in relation to the normative aspect of originality arising from disagreement surrounding the philosophical underpinnings of copyright law necessarily injects uncertainty into the concept of authorship. This complicates the role of authorship within the statutory scheme, which seems to reflect more than one rationale for protection.[29] Equally as important as economic incentives, the author title also provides valuable non-economic benefits, including moral rights and social recognition.[30]

---

[27] Bently et al. 96; S Ricketson, 'The Concept of Originality in Anglo-Australian Copyright Law' (1991) 9(2) Copyright Reporter 1.

[28] The main views are helpfully summarised in W Fisher, 'Theories of Intellectual Property' in S Munzer (ed) *New Essays in the Legal and Political Theory of Property* (2001) <www.tfisher.org/publications.htm>.

[29] Fisher, ibid. On the limits of the 'incentive story': D Zimmerman, 'Copyright as Incentives: Did We Just Imagine That?' (2011) 12 Theoretical Inquiries in Law 29; N Elkin-Koren, 'Tailoring Copyright to Social Production' (2011) 12(1) Theoretical Inquiries in Law 309.

[30] Attribution is an important incident of authorship, as seen in a number of aspects of literary property law. The right to object to false designation of authorship is venerable and attribution is a precondition for relying upon a number of the fair dealing defences. W Cornish, D Llewelyn and T Aplin, *Intellectual Property: Patents, Copyright, Trade Marks and Allied Rights* (8th edn, Sweet & Maxwell 2013) 505.

Originality is a matter of fact and degree. And the apparent philosophical tension between UK and European notions of authorship plays out in its interpretation.[31] UK courts have typically expressed originality in terms involving an individual's skill, labour and/or judgement, although many linguistic variations of the test exist.[32] In some cases, mostly involving compilations or tables, UK courts seem to have recognised mere routine labour, or 'sweat of the brow', to be sufficient to confer the requisite originality upon a work.[33] Yet, these decisions often appear motivated by a desire to remedy unfair competition rather than to recognise an act of authorship, and so fit uneasily within the copyright regime as a whole.[34] In any event, following *Infopaq*, there may no longer be room for such an approach.

In *Infopaq*, the CJEU considered the scope of the reproduction right, harmonised in the InfoSoc Directive, in relation to the activities of a media monitoring company which produced excerpts of Danish newspaper articles using a data-capture process.[35] In determining how much of a work must be taken to infringe copyright, the court found it necessary to form a view about the scope of copyright protection. This led it to consider two core aspects of copyright subsistence: the scope of the work and the threshold for protection. The CJEU held that the unauthorised reproduction of an eleven-word text excerpt might constitute copyright infringement if through the choice, sequence and combination of those words, the author has expressed his or her creativity in an original manner which resulted in an intellectual creation.[36] The court relied upon Recital 9 of the InfoSoc Directive to extend this 'intellectual creation' standard to all authorial works – a manoeuvre

---

[31] Although these approaches are not without their commonalities: Ginsburg (n10).

[32] Bently et al. 97 also cite: 'work, capital, effort, industry, time, knowledge, taste, ingenuity, experience or investment'.

[33] For example, *Ladbroke v William Hill* [1964] 1 All ER 465 (HL) 478 (Lord Devlin); *Waterlow Directories v Reed Information Services* [1992] FSR 409 (Ch); *Blacklock v Peterson* [1915] 2 Ch 376; *University of London Press* (n26); *Elanco Products v Mandops* [1979] FSR 46; [1980] RPC 213 (CA); *Football League v Littlewoods Pools* [1959] Ch 637.

[34] Cornish et al. 438–439 observe that copyright tends to be denied in these sorts of cases where some other form of relief against unfair competition is available, citing *Exxon v Exxon Insurance* [1982] Ch 119 (CA). L Bently and B Sherman, *Intellectual Property Law* (OUP 2009) 106 note that instead of focusing on whether the work is original, courts in these cases tend to start from the premise that any labour or effort exerted in the production of the work ought to be protected (as long as a quantitative threshold is met) citing the 'maxim': 'what's worth copying is prima facie worth protecting'. This approach is concerningly close to granting protection against unfair competition or the misappropriation of a valuable intangible per se, which has been rightly resisted in a number of notable cases: *L'Oréal v Bellure* [2007] EWCA Civ 968; *Victoria Park Racing & Recreation Grounds Co Ltd v Taylor* [1937] HCA 45, (1937) 58 CLR 479 (High Court of Australia).

[35] *Infopaq* (n5) discussed in more detail in, e.g., E Derclaye, 'Case comment: Infopaq International A/S v Danske Dagblades Forening (C-5/08): wonderful or worrisome? The impact of the ECJ ruling in Infopaq on UK copyright law' (2010) 32(5) EIPR 247.

[36] *Infopaq* ibid [45].

which has been described as a 'judicial sleight of hand'.[37] Previously, it was widely understood to apply to software, databases and photographs only, since the legislation protecting these works explicitly employs the term intellectual creation.[38] Although the CJEU's elaboration of the intellectual creation standard initially arose in the context of infringement, it has subsequently been applied to determine questions of copyright subsistence (e.g., in relation to a graphic user interface[39] and a football match[40]). In *Football Dataco*, the CJEU referred to the line of cases following *Infopaq* to suggest that a harmonised originality test now exists across all categories of work.[41]

In *Infopaq* the CJEU drew an analogy between its own elaboration of the intellectual creation standard and the provisions of the Berne Convention. Subsequent cases, however, seem to reveal a narrower interpretation of this term by the CJEU than that suggested by Ricketson and Ginsburg in the context of Berne. Similar to the UK approach, the work must be the author's *own* intellectual creation in that the author must be its originator (the factual/causative dimension of authorship). The work must also reflect the author's personality in the sense that the author has been able to express his or her creative ability by making free and creative choices in the process of creation,[42] thus, stamping his or her 'personal touch' on the work.[43] Some scholars consider this to be a requirement for creativity and therefore, a higher standard than the UK's traditional approach to originality.[44] The fact that this language appears closer to the language used in continental legal systems, which have a preference for natural rights personality-based justifications, suggests to some that *Infopaq* entails a fundamental change in the normative dimension of originality.[45] The need for such a paradigm shift, however, is by no means clear. The words 'intellectual

---

[37] Cornish et al. 440.
[38] Database Directive, Art 3; Term Directive, Art 6; Software Directive, Art 1(3).
[39] C-393/09 *Bezpečnostní softwarová asociace v Ministerstvo Kultury* [2010] ECR I-0000, [2011] ECDR 3, [2011] FSR 18 (*BSA*) [45].
[40] Joined Cases C-403/08 and C-429/08 *Football Association Premier League and Others* [2011] ECR I-0000 [97].
[41] Case C-604/10 *Football Dataco v Yahoo! UK Ltd* ECLI:EU:C:2012:115, [2012] ECDR 10 [42]–[44].
[42] *Infopaq* (n5) [45]; *BSA* (n39) [50]; C-145/10 *Painer v Standard Verlags* [2012] ECDR 6 [87]–[89]; *Football Dataco* ibid [37]–[38].
[43] *Painer* ibid [21]; *Football Dataco* ibid [38]; cf. *Newspaper Licensing Agency v Meltwater* [2011] EWCA 890 [20].
[44] Derclaye (n35) 248–249; M van Eechoud, 'Along the Road to Uniformity – Diverse Readings of the Court of Justice's Judgments on Copyright Work' (2012) 1 JIPITEC 60; E Rosati, 'Originality in a Work, or a Work of Originality: The Effects of the Infopaq Decision' (2011) 33(12) EIPR 746.
[45] Cf. A Rahmatian, 'Originality in UK Copyright Law: The Old "Skill and Labour" Doctrine Under Pressure' (2013) 44 IIC 4 who argues that this is not the case.

creation' are not particularly revelatory of themselves and the context in which this standard was derived does not provide much assistance in its interpretation.[46]

It is still too early to assess the full impact of these decisions on UK copyright law.[47] Some judges have proceeded on the basis that *Infopaq* has not altered the position in the UK.[48] Others seem to hedge their bets by referring to both UK and CJEU formulations of the originality test.[49] In *SAS Institute v World Programming*, the UK Court of Appeal seemed to suggest that the CJEU's intellectual creation test may have raised the standard.[50] There has been a discernible shift in language in recent cases which have

---

[46] Rahmatian, ibid, 11, 18 describes the intellectual creation standard as neutral and chameleonic.

[47] It is worth noting a curious result that might flow from *Infopaq* (n5). In defining the scope of the protected work the CJEU stressed that the parts of a work should not be treated any differently from the work as a whole as they share the originality of the work and that 'the various parts of a work thus enjoy protection ... provided that they contain elements which are the expression of the intellectual creation of the author of the work' ([38]–[39]). In a subsequent line of cases the CJEU has held that copyright might subsist in subject matter that would have been denied copyright protection in the UK on the basis that it falls outside of the CDPA's closed list of subject matter if it passes the intellectual creation test (e.g., *BSA* (n39), *Football Association Premier League* (n40)). Indeed, the concept of the 'work' does not take obvious prominence in these decisions, which may seem to suggest that *Infopaq* leaves no room for any threshold requirements for a copyright 'work' to exist. If this is the case, it may not be permissible for Member State courts to use the characteristics of particular kinds of works to restrict the types of contributions which might result in authorship (for example, to contributions that are relevantly musical, artistic, etc.). Furthermore, copyright protection could conceivably be available in respect of the products of a broader range of creative activities than have tended to be conceived of as authorial in the UK to date as long as they are capable of being expressed in a precise and objective manner, see Case C-310/17 *Levola Hengelo* EU:C:2018:899 (the taste of a cheese not a copyright work).

[48] *NLA v Meltwater* (n43) [20] (Sir Andrew Morritt C): 'I do not understand the decision of the European Court of Justice in Infopaq to have qualified the long standing test established by the authorities' [referring to *University of London Press* (n26) and *Ladbroke* (n33)].

[49] *Temple Island Collections v New English Teas* [2012] EWPCC [27] (Birss J) 'skill and labour (or intellectual creation)'. *Taylor v Maguire* [2013] EWHC 3804 [6]–[7] (Clark DJ): 'an original artistic work is a work in which the author/artist has made an original contribution in creating it, for example by applying intellectual effort in its creation ... it must have been produced as a result of independent skill and labour by the artist'. *Abraham Moon v Thornber* [2012] EWPCC 37 [56] (Birss J): 'skill, labour and judgment ... it is his own intellectual creation'.

[50] *SAS* (n5) [36]–[37] (Lewison LJ): 'This test may not be quite the same as the traditional test in English law ... If the Information Society Directive has changed the traditional domestic test, it seems to me that it has raised rather than lowered the hurdle to obtaining copyright protection'. Lewison LJ cites AG Mengozzi in *Football Dataco* (n43) who suggests that the test resembles the continental European approach and is, therefore, probably a higher standard than the traditional UK approach in that it excludes mere mechanical effort.

found originality by reference to the work reflecting the creator's personal vision rather than purely their time, effort or investment[51] (using terms such as 'intellectual creativity',[52] 'personality of the author',[53] 'significant creative contribution'[54]). This may indicate the acceptance of the evolution of the test towards a requirement for some creativity,[55] although it is clear that the standard remains fairly low.[56]

It is important not to overstate the significance of this shift in focus. The new language is not very far removed from terms such as 'judgement' or 'taste' that have been used to elaborate the originality test in the UK well before *Infopaq*. It can now be said that mere 'sweat of the brow' will never suffice, but even this was a matter of debate prior to *Infopaq*.[57] Although this new formulation of the originality standard may make little difference to many outcomes, the linguistic shift is a significant, positive development for copyright law. By articulating originality in terms of creative input rather than investment, judges have the opportunity to define copyright's limits in a way that is more likely, over time, to elucidate a clearer concept of authorship. This will consign to history formulations of the copyright protection threshold founded upon more nebulous notions of misappropriation or unfair competition.[58] The need to define the boundaries of authorship is likely to become more urgent in the light of recent technological and cultural developments.[59]

It is difficult to pin down the normative dimension of authorship when it is treated as a proxy for what copyright protects or ought to protect.[60] In

---

[51] For example, *Taylor v Maguire* (n49), *Abraham Moon v Thornber* (n49), *Temple Island Collections* (n49). The language used in these cases approaches the way in which the CJEU describes authorship in cases such as *Painer* (n42).
[52] *Martin & Anor v Kogan & Ors* [2017] EWHC 2927 (IPEC) (Hacon J) [43]: 'Here I use "skill" as a shorthand term for the intellectual creativity of an author required for copyright protection within the meaning discussed in *Infopaq* . . . '.
[53] *Mei Fields Designs v Saffron Cards and Gifts* [2018] EWHC 1332 [77].
[54] *Bamgboye v Reed* [2002] EWHC 2922, [2004] 5 EMLR 61 [54] (preceding *Infopaq*).
[55] This is how the continental approach is often characterised: van Eechoud (n44).
[56] Although there must be some room for creative choice (*BSA* (n42)), a simple portrait photo might meet this standard (*Painer* (n42))
[57] Bently et al. 108–110. Routine labour or sweat of the brow has only been sufficient to confer originality in limited situations, largely in respect of tables or compilations. Thus, sweat of the brow may not have survived the implementation of the Database Directive, which resulted in the author's own intellectual creation standard being applied for the subsistence of copyright in databases (the wording of s3(1)(a) suggests that where a work is both a database and a compilation it should be treated as a database only; and as the definition of a database in s3A(1) is very broad, most compilations will now be treated as databases, see further p 84–85). See also M Spence, *Intellectual Property* (OUP 2007) 89.
[58] On the difficulty of distinguishing fair from unfair competition: *L'Oréal v Bellure* (n34) (Jacob LJ) [139]–[141]. Also Spence ibid 36.
[59] See Chapter 1, n28.
[60] Ginsburg (n10) 1067 highlighting the problem of consequentialist reasoning.

the absence of a clear guiding account of the purpose of copyright law, some courts have preferred a negative definition of authorship: *not* a contribution merely of ideas;[61] *not* a mechanical contribution to fixation;[62] *not* interpretation or performance;[63] or *not* activities akin to proof-reading.[64] Indeed, the most conservative view of the recent CJEU case law is that it simply establishes that there can be no authorship where there is no creative freedom at all.[65]

The positive aspects of authorship are less clear. The aesthetic quality of the contribution is sometimes a relevant factor in the UK, as on occasion the sorts of contributions that count have depended upon the type of work (i.e., literary, dramatic, musical or artistic work). For example, contributions which affect the playability of a musical work might be authorial;[66] whilst contributions which do not affect an artistic work in a visually significant way will not be authorial.[67] In this way the categories of works have been used to constrain authorship entitlement.[68] This provides an entry point for judges to take into account creative practices, as the CDPA provides only skeletal definitions of the categories of work.[69] Some suggest that this approach may no longer be permissible following *BSA* and *Football Association Premier League*, which seem to suggest that the categories of work are no longer relevant.[70] Yet, it is likely that the category of work will be pertinent in identifying the sorts of choices that might be relevant in determining whether a work amounts to an intellectual creation. For example, choices related to lighting, setting and pose

---

[61] *Donoghue v Allied Newspapers* [1938] 1 Ch 106 (Ch).
[62] Such as a clerk taking dictation: *Walter v Lane* (n23) 554 (Lord Justice James).
[63] *Hadley v Kemp* [1999] EMLR 589 (Ch); *Brighton v Jones* [2004] EWHC 1157, [2005] FSR 288.
[64] *Fylde Microsystems v Key Radio Systems* [1998] FSR 449 (Ch).
[65] *Football Association Premier League* (n43); *BSA* (n43).
[66] *Sawkins v Hyperion Records* [2005] EWCA 565, [2005] 3 All ER 636, 648 (Mummery LJ): 'The work of Dr Sawkins has sufficient aural and musical significance to attract copyright protection'.
[67] *Interlego v Tyco Industries* [1989] AC 217 (PC); *Lucasfilm v Ainsworth* [2009] FSR 2.
[68] Whether or not this is ought to be the case post-*Infopaq* is unclear, see n47 and n70.
[69] The statutory presumptions as to authorship also oblige the court to take into account attribution as an author on a work (which is likely to be affected by predominant creative practices): s104, s105.
[70] van Eechoud (n44) 70–71. In *SAS Institute Inc v World Programming Ltd* [2013] EWHC 69 (Ch) [27] Arnold J opined it may now be possible to make the argument that the categories of work in the CDPA's closed list do not narrowly prescribe the limits of protectable expression (although in his view, any putative copyright subject matter would still need to satisfy the definition of 'literary or artistic work' in the Berne Convention, Art 2(1)). In *Abraham Moon v Thornber* (n49) [99], on the other hand, Birss J dismissed the argument 'however tempting it might be' that the different ways in which literary and artistic works are treated in the CDPA are no longer justified.

affect the artistic qualities of portrait photograph, and thus allow an author to stamp his or her personal touch upon it.[71]

The different protection offered to entrepreneurial (as compared to authorial) works may offer further insight into the meaning of authorship.[72] Entrepreneurial works have always been treated differently on the very basis that they result from investment, not authorship.[73] For these works, copyright is generally conferred on the party bearing the financial risk, the entrepreneurial or other driving force behind the project.[74] For a film, for example, the producer was designated as author.[75] Indeed, the 1956 Act referred to the first owner of copyright in an entrepreneurial work as its 'maker' rather than its 'author'. This is an aspect which has been reformed under European harmonisation.[76] The CDPA now provides that certain nominees are 'taken to be' the author of an entrepreneurial work. This phrasing echoes the historical hesitation to label those whose main contribution was to direct the project or to carry the financial risk, 'authors'.[77] It suggests that here the word 'author' is used as a shorthand to refer those individuals who do not have the inherent qualities of a *true* copyright author because they are *not* creators.[78] This reinforces that use of the word 'creates' in CDPA's definition of authorship (rather than 'makes' or 'produces') tells us something meaningful about authorship. It underscores the ordinary meaning of 'create' which involves creativity, imagination or innovation. This also goes some way to explaining why (so-called) 'authors' of entrepreneurial works are generally not granted moral rights.[79]

---

[71] *Painer* (n42).   [72] Bently et al. 118.
[73] The Gregory Report argued for a fixation-only form of copyright protection for film on the basis that it resembled an industrial product more than an authorial work: 'Report of the Board of Trade Copyright Committee' (HMSC, October 1952) Cmd 8662. See further 6.2.1.
[74] Cornish et al. 450.
[75] Now the principal director is also considered to be an author, see further 6.2.3.
[76] In particular, implementing the Rental and Related Rights Directive and the Term Directive. KM Garnett, G Davies, G Harbottle, WA Copinger and EP Skone James, *Copinger and Skone James on Copyright* (16th edn, Sweet & Maxwell 2011) 251 [4-47]; G Dworkin, 'Authorship of Films and the European Commission Proposals for Harmonising the Term of Copyright' [1993] EIPR 151.
[77] Ricketson and Ginsburg (n11) Ch 7 (particularly 7.10).
[78] Copinger et al. 248 [4–40]: in this context ' ... the expression [author] is not in fact used otherwise than as a shorthand in the process of identifying the first owner of the copyright'. Although it might be argued that this is just a drafting technique used for the avoidance of doubt and that it should not impact the definition of 'author' (or if it should, it should favour a broad interpretation) – the history of the introduction of these provisions records a hesitation to call such contributors 'authors', see Gregory Report (n73). This is also evident in the different way in which the court approaches the task of determining the authorship of a musical work from the task of determining the authorship of the sound recording upon which it was fixed in *Bamgboye v Reed* (n54) [87].
[79] With the exception of those who are also creative contributors (closer to true authors), e.g., the principal director of a film and the performer of a broadcast or sound recording.

The mere existence of 'deemed' authors suggests that authorship under UK copyright law does indeed require at least a modicum of creative or intellectual effort.[80] It also implies that a true author must be a natural person.[81] This view is reinforced by the provisions covering works made in the course of employment. Here, although the employer (often a company) is presumed to be first owner of copyright in the work, the author is still the individual employee who created it.[82] So, we may surmise that a 'true' (rather than a deemed) author is a natural person who has contributed more than simply assuming any financial risk or overseeing the creative process. Seen from this angle, it is hard to conclude other than that the CDPA requires an 'author' to have created a work in *both* relevant senses of the word; i.e., a ('but-for') causal connection is a necessary, but not sufficient condition of authorship. An author must do something more than just 'make' or 'produce' a work, meaning at least a modicum of 'creativity' is hardwired into the concept of authorship in the CDPA.[83] Thus, the concept of authorship in the CDPA may be more aligned with the European concept of intellectual creation than some suppose. In the third part of this chapter, I propose that the judicial commitment to aesthetic neutrality is one reason why UK case law rarely acknowledges this inherent requirement for creativity.[84]

Since copyright has often been used as a tool to protect investors and entrepreneurs, some suggest that copyright law is primarily concerned with ensuring the dissemination (rather than creation) of works.[85] Yet, the fact that it might be necessary for creators to divest some of their rights to entrepreneurs to ensure that their works are disseminated, does not undermine the importance of granting them these rights in the first

---

Moral rights recognise the personal connection between a creator and their creation which arises due to the nature of the creative process.

[80] Thus, in the case of entrepreneurial works and computer-generated works the author is merely a legal fiction used to allocate rights: Bently et al. 126.

[81] S Ricketson, 'People or Machines? The Berne Convention and the Changing Concept of Authorship' (1991) 16 Columbia J of L and the Arts 1, 28 arguing that the Berne Convention requires an author to be a natural person; thus considering that US 'work for hire style' principles run counter to the basic premises of the concept of authorship in the Convention. See also: A Dietz, 'The Concept of Authorship Under the Berne Convention' (1993) 155 Revue Internationale du Droit d'Auteur 3.

[82] Cf. US copyright law, which provides that an employer is the author as well as the first owner of copyright subsisting in a work for hire, Copyright Act 1976 (US), s201.

[83] This is reflected in the different approach to determining joint authorship of a sound recording and of a musical work in *Bamgboye v Reed* (n54) ([46]–[50], [87], Williamson QC distinguishing 'making' from 'creating').

[84] The other probable reason is a temptation to expand copyright protection in order to compensate for the lack of a tort of misappropriation or unfair competition. Spence (n57) 80–82.

[85] LJ Lacey, 'Of Bread and Roses and Copyright' [1989] Duke LJ 1532.

place.[86] Indeed, authorship is one of the central organising concepts in copyright law *because* copyright law derives its legal and moral force from the act of creativity.[87] In this section, I have argued that the concept of authorship is linked to the act of creativity and that it requires, at least, a more than de minimis contribution of creative choices or intellectual input to the protected expression of a copyright work. This conception comes even more clearly to the fore in light the CJEU's elaboration of the author's own intellectual creation standard. This stable core concept of authorship remains at the heart of copyright law regardless of the normative justification, combination of justifications or none, appealed to in an instant case.[88]

2.2 The Joint Authorship Test

Armed with a basic understanding of the meaning of authorship, we are now better placed to consider the joint authorship test. Section 10(1) of the CDPA defines a 'work of joint authorship' as a 'work produced by the collaboration of two or more authors in which the contribution of each author is not distinct from that of the other author or authors'. In addition, case law establishes that joint authorship only applies for those who contribute a significant part of the protected skill, labour or judgement – sometimes termed the 'authorship' limb of the test.[89] In sum, a contributor is only a joint author under the CDPA, if they have:

(i) made a contribution which is not distinct;
(ii) which is made in pursuance of a common design (or collaboration); and
(iii) which amounts to a significant contribution of the right kind.

In this part, I evaluate each limb of the test, drawing out common themes from the case law, and filling any gaps identified, where possible, with reasoning from first principles.

---

[86] M Handler, 'Continuing Problems with Film Copyright' in F Macmillan (ed) *New Directions in Copyright Law: Volume 6* (Edward Elgar 2007) 173.

[87] W Cornish, 'The Author as Risk-Sharer' (2002) 26 Columbia J of L & the Arts 1, 12. L Bently, 'R v Author: From Death Penalty to Community Service' (2008) 32(1) Columbia J of L & the Arts 1, 94: ' ... authorship remains at the heart of what most people think, and most legal systems say, copyright is about'.

[88] Similar to a mid-level principle that ties together the disparate practices bridging the gaps between different views of the theoretical underpinnings of the law. On mid-level principles see: R Merges, *Justifying Intellectual Property* (Harvard UP, 2011). Also: R Merges, 'Foundations and Principles Redux: A Reply to Professor Blankfein-Tabachnick' (2013) 101 California LRev 1361 elaborating on the idea of mid-level principles or meta-themes as types of incompletely theorised agreements. On the latter: C Sunstein, 'Incompletely Theorized Agreements' (1995) 108 Harvard LRev 1733.

[89] *Godfrey v Lees* [1995] EMLR 307, 325–328; *Ray v Classic FM* (n22) 636; *Hadley v Kemp* (n63).

2.2.1 A Contribution That Is Not Distinct

The requirement that a contribution is 'not distinct' is open to two possible interpretations.[90] It could refer to whether it is possible to separately identify or distinguish the contribution. Alternatively, it might relate to whether the contribution forms an integral part of the work such that without it, the work would be different in character.[91] *Beckingham v Hodgens* suggests that the latter interpretation prevails (although the court applied the joint authorship test in the 1956 Act which specified 'not separate', rather than 'distinct'). The court held that the violin part of a song was not separate because it was:

... heavily dependent upon what is there already. Stripped of the voices and other instruments, the violin part would sound odd and lose meaning. The final musical expression – what the audience will hear – is a joint one.[92]

This quote underlines that a work of joint authorship is not a collection of (separate) works, e.g., two separate essays in the same book. Rather, a work of joint authorship involves the combining, merging or mixing of contributions.[93]

Where a contribution is distinct it may be a separate copyright work or it may not be protected by copyright at all (for example, if it is too trivial or lacks originality).[94]

---

[90] Very little case law directly addresses this question. *Beckingham v Hodgens* [2002] EWHC 2143 (Ch), [2002] EMLR 45 is a notable exception. In *Hadley v Kemp* (n63) (Park J, 650) the suggestion that a saxophone fill might be considered 'separate' was raised but largely left unexplained. Some Australian cases appear to tie the finding that a contribution is 'separate' to a lack of collaboration among contributors: e.g., *Primary Healthcare v Federal Commissioner of Taxation* [2010] FCA 419, [121]–[122]; *Acohs v Ucorp* [2010] FCA 57 [57]–[59]; approved [2012] FCAFC 16 [86]. This approach seems to collapse these two limbs of the test. It would be preferable for the scope/boundary of the joint work to be approached as a matter of objective determination (to which the creative context might be relevant, but which is not solely determined by the attitudes of contributors) so as to avoid an artificial proliferation of layers of copyright protection.

[91] Copinger et al. [4–37].

[92] At first instance [2002] EWHC 2143 [46]. In *Cala Homes* (n22) 834 (n5 of the judgement) it was accepted that there was no material difference between the wording of the test in 1956 and 1988; similarly, *Brown v Mcasso* [2005] FSR 846 (EWPCC) [40].

[93] Cf. 'joint work' in the US which includes interdependent as well as inseparable parts (Copyright Act 1976 (US), s101). Despite the differing definitions of joint authorship, in both jurisdictions courts tend to find separate (rather than joint) works wherever possible. On the disaggregation of authorship and bias in favour of individual authorship: P Jaszi, 'On the Author Effect: Recovering Collectivity' in M Woodmansee and P Jaszi (eds) *The Construction of Authorship: Textual Appropriation in Law and Literature* (Duke UP 1999) 29, 51–56.

[94] In *Redwood Music v Chappell* (1982) RPC 109 (QB), for example, music and lyrics to a song were distinct contributions amounting to two separate works – a literary and a musical work. There is, however, no need to prove that a distinct contribution is a copyright work: P Kamina, *Film Copyright in the European Union* (2nd ed, CUP 2016)

2.2.2 Collaboration or Common Design

The test's requirement for 'collaboration' distinguishes a work of joint authorship from a derivative work.[95] A derivative work is created where an existing work is modified by a subsequent author working independently of the original author (for example, a translation). In order to be joint authors, contributors must have some sort of preconcerted common design to produce the work or at least a loose plan to work together. This does not require joint authors to be located in the same place or to make their contributions simultaneously. Collaboration is usually assessed at the time of the creation of the particular work in question, such that where works have evolved over time, courts might look for co-operative acts by the putative authors in relation to the specific draft in issue.[96]

Beyond this, case law fails to provide much clear guidance. In *Levy v Rutley*, the introduction of a new scene together with some alterations to the play's dialogue undertaken without the co-operation of the commissioned writer, was found not to be made in furtherance of a common design ('mere additions' to a complete piece, only intended to make the play more attractive to the audience, were insufficient to demonstrate collaboration).[97] Yet in *Springfield v Thame*, it was suggested a sub-editor's finessing of a paragraph composed by another might result in joint authorship of the final newspaper article.[98] Decided cases seem to suggest that a contributor providing input either too early or late may

---

156, 159 (commenting on the 1956 Act). A number of distinct contributions might together be a collective work: s178. On the distinction between co-authors and joint authors, see Copinger et al. [4-17], [4-44].

[95] *Beckingham v Hodgens* (n90) [45] (Floyd QC) citing *Levy v Rutley* (1871) LR 6 CP 523 distinguishing 'joint labouring in the furtherance of a common design' from the 'subsequent independent alteration of a finished work'.

[96] *Martin v Kogan* (n52) [25] (Hacon J) 'cooperative acts by the authors at the time the copyright was created, which led to its creation'. In this case, following a relationship breakdown, there was no relevant collaboration between authors on the final draft of a screenplay despite such collaboration being present in relation to earlier drafts. Also: *Brighton v Jones* (n63) [32], [67]–[69].

[97] (1871) LR 6 CP 523. The court failed to discover 'any cooperation of the two in the design, or execution of the piece, or in any improvements either in the plot or general structure' (529, Keating J); 'The additions do not disturb the drama composed by Wilks: they were made for the mere purpose of improving or touching up some of its parts. It would be strange indeed, if not unjust, if the author's rights could be thus merged into a joint-authorship with another. There are probably very few instances, at least in modern times, of a play being put upon the stage without some alteration by the manager' (530, Montague Smith J).

[98] (1903) 89 LT 242 (Ch). Laddie et al. [3.97] consider that collaboration might have been assumed in this case on the basis that both were employed by the same newspaper.

struggle to establish joint authorship.[99] Although such findings are not always explained in terms of a lack of collaboration, they do seem to reflect the court's perception of when the creative process had begun and ended, thereby defining the window of opportunity during which collaboration might occur.[100] Thus, it might be possible to explain divergent approaches in specific cases as attributable to variation between different creative sectors which, in turn, influences perceptions about the creative process and the role of different contributors. In *Brighton v Jones*, for example, contributions made to a play by an actor or director that might normally be expected to arise during rehearsals (i.e., after the play-writing stage was over) pointed away from collaboration with the scriptwriter.[101] Some courts, however, are wary of simply adopting the industry view on who should count as authorial collaborator, since this tends to reflect power dynamics which might unfairly deny authorship credit to less influential contributors.[102]

In *Levy v Rutley* the court seems to have considered authorial intent to be relevant.[103] In *Beckingham v Hodgens*, however, the Court of Appeal clarified that a 'common design' did not require the existence of a common intention as to joint authorship.[104] However, it must be incorrect to

---

[99] Contributions made too early might constitute separate works (e.g., Brighton's draft opening script in *Brighton v Jones* (n63) [32], [67]–[69]; *Martin v Kogan* (n52) [17]–[19]) or mere ideas which another has subsequently, independently, turned into a protectable copyright work (*Donoghue v Allied Newspapers* (n61)). Contributions made too late might not be seen to relate to the creation of the work, for example, because they relate to its performance (*Hadley v Kemp* (n63)) or because they are akin to proof-reading (*Fylde Microsystems* (n64)).

[100] Sometimes this is said to indicate that the contribution is not of the *right kind* or of an authorship-type (e.g., *Hadley v Kemp*, ibid).

[101] (n63) [48]–[49], [56]. Similarly, in *Hadley v Kemp* (ibid, 646) the court distinguishes performance creativity from authorial creativity, suggesting the creative process was complete once Kemp had fixed the musical work in his musical consciousness and that subsequent contributions of band members were equivalent to the contributions of session musicians who are not usually credited as authors ('The members of the band ... did what any good musician does').

[102] *Bamgboye v Reed* (n54) [79]; *Brown v Mcasso* (n92) [44]; *Fisher v Brooker and Onward Music* [2006] EWHC 3239, [2007] FSR (12) 255 [45], [46], [60], [62].

[103] The requirement for intention appears more explicitly in the Law Times Report of the case than it does in the Law Report version: (1871) 24 LT 621, 623 (Montague Smith J) 'There seems to have been no agreement between the two, or intention on Wilk's part, that they should have been joint authors originally'; 622 (Keating J) 'If they agreed to rearrange the play together, they might be joint authors ... And if they agree to a general design and structure they might divide their parts and work separately'. E Cooper, 'Joint Authorship in Comparative Perspective: *Levy v Rutley* and the divergence between the UK and USA' (2005) 62(2) J of the Copyright Society of the USA 245, 256–257, 269–270 noting that early editions of Walter Copinger's copyright treatise cited the Law Times Report of the case and considered intention to be relevant.

[104] *Beckingham v Hodgens* [2003] EWCA Civ 143 (Jonathan Parker LJ). The court rejected the approaches taken in Canadian and US cases, which required intention to be

interpret *Beckingham v Hodgens*, as meaning that intent has no role to play at all, since a common design can only exist when there is some intention to work together.[105] To hold otherwise would stretch the word 'collaboration' well beyond its ordinary meaning. Rather, the court's decision should be construed to mean that there is no need to prove a subjective intention to jointly author in the copyright sense. Instead, the proper focus is on creative realities.[106] Were the contributors in fact working together? Did they have a common design? Factors such as job title or industry customs of sharing authorial credit provide only very limited assistance as they may tend to reflect traditional inequalities within particular cultural spheres (rather than the actual nature of the contributors' working relationship).[107]

The US experience illustrates the hazards of requiring proof of intention. The US Copyright Act 1976 defines a 'joint work' as one 'prepared by two or more authors with the intention that their contributions be merged into inseparable or interdependent parts of a unitary whole'.[108] Over time, the explicit intention requirement has taken on greater importance in decisions on joint authorship.[109] Dominant contributors seem to have been able to retain sole authorship of a work by asserting that it was never their (subjective) intention to collaborate, effectively excluding others who have provided creative, copyrightable input from sharing in the benefits of authorship of the final work.[110] In determining the parties' intentions, US courts have been persuaded by evidence of 'objective manifestations of intent'. These have included billing, control over the creative process and other aspects of managerial status, including the authority to enter into

established, as looking 'beyond the [statute] into the uncertain realm of policy' and introducing undesirable requirements of proof, referring to *Childress v Taylor* 945 F2d 500 (2nd Cir, 1991) and *Neudorf (Darryl) v Nettwerk Productions Ltd* [2000] RPC 935 (British Columbia SC) [52]. Cf. L Zemer, *The Idea of Authorship in Copyright* (Ashgate 2007) 217, arguing that despite this decision UK courts tend to silently embrace a requirement for intention to some extent. See also: Ginsburg (n10).

[105] L Zemer, 'Is Intention to Co-author an Uncertain Realm of Policy?' (2007) 30(4) Columbia J of L and the Arts 611, 617.

[106] There are a number of examples of this approach: *Brown v Mcasso* (n92), *Bamgboye v Reed* (n54); *Beckingham v Hodgens* (n90), (n104) (to name a few).

[107] *Bamgboye v Reed* (n54) [61]: 'It really is not, therefore, a question of whether Mr Bamgboye would have been thought of as a "collaborator", in the way that word might normally be used in the industry. The question is, was Mr Bamgboye, in fact, instrumental in having creative input into the music as it became created in the version that finally became recorded?'.

[108] s101.

[109] L Zemer, 'Contribution and Collaborations in Joint Authorship: Too Many Misconceptions' (2006) 1(4) JIPLP 283. See, for example, *Childress v Taylor* (n104).

[110] *Thomson v Larson* 147 F3d 195 (2nd Cir, 1998) where this argument was made by the late Larson's estate as copyright owner.

contracts with third parties.[111] US commentators have expressed concern that linking authorship to the ability to demonstrate objective manifestations of intent automatically favours the more powerful contributors in an enquiry which should be concerned with the magnitude each party's creative contribution.[112] Inevitably, this tends to concentrate authorship in the hands of producers, managers, etc., with most control over the creative process, thereby distancing copyright authorship from the originators of the protectable expression (creators).[113]

In the UK, most cases focus almost exclusively on the authorship limb, which means that decisions on joint authorship tend to hinge on the characterisation of the nature of a contribution. As a result, the collaboration limb is under-developed and its impact on the other parts of the test unknown.[114] For example, does the nature of the common design shed any light on whether a contribution is distinct or whether it is significant? The relative neglect of the collaboration limb in favour of the requirement for authorship deviates from the plain language of section 10, which specifically requires the former and only implies the latter. This impoverished understanding of collaboration makes the joint authorship test particularly difficult to apply to works of collective authorship.[115]

Clearly, the common design requirement cannot simply be ignored altogether. Whilst there are good reasons to resist an interpretation which requires proof of intention to create a work joint authorship, the collaboration limb ought to take more prominence in decisions. When taken together, the requirements for collaboration and for contributions which are not distinct indicate that joint authorship involves working together to create a work which is *greater* than the sum of its parts. In this book I argue that this conception should guide the application of joint authorship test.

---

[111] *Thomson v Larson* ibid; *Aalmuhammed v Lee* 202 F3d 1227 (9th Cir, 2000); *16 Casa Duse v Merkin* 791 F3d 247 (2nd Cir, 2015).

[112] FJ Dougherty, 'Not A Spike Lee Joint? Issues in the Authorship of Motion Pictures Under US Copyright Law' (2001) 49 UCLA LRev 225.

[113] Criticising the apparent circularity of granting control over the subsequent uses of copyright work to the party who already has most control over the work: A Casey and A Sawicki, 'The Problem of Creative Collaboration' (2017) 58 William & Mary LRev 1793, 1830.

[114] Cooper (n103) 246–247 considers this requirement to have taken on greater significance in some cases in New Zealand and Australia, particularly, *Land Transport Safety Authority of New Zealand v Glogau* [1999] 1 NZLR 261, 271; *Milwell v Olympic Amusement* (1999) 85 FCR 436, 446-47; *Primary Healthcare* (n90) [121]–[122]; *Acohs v Ucorp* (n90)[57]–[59]; *Telstra v Phone Directories* [2010] FCA 44 [337], [2010] FCAFC 149.

[115] This problem is particularly acute in relation to a perpetual work in progress like Wikipedia. The current test for collaboration fails to convincingly resolve the issue of whether Wikipedia is best seen as a series of derivative works or a work of joint authorship, see 3.2.1.

2.2.3 A Significant Contribution of the Right Kind

As has been foreshadowed already, the authorship limb of the test has been the overwhelming focus for UK case law involving joint authorship despite being an implicit requirement, which does not appear in the text of the statute. In order to be a joint author, a contributor must have made a significant contribution of the right kind. Decisions on joint authorship are often said to be limited to the specific facts, which gives the test the flexibility to adapt different creative contexts, although this also makes it challenging to draw out common themes. It is well established that joint authors do not need to contribute equally.[116] In applying the authorship limb, courts consider the nature of the work at issue, as well as the quantity and quality of the contribution in question.[117] Beyond this, it is difficult to identify any over-arching guiding principles from the case law. For example, when adopting a qualitative approach, reasoning often does not elucidate whether the qualities considered relate to the 'significance' of the contribution, to whether it is of the 'right kind' or to both. Although it might be debated whether this limb of the test comprises one part or two, here I shall consider each aspect separately: first the need for a *significant* contribution, and then the requirement that the contribution is of the *right kind*.

There is very little judicial guidance on the meaning of 'significant'. This is complicated because some courts elide this question with the evaluation of the kind of contribution which has been made. Commonly, a court identifies significance as a requirement, then states a conclusion that it has been satisfied (or not), with little explanation of the relative weight given to different factors which may have influenced the court's decision.[118] In *Fisher v Brooker*, the first instance judge considered that 'significant' meant 'more than merely trivial'[119] (although he also acknowledged that the relevant contribution in that case was

---

[116] *Godfrey v Lees* (n89) 325 (Blackburne J): 'It is not necessary that his contribution to the work is equal in terms of either quantity, quality or originality to that of his collaborators'.

[117] *Brown v Mcasso* (n92) (affirmed on appeal [2005] EWCA Civ 1546); *Martin v Kogan* (n52) [54].

[118] E.g., *Beckingham v Hodgens* (n90) [50]; *Hayes v Phonogram* [2002] EWHC 2062 (Ch), [2003] ECDR 11; *Godfrey v Lees* (n89) 325–328; *Stuart v Barrett* [1994] EMLR 448, 463.

[119] [2006] EWHC 3239, [2007] FSR 255 [46]; a similarly low standard appears to have been applied in *Minder Music v Sharples* [2015] EWHC 1454. In *Fylde Microsystems* (n64) [25] Laddie J thought the relevant question was whether the contribution was 'big enough', which also seems to imply a quantitative standard. In *Beckingham v Hodgens* (n90) [45] Floyd J expressed the view that 'trivial contributions will not qualify the contributor as a joint author', but then took a qualitative approach taking into account expert evidence that the violin riff concerned was memorable and catchy ([49]).

substantial on any view[120]). Some approve of this de minimis, quantitative approach to significance as it seems to support aesthetically neutral decision-making.[121] This is seen as a virtue in copyright cases generally, but might appear particularly appealing in the context of joint authorship where determinations have been criticised for appearing subjective and arbitrary,[122] or for their over-reliance on evidence that may be insensitive to the particular features of the relevant genre.[123] Yet, such a standard would add little, if anything, to the test since it already requires a contribution of the *right kind* (i.e., an authorial contribution) and it is well established that trivial contributions will not amount to authorship. Thus, it has been suggested that the requirement for a significant contribution may be an unnecessary gloss.[124]

More recently, in *Martin v Kogan*, Hacon J states that significance is a 'sufficiency' test having both qualitative and quantitative aspects.[125] Yet, he then equates this test to the substantiality requirement in the infringement context, which requires that a defendant's use is enjoined only if a 'substantial part' of the Claimant's work is taken (post-*Infopaq* this amounts to no more than taking elements which express the author's own intellectual creation).[126] Once again, this would seem to duplicate the requirement that the contribution is of the right kind to be protectable.

Overall, however, the case law does not seem to support the view that the significant contribution requirement is an unnecessary gloss, since the value (significance) of a putative joint author's contribution appears as a guiding consideration in many determinations of joint authorship.[127] In

---

[120] Ibid [98]; partially reversed by the Court of Appeal considering it to be an 'extremely unusual case' ([2008] EWCA Civ 287 [34]); then, upheld in the House of Lords ([2009] UKHL 41). Blackburne J's ruling on joint authorship was not challenged in either appeal.
[121] Bently et al. 131–132. L Bently, 'Authorship of Popular Music in UK Copyright Law' (2009) 12(2) Information Communication & Society 179, 197 acknowledging that it might not be possible, or even always desirable, to completely exclude aesthetic value judgements from copyright decision-making.
[122] Zemer (n109) 287. Bently has argued that the requirement for a significant contribution has tended to invite judges to make value judgements about the quality of particular contributions: ibid, 190.
[123] Bently ibid 198 arguing that inappropriate weight has been given to the evidence of classically trained musicologists in cases involving popular music.
[124] D Vaver, *Intellectual Property: Copyright, Patents and Trade-Marks* (2nd ed, Irwin Law 2011) 120–121 (writing in the Canadian context, where the joint authorship test is similarly worded).
[125] (n52) [48].
[126] *Designers Guild Ltd v Russell Williams (Textiles) Ltd* [2001] 1 WLR 2416; [2001] FSR 11; [2001] ECDR 10 as affected by *Infopaq* (n5), which now applies, see *SAS* (n5) [82].
[127] A significant contribution is expressed as a separate requirement in *Hadley v Kemp* (n63) 636 and *Cala Homes* (n22) 834. Even where the separate requirement for a significant

Beckingham v Hodgens, for example, the court took into account that the violin riff was memorable and catchy.[128] In *Brown v Mcasso*, the court upheld Brown as a joint author despite the quantitatively modest changes made, as it was his contribution which gave the song an 'authentic rap feel'.[129] Similarly, in *Hadley v Kemp*, the improvisations of a saxophonist were found to be insignificant – not 'particularly memorable, tuneful or original ... just the sort of thing which any accomplished professional saxophonist would have provided'.[130] Yet in one song where the saxophone fill was 'memorable', 'particularly attractive' and 'felicitous', it was still not a significant contribution as it lasted less than 10% of the duration of the track – thus, quantity was not irrelevant.

Different qualitative factors have been considered pertinent to the question of significance. Courts have assessed whether the contribution is relevant, attractive or valuable in the creative context concerned.[131] A court may be persuaded that a contribution is significant if it forms a distinctive part of the work or serves to distinguish that particular work from others in the same genre.[132] Equally, a court might be swayed if the contribution improves the appeal of the work to its intended audience, is memorable or has become famous.[133] Significance may be described in fairly vague terms, for example, contributions that made the work more 'interesting'[134] or gave it 'shape' or 'drive'.[135] In music cases, judges have often been influenced by the evidence of musicologists who may appear to provide a more objective expert perspective on the significance of a contribution.

Uncertainty about the content of the significant contribution requirement is compounded by a lack of clarity about the role of this part of the joint authorship test.[136] It will be recalled that authorship has a factual

---

contribution is not explicitly stated, there are few cases in which courts do not rely on aspects of the quality or quantity of a contribution beyond the question of whether the contribution is of the right kind.

[128] (n90) [49]. [129] [2005] FSR 40 [30].
[130] [1999] EMLR 589, 650 according to evidence of a musicologist which was accepted by the court.
[131] *Brown v Mcasso* (n92) [46]: 'In rap, the words are of greater importance than in many other music forms and that is no less so in this case. Mr Brown's choice of words depended upon inter alia correct vernacular usage, fitting chosen words into the backing and in the overall idiom itself'; *Bamgboye* (n54) [72].
[132] *Hadley v Kemp* (n63) 650; *Beckingham v Hodgens* (n90) [49].
[133] *Brown v Mcasso* (n92) [30] (contributions that gave a rap song for use in an advertisement the required authentic feel established joint authorship). In *Fisher v Brooker* (n102) [23], [10], [3] the court was influenced by the fact that Fisher's organ solo was distinctive and famous.
[134] *Bamgboye v Reed* (n54) [27].
[135] *Stuart v Barrett* (n118) 460 in relation to the (significant) contribution of a drummer.
[136] Hacon J attempted to consider this question in *Martin v Kogan* (n52), although this section has argued that his approach tends to elide the requirement of a significant contribution with the requirement that the contribution be of the right kind.

causative dimension (an author is an originator) and a normative one (an author undertakes an activity of the sort which copyright protects). As the requirement for a contribution of the 'right kind' relates to the latter dimension, I would argue that the requirement for significance should be seen as relating to the former. The question of origination is far more complex for jointly authored works than it is for individually-authored works. In this context a significant contribution ought to be interpreted as requiring a contribution that is meaningful/valuable in the particular context, such that the contributor who made it can fairly be considered responsible for the copyright work as one of its authors. In light of the importance of the requirement of collaboration (as indicated by the wording of s10), I suggest that the significance requirement is best approached in light of the contributors' common design. This would require a qualitative approach which takes account of aesthetic criteria drawn from the relevant creative context (rather than acontextual or abstract aesthetic criteria, determined externally).[137]

As I have just suggested, it is not enough to make a significant contribution, a joint author must also make a contribution of the *right kind* and this part of the test is an entry point for much of the normative content of the concept of authorship. Although there is no requirement the contribution must be separately copyrightable, the jurisprudence relating to originality is relevant when assessing this aspect of a contributor's input.[138] Thus, it seems that the intellectual creation test will be relevant to the joint authorship test, although its impact, if any, is still largely unknown.[139]

For a contribution to be of the 'right kind', it must be a contribution in the nature of authorship i.e., relating to the *creation* of the work.[140] Consequently, this part of the test will rarely be satisfied if suggestions are made *after* the substance of the creative process has taken place.[141] The right kind of contribution can also depend upon the type of the

---

[137] I argue that there is a reliable external standard from which to judge the significance of a contribution: the common design of the contributors as revealed by the social norms which regulate their collaborative activities (see Chapters 7 and 8).

[138] Cf. US cases which have sometimes required a joint author to provide a separately copyrightable contribution, e.g., *Childress v Taylor* (n104), *Erickson v Trinity Theatre* 13 F3d 1061 (7th Cir, 1994), *Thomson v Larson* (n110). Cf. *Gaiman v McFarlane* 360 F3d 644 (7th Cir, 2004).

[139] In *Martin v Kogan* (n52) 30, Hacon J considered the question of significance to amount to a single multi-purpose 'sufficiency' test which applies: (i) in determining whether a contribution establishes joint authorship; (ii) in establishing whether a derivative work is sufficiently different from the work upon which it is based to be protectable in its own right; and (iii) in determining whether a Defendant has taken a substantial part of the Claimant's work to establish copyright infringement.

[140] *Hadley v Kemp* (n63) 643.   [141] Ibid; *Brighton v Jones* (n63).

work in issue.¹⁴² For example, contributions relating to the performance of a musical work did not yield authorship rights in that musical work;¹⁴³ suggestions relating to the interpretation and theatrical presentation of a play were not of the right kind to vest authorship in the underlying dramatic work;¹⁴⁴ and contributions akin to proof-reading did not amount to authorship of a literary work.¹⁴⁵

In *Martin v Kogan*, Hacon J attempted to explain the complex joint authorship case law landscape by identifying a distinction between an exercise of 'primary' and 'secondary' skills in the following terms:

> In the case of an artistic work for instance, the primary skill lies in the use of a pencil, brush, computer program or other means to create an image. In the case of a literary work such as a novel or screenplay, the primary skill is in the selection and arrangement of words in the course of setting them down.
>
> Examples of secondary skills for, say, a painter are composition and selection of colour. For an author of a novel or screenplay, secondary skills include inventing plot and character.¹⁴⁶

Thus, he appears to distinguish between those who make choices which are closely related to the recording or fixing of a work (primary skills); and those who make preparatory choices related to nonliteral aspects concerning the work's content (secondary skills). Although either skill-types might suffice, Hacon J suggests that as a practical matter, it will be more difficult for those using only secondary skills to establish their joint authorship, since they must demonstrate that their contributions are protectable by copyright, and not 'mere ideas'. Still, the language used in the judgement seem to imply a burden that is greater than an evidentiary one (contributions of primary skills need only satisfy a substantiality test akin to the 'substantial part' test; but, in relation to contributions of secondary skills 'the case law sets the bar high'¹⁴⁷). It is difficult to escape the conclusion that this distinction between primary and secondary skills adds complexity without improving analytical clarity.

There is further evidence that some courts seem to require a higher standard of 'authorship' for joint authorship than for individual authorship.¹⁴⁸ Putting aside the merits of the distinction between primary

---

¹⁴² This may not survive *Infopaq* (n5), see n47 and n70 above. ¹⁴³ *Hadley v Kemp* (n63).
¹⁴⁴ *Brighton v Jones* (n63). ¹⁴⁵ *Fylde Microsystems* (n64). ¹⁴⁶ (n52) [45]–[46].
¹⁴⁷ *Martin v Kogan* (n52) [49]–[51]. This is also evident in Hacon J's discussion of *Cala Homes* (n22) and *Ray v Classic* (n22) [50]: 'If, for instance, an individual were to create the entirety of the plot of a novel or play and all the characters featured in it, and a collaborator were left to do the writing with discretion as to wording, such that the collaborator could not be dismissed as a scribe, I doubt that the possibility of joint authorship *could be ruled out*' (emphasis added).
¹⁴⁸ *Hadley v Kemp* (n63) 644 the court required 'significant creative originality' in a passage described as odd by R Arnold, 'Are performers authors?' (1999) EIPR 464, 467.

and secondary skills, Hacon J's approach typifies two trends which operate in some (but not all) cases. These serve to concentrate authorship in the hands of fewer contributors by favouring the authorship claims of dominant collaborators who control the creative process; and/or those most directly involved in the fixation of the work. These trends are not evident in the cases that take an inclusive approach to joint authorship, but where a restrictive approach is taken one or the other of these trends will usually be present.

First, it is apparent that some courts conclude that a contributor who does not have control of the creative process is unlikely to have made the right kind of contribution. Thus, in *Brighton v Jones*, the court reasoned that Jones' contributions to a play did not entitle her to joint authorship because Brighton had sole discretion to accept or reject her input (characterised as mere suggestions), irrespective of whether Brighton did in fact act upon some of Jones' suggestions. Similarly, in *Hadley v Kemp*, the court held that one member of the band Spandau Ballet was the sole author of most of the band's repertoire. Since Kemp was in charge of the rehearsal process, he could ensure that the songs were made to his vision, and he had the last word on any changes.[149] The court seemed to overlook the musical skills employed by other band members to translate the 'Kemp vision' on their own instruments.

Extrapolating from joint authorship cases such as these, in *Martin v Kogan*, Hacon J distils a factor which he labels as being influential in joint authorship cases: the 'ultimate arbiter'.[150] When a court adopts control over the creative process as the guiding consideration, the resulting work is more likely to be held to be one of individual, rather than joint, authorship.[151] While this outcome may be well have been correct on the specific facts of those cases, an ultimate arbiter approach introduces a bias towards individual ownership of the fruits of collaborative efforts. This risks undermining copyright's incentives in collaborative contexts, making the joint authorship test unsuited to works of collective authorship. The more nuanced approach taken to the question of control in *Bamgboye v Reed* ought to be preferred. Here, the court recognised that Reed, having control over the creative process, had made a more *significant* contribution, but this did not preclude recognition of Bamgboye as a joint author, albeit sharing only one third of the copyright interest.[152]

---

[149] For another example, see: *Fylde* (n64) [40]. Also: *Hatton v Kean* (1859) 7 CB NS 268; 141 ER 819 (Erie CJ).

[150] (n52) [29]; this factor appeared to weigh heavily in the reasoning in that case.

[151] This is not always the case, note, for example in *Cala Homes* (n22) a design director's control over the creative process lead to a broader view of authorship (both he and the draftsmen were joint authors); similarly, see *Heptulla v Orient Longman* [1989] 1 FSR 598 (Indian High Court) and *Hatton v Kean* (n149).

[152] *Bamgboye v Reed* (n54) [29], [74], [77].

It is well accepted that the idea/expression dichotomy has a role to play. A contribution of the right kind must be more than a contribution of mere ideas, it must be reflected in the protected expression.[153] The idea/ expression boundary, however, is notoriously slippery. In *Cala Homes*, the court accepted that joint authorship of an artistic work might arise from purely verbal contributions. According to Laddie J, merely asking 'who pushed the pen is too narrow a view of authorship',[154] since this would prioritise physical/mechanical contributions over other equally important conceptual contributions.[155] Lightman J took a narrower approach in *Robin Ray v Classic FM*, labelling *Cala Homes* as an exceptional case and distancing himself from the notion that 'there is no restriction on the way in which a joint author's contribution may be funnelled into the finished work'.[156] Ostensibly restoring the primacy of the idea/expression dichotomy, Lightman J insisted that a joint author of a literary work must 'participate in the writing'.[157] This seems to present an unduly narrow view of authorship that fails to appreciate the distinction between the expression (the intangible 'work' in which copyright subsists) and its fixation (the physical instantiation or record of the work), meaning that it does not sit well with other case law.[158]

Ray v Classic FM links in with the second case law trend – the focus on fixation – which may result in the concentration of authorship.[159] In *Brighton v Jones*, for example, the court prioritised contributions to the fixation. It acknowledged that Brighton had contributed to the play's concepts and dialogue, but found that Jones was the sole author in light of the fact that she was the one who actually recorded those words on her

---

[153] *Donoghue v Allied Newspapers* (n61); *Brighton v Jones* (n63).
[154] *Cala Homes* (n22) 835–836.
[155] Ibid, 835 (Laddie J): 'It is both the words or lines and the skill and effort involved in creating, selecting or gathering together the detailed concepts, data or emotions which those words or lines have fixed in some tangible form which is protected'.
[156] *Ray v Classic FM* (n22) 636 (Lightman J): 'it appears to me the architects in [*Cala Homes*] were in large part acting as "scribes" for the director. In practice such a situation is likely to be exceptional.'
[157] Ibid, 636 Lightman J stresses '[w]hat is essential is a direct responsibility for what actually appears on the paper'. Similarly at 637 when Lightman J states 'the plaintiff ... was in no wise a collaborator in its production' he seems to be referring to the physical fixation of the work.
[158] For example, *Heptulla v Orient Longman* (n151); *Donoghue v Allied Newspapers* (n61) 109. E Adeney, 'Authorship and Fixation in Copyright Law: A Comparative Comment' (2011) 35 Melbourne University LRev 677 argues that Australian courts have even more explicitly, and in her view erroneously, linked authorship to responsibility for the material form, or fixation, of the work rather than its expression. Tehranian (n2) makes a similar criticism in the US context.
[159] There was also an emphasis on contributions which are fixed in *Tate v Thomas* [1921] 1 Ch 503 and *Tate v Fullbrook* [1908] 1 KB 821 (CA) although those cases concerned the Dramatic Copyright Act 1833.

laptop.[160] Similarly, in *Martin v Kogan*, the primary skills most likely to yield authorship are those contributions which are more directly related to the fixation of a work.

While it is understandable that courts may be generally unsympathetic to claims based upon fuzzy contributions which cannot be precisely tied to an identifiable part of the fixation,[161] copyright protects the expression of a work and not its fixation. There is simply no basis in the CDPA, or its legislative context, for adopting a stricter approach to authorship where there is a plurality of contributors than is taken in the case of a work of individual authorship. Laddie J, in *Cala Homes*, seems alive to this risk, when he stresses that authorship hinges upon responsibility for the content of the *expression* (not its fixation). It will be evident that this approach is preferred to Lightman J's focus upon responsibility for fixation, because it is more attuned to the way in which groups of authors work together to create a copyright work (as the following four chapters will show). Despite this, there is a real risk that courts look to take a restrictive approach to joint authorship for pragmatic reasons, which I discuss in the third part of this chapter.[162]

2.3   A Critique of the Application of the Joint Authorship Test

Having explored the general contours of the joint authorship test, it is difficult to predict how it would be applied to works of collective authorship. First, the cases depend very much upon their facts. But it is not just factual specificity that makes it difficult to draw much guidance from the case law, it is also a lack of analytical clarity in the application of the test.[163] I suggest that the reasons behind this lack of analytical clarity are two-fold: a pragmatic concern to reduce the number of potential joint owners of copyright (who might disagree, potentially inhibiting the economic exploitation of the work); and concerns about aesthetic neutrality when evaluating different types of contribution.

---

[160] (n63) [42], [56].
[161] See, e.g., *Martin v Kogan* (n52) where the lack of clarity in the presentation of Kogan's contributions did not impress the court; *Minder Music v Sharples* (n119) where the court did not accept that a producer's claim to have 'steered' the lyrics of a song in an organic way; *Hayes v Phonogram* (n118) rejecting an argument that the sonoric qualities of rap lyrics influenced subsequent non-rap remixes of the music. But Cf. *Stuart v Barrett* (n118) 455, 459 where the court puts specific weight on the organic and reciprocal nature of a creative process that involved collective jamming.
[162] 2.3. See M Rimmer, 'Heretic: Copyright Law and Dramatic Works' (2002) 2(1) QUT LRev 131, 139, 144.
[163] Indeed, some textbooks and commentaries resort to giving long lists of examples to give the reader a feel for the various circumstances in which joint authorship has and has not been granted, e.g., H Laddie, P Prescott and M Vitoria, *The Modern Law of Copyright and Designs* (4th edn, LexisNexis 2011) [3.97].

This section explores these three themes in order to foreshadow the insights for copyright law that emerge from the consideration of the case studies of collective authorship in the following chapters.

2.3.1 Factual Specificity

It is frequently said that joint authorship is a question of degree which turns on the facts of the case.[164] In such situations, a significant body of case law is required for the jurisprudence to mature and settle into coherent legal principles. This makes it difficult to predict an outcome, particularly where there is no direct precedent, as is the case for collective authorship.[165] But, this uncertainty is also a strength because there is inbuilt flexibility which permits the concept of authorship to adapt over time to new creative forms and techniques.[166] Factual specificity allows judges to calibrate the provisions of the joint authorship test to the specific creative context in which authorship occurs. It makes a one-size-fits-all joint authorship test a workable framework, implementable across a diverse range of creative endeavours.

Spence and Endicott have argued that a degree of vagueness is not a defect in the law, provided that it is controlled by a clear articulation of the purpose of the enquiry and the principles that guide decision-making.[167] Two reasons why the joint authorship test currently lacks the clear articulation required for this beneficial vagueness are discussed in the following sections.

2.3.2 The Pragmatic Instrumental Approach

I suggest that pragmatic concerns about joint ownership may sometimes compel judges to take a restrictive approach to joint authorship. Here, a

---

[164] *Brighton v Jones* (n63) [31] (Park J): ' . . . to a considerable extent the question whether a person is or is not the author of a work within [s10] is one of fact, assisted of course by the wealth of case law which has considered the matter'; *Brown v Mcasso* (n92) [43] (Fysh J): 'Each case stands on its own facts'.

[165] This is the case in the UK. There have been examples in Australia of works which might be argued to be works of collective authorship, but where joint authorship has not been found: *Bulun Bulun v R & T Textiles* (1998) 86 FCR 244 (Fed. Ct. of Australia) (an Indigenous elder claimed that his tribe had a communal authorship interest in an artwork produced in accordance with customary law) (4.2); *Telstra Corporation Ltd v Phone Directories Co Pty Ltd* (2010) 194 FCR 142 (Full Fed. Ct. of Australia) (copyright did not subsist in telephone directories due to insufficient evidence of collaborative authorial input in their creation).

[166] For an example of the benefits of this in another context, consider the change in the way that photography has been treated by copyright law: Bently and Sherman (n 34) 96.

[167] M Spence and T Endicott, 'Vagueness in the Scope of Copyright' (2005) 121 LQR 657 make this argument in the context of copyright scope, considering the idea/expression dichotomy and the substantial part test.

'restrictive approach' is one which imposes an apparently higher standard for authorship of joint works than for single-author works. I argue that this sort of instrumental reasoning hinders a thorough, analytical application of the joint authorship test resulting in uncertainty.[168] Both the restrictive approach and the resulting uncertainty in the law might risk chilling collaborative creativity.

Subject to any over-riding agreement, joint authors will also be the first owners of the copyright that subsists in a joint work.[169] Typically, joint owners of a copyright work will be tenants in common,[170] with a presumption that each joint owner owns an equal share of the copyright interest.[171] However, there are instances where this presumption has been rebutted and ownership allocated in unequal shares according to the significance of each joint author's contributions.[172] Consent is required from each joint owner either to assign rights in the joint work or to licence a third-party to do any of the protected acts, no matter how large their share and regardless of whether the licence is exclusive or non-exclusive.[173] Additionally, the CDPA does not provide that a joint owner cannot unreasonably withhold consent. Thus, the joint ownership rules may appear poorly adapted to situations involving multiple owners.[174] A single contributor, who may have made a relatively small contribution, yields a seemingly disproportionate power to preclude other contributors from exploiting 'their' work by generating licensing royalties. This might be thought to affect creators'

---

[168] This is not the only example of consequentialist reasoning in copyright decision-making. A classic example is the 'principle' that what is copying is worth protecting, which seems to be a sleight of hand designed to transfer complicated considerations of policy to the infringement side of the analysis shifting focus from the proper scope of the rights of the copyright owner to the conduct of the potential infringer.

[169] s11(1), s10(3).

[170] *Lauri v Renad* [1892] 3 Ch 402. They may sometimes hold their copyright interest as joint tenants: *Mail Newspapers v Express Newspapers* [1987] FSR 90 (although the circumstances of this case were unusual).

[171] *Prior v Lansdowne Press* [1977] FLR 59, [1977] RPC 511; *Stuart v Barrett* (n118); *Beckingham v Hodgens* (n90).

[172] For example, *Bamgboye v Reed* (n54) [42] (ownership divided in one third and two third shares); *Fisher v Brooker* [2009] UKHL 41 (Fisher's organ solo entitled him to ownership of 40 per cent of the copyright in the song 'A Whiter Shade of Pale').

[173] *Powell v Head* (1879) 12 Ch D 686. One joint owner can independently sue in relation to an infringement of copyright subsisting in the work, but they may have to account to the other owners. A joint owner may also independently assign his or her ownership share. See further 8.6.1.

[174] Copyright law also provides little guidance as to contributors' rights with respect to one another and in relation to the work as a whole: Elkin-Koren (n29); RC Dreyfuss, 'Collaborative Research: Conflicts on Authorship, Ownership and Accountability' (2000) 53 Vanderbilt LRev 1161.

willingness to collaborate and also potentially undermines the general public's interest in the wide dissemination of creative works.[175]

Given this ownership framework, the trend to apply the joint authorship test in a restrictive manner is understandable. Judges may (whether consciously or sub-consciously) seek to minimise the number of joint owners of a work to reduce the possibility that one contributor might hold-up the exploitation of the work.[176] Simplifying ownership might also mean that assignments and licences of copyright are easier and cheaper to effect.[177] Pragmatic, instrumental reasoning of this type is long evident in the case law, although not always explicitly. In *Levy v Rutley*, one of the first joint authorship cases, the court notes the potential 'inconvenient multiplication of rights and remedies'.[178] Later, in *Hadley v Kemp*, Park J comments that: '... [i]t would be surprising if a slight contribution was enough to make a person a joint author and thereby make him an equal owner with another or others who had contributed far more than he had'.[179] Although this conclusion seems premised upon the misassumption that joint authors are always owners in equal shares, Park J repeats this sentiment in *Brighton v Jones*.[180]

The given quote from *Hadley v Kemp* seems to suggest that the reasons for adopting a restrictive approach might also be intermingled with concerns about fairness. In relation to revenue-sharing, fairness can be adequately ensured by the allocation of appropriate ownership shares according to the significance of each joint author's contribution. But

---

[175] Cf. the US, where one joint owner can non-exclusively licence any use of the work (as long as they account to the other joint owners). Nonetheless, a restrictive approach has also found favour here motivated by a concern that creators may refrain from asking for suggestions of others out of fear that they might claim authorship and gain control over subsequent uses of the work: for example, *Aalmuhammed v Lee* (n111) 1235.

[176] This explanation is also offered by others: D Vaver, *Copyright Law* (Irwin Law, 2000) 76; D Vaver (n124) 121; Rimmer (n162); L Bently, 'Copyright and the Death of the Author in Literature and Law' (1994) 57 MLR 973; C Waelde, 'What Is beyond the Score?' in A Rahmatian (ed) *Concepts of Music and Copyright: How Music Perceives Itself and How Copyright Perceives Music* (Edward Elgar 2015) 23, 33.

[177] Bently ibid.

[178] *Levy v Rutley* (n95) 531 (Montague Smith J); 528 (Byles J) (in relation to the requirement for a common design): 'The plaintiff was ... the contributor of a very small part of the entire piece at a subsequent time ... the consequence of holding [him to be a joint author] ... would be that so many persons as may have contributed separate scenes or portions of a dramatic piece might each have separate and concurrent actions for penalties against a person who may have represented the whole or particular parts of it, without any means on his part of knowing that there was a plurality of authors, or who they were.' See also *Hatton v Kean* (n149) Erie CJ: 'One cannot but perceive, that, if the plaintiff were right in his contention, the labour and skill and capital bestowed by the defendant upon the preparation of the entertainment might all be thrown away, and the entire object of it frustrated, and the speculation defeated, by any one contributor withdrawing his portion.'

[179] *Hadley v Kemp* (n63) 643.   [180] (n63) [34], correcting the point on equal shares.

when it comes to the power to control the exploitation of the work, such a graduated approach is not possible. As a default position, the law provides each joint owner with a veto power to forbid any use of a work, potentially at whim.[181] It is not clear, however, that this outcome is unfair, particularly in relation to the alternative: excluding those who have made (comparatively smaller) authorial contributions from the benefits to which they seem entitled.[182] If, as I have argued, a joint work is best conceived of as something *greater* than the sum of its parts – then, the work would simply not exist but for *all* these contributions. Viewed in this light, it seems proper that all authors must agree to exercise any of the exclusive rights. Furthermore, where disagreements among joint owners are seen to be problematic surely this is better addressed in the law of joint *ownership*, than by reading in stricter requirements for authorship of a joint work than can be justified by the wording in s10 or the general law on authorship.[183]

Another explanation for the restrictive approach may lie in the practical difficulties that arise in establishing evidence of the creative process when putative joint authors come forward after the passage of much time. Yet there are other legal doctrines, including laches and estoppel, which are apt to deal with some of these concerns.[184] Surely evidentiary difficulties should not, of themselves, be taken as sufficient justification to deny the benefits of copyright ownership to a putative joint author. It is the putative joint author who bears the burden of establishing their claim and spurious claims will no doubt be given short shrift by courts.

When faced with the objective of restricting the number of authors of a collaborative project, judges might adopt a combination of strategies, which reveal themselves in the interpretation of the joint authorship test. One is to rule that a contribution is too small. Another is to privilege some contributors or types of contributions over others; for example, finding that there has not been a contribution of an authorship-type (e.g., contribution to interpretation or performance, rather than creation).[185] Similarly, a contribution might fail to be 'significant' unless

---

[181] There are no special rules governing rights of joint owners who are also joint authors and the relationship of one joint owner to another is the same as their relationship to a third party, see further 8.6.1.

[182] The rhetorical power of the romantic author construct might have some role to play in lending plausibility to dominant contributors' claims to sole authorship of joint works, see 2.5.1.

[183] See 8.6.

[184] Delay was a matter of concern in *Hadley v Kemp* (n63), *Brighton v Jones* (n63) and *Godfrey v Lees* (n89). In all these cases estoppel arguments were made.

[185] *Hadley v Kemp* (n63). *Brighton v Jones* (n63) [49], [56] distinguishing a director's contribution from a writer's contribution. Similarly a contribution might be akin to

it is a stand-out part of the work or unexpected type contribution given the designated role of the contributor in the creation of the work. It is these strategies which seemingly impose a de facto higher standard for joint authorship than individual authorship.[186] Often, these findings rely on unsupported and unarticulated assumptions about the scope of the creative process: when it began, when it ended, and what it entailed. Rarely is analysis of the contribution undertaken in a step-by-step fashion, considering each limb of the joint authorship test in turn. More often, one is left to wonder whether a putative joint author's contribution did not suffice because it was not 'significant', not of the 'right kind', or because it was not made pursuant to a 'common design'.[187]

The fact that decisions depend so much on their facts makes it even easier to employ the pragmatic instrumental approach. Comparing cases gives a good flavour of the inconsistencies which result. In *Brighton v Jones*, the judge's focus was on contribution to the fixation (Jones was held sole author in part because she was the one who wrote down the words of the play),[188] whereas in *Hadley v Kemp*, the actual process of fixation seems to have been completely disregarded. Indeed, there the musical works were treated as 'fixed' in Gary Kemp's musical consciousness before he presented his efforts to the band, making him sole author.[189] Authorship, thus, appears as a shapeshifter, expanding in one direction or contracting in another to reach the same result: a concentration of rights in singular rather than plural hands.[190]

---

proof-reading (*Fylde* (n64)) or merely useful criticism (*Wiseman v George Weidenfeld & Nicolson Ltd* [1985] FSR 525) rather than authorship.

[186] For example, see the discussion of *Martin v Kogan* (n52) above p 40–42. Also *Hadley v Kemp* (n63) 634–664, *Brighton v Jones* (n63) [34].

[187] See *Beckingham v Hodgens* (n90) [50] or *Hayes v Phonogram* (n118) where the limbs of the joint authorship test are not even set out in the judgement. In *Brighton v Jones* (n63), a director did not make enough of the right kind of contribution to be a joint author despite the judge describing her contribution as 'valuable and important'. In other parts of the judgement the court suggests that Brighton's contributions were not made at the right time, as they were made when the dramatic work was already complete: [56] point (ii).

[188] (n63) [56].

[189] (n63) 639. The band members were said to be 'interpreting', not creating. Cf. D Free, 'Beckingham v Hodgens: The Session Musician's Claim to Music Copyright' (2005) 1 (3) Entertainment and Sports LJ 93, who argues that if they were interpreting something, it was not something created by Gary Kemp.

[190] In light of the relatively small number of joint authorship cases (few of which contain thorough reasoned discussion of the application of the joint authorship test), it could be argued that these cases have taken on more importance than might be warranted given their specific facts. Although they might be unusual cases, rightly or wrongly, they have had an undeniable influence on the way in which the general jurisprudential approach to joint authorship is understood.

If courts view their task as minimising the number of owners, then their approach is often to find the one, or a small number of individuals, who seem most deserving of copyright ownership. This explains the restriction of authorship to those who are responsible for most of the valuable work to the exclusion of contributors who have made less significant contributions.[191] Inevitably, this also favours those individuals who have exercised most control over the creative process.[192] As we have seen, the presence of a dominant contributor, who is also the 'ultimate arbiter' of the creative process, might typically persuade a court to see a work as one of individual, rather than joint, authorship.[193]

Authorship, on this model is thus likely to gravitate to the most powerful in the relevant industry.[194] These players might also seem to deserve copyright protection most as they may appear best-placed to ensure the work's effective exploitation. Granting authorship based upon the ability to exploit the work, at the expense of other creative contributors arguably distances 'authorship' from its core meaning in copyright law, i.e., a contribution of creative choices to the protected expression.[195] While it might be tempting to deny authorship to those who have made more nebulous, non-literal contributions to the creative process when there is a dominant contributor who has been directly involved in the fixation of the work,[196] this approach is ill-fit for a test which on a plain reading simply requires a merging of contributions pursuant to a common design (even allowing for the additional implied authorship requirement).

Imposing a higher standard of authorship in respect of joint works does not make much sense on the conceptual level, as 'authorship' implies the same consequences, and has the same role in the CDPA, whether a work is

---

[191] In *Hadley v Kemp* (n63) the court considers the only exception to this approach to be where there is a very egalitarian environment, e.g., the 'collective jamming' in *Stuart v Barrett* (n118).

[192] For example, in *Hadley v Kemp* (n63) 641 Gary Kemp was described as a 'control freak' and the band as 'not a democracy'; see also *Brighton v Jones* (n63) [43], [56]. RR Kwall, 'Author-Stories: Narrative's Implications for Moral Rights and Copyright's Joint Authorship Doctrine' (2001) 75 Southern California LRev 1, 5 warns that the even more restrictive application of the US joint authorship test tends to privilege dominant contributors.

[193] *Martin v Kogan* (n52) [29] (Hacon J). Cf. *Bamgboye* (n54) [77], [79] considering creative control to indicate the greater significance of the controlling party's contribution (rather than negating the contribution of non-dominant party).

[194] On the dangers of allowing authorship to gravitate to the most powerful players, see Dreyfuss (n174) 1206, 1209. Also 8.2.

[195] This can be seen in the US where control has become an important part of the joint authorship test, Dougherty (n112).

[196] *Ray v Classic FM* (n22), *Donoghue v Allied Newspapers* (n61).

individually or jointly authored.[197] If short snippets of text are eligible for protection as sole-authored literary works, then why is the same level of input insufficient to claim joint authorship of a literary work? Collaboration is becoming an increasingly important (and in some cases an essential) way of working, not least because groups can sometimes create works that individuals cannot.[198] On the premise that copyright protection seeks to promote cultural flourishing by ensuring society enjoys a wide choice of available works, it would seem perverse to encourage individual authorship at the expense of collaborative endeavours. Equally, if copyright's goal is to reward and/or incentivise authors, then there seems little basis to disincentivise or penalise contributors to a valuable collaborative project[199] in the search of a small number of potential owners.[200] Surely concerns over ownership ought to be addressed, if needs be, by re-evaluated rules on joint *ownership* rather than tinkering with the concept of *authorship*.[201]

It should also be appreciated that denying authorship to contributors of creative content also results in the denial of moral rights.[202] Yet, the case studies will show that authorial credit (attribution) might be more significant to creators than copyright ownership. Thus, such a pragmatic instrumental approach may ignore the realities of collaboration by potentially overlooking what actually incentivises individuals to undertake collaborative work.[203] Additionally, since pragmatic instrumental concerns are accommodated at the expense of a principled analysis of the joint authorship test, case law fails to provide increasing certainty over time, which itself may have a chilling effect.[204] Given the concept of

---

[197] On the possibility of different notions of authorship for the other guises which this concept might take on in the CDPA: L Bently and L Biron, 'Discontinuities between legal conceptions of authorship and social practices: What, if anything, is to be done?' in M van Eechoud (ed) *The Work of Authorship* (Amsterdam UP 2014) 237 suggesting broader attribution rights to address the discontinuities between legal conceptions of authorship and social practices.

[198] A Bell and G Parchomovsky, 'Copyright Trust' (2015) 100(5) Cornell LRev 1015.

[199] In some cases, a work may not have existed at all without the efforts of a large number of people, Vaver (n124) 52–53.

[200] Kwall (n192) 58.

[201] The pragmatic instrumental approach is arguably worse than this, as it appears to empty the concept of authorship of most of its meaning – treating it as a placeholder for the separate concept of ownership. For suggestions on how the rules of joint ownership might be better adapted to collective authorship, see 8.6.3.

[202] This might, perhaps, be understandable in light of the half-hearted implementation of moral rights in the CDPA: J Ginsburg, 'Moral Rights in the Common Law System' [1990] Ent LR 121, 129.

[203] Bently (n176) 981 noting that copyright law prefers to minimise the number of authors rather than reflect the realities of collaboration.

[204] PS Fox, 'Preserving the Collaborative Spirit of American Theatre: The Need for a "Joint Authorship Default Rule" in Light of the Rent Decision's Unanswered Question' (2001) 19 Cardozo Arts & Entertainment LJ 497, 498.

authorship is at the crux of the entire copyright legislative scheme, this is also detrimental to the coherence of copyright law as whole.

The impoverished understanding of 'collaboration' combined with the diminished importance of this part of the test in the UK increases the difficulty of conceptualising collaborative creative processes. The term 'author' then risks becoming a proxy for the most obvious/substantial/dominant contributor, which contradicts the actual legal test for authorship. In this way, the pragmatic instrumental approach (with its failure to contemplate that a variety of contributions may add important value to a work) might seem an instantiation of the romantic authorship myth: the assumption that creativity is the product of the mind of a singular genius figure (see 2.5.1). I will argue that such an approach fails to take collaborative authorship seriously and that the cases which resist this trend provide better precedent.[205]

2.3.3 A Preoccupation with Aesthetic Neutrality

I have suggested that concerns arising from the lack of analytical clarity in the application of the test are compounded by an unwillingness to consider relevant aesthetic considerations explicitly in joint authorship cases.[206] The principle that originality does not require any 'novelty, usefulness, inventiveness, aesthetic merits, quality or value' is a longstanding feature of copyright law.[207] In this part, I argue that the (valid) concern that copyright decisions ought not to depend upon the aesthetic *merit* of a work has evolved into a general collective judicial anxiety about making any sort of aesthetic value judgement.[208] This preoccupation with aesthetic *neutrality*, however, is misplaced in (joint) authorship cases because aesthetic criteria are inescapably relevant to a determination of authorship according to the established test.[209]

---

[205] Cases which have taken a more inclusive approach which better reflects the nature of collaboration as a working together to create something that is greater than the sum of its parts include: *Stuart v Barrett* (n118), *Cala Homes* (n22), *Heptulla v Orient Longman* (n151), *Godfrey v Lees* (n89).

[206] Making this argument in relation to US copyright law more generally: RK Walker and B Depoorter, 'Unavoidable Aesthetic Judgments in Copyright Law: A Community of Practice Standard' (2015) 109(2) Northwestern University LRev 343. This trend is mirrored in academic writing: J Cohen, 'Creativity and Culture in Copyright Theory' (2007) 40 U of California Davis LRev 1151 discusses copyright scholars' preoccupation with neutrality and abstraction.

[207] *Sawkins v Hyperion* (n66) [31].

[208] *Burge v Swarbrick* [2007] HCA 17 (High Court of Australia) [63]: the 'supposed terrors for judicial assessment of matters involving aesthetics'.

[209] Barton Beebe has discussed the role of the concept of aesthetic progress in the US copyright tradition in 'Bleistein, the Problem of Aesthetic Progress, and the Making of American Copyright Law' (2017) 117 Columbia LRev 319.

The preoccupation with aesthetic neutrality is based upon a legitimacy concern: judges are poorly placed to make aesthetic judgements about the aesthetic quality of a work.[210] As Lord Reid puts it:

> Judges have to be experts in the use of the English language but they are not experts in art or aesthetics. ... we must avoid philosophic or metaphysical argument about the nature of beauty, not only because there does not seem to be any consensus about this but also because those who are ignorant of philosophy are entitled to have opinions about what is artistic.[211]

Despite attempts to maintain neutrality, a number of scholars have argued convincingly that copyright cases are affected by cultural[212] and aesthetic biases.[213] This suggests that aesthetic value judgements do, in fact, slip in to judicial decisions.[214]

It is difficult to make sense of the concept of authorship, especially as it is framed in the CDPA, without any resort to aesthetic criteria.[215] In determining authorship, judges often assess the nature of a putative author's contribution relative to the category of work concerned. But, as case law illustrates, it is difficult to assess the literary, dramatic, musical or artistic nature of a contribution without resort to aesthetic judgement about what makes something literary, dramatic, etc.[216] In *Norowzian v Arks*, the court held that dramatic work must be a work of action capable of being performed;[217] in *Lucasfilm v Ainsworth*, a sculpture was held to be something that is intended to be enjoyed visually, not something that is merely utilitarian or functional;[218] in *Sawkins v Hyperion Records* a musical work

---

[210] Cf. *George Hensher v Restawile* [1976] AC 64, 97 Kilbrandon LJ did not think that aesthetic matters were difficult or unseemly for a court to decide (although he thought this unwarranted in that case).
[211] *George Hensher* ibid 78, also 94 (Simon LJ), 96 (Kilbrandon LJ).
[212] A Barron, 'Copyright Law and Musical Practice: Harmony or Dissonance?' (2006) 15(1) Social and Legal Studies 25 discusses copyright law's complicity with the cultural bias against the popular. K Bowrey, 'The Outer Limits of Copyright Law – Where Law Meets Philosophy and Culture' (2001) 12 L and Critique 75 reveals the influence of Western views about creativity in denying the communal authorship claim of an Australian Indigenous tribe, see 4.2.
[213] C Buccafusco, 'Making Sense of Intellectual Property Law' (2012) 97 Cornell LRev 501; B Heile, 'Who Wrote Duke Ellington's Music?' in A Rahmatian (ed) *Concepts of Music and Copyright: How Music Perceives Itself and How Copyright Perceives Music* (Edward Elgar 2015) 123, 125.
[214] Arguing that this is unavoidable: Walker and Depoorter (n206) 343. Arguing that aesthetic neutrality is a cloak to hide biases, rather than remove them: Beebe (n209).
[215] Walker and Depoorter, ibid 345, describe such attempts as 'analytical jujitsu'.
[216] Only very minimal guidance about the meaning of these terms can be found in the CDPA. It is a matter that has been essentially left to case law for definition, see further, J Pila, 'An Intentional View of the Copyright Work' (2008) 71(4) MLR 535.
[217] *Norowzian v Arks (No 1)* [1998] FSR 394 (Ch).
[218] *Lucasfilm v Ainsworth* [2008] EWHC 1878, [2009] FSR 103.

required something more than 'mere noise';[219] and the Court of Appeal in *Hollinrake v Truswell* considered that a literary work must be 'intended to afford either information and instruction, or pleasure in the form of literary enjoyment'.[220] Thus, a literary contribution requires something more than proof-reading[221] or helpful criticism,[222] and a musical contribution is something other than one relating to the performance or interpretation of a musical work.[223] In light of this preoccupation with aesthetic neutrality, it becomes apparent why judges have been hesitant to associate authorship with a requirement for creativity. However, as I have argued already in this chapter, the requirement for some creativity is built into the CDPA. Indeed, consideration of aesthetic criteria seems unavoidable, when tasked with distinguishing a 'creator' from a 'maker' or a 'producer', because these criteria pertain to the very act of creation.

The requirement of authorship is often seen as a shorthand way of asking: is this the sort of thing that copyright ought to protect? This enquiry is far from value-neutral. Indeed, in many cases, the application of copyright's rules of subsistence appears to have been influenced by public policy concerns.[224] Of course, it is essential to consider policy concerns and to use aesthetic criteria to guide decision-making where these yield principles which shed light on the meaning of the CDPA. However, the elision of such matters has led to unhelpfully opaque reasoning, as is evident in many of the joint authorship cases.

Judges, faced with assessing the value and significance of one party's contribution to a work relative to another's, need to have regard to aesthetic matters. In *Beckingham v Hodgens*, for example, what was determinative was that the session musician's violin riff was memorable and catchy. Similarly, in *Brown v Mcasso*, it was the very changes made to the song's lyrics by the junior contributor which gave it an 'authentic' rap feel. Yet, as we have seen, the reasoning provided in these decisions leaves unclear whether these considerations are relevant to determine whether the contribution was significant or of the right kind (or both). Ironically, avoiding explicit discussion of aesthetic criteria can result in courts relying upon their own subjective intuitions in an ad hoc manner.[225] Unsurprisingly, then, the case law on joint authorship faces criticism for appearing arbitrary and subjective.[226]

---

[219] (n66) [53] (Mummery LJ) considering that music is also 'intended to produce effects of some kind on the listener's emotions and intellect'.
[220] [1894] 3 Ch 420 (CA), 428 (Davey LJ); approved in *Exxon* (n34) 142–143 (Stephensen LJ).
[221] *Fylde Microsystems* (n64).
[222] *Wiseman v George Weidenfeld & Nicolson Ltd* [1985] FSR 525 (Ch).
[223] *Hadley v Kemp* (n63).   [224] Spence (n57) 80–82.
[225] Walker and Depoorter (n206) 353.   [226] Zemer (n109).

Instead of striving for complete neutrality, I suggest that it would be better to only avoid subjective judgements of the aesthetic *merit* of a work. This would free up judges to engage directly and openly with questions concerning identification of the aesthetic characteristics of a contribution, which aesthetic criteria should apply in different cases, and how best to evaluate this.[227] This might include consideration of the appropriate weight to place upon the intentions of collaborators, the views of experts, the features of the relevant genre, the impact on the audience and social norms which operate in the particular creative context. An explicit, analytical approach is more likely to enhance the perceived legitimacy of judicial decisions than any surreptitious consideration of aesthetic criteria. Such an approach is also likely to result in greater analytical clarity helping to build up a body of case law that provides increased certainty and a solid foundation for jurisprudential development.[228]

2.4 The Factual and the Normative Dimensions of the Joint Authorship Test

Given the lack of analytical clarity in the case law, it may be useful to suggest a more defined structure. A logical starting point would be to try to separate the parts of the joint authorship test which ought to be treated as questions of law from the parts that ought to be treated as questions of fact. Although vital in many areas of law, the distinction between questions of law and fact is notoriously difficult to justify.[229] The scholarship on this point is primarily focused on public law, where this distinction serves an important role in distributing decision-making power and responsibility. In this context, the predominant view has been that the allocation is ultimately a pragmatic one.[230] Some commentators do argue, however, that an analytical approach is possible.[231] Although it is

---

[227] The CJEU's intellectual creation test might potentially provide a convenient entry point as it directs judges to consider the impact of creative choices.
[228] Walker and Depoorter (n206) 343.
[229] It has been described as 'vexing' by the US Supreme Court in *Pullman–Standard v Swint* 456 US 273 (USSC, 1982), 288. See also: MJ Beazley, 'The Distinction between Questions of Fact and Law: A Question without an Answer?' (2013) 11 The Judicial Rev 279.
[230] P Craig, *Administrative Law* (4th ed, Sweet & Maxwell 1999) 266.
[231] T Endicott, 'Questions of Law' (1998) 114 LQR 292; JW Smith, 'The Analytic Distinction between Questions of Fact and Questions of Law' (2009) 34 Australian Journal of Legal Philosophy, 69. These attempts to determine an analytical basis for the distinction are not without their detractors, for example RJ Allen & MS Pardo, 'Facts of law and facts in law' (2003) 7 International J of Evidence and Proof 135; M Phillis, 'Skepticism about an Analytical Distinction between Law and Fact' (Draft for 2011 ASLP PhD students' workshop, August 1, 2011) at: <ssrn.com/abstract=1956324>.

not necessary to evaluate this scholarship in depth, certain insights from one pre-eminent jurist, Endicott, are worth outlining.

Endicott's careful analysis demonstrates that an analytical approach is possible.[232] He begins by asking what the *point* of is treating certain questions as questions of law.[233] He argues that questions of law are those where the law requires a particular answer to the question.[234] In this way, we might see legal questions as those that have a normative importance in a particular context. They are general questions.[235] On the other hand, in his view, questions of fact are capable of decision either way, in the sense that they require an objective determination (i.e., that a certain state of affairs does or does not exist). These are more particular questions. They are empirical/observational questions that do not bear a normative load per se (although, of course, a determination of fact may have normative consequences).

Even if one does not accept Endicott's analytical approach, it is clear that as a matter of practice, whenever judges, lawyers and scholars refer to questions of law (or questions of fact), they understand each category to share particular attributes.[236] In this sense, the distinction has some identifiable semantic meaning (even for those who believe it to be on shaky analytical grounds). *Ballentine's Law Dictionary* defines a question of law as a question 'as to the terms of the law by which the case is to be adjudicated' and a question of fact to be a question 'of the truth to be decided upon conflicting evidence'.[237]

If questions of law are those that require elaboration of the law (either because of their nature or for pragmatic/functional reasons), which parts of the joint authorship test ought to be considered to be questions of law?

I have already argued that authorship has both a factual and a normative dimension. As an important organising concept in the CDPA, 'authorship' is shaped by the purpose of copyright law (e.g., is this the

---

[232] Endicott, ibid, 318–319. Allen and Pardo, ibid, argue that Endicott's account is ultimately pragmatic as they see it collapsing into a functional account of how to allocate decision-making authority (who should decide a particular question and why). Endicott admits that his approach incorporates both pragmatic and normative considerations. He claims that his approach is analytical, as it starts by asking 'what would make sense of this question?', rather than 'what answer to this question would be convenient?', which is how he characterises the pragmatic approach.

[233] Endicott, ibid.

[234] Endicott, ibid, 318 explains that this might the case in 'a *clear* case of the application of the statutory language, and (ii) when the court exercises its legal power to elaborate the law so as to require (*or* interprets the statutory standard to require) one answer.'

[235] Ibid 293: for example, the question 'what is the offence?'.

[236] P Kirgis, 'Questions of fact in the practice of law: A response to Allen and Pardo's "Facts in Law and Facts of Law"' (2004) 8 International J of Evidence and Proof 47.

[237] *Ballentine's Law Dictionary* (2010, electronic version accessed via LexisLibrary).

sort of thing which copyright law should protect?) and policy concerns that limit its scope (e.g., has enough creative effort been exerted to warrant protection?).[238] The case law establishes that the authorship limb of the joint authorship test is derived from the general requirement for authorship in the CDPA, as such, it too must have a factual and a normative dimension. The normative dimension of authorship must clearly entail a question of law insofar as it probes the underlying purposes of copyright law. Thus, when it comes to determining whether, or not, a contribution is 'of the right kind', this is a question for which copyright law requires a particular answer − the law limits the sorts of activities which amount to authorship. Pragmatically, courts with their copyright expertise and skills of legal interpretation are best placed to answer such a question. However, this is not to say that the facts are irrelevant, as this part of the test must still be applied in light of the facts.[239]

The lack of certainty in relation to the normative underpinnings of copyright does not make this any less of a legal question. The answer to the question 'what is a contribution of the right kind?' cannot be found in prevailing social norms in creative communities. Such norms might conflict with other important policy goals that the law seeks to uphold. Indeed, although it is recognised that contributors might agree in advance who owns the copyright in a work, they cannot contract who will count as an author of the work.[240] In this sense, copyright law provides a source of authorship standards, which are independent of any power imbalances, etc., found in creative communities.[241]

Accepting questions of fact are questions of the truth to be decided upon conflicting evidence (because the law does not require a specific answer to those questions or for pragmatic/functional reasons), which parts of the joint authorship test ought to be considered questions of fact?

Authorship's factual, causative dimension manifests itself in a fairly straightforward manner in cases of singular authorship. It is generally easy to attribute individual responsibility (or not) for the protectable

---

[238] In the words of B Kaplan, *Unhurried View of Copyright* (Columbia UP 1967) 46 'to make the copyright turnstile revolve, the author should have to deposit more than a penny'. In this way copyright law provides a source of authorship standards, see further 8.5.

[239] The creative context might be of assistance in assessing the artistic, musical, literary, etc., character of a particular contribution and in some cases might even shed light on whether a contribution is of a mere idea or is reflected in the protected expression. See further 8.1, 8.5.

[240] Copinger et al. [4-38]; *Samuelson v Producers Distributing* [1932] 1 Ch 201, (1932) 48 RPC 580, 586; *Wiseman v Weidenfeld* (n222).

[241] The importance of the legal dimension of authorship in the application of the joint authorship test is discussed in Chapters 7 and 8, with the limits of social norms considered in more detail at 7.4.3. Of course, greater certainty about the content of 'authorship' would make copyright law an even more valuable source of standards.

expression. When it comes to collaborative authorship, the case studies in this book will demonstrate that the creative process requires a division of labour in which creative control is shared among a number of contributors. This complicates the factual, causative dimension of authorship. The question is who among these (many) contributors is *responsible*, in a copyright sense, for the protected expression; i.e., who of all the contributors has made a 'significant' contribution? Case law appears to imply that for authorship to ensue, a contribution is 'significant' if it is meaningful in a relevant sense. The question arises, therefore, from whose perspective ought this to be addressed?

The requirement for a 'significant' contribution might appear on its face as a sort of threshold requirement for joint authorship. This might lead one to treat it as a legal question, which would imply that the content of this standard ought to be a matter set by the law. Some cases appear to imply that there is a higher standard of authorship required for joint authorship than for singular authorship (see 2.3.2). Yet, as the standard is raised for pragmatic reasons, judges do not tend to articulate a legal standard for the quantum of contribution required. Indeed, copyright law provides no standard for assessing the meaningfulness of a particular contribution. This may be why, in *Fisher v Brooker*, Blackburne J suggests that the requirement for a significant contribution is a de minimis standard, or why Hacon J, in *Martin v Kogan*, appears to elide this requirement with the requirement that the contribution be of the right kind. Yet, more typically, judges appear to allocate authorship based upon whether a contribution is *meaningful* or *valuable* by considering the relevance, attractiveness or value of the contribution within the creative context concerned.[242] Courts have considered, for example, whether a contribution forms a distinctive part of a work or contributes to the aspect of the work which distinguishes it from others of the same genre.[243] Occasionally, they have considered whether the contribution improves the appeal of the work to its intended audience.[244] Although these comments might not always appear clearly tethered to the requirement for a *significant* contribution – I suggest that this appears to be the most logical part of the test in which to incorporate such concerns.

It seems that 'significant' might be understood either as a de minimis quantitative standard or as a qualitative standard which requires a *meaningful* contribution. The former adds little to the test, whilst the latter

---

[242] E.g., *Brown v Mcasso* (n92) [46]; *Bamgboye* (n54) [72].
[243] *Hadley v Kemp* (n63) 650; *Beckingham v Hodgens* (n90) [49].
[244] In *Brown v Mcasso* (n92) [30] contributions that gave a rap song to be used in an advertisement the required authentic feel were significant contributions of the right kind. In *Fisher v Brooker* (n102) [3], [10], [23] the court was influenced by the fact that Fisher's organ solo was distinctive and famous.

requires discerning the relative value of particular contributions. This book argues that the 'significance' of a contribution ought to be assessed by reference to its value in a particular context (not in the abstract). This leaves issues with a likely aesthetic dimension to be answered from the perspective of those (creators) best-placed to answer such questions (see 8.5).[245] Creative communities often have very nuanced contextually sensitive understandings of the meaningfulness or value of particular contributions. The case studies evidence the wide variety of contexts in which collaboration might occur. A fixed legal standard of 'significance' is likely to be far too inflexible to sensibly apply across the range of creative circumstances to which copyright law must be applied.[246] For these reasons, I would argue that the requirement for a significant contribution should be treated as a question of fact.

The joint authorship test also requires joint authors to be collaborating or working with a common design, and their contribution must not be distinct. I have argued that these elements of the test simply indicate that a work of joint authorship involves a working together to create something that is more than sum of its parts. These are matters that are capable of decision either way; that is, copyright law does not require a particular answer to these questions. They are not terms to which copyright ascribes any particular meaning and they do not appear to bear any normative weight, so they too ought to be seen as questions of fact.

In this book, I argue that whether or not there is collaboration is best determined in light of the shared understanding of the contributors objectively construed. Whether or not a contribution is distinct should be determined in accordance with the ordinary meaning of 'distinct' and in light of the creative context.[247] This latter question requires a determination of the scope of a joint work. The scope of a work is something that has usually been treated under UK law as a matter of objective determination.[248] Insofar as dicta from the CJEU in *Infopaq* has been interpreted to mean that parts of a work are separately protectable,[249] this

---

[245] Endicott (n231) 294 argues that the most common use of the notion of questions of law or fact is to distribute decision-making power and responsibility.

[246] On the value of the judicial employment of devices that allow the application extra-legal standards, see J Gardner, 'The many faces of the reasonable person' (2015) 131 LQR 563 (discussing the reasonable person standard).

[247] On the proper approach to determining questions of fact: *Cozens v Brutus* [1973] AC 854, 861 (Lord Reid); *Moyna v Secretary of State for Work and Pensions* [2003] UKHL 44, [2003] 1 WLR 1929.

[248] *IPC Media v Highbury-Leisure Publishing* [2004] EWHC 2985, [2005] FSR 20 [23] (Laddie J) approved in *Coffey v Warner/Chappell Music* [2005] EWHC 449 (Ch) [10] (Blackburne J).

[249] *Infopaq* (n5) [38]–[39], discussed at n47. This has been interpreted as a move away from objectively construing the boundaries of a copyright work, resulting in the potential

may transform the question of what constitutes a 'distinct' contribution into a legal question as the requirement for a work begins to collapse into the originality requirement. This is one reason to doubt the correctness of such an approach.

A key objective of this book is to determine the best way of interpreting the joint authorship test such that it is capable of application to works of collective authorship. In the next section, I glean insights from theories of authorship in scholarly literature. This forms a springboard for a foray into creative practice. Four case studies of collective authorship follow in the subsequent chapters which outline how issues of authorship are dealt with in 'real life' scenarios. The final chapter will bring these two aspects together. Chapter 8 sets out a more elaborated analytical framework for the application of the joint authorship test informed by theory and practice.

2.5 Copyright Scholarship: Theories of Authorship

The critique offered in the previous section reveals the difficulty of predicting how the joint authorship test might apply to any collaboration. This complicates the task of assessing whether the current test can provide a suitable mechanism for determining the authorship of a work of collective authorship. In this section, I consider whether the scholarly literature might shed some light on this question. I begin with the scholarship criticising the influence of the 'romantic author' on copyright law (2.5.1). I note that this critique has led to few concrete, implementable suggestions on how the authorship of collaborative works ought to be determined. Then, I situate this book in the context of broader scholarship addressing the concept of authorship in copyright law, particularly, the influential work of Jane Ginsburg (2.5.2). In 2.5.3 I consider the debate in the US, where an extremely restrictive approach to joint authorship has been taken. Finally, 2.5.4 considers recent trends in copyright scholarship which stress the value of taking into account the context in which creativity occurs and concludes with a comment on the interrelationship of legal and cultural notions of authorship, which underlies the method of this book.[250]

---

dematerialisation of copyright protection (J Griffiths, 'Dematerialization, Pragmatism and the European Copyright Revolution' [2013] Oxford Journal of Legal Studies 1) or the conflation of the concept of the work with the requirement of originality (C Waelde, 'What is beyond the score?' in A Rahmatian [ed] *Concepts of Music and Copyright: How Music Perceives Itself and How Copyright Perceives Music* [Edward Elgar 2015] 23, 34).

[250] See 1.2.

2.5.1 The Romantic Author

The debate on the role of literary theory and the influence of the 'romantic' conception of authorship in copyright law has fuelled many pages of academic writing. The romantic literary tradition of the solo genius conceives of an author's work as an organic emanation from one individual and the embodiment of his or her personality. This conception might be contrasted with a postmodern vision of authorship as a process of cultural negotiation between author and audience in which the work functions as a cultural pastiche.[251] Some commentators view the conception of authorship in copyright law as being intertwined with the traditional romantic authorship model.[252] The typical observation made is that whilst literary theory has progressed under the influence of postmodernist and post-structuralist ideas, copyright law's conception of authorship has remained static, and is still dominated by the romantic model.[253] This blinkered view is blamed for supporting a copyright system which is perceived to grant rights which are too broad in scope, but which also denies protection too often.[254]

There does appear to be some foundation to support this critique in that the basic concepts of copyright subsistence appear inadequate to deal with some situations. In particular, the concepts of a 'work' and of the 'author' have been criticised for being too inflexible to encompass certain creations or creators that ostensibly merit copyright protection

---

[251] JP Barlow, 'The Economy of Ideas: Selling Wine without Bottles on the Global Net' (1993) <homes.eff.org/~barlow/EconomyOfIdeas.html>.

[252] This argument is often combined with the critique that the romantic view of authorship was never a particularly apt view of creative practice. See Woodmansee and Jaszi (n93); J Boyle, *Shamans, Software and Spleens: Law and the Construction of the Information Society* (Harvard UP 1996); D Saunders, *Authorship and Copyright* (Routledge 1992); M Rose, *Authors and Owners: The Invention of Copyright* (Harvard UP 1993); M Rose, 'The Author as Proprietor: *Donaldson v Beckett* and the Geneology of Modern Authorship' (1988) 23 Representations 51. Cf. M Lemley, 'Romantic Authorship and the Rhetoric of Property' (1997) 75 Texas LRev 873; A Adler, 'Against Moral Rights' (2009) 97 California LRev 263. See also discussion in Bently (n176).

[253] For example: M Woodmansee, 'On the Author Effect: Recovering Collectivity' in Woodmansee and Jaszi (n93) 15; M Woodmansee, 'The Genius and the Copyright: Economic and Legal Conditions of the Emergence of the "Author"' (1983–1984) 17 Eighteenth Century Studies 425; D Nimmer, 'Copyright in the Dead Sea Scrolls: Authorship and Originality' (2001) 38(1) Houston LRev 1.

[254] Woodmansee and Jaszi (n93) 10; A Chander and M Sunder, 'The Romance of the Public Domain' (2004) 92 California LRev 1331; P Jaszi, 'Towards a Theory of Copyright: The Metamorphoses of Authorship' (1991) 2 Duke LJ 455 argues that this romantic conception of authorship in copyright law operates to conceal the influence of economic forces in discussions of literary property; M Rose, *Authors and Owners* (n252) 133: 'The story of copyright ... is one of steady expansion'. Cf. Lemley (n252); O Bracha, 'The Ideology of Authorship Revisited: Authors, Markets, and Liberal Values in Early American copyright (2008) 118 Yale LJ; Bently (n176).

(notably including collaborative work).[255] Other aspects of copyright law, however, are at odds with a romantic view of the author,[256] for example:
- the low standard of the originality test (which does not imply novelty);
- the idea/expression dichotomy (which recognises that authors are not the source of original knowledge, but rather are compilers assembling their works from a pre-existing stock of ideas which belong to the public domain);
- judicial reluctance to award protection based upon aesthetic merits;
- the restrictive and narrow provisions on moral rights (which most directly protect an author's personality); and
- a bias in favour of corporations over individuals (rules which automatically vest ownership of copyright in works created by employees in the hands of employers, and prioritise ease of transferring copyright interests, etc.).

These aspects suggest that even if copyright law did once reflect a romantic notion of authorship, this notion does not provide a complete explanation of the modern legal rules for determining the subsistence of copyright.[257] Perhaps this is unsurprising, as law and literary theory are engaged in two very different enterprises.[258] Literary theory seeks conceptions of authorship which aid in understanding the meaning of a text. In this context, postmodern ideas about authorship may well be revealing. Copyright law is usually thought to be much less concerned with the meaning of a work, seeking instead to grant property rights to particular identifiable authors in respect of original works.[259]

---

[255] R Merges, 'Locke for the Masses: Property Rights and the Products of Collective Creativity' (2008) 36(4) Hofstra LRev 1179; DJ Halbert, *Intellectual Property in the Information Age: The Politics of Expanding Ownership Rights* (Quorum 1999); A Stokes, 'Authorship, Collaboration and Copyright a View from the UK' (2002) Entertainment LRev 121.

[256] Lemley (n252) 883.   [257] Ibid, 879; Adler (n252); Bently (n176).

[258] M Price and M Pollack, 'The Author in Copyright: Notes for the Literary Critic' in Woodmansee and Jaszi (n93) 439; Saunders (n252) 233: '... to have believed that a mutation in the literary theory of authorship must produce a corresponding mutation in the law of copyright was perhaps a sign of naivety or aesthetic arrogance'; R Posner, *Law and Literature. A Misunderstood Relationship* (Harvard UP 1988) 17: '... the problems of literary and of legal interpretation have little in common except the word "interpretation"'. Posner argues that literature and literary theory are unlikely to help lawyers and judges to interpret legal texts.

[259] Insofar as questions of entitlement and copyright scope hinge on conceptions of the meaning of a text there might remain a role for insights from literary theory or other scholarship which relates to textual meaning, such as aesthetics or art theory. For an interesting discussion of difficulties of using aesthetics to inform legal scholarship: E Lavik, 'Romantic authorship in copyright law and the uses of aesthetics' in van Eechoud (n197) 45.

Regardless of whether the romantic author model is an adequate explanation of current copyright law,[260] it is generally agreed that copyright is not well-adapted to collaborative authorship.[261] Critiques of the supposed romantic notion of authorship in copyright law have, however, offered few concrete solutions to the problem of determining the authorship of a collaborative work.[262] A truly postmodern definition of authorship equates to a definition of non-authorship, that marks the 'death of the author' to make way for the 'birth of the reader' in its stead.[263] Zemer's work arguably approaches a postmodern concept of authorship. He argues that the general public ought to be considered joint authors of all creative works, because any work is the product of a cultural discourse that is constituted by the general public.[264] Although well-argued and conceptually attractive in some ways, Zemer's proposal would prove extremely difficult to implement.[265] From a practical view, there seems little difference between granting everyone authorship rights and granting no one authorship rights. Once we all become an author of every work, the author label is emptied of any meaning because it cannot distinguish between readers, writers and the general public, even though they each have a different relationship to a work. In addition, such a conception does not reveal any criteria for determining rights between primary and derivative authors.[266]

Arguably, neither a romantic nor a postmodern view of authorship is helpful in clarifying the boundaries and content of the concept of the

---

[260] Arguing that the romantic notion of authorship may not have existed or might be greatly exaggerated: A Rahmatian, *Copyright and Creativity: The Making of Property Rights in Creative Works* (Edward Elgar 2011).

[261] Stokes (n255) 121, 124: ' ... hopes for a simple, pragmatic, fair and meritocratic solution to the questions "who owns a collaborative work" and "what is each collaborator's share of it" are comprehensively dashed by the actual operation of the CDPA'.

[262] Commentators have tended to focus on the infringement side of the analysis, suggesting a more liberal approach to copyright defences/exceptions.

[263] R Barthes, 'The Death of the Author' in S Heath (ed) *Image, Music, Text* (Fontana 1977); M Foucault, 'What is an author?' in D Bouchard (ed) *Language, Counter-Memory, Practice: Selected Essays and Interviews by Michel Foucault* (Cornell UP 1977). It should not be surprising that this proves relatively unhelpful from a legal perspective as this scholarship was directed towards identifying the interpreter who creates the meaning of a text rather than entitlement to copyright ownership.

[264] Zemer (n63), although he does not consider his work in these terms: 'I do not announce the "death of the author"' (228); 'I distance my approach from Foucault and Barthes' (1450). For an argument in favour of 'postmodern law': A Todd, 'Painting a Moving Train: Adding "Postmodern" to the Taxonomy of Law' (2008) 40(1) U of Toledo LRev 105.

[265] RR Kwall, 'The Author as Steward "for Limited Times": A Review of "The Idea of Authorship in Copyright" (Lior Zemer, Ashgate Press, 2007)' (2008) 88(3) Boston U LRev 685.

[266] Lemley (n252) 885. On the value of a postmodern approach in considering questions of copyright scope: P Jaszi, 'Is There Such a Thing as Postmodern Copyright' (2009) 12 Tulane J of Technology & IP 105.

'author' in copyright law. The case studies that follow, however, demonstrate the profound cultural impact the romantic view has had on the way in which authorship has been historically understood in different disciplines.[267] The enduring rhetorical power of the romantic author figure may, thus, provide an additional explanation for the trend in some cases towards a restrictive approach to joint authorship, as the discourse of romantic authorship helps lend cultural credibility to the claims of dominant contributors allowing them to present themselves as more self-evidently authorial than their collaborators.

2.5.2 Ginsburg's Search for Copyright's Author

The concept of authorship is surprisingly under-theorised given its importance as an organising concept in the CDPA, and copyright law more generally. Whilst many scholars have opined about the different theoretical justifications of copyright law, few have attempted a comprehensive theory of authorship. Despite the difficulties of deriving a fully articulated, coherent concept of authorship from case law,[268] some scholars have taken positive steps in this direction.[269] This part develops some suggestions made by one such scholar – Jane Ginsburg.

'In search of an author', Ginsburg has identified six principles which characterise how legal systems typically attempt to identify the author of a copyright work.[270] Ginsburg argues that an 'author' in copyright law generally refers to the person who conceptualises and directs the development of a work, rather than a person who follows those directions to execute it.[271] (This resonates with Laddie J's flexible view in *Cala Homes*, which characterises authorship as more than who pushed the pen.) Ginsburg notes that authorship is a shifting concept that is sensitive to context and that might depend upon the nature of a work and the number of putative authors. Thus, she acknowledges its flexibility to adapt to new creative practices. Ginsburg argues that much of the confusion surrounding authorship arises from an eliding of issues concerning authorship and

---

[267] See 4.2.3, 5.1, 6.1.   [268] Saunders (n252) 213, 235; Ginsburg (n10) 1066.
[269] R Versteeg, 'Defining "Author" for Purposes of Copyright' (1996) 45 American U LRev 1323 argues that the heart of the concept of authorship is the communication of original expression. A Drassinower, 'From Distribution to Dialogue: Remarks on the Concept of Balance in Copyright Law' (2009) 34(4) J of Corporation L 991 presents a concept of authorship as a mode of communication or public address. A similar definition of authorship has been adopted by C Graber and G Taubner, 'Art and Money: Constitutional Rights in the Private Sphere?' (1998) 18 OJLS 61. See also ch 1, n23.
[270] Ginsburg's principles point to characteristics that sometimes indicate authorship, such as, sweat of the brow, highly skilled labour, intent to be a creative author, and investment: (n10) 1071.
[271] Ibid, 1072 noting that *Walter v Lane* (n23) may not sit perfectly with this.

those concerning to ownership (see 2.3.2). In this book, I reassert the importance of preserving a distinction between these two concepts.

Ginsburg calls for emphasis to be placed on those principles which focus on the author themselves and the act of creating.[272] According to Ginsburg, an 'author' for the purposes of copyright law is, or should be:

> ... a human creator who, notwithstanding the constraints of her task, succeeds in exercising minimal personal autonomy in her fashioning of the work. Because, and to the extent that, she moulds the work to her vision ...[273]

This definition has much in common with the CJEU's elaboration of an intellectual creation test of originality which requires creative choices that reflect the author's personality.[274] A further point of commonality between Ginsburg and Laddie J (in *Cala Homes*) is that both suggest that authorship concerns a link between the subjectivity of the author and his or her creation that is difficult to express in precise terms.[275] I have considered that this might best be expressed as a threshold requirement for a more than a de minimis contribution of creative choices or intellectual input to the protected expression.

2.5.3 Nimmer v Goldstein (and Beyond)

Although in terms of joint authorship, US and UK copyright law are different in crucial respects,[276] it is interesting to canvas the views of two eminent US copyright scholars who have disagreed on the proper approach to determine the authorship of collaborative work.[277] The late Melville Nimmer's considered it paramount that the test operate to incentivise and reward collaborators and so took a broad approach to

---

[272] Ginsburg is not alone in calling for renewed focus on authorship in copyright law, see: Bently (n176).
[273] (n10) 1092.
[274] E.g., *Painer* (n42) [92]: 'By making those various choices, the author of a portrait photograph can stamp the work created with his "personal touch".'
[275] Also, Nimmer (n253) 159: '... copyright protection arises only for works that reflect an intent to produce something personal or subjective'.
[276] The wording of the relevant test differs significantly in the US, requiring intention and permitting interdependent as well as inseparable contributions (Copyright Act 1976 (US), s101: 'a work prepared by two or more authors with the intention that their contributions be merged into inseparable or interdependent parts of a unitary whole'). The US test needs to be read in light of its legislative context (which contains work for hire and joint ownership provisions which vary significant from the CDPA). Its interpretation might also be constrained by the origin of the Federal power to enact copyright legislation 'to promote the progress of science and useful arts, by securing for limited times to authors and inventors the exclusive right to their respective writings and discoveries' (US Constitution, Art 1, s 8, cl 8).
[277] On this disagreement: M LaFrance, 'Authorship, Dominance, and the Captive Collaborator: Preserving the Rights of Joint Authors' (2001) 50 Emory LJ 193,

the question of joint authorship. He proposed that all collaborators ought to be recognised as joint authors provided they made a more than de minimis contribution of an authorship-type, pursuant to a common design.[278] Paul Goldstein, on the other hand, argued that to count as a joint author more is required and a contributor must make an independently copyrightable contribution.[279] US courts have tended to favour Goldstein's approach and have taken increasingly restrictive approaches to joint authorship.[280] The US scholarship critical of these developments might provide a timely warning for UK courts yet to apply the joint authorship test in the context of collective authorship.

The trend in recent US case law, particularly regarding film copyright, is to go even further than Goldstein advocated, concentrating the authorship of highly collaborative works in the hands of a single mastermind/ dominant author.[281] This has been driven by a concern that too many owners, each willing to grant licences, may drive the price down and dissipate all profit, since US law grants each joint owner the independent right to grant a non-exclusive licence in respect of the joint work.[282] In this way instrumental concerns have affected the interpretation of the statutory requirements for joint authorship. Thus, control over the project has sometimes been equated to intent to joint author (explicitly required in the US) with the effect of excluding contributors who lack

---

196–197, 259–261; PS Fox, 'Preserving the Collaborative Spirit of American Theatre: The Need for a "Joint Authorship Default Rule" in Light of the Rent Decision's Unanswered Question' (2001) 19 Cardozo Arts & Entertainment LJ 497, 507–509; T Huang, 'Gaiman v McFarlane: The Right Step in Determining Joint Authorship for Copyrighted Material' (2005) 20(1) Berkeley Technology LJ 673.

[278] MB Nimmer and D Nimmer, *Nimmer on Copyright* (1976 edition) 283 ('more than a word or a line'); (2011 edition): '... copyright's goal of fostering creativity is best served, particularly in the motion picture context, by rewarding all parties who labor together to unite idea with form, and that copyright protection should extend both to the contributor of the skeletal ideas and the contributor who fleshes out the project'. For an argument that even contributors of 'substantial ideas' ought to be considered joint authors, see: T McFarlin, 'An Idea of Authorship: Orson Welles, *The War of the Worlds* Copyright, and Why We Should Recognize Idea-Contributors as Joint Authors' (2016) 66(3) Case Western LRev 701.

[279] P Goldstein, *Copyright: Principles, Law and Practice* (Little Brown & Co 1989) 4.2.1.2.

[280] The result has been that often only one or two dominant contributors have been considered authors. This has coloured the interpretation of the requirement for mutual intent to be joint authors, and resulted in the use of control as a proxy for authorship in *Aalmuhammed v Lee* (n111) discussed following and also at 6.2.5.

[281] J Dougherty, 'The Misapplication of "Mastermind": A Mutant Species of Work for Hire and the Mystery of Disappearing Copyrights' (2016) 39 Columbia J L & Arts 463 considers these terms to refer to roughly the same concept.

[282] Subject only to a requirement to account to the other owners: *Erickson v Trinity Theatre* (n138) 1069–1071 (7th Cir, 1994); *Childress v Taylor* (n104) 506–507; *Aalmuhammed v Lee* (n111) 1235–1236; *16 Casa Duse v Merkin* (n111) [7], see further 6.2.5 and 8.6.2.

control over the creative process from authorship benefits.[283] So, in *Thomson v Larson*, it was held that a dramaturg was not a joint author, because it was the scriptwriter who retained sole decision-making authority on the play's content and was billed as sole author.[284] This was accepted as an objective manifestation of the scriptwriter's lack of intent to share authorship of the work.[285] As we have seen, this approach raises the concern that dominant contributors with more control over the creative process will find it easier than other contributors to demonstrate such objective manifestations of intent.[286] The risk is then that the intent requirement becomes a stand-in for control rather than indicating collaboration.[287]

Control has taken on an even greater significance is some subsequent cases, even appearing to serve as a proxy for authorship. In *Aalmuhammed v Lee*, the court held that Aalmuhammed's contributions to a film, although 'substantial and valuable', were insufficient to entitle him to joint authorship for want of 'superintendence' over the work.[288] The court defined the author as the person to whom the work owes its origin and who superintended the whole work, the 'mastermind'. In the court's view, this would generally limit authorship of a film to 'someone at the top of the screen credits, sometimes the producer, sometimes the director, possibly the star, or the screenwriter – someone who has artistic control'.[289] The court expressed concern that a more inclusive approach might actually discourage creators from consulting with others, for fear of loss of sole author status.[290] Unsurprisingly, scholars have criticised this case for adopting instrumental reasoning that foreclosed any meaningful deliberation on the value of particular contributions to a collaborative work.[291] Furthermore, the restrictive approach fails to incentivise collaborators and provides a standard that is vague, unpredictable and unworkable in the context of highly collaborative work[292] (the latter view is

---

[283] Copyright Act 1976 (US), s101: 'a work prepared by two or more authors with the *intention* that there contributions be merged into inseparable or interdependent parts of a unitary whole' (emphasis added).

[284] (n110) 203–204. The author portrayed himself as sole playwright in contracts with third parties and 'was steadfast in his determination to make *Rent* "entirely his own project."'

[285] Ibid, 201.   [286] Also, Kwall (n192) 57.

[287] Tehranian (n2) 1364. For a critique of the way in which the intent requirement has been interpreted: S Balganesh, 'Unplanned Coauthorship' (2014) 100 Virginia LRev 1683; LaFrance (n277).

[288] (n111) 1235 drawing on *Burrow-Giles Lithographic v Sarony* (1884) 111 US 53, quoting *Nottage v Jackson* (1883) 11 QBD 627. Questioning this approach: Dougherty (n112) 278–279.

[289] (n111) 1233, 1235–1236.   [290] *Aalmuhammed v Lee* (n111) 1235.

[291] J Ginsburg, 'Response to David Nimmer' (2001) 38 Houston LRev 231, 235.

[292] Dougherty (n281) 464. Under this test many highly collaborative works may appear authors-less: Nimmer (2011 edn) (n278) 6.07[A][3][c] citing, in particular, the opinion of Judge Posner in *Gaiman v McFarlane* (n138) 659 that in some cases this would result in 'peeling the onion until it disappeared' and Dougherty (n112).

shared even by those who advocate the concentration of ownership rights in works of collective authorship[293]).

16 Casa Duse v Merkin takes this reasoning a step even further. In its search for a dominant author,[294] the court viewed as significant that it was the producer who 'had initiated the project; acquired the rights to the screenplay; selected the cast, crew and director; controlled the production schedule; and coordinated (or attempted to coordinate) the film's publicity and release'.[295] As a result, the film's director was denied joint authorship despite his control over creative (rather than managerial) aspects of the film. Unsurprisingly, this decision has also attracted much criticism from scholars.[296] Dougherty, noting that the statute itself makes no reference to control, makes the following important point:

> Control can be relevant to distinguish mere fixation from original expression, and may be a factor in determining whether or not the creator is an employee, but control is otherwise irrelevant to authorship. Control, in the sense of a right to accept or reject a contribution and use it in a work, is not authorship.[297]

There appear to be only pragmatic, instrumental reasons to hold that a substantial and valuable contribution to a collaborative work is insufficient for joint authorship. Thus, Dougherty argues that the mastermind/dominant author concept untethers copyright law from its fundamental principles. Additionally, this approach results in intolerable uncertainty because control is not always easily located in collaborative creative processes.[298] Thus, US case law serves as a cautionary tale to demonstrate how emphasis on control might skew decisions on joint authorship towards powerful contributors and distance copyright from its core justification: incentivising and rewarding authors.

---

[293] A Casey and A Sawicki, 'Copyright in Teams' (2013) 80 U of Chicago LRev 1683, 1721; also (n113) 1830 and 1835 arguing that there is an unhelpful circularity in using control as a proxy for authorship (determining who ought to have control over the form and subsequent uses of a work by enquiring who has most control over that work).

[294] *16 Casa Duse v Merkin* (n111) 260 the court considered that when 'multiple individuals lay claim to the copyright in a single work, the dispositive inquiry is which of the putative authors is the "dominant author"'.

[295] Ibid, 260.   [296] Dougherty (n281); Tehranian (n2) 1359.

[297] Dougherty (n112) 279.

[298] Control might change over time and ultimate control may not be evident until after the work is complete: Dougherty (n112) 275; (n281) 468. Dougherty links the rhetorical power of this view of authorship in terms of control over the creative process to the romantic author concept. Yet, the dominant approach, in reality, has little to do with the romantic author ideal insofar as it risks concentrating authorship in the hands of orchestrators, rather than creators. Indeed, Dougherty argues that this standard is actually more of a mutant work-for-hire concept.

The US debate is enlightening not only because scholarship highlights the limitations of a restrictive approach, but also because it reveals a more inclusive alternative. The current UK approach still hovers somewhere between the Goldstein/Nimmer extremes.[299] Although there are relatively few cases on joint authorship in the UK, there are troubling trends in some cases to concentrate authorship in the hands of dominant contributors.[300] The powerful critiques offered by US scholars provide a good reason to be sceptical of the usefulness of control (especial understood in terms of decision-making control) as a proxy for authorship.[301] They demonstrate how the pragmatic, instrumental approach can cause an unjustifiable disconnect between the reasoning adopted in joint authorship cases and the concept of authorship at the heart of copyright law. This book follows the path lit by Nimmer, arguing for an inclusive approach to the application of the joint authorship test.

2.5.4 The Value of Social and Cultural Conceptions of Authorship

Increasingly, commentators are noting a gap between social practices and copyright law's concept of authorship.[302] Dreyfuss offers a new concept of the 'collaborative work' to realign copyright law with social practices in large scientific collaborations.[303] Biron and Cooper offer insights from aesthetics, arguing that concepts such as role, intention and authority might be usefully employed to enhance copyright law's flexibility and make it more adaptable to changes in creative practice over time.[304] Kwall stresses the importance of considering the perspectives of authors (as reflected in the narrative of creation).[305] These theorists are part of a growing body of literature that stresses the relevance of the context in

---

[299] Zemer (n109) 288 considers it to be closer to the Nimmer approach, although he writes prior to the court in *Martin v Kogan* (n52) [29] clearly specifying the 'ultimate arbiter' as a factor relevant to joint authorship determinations.

[300] 2.2.3 and 2.3.2.

[301] The case studies in the following chapters show that such a standard is disconnected from the reality of the collaborative process, where creative control is necessarily dispersed, see 7.1. See also Tehranian (n2) 1365; Casey and Sawicki (n293) 1720.

[302] Bently and Biron (n197). On the gap between copyright law and practices of attribution see also: C Fisk, 'Credit Where It's Due: The Law and Norms of Attribution' (2006) 95 Georgetown LJ 49; G Lastowska, 'The Trade Mark Function of Authorship' (2005) 85 Boston U LRev 1171.

[303] Dreyfuss (n174).

[304] L Biron and E Cooper, 'Authorship, Aesthetics and the Art World: Reforming Copyright's Joint Authorship Doctrine' (2016) 35 Law and Philosophy 55, referring to the relational theories of Arthur Danto, George Dickie and Jerrold Levinson.

[305] Kwall (n192).

which creativity occurs.[306] Some scholars even take this even further, arguing that in some cases social practices might provide an effective substitute for copyright law.[307] In Chapter 8, I argue that there are some good reasons for copyright law to have regard to social practices, as well as some potential dangers.

It should also be kept in mind that copyright law is not alone in establishing a specific notion of authorship. Aside from its legal dimension (who the law considers to be an author for the purposes of copyright law and related rights), authorship has many other possible dimensions including: a historical dimension (located temporally); a social dimension (who judges who is an author); a cultural dimension (what it means to be an author of a work); and a technological dimension (the mechanical aspects of creation).[308] In cultural terms, whether (or not) a creator is an author is a socio-historical question based upon technology and politics.[309] In this context, what it means to be an author will be different to different interpretative communities (i.e., literary critics, authors, copyright lawyers and the public). In cultural terms, the label 'author' is important in ensuring that creators are accountable for what they create by identifying an originator of a work who is socially and legally responsible for its content.[310] Thus, authorship has a specific meaning which allows readers to make generalisations about the truth and reliability of a work by reference to broadly located sources of meaning in respect of the particular author and in respect of the aesthetic or expressive tradition to which the work belongs.[311]

Scholars agree that the legal definition of authorship might be influenced by other dimensions of authorship (i.e., what it means to be an author or to

---

[306] LJ Murray, S Tina Piper and K Robertson, *Putting Intellectual Property in Its Place: Rights Discourses, Creative Labor, and the Everyday* (OUP 2014); Cohen (n206).

[307] Casey and Sawicki (n113). E Rosenblatt, 'A Theory of IP's Negative Space' (2011) 34 (3) Columbia J of L and the Arts 317; the scholarship on intellectual property's negative spaces referred to in Chapter 1, n65.

[308] J Griffin, 'The Changing Nature of Authorship: Why Copyright Law Must Focus on the Increased Role of Technology' (2005) IPQ 135, 137 argues that technology is a central component of authorship.

[309] M Ross, 'Authority and Authenticity: Scribbling Authors and the Genius of Print in Eighteenth Century England' (1992) 10 CAELJ 495, 495.

[310] Griffin (n308) 193: 'authorship is used as a method of quality control by readers'; Lastowska (n302); J Ginsburg, 'The Author's Name as a Trade Mark: A Perverse Perspective on the Moral Right of "Paternity"?' (2005) 23 Cardozo Arts and Entertainment LJ 379.

[311] Shapin considers the significance of trust and its relation to cultural ideas about the location of textual authority in constituting knowledge: S Shapin, *A Social History of Truth: Civility and Science in Seventeenth-Century England* (U of Chicago P 1994); also J Pila, 'Authorship and e-Science: Balancing Epistemological Trust and Skepticism in the Digital Environment' (2009) 23 Social Epistemology 1 on the role of authorship in balancing epistemological trust and skepticism in e-science.

create a literary work in social and cultural terms, etc.).[312] Coombe argues that the relation between law and culture is best conceived of as one of 'mutual rupturing'.[313] The attribution of the label of 'author' in copyright law has significance for the public at large because the law can serve as a valuable source of default rules, policy and public interest safeguards.[314] By defining who is an author, copyright law has an important role to play in constituting textual authority (who can be held responsible for that work).[315] The wider interpretative community's attribution of textual authority is necessarily influenced by whom copyright law recognises as an author. But because the relationship between law and culture is not simple or linear, it may be informative to consider significant reasons for the attribution of authorship that are external to the legal definition.[316]

Cultural ideas have a place within legal notions of authorship. Once it is acknowledged that it is virtually impossible to decide who counts as an author without reference to aesthetic criteria, it must be recognised that there are better sources of information about these criteria external to legal discourse. Musicians, for example, have a valuable perspective, and greater knowledge, of what constitutes a musical contribution than judges or lawyers. The creative context might provide important information that can help courts answer questions of fact. It may shed light on what contributors intend to do, how they see each other, and which aspects of the creation are meaningful to them.[317] These perspectives are particularly relevant to the determination of whether a contribution is 'distinct', whether it is 'significant', and whether contributors are 'collaborating'. Perhaps the most important reason for a link between the legal conception of authorship and social or cultural understandings of authorship is that this is important for copyright law's legitimacy and credibility.[318]

---

[312] Pila (n216) 557 argues that legal conceptions of authorial works ought to be anchored in non-legal conceptions of them.
[313] R Coombe, 'Contingent Articulations: A Critical Cultural Studies of Law' in A Sarat and T Kearns (eds) *Law in the Domains of Culture* (U of Michigan P 1998); R Coombe, 'Fear, Hope and Longing for the Future of Authorship and a Revitalized Public Domain in Global Regimes of Intellectual Property' (2003) 52 DePaul LRev 1171.
[314] Pila (n311); Dreyfuss (n174); R Coombe, *The Cultural Life of Intellectual Properties: Authorship, Appropriation and the Law* (Duke UP 1998) particularly the Introduction.
[315] Saunders (n252) 213: 'in a culture as juridified as ours, the phenomenon of authorship cannot be defined independently of, or prior to, its legal conditions'.
[316] Ibid.
[317] Some see intention as a crucial aspect of the determination of copyright subsistence: Nimmer (n253); Pila (n216); Buccafusco (n2).
[318] Bently and Biron (n197); A Barron, 'Copyright and the Claims of Art' (2002) 4 IPQ 368, 399: '... the relation between art and copyright law *matters*; and in particular that copyright law is in some important sense answerable to the claims of art, and amenable to being judged by reference to whether and how it responds to those claims'. See also 8.1.

70   Copyright and Collective Authorship

I will consider how far legal decisions can be usefully informed by social norms in Chapters 7 and 8.

2.6 Conclusion

Although the contours of the concept of authorship in copyright law are uncertain, I have argued that authorship does have a stable core meaning, which requires a more than de minimis contribution of creative choices or intellectual input to the protected expression of a copyright work. A number of scholars propose that copyright law's rules of subsistence are poorly adapted to collaborative activities, because of the remaining influence of the out-dated literary trope of the romantic author. Whether this is best explanation, or not, is unclear; but my analysis does identify a tendency in some cases to concentrate authorship in the hands of one or two dominant contributors. I have argued that this approach is not mandated by the wording of CDPA provisions on joint authorship, but results from the way in which those provisions have been applied, and based on a particular pragmatic, instrumental objective. If the romantic author has any impact at all, it is likely to be on those who apply the law, due to its power as a rhetorical tool to tap into cultural discourses about authorship which may tend to lend credibility to the claims of some contributors at the expense of other collaborators. Ultimately, it is difficult to predict how the joint authorship test would apply to a work of collective authorship because of the factual specificity of the test and the lack of analytical clarity in the limited body of case law. These factors combine to create significant legal uncertainty which has the potential to chill collaborative creativity.

I presented three themes which emerge in the application of the joint authorship test. The first, factual specificity, is a positive aspect of the test allowing it to adapt to different creative contexts. The second theme is the tendency to apply a restrictive approach to the joint authorship test with the aim of concentrating copyright ownership in the hands of a few (primarily for pragmatic reasons). This approach is undesirable because it risks divorcing the test from the core meaning of authorship in copyright law. The third theme is a judicial preoccupation with aesthetic neutrality. Courts' reluctance to refer to aesthetic criteria when discussing individual contributions to a work for appearing to judge it on its merits makes it difficult to take the context of creativity into account. This leaves the joint authorship test without adequate tools to differentiate between authors and mere contributors, particularly where responsibility for the creative or intellectual content of a work is shared between many. These final two themes suggest that the joint authorship test as currently applied may determine the authorship of a work in a way that fails to reflect the reality of collective authorship.

The working premise of this book is that analysis of the manner in which creative communities, engaged in collective endeavours, regulate collective authorship themselves can enrich our understanding of how authorship of such works should be determined for copyright's purposes. The aim is to assess how the joint authorship test ought to be applied so as to retain the strengths of the current law, particularly, the flexibility of the concept of authorship, while more accurately tracking the law's purpose to incentivise and reward authors, being those who make minimally creative or intellectual contributions to protected expression. It is proposed that the best approach is one which enhances, or at least does not detract from, the credibility of copyright law as a tool for regulating authorship.

The case studies contained in the next four chapters reveal that there are good reasons for UK courts to follow Nimmer's lead and adopt an inclusive approach when applying the joint authorship test in cases of collective authorship. They will show that the pragmatic instrumental approach is based upon assumptions which are far-removed from the reality of collective authorship. Taking this on board, I recommend an approach which is *inclusive* (because it includes all those who would qualify as authors), and *contextual* (as it takes the social norms which govern creativity in collective authorship groups into account in answering relevant questions of fact).

3   Wikipedia

Wikipedia, the popular online encyclopaedia, is one of the most visited websites on the internet.[1] It is the site for a unique form of creativity that is interactive, dynamic and highly iterative. Wikipedia promotes a model of creativity that intentionally blurs the distinction between reader and writer. It is an example of the increasing use of applications which facilitate the interactive and collaborative use of the internet, which is often described as Web 2.0.[2] Web 2.0 technology has transformed processes of cultural production by providing authors with new sources of inspiration and greatly facilitating the creation, dissemination and publication of works, thereby permitting more people than ever before to participate in creative processes. A number of commentators have observed that copyright law provides a significant impediment to much of the innovation facilitated by Web 2.0.[3] Some claim that copyright law is at a moment of crisis,[4] or at least, in need of substantial reform as many of its concepts seem to conflict with norms and community expectations which have developed in the context of this new digital environment.[5] As the 'poster child for the collaborative construction of knowledge and truth that the new, interactive Web facilitates',[6] Wikipedia makes an interesting case

---

[1] At the time of writing, Alexa ranked www.wikipedia.org fifth globally in terms of internet traffic: <www.alexa.com/siteinfo/wikipedia.org>. This book primarily refers to the English language version of Wikipedia, see <en.wikipedia.org/wiki/Main_Page>.

[2] T O'Reilly, 'What Is Web 2.0?' <www.oreillynet.com/pub/a/oreilly/tim/news/2005/09/30/what-is-web-20.html>.

[3] L Lessig, *Remix: Making Art and Commerce Thrive in the Hybrid Economy* (Penguin Press 2008); D Tapscott and A Williams, *Wikinomics: How Mass Collaboration Changes Everything* (Atlantic Books 2008) 25–27; N Elkin-Koren, 'Tailoring Copyright to Social Production' [2011] 12 Theoretical Inquiries in Law 309.

[4] S Corbett, 'Creative Commons Licences, the Copyright Regime and the Online Community: Is There a Fatal Disconnect?' (2011) 74(4) MLR 503.

[5] R Merges, 'The Concept of Property in the Digital Era' (2008) 45(4) Houston LRev 1239 provides a summary and critique of some of these arguments. See also Lessig (n3); DJ Halbert, *Intellectual Property in the Information Age: The Politics of Expanding Ownership Rights* (Quorum 1999).

[6] W Richardson, *Blogs, Wikis, Podcasts, and Other Powerful Web Tools for Classrooms* (Corwin Press 2006) 61–62.

study of collective authorship and the challenges that it might pose to copyright law's joint authorship test.

This chapter begins by considering the dynamics of creativity on Wikipedia: briefly describing how it works; and suggesting some reasons why it works. I explain that authorship on Wikipedia is understood as a donation of creative efforts to an altruistic community project. In the second section, I consider the subsistence of copyright on Wikipedia, asking whether: (i) Wikipedia as a whole, or individual Wikipedia pages, would be recognised as original literary works in which copyright subsists for the purposes of CDPA; and (ii) whether Wikipedia contributors would be recognised as joint authors and thus copyright owners. I conclude that it is at least unlikely, and at most uncertain, that Wikipedia contributors would be considered to be joint authors of individual pages to which they have contributed. The third section examines the role of copyleft licences in sustaining collective creativity on Wikipedia. I argue that copyleft licences are more effective as a means of reinforcing Wikipedia's sharing norms, than they are as legal instruments. The fourth section concludes with some insights for copyright law that arise from this case study.

3.1 Authorship Dynamics: Promoting Sharing

This section considers the dynamics of authorship on Wikipedia. These dynamics are influenced by three significant features of Wikipedia, namely that: (i) it is a perpetual work in progress; (ii) created collaboratively by people all over the world who may have never met, who work incrementally and autonomously;[7] and (iii) it relies upon social norms that reflect community values, in particular, sharing. On Wikipedia, authorship is a very inclusive notion that is defined in terms of participation in a non-profit community project with public-minded goals.

Wikipedia calls itself 'the free encyclopedia that anyone can edit'.[8] There are many differences between Wikipedia and traditional paper encyclopaedias like *Encyclopaedia Britannica*. *Encyclopaedia Britannica* commissions experts to write articles which are presented as an evaluative synthesis of views which approach the 'truth' on a subject. The subject of

---

[7] Although most contributors will not have met one another, the platform provides a tool for instant communication which facilitates and encourages collaboration. Some groups of contributors organise local face-to-face meetings with each other: <en.wikipedia.org/wiki/Wikipedia:Meetup>. There is also an annual international Wikimania Conference for users of projects operated by the Wikimedia Foundation (<en.wikipedia.org/wiki/Wikimania>).

[8] <www.wikipedia.org>.

each article is chosen by an editorial board with almost no input from readers and each edition is published (and sold) only when complete. Wikipedia, by contrast, is created by an extensive, loose, global network of collectively-organised volunteers and is made freely available to anyone with an internet connection.[9] It aims to present a selection of currently prevalent representations of knowledge, rather than the truth on any subject.[10] Contributors have a great degree of freedom to determine its content and scope. Authorial freedom is limited by three core policies ('No Original Research', 'Verifiability' and 'Neutral Point of View'), which have been adopted, and are enforced, by the community of Wikipedians. These policies aim to ensure that Wikipedia's content is factual, attributable to reliable published sources and all sides of a dispute are fairly presented.

Contributions can be made by anyone, regardless of their level of expertise, at any time.[11] Wikipedia is a constant work in progress that grows by the accumulation of a great many relatively small contributions. Wikipedia works on the assumption that many different users will continually refine or 'refactor' each individual page until the page stabilises and comes to represent the voice of the community.[12] In this way, it makes more sense to think of Wikipedia as a creative *process* than a creative *product*. Indeed, Wikipedia is best conceived of as a perpetual work in progress. Although it may seem that such a process could only result in chaos, Wikipedia has organised itself over time through the consensus-driven activities of its community of regular contributors.

---

[9] This is made possible by wiki software which allows web pages to be created, edited and linked to one another by anyone in real time using a common web browser: A Ebersbach, M Glaser and R Heigl, *Wiki: Web Collaboration* (Springer 2006) 14–17. Although Wikipedia is collectively organised, Jimmy Wales, (co-founder of Wikipedia and sometimes referred to as its benevolent dictator) is an influential figure; and the inner core of highly active contributors have a particularly important role in steering its course. For a nuanced discussion of leadership on Wikipedia, see JM Reagle, *Good Faith Collaboration: The Culture of Wikipedia* (MIT 2010) Ch 6.

[10] A Bruns, *Blogs, Wikipedia, Second Life, and Beyond: from Production to Produsage* (Peter Lang 2008) 114. The debate on the reliability of Wikipedia is outside the scope of this book, but see A Keen, *The Cult of the Amateur: How Today's Internet Is Killing our Culture* (Doubleday/Currency 2007); L Sanger, 'WHO SAYS WHAT WE KNOW: On the New Politics' (*The Edge*) <www.edge.org/3rd_culture/sanger07/sanger07_index.html>; cf. Bruns 121.

[11] To adopt Eric Raymond's oft-quoted observation on the creation of Linux, Wikipedia is not built like a cathedral 'carefully crafted by individual wizards', but more like 'a great babbling bazaar of different agendas and approaches ... out of which a coherent and stable system could seemingly emerge only by a succession of miracles': 'The Cathedral and the Bazaar' <www.catb.org/~esr/writings/cathedral-bazaar/cathedral-bazaar/>.

[12] Bruns (n10) 321.

In the 'Village Pump' section of Wikipedia, users collaborate to create policies, style guides, codes of conduct and other self-governing mechanisms to regulate the community's activities. Perusal of this behind-the-scenes space reveals that Wikipedia sees itself as defined by five fundamental principles, or 'pillars':
• Wikipedia is an encyclopaedia;
• Wikipedia is written from a neutral point of view;
• Wikipedia is free content that anyone can use, edit, modify and distribute;
• Editors should treat each other with respect and civility; and
• Wikipedia has no firm rules.[13]

Wikipedia has developed complex dispute resolution mechanisms for dealing with editorial and other conflicts.[14] This transparent process of holding one another accountable helps promote the collaborative culture Wikipedia depends upon for its success.[15] Thus, a sense of what it means to be a 'good' Wikipedian emerges in the resolution of disputes and in the fashioning and applying of community policies.

Wikipedia contributors might undertake a variety of different activities including: contributing content, editing, correcting spelling and grammar, devising and running 'bots'.[16] creating and enforcing community policy, helping to resolve disputes, etc. Many of these are community sustaining activities rather than purely content creating activities. There are a variety of levels of access to the functionalities of Wikipedia's wiki software which a user might attain over time if they participate as a good Wikipedia community member. Each Wikipedia page has a history page associated with it which allows users to see previous versions of the page so that quick reversions might be made if it is affected by vandalism or spam and so that contributions might be clearly identified by user name (for a registered user) or IP address (for an 'anonymous' user).[17] Every time a contributor edits a Wikipedia page that page is reproduced and published online. In order to avoid future claims of copyright infringement, when a contributor adds anything to Wikipedia he or she must

---

[13] <en.wikipedia.org/wiki/Wikipedia:Five_pillars>.
[14] <en.wikipedia.org/wiki/Wikipedia:Dispute_resolution>. This may include editor-moderated discussion, seeking a third opinion, community input, input from a more experienced editor, formal mediation or, as a last resort, arbitration.
[15] Reagle (n9) discusses the importance of good faith and pro-social norms in fostering this culture.
[16] These are semi-automated tools or 'robots' which carry out mundane or repetitive tasks.
[17] This aids openness and transparency which increases accountability and helps socialise newcomers. Editorial disputes can also have an important role in constructing Wikipedia's collaborative culture: Reagle (n9) 51.

agree to allow that contribution to be reproduced or modified by anyone for free (under certain conditions) pursuant to copyleft licences.[18]

Wikipedia works because the barriers to contribution (money, technical expertise, time, etc.) are minimal. A sense of community is often seen as a key factor in ensuring that there are more positive than negative contributions.[19] Wikipedia fosters this sense of community through the activities of its welcoming committee,[20] the discussion pages linked to each page, the use of consensus-driven policies[21] and the principle of Wikiquette.[22] People contribute to Wikipedia for a variety of non-financial reasons: because they want to teach the world about something that they are enthusiastic about, out of a sense of altruism, just for fun, or 'because there's nothing better on television'.[23] Some contributors might be motivated by a desire to attain status and respect within this community. Contributors grant each other 'barnstars' for positive contributions to Wikipedia and its community.[24] Although contributors to Wikipedia might have different motivations, they are bound together by the act of contributing towards the shared goal of the community: providing a free encyclopaedia that anyone can edit.[25]

Cass Sunstein suggests that the concept of authorship makes no sense in the context of Wikipedia.[26] This is because of the unique way in which

---

[18] When a contributor makes changes to Wikipedia, he or she sees the following message displayed above the 'Save Page' button: 'By publishing changes, you agree to the Terms of Use, and you irrevocably agree to release your contribution under the CC-BY-SA 3.0 License and the GFDL. You agree that a hyperlink or URL is sufficient attribution under the Creative Commons license' (including hyperlinks to the licences and Terms of Use).

[19] Bruns (n10) 110; S Rafaeli and Y Ariel, 'Online Motivational Factors: Incentives for Participation and Contribution in Wikipedia' in A Barak (ed) *Psychological Aspects of Cyberspace: Theory, Research, Applications* (CUP 2008). It is also important to have enough contributors for this to work. Wikipedia has a very active core of regular contributors. In April 2018, for example, English Wikipedia had 34,251,800 registered users, of which only 120,446 had made edits in the previous 30 days: <en.wikipedia.org/wiki/Wikipedia:Wikipedians>.

[20] <en.wikipedia.org/wiki/Wikipedia:Welcoming_committee/Welcome_to_Wikipedia>.

[21] <en.wikipedia.org/wiki/Wikipedia:List_of_policies_and_guidelines>.

[22] <en.wikipedia.org/wiki/Wikipedia:Etiquette>. See also Reagle (n9) on the importance of good faith to Wikipedia's collaborative culture.

[23] Bruns (n10) 112; Lessig (n3) 162.

[24] <en.wikipedia.org/wiki/Wikipedia:Barnstars>. Barnstars are displayed on a contributor's userpage and are available to reward virtually any type of contribution. Some examples include: the Barnstar of Good Humour (for lightening the mood); the Anti-Vandalism Barnstar; the Barnstar of Diplomacy; the Copyright Clean-up Barnstar. Giving barnstars, when they are earned, is particularly encouraged by a group of contributors who have formed what is known as the 'Kindness Campaign'.

[25] There is a more ambitious ultimate vision for Wikipedia as a tool for disseminating the sum of human knowledge to everyone on the planet.

[26] C Sunstein, *Infotopia: How Many Minds Produce Knowledge* (OUP 2006) 153.

the wiki software it relies upon allows people to add, delete, and change the content of any page in real time. Implicit in Sunstein's suggestion is that the notion of authorship necessarily implies control or dominion over a work, a notion of authorship that appears linked to a particular view of copyright's notion of the author as first owner of copyright's exclusive rights.[27] This view tends to conflate authorship and ownership, concepts which I have argued ought to remain distinct.[28] In Chapter 2, I also expressed reservations about the use of control as a proxy for authorship because of the potential of this approach to distance authorship from the creator(s) of the protected expression.

Rather than being a space of non-authorship, I would suggest that the Wikipedia community crafts its *own* concept of authorship. In doing so the community taps into some of the values of copyright's proprietary notion of authorship, whilst discarding other aspects of it. Wikipedians have created their own concept of authorship which is tailor-made to the project's needs. Authorship on Wikipedia is an extremely inclusive and community-orientated notion built on sharing rather than exclusion. It is a dynamic concept that is defined in terms of participation in a shared project with altruistic goals. Participation is shaped by adherence to a set of community-developed policies and norms that are crafted to reflect the project's aims.[29] This alternative view of authorship means that some activities which Wikipedians conceive of as vital to the creative process might not count as authorial activities in a copyright sense.

A crucial feature of Wikipedia's sense of community is the notion that Wikipedia is a sharing economy which operates in the absence of the 'usual' notions of authorship in the sense of the ownership and control of works.[30] Contributors make their contributions for free and expect others to modify or even destroy them. Wikipedia is thought of as owned by no one, to be shared by all.[31] The next section considers whether Wikipedia is in fact owned by no one in copyright terms; and the following section considers whether the operation of copyleft licences really does ensure that content may be shared by all.

---

[27] This view also assumes a conception of authorship aligned with the romantic author model that is not a good fit both for copyright law and for creative practice, see 2.5.
[28] See Chapter 2.
[29] So, for example, the no original research policy reflects the anti-expertise bias of the site; and the neutral point of view policy reflects the desire to create a factual work of reference.
[30] Sunstein (n26) 153.
[31] <en.wikipedia.org/wiki/Wikipedia:Ownership_of_articles> still substantially reflecting the statement made in 24 September 2003, on the original version of this page, that: 'No one person "owns" the articles in the Wikipedia. They are the common property of all humankind. The license known as [[GFDL]] guarantees this.'

3.2 Copyright Subsistence on Wikipedia

Wikipedia encourages users to download and print pages and even to create books of collections of Wikipedia pages.[32] Whilst there are many pages of discussion dedicated to dealing with the problem of identifying and removing copyright infringing material, the Wikipedia community spends considerably less time considering the extent to which copyright subsists in Wikipedia itself and which contributors, if any, might own that copyright.[33] Presumably, this is because the act of contributing to Wikipedia is often seen to imply the relinquishment of the usual incidents of authorship, such as the right to control certain reproductions of the work, for the greater good of the Wikipedia project (the creation of a free encyclopaedia that anyone can edit) in the spirit of its ethic of sharing.[34] Nonetheless, this question merits some consideration.

3.2.1 Is Wikipedia (or Parts Thereof) an Original Literary Work?

Section 1(1)(a) of the CDPA provides that copyright subsists in an 'original literary, dramatic, musical or artistic work'. Copyright may subsist in: an individual Wikipedia page as a literary work; or in Wikipedia as a whole as a literary work which is a compilation or a database. Individual Wikipedia pages are clearly 'literary' in the relevant sense.[35] They are also likely to be original as long as they are an 'intellectual creation', the result of creative choices (or skill, labour and judgement).[36] Some 'stub' pages may not be sufficiently substantial or original for copyright to subsist in them.[37] It is difficult to define the

---

[32] Facilitated by links on the left-hand side of each Wikipedia page.
[33] To the author's knowledge no court has considered the subsistence of copyright in Wikipedia to date. Wikipedia's copyright policy can be found at: <en.wikipedia.org/wiki/Wikipedia:Copyrights>.
[34] There is, however, a notion of the integrity of contributions. Thus, there is a preference to improve, rather than delete, salvageable text. Changes must also be accompanied by an explanation as to why they were necessary. See: <en.wikipedia.org/wiki/Wikipedia:Dispute_resolution> and <en.wikipedia.org/wiki/Wikipedia:Editing_policy#Try_to_fix_problems>.
[35] s3(1), s178.
[36] Usually a low threshold test: *University of London Press v University Tutorial Press* [1916] 2 Ch 601, 608–609 (approved in *Ladbroke v William Hill* [1964] 1 WLR 273, [1964] 1 All ER 465 (HL)), although there remains considerable uncertainty as to whether the CJEU raised the bar in Case C-5/08 *Infopaq Intl v Danske Dagblades Forening* [2009] ECR I-6569 and subsequent decisions, see 2.1.
[37] Stub pages usually consist of a short title or a few sentences, which act as an invitation to the reader to add content. Very short works such as titles have sometimes been held either not to be substantial enough to constitute a protectable work or insufficiently original; although there have been some exceptions. See: *Francis Day and Hunter v 20th Century Fox* [1940] AC 112; *NLA v Meltwater* [2011] EWCA 890 [19]–[22] (newspaper headlines might be original

contours of a literary work on Wikipedia due to the interactive and transient nature of most of its content.[38] A Wikipedia page could, for example, be conceived of either as a series of different works or as a series of draft versions of one final work. The latter conception appears most apt, although a truly final version of a Wikipedia page may never exist. Indeed, Wikipedia presents itself as a perpetual work in progress with almost every page inviting the reader to interact with it by editing it or commenting on its content on the associated 'talk' page.

It is unclear how copyright law would deal with such a situation. Although copyright generally does not subsist in mere copies of a work with minor alterations,[39] each draft version of a final work is likely to create a new copyright work.[40] In *LA Gear v Hi-Tec Sports*, for example, Nourse LJ said that,

> If, in the course of producing a finished drawing, the author produces one or more preliminary versions, the finished product does not cease to be his original work simply because he adapts it with minor variations, or even if he simply copies it, from an earlier version. Each drawing having been made by him, each is his original work.[41]

Bently and Sherman have suggested that this approach only applies in cases where draft versions have the same author.[42] Where the same author creates a number of drafts, courts have adopted a more relaxed approach that takes

---

literary works); *Infopaq* [45] (an 11 word phrase might meet the intellectual creation test). The most simple works might be unprotectable ideas or may lack the intelligibility necessary for a literary work (*Hollinrake v Truswell* [1894] 3 Ch 420 (CA) 428 (Davey LJ) if they are not 'intended to afford either information or instruction, or pleasure in the form of literary enjoyment', approved as a guideline of what constitutes a literary work in *Exxon v Exxon* [1982] Ch 119 (CA) 142–143 (Stephensen LJ)).

[38] M Chon, 'New Wine Bursting from Old Bottles: Collaborative Internet Art, Joint Works, and Entrepreneurship' (1996) 75 Oregon LJ 257, 263.

[39] *Interlego AG v Tyco Industries* [1989] AC 217 (PC): 'a well-executed tracing' is not sufficiently original. This decision may have been affected by the court's perception that Interlego were attempting to obtain a perpetual monopoly by making minor alterations to their Lego bricks (255–256). Similarly, an enlarged facsimile copy of a drawing will not suffice: *The Reject Shop v Manners* [1995] FSR 870.

[40] *Brighton v Jones* [2004] EWHC 1157 [32] (adopting Lightman J's comments in *Robin Ray v Classic FM* [1998] FSR 622, 638 that where an earlier work is used as a basis for a later work, copyright in the earlier work is not somehow 'subsumed' into copyright in the later work).

[41] [1992] FSR 121 (CA)136 (Staughton LJ and Sir Michael Kerr agreeing), approved in *Taylor v Rive Droite Music* [2004] EWHC 1605, [2004] All ER 88 [247]–[248] Lewison J noting that copyright is capable of subsisting in unfinished versions, but that a new composition will not be created by simply reworking a previous version of a work unless the reworking is so extensive as to produce a recognisably new work or a new arrangement of the previous work.

[42] L Bently and B Sherman, *Intellectual Property Law* (OUP 2009) 103.

into account the iterative nature of the creative process, tending to consider each draft to be a potentially independent copyright work even where only small changes have been made.[43] In taking this approach, judges have sometimes thought the point not to be of great consequence since, as a practical matter, even if a later draft is not an independent work in which copyright subsists (because it lacks originality), it might still be used as evidence of an earlier draft which is an original work.[44] Yet, determining which of a series of drafts constitute an original work becomes important where the author does not own copyright in each draft[45] or where a party appears to be attempting to create a perpetual monopoly.[46] It might also be important for calculating the term of copyright protection.[47]

Where a series of drafts involves the work of different people (as would usually be the case on Wikipedia), one must turn to the complex case law on derivative works for assistance. It may be difficult to distinguish between an infringing copy and a derivative work in which copyright subsists (especially given that a work might be both[48]). In such cases, judges might be disinclined to find that a new derivative work has been created where there appears to have been some misappropriation of the labour of previous authors.[49] Generally, some material change in

---

[43] For example, *Sweeney v Macmillan Publishers* [2002] RPC 35 (HC) [34] (Lloyd J): 'In the case of a creative process as complex as that of Ulysses, it may be unclear, now, in what form the author's text, as a whole, stood at any given moment of time'.

[44] *Cala Homes v Alfred McAlpine Homes* [1995] FSR 818 (Laddie J); *Sweeney v Macmillan* ibid (although the court may have been influenced by the fact that the previous versions were unpublished).

[45] *Ultra Marketing v Universal Components* [2004] EWHC 468 where the author did not own copyright in the latest and most detailed draft of a drawing; *Biotrading and Financing Oy v Biohit* [1996] FSR 393, 395 (HC) (upheld on appeal [1998] FSR 109 (CA)) where it seemed likely there was no copyright in the earliest drawing.

[46] *Interlego* (n39) 255–256 (Lord Oliver of Aylmerton). *Biotrading v Biohit* ibid, 395 (upheld on appeal [1998] FSR 109 (CA)) where it was suggested that earlier drawings cannot be relied upon as proof of the originality of almost identical later drawings to avoid the possibility of creating a perpetual copyright monopoly in an image (referring to *Interlego*); cf. *Rexnold v Ancon* [1983] FSR 245, 260 (HC) where it was considered arguable that later drawings might be sufficiently original if there were some differences between these and earlier drawings. These cases might also be explained by the need to ensure certainty in the subject matter of copyright: *IPC Media v Highbury-Leisure Publishing* [2004] EWHC 2985, [2005] FSR 20 [7] referring to *Green v Broadcasting Corp of New Zealand* [1989] RPC 700.

[47] The long duration of copyright protection means that this is rarely at the heart of disputes, although it did appear to impact very early decisions on joint authorship when copyright term was significantly briefer: E Cooper, 'Joint Authorship in Comparative Perspective: *Levy v Rutley* and the Divergence between the UK and USA' (2005) 62(2) J of the Copyright Society of the USA 245.

[48] *Redwood Music v Chappell* (1982) RPC 109 (QB).

[49] For example: *Elanco Products v Mandops* [1980] RPC 213 (CA) 228 (Goff LJ); 231 (Buckley LJ) 'on the material before the court there is a distinct possibility that it might be held that they have not done sufficient independent work to eradicate the vice of copying'.

character or quality must be brought about in the new work for it to be considered sufficiently 'original'. It seems that the skill, labour or judgement applied in creating the derivative work must exhibit some 'individuality', which the Privy Court's decision in *MacMillan v Cooper* might lead one to believe is an exacting standard, implying the addition of a new quality or character which the raw material did not possess.[50] The change must also be of the right kind in relation to the type of work considered (i.e., having a literary, artistic, dramatic or musical character).[51] The amount and type of change required appear to vary between categories of work and even between sub-categories of work.[52] On the strict view established in *MacMillan v Cooper*, it might seem that few newly updated versions of Wikipedia pages would qualify as independent original literary works. Yet, this would be to disregard case law in which judges have taken a less stringent view making allowances for a creative process that involves building upon pre-existing ideas and works[53] or taking into account the public interest in encouraging the creation of particular types of derivative works such as high-quality restorations.[54]

For some theorists, the heart of the matter is whether there has been an injection of the author's subjectivity in the derivative work.[55] Although this approach might have more currency in the UK following the CJEU's decision in *Infopaq* and subsequent cases, it remains unclear how it might be used to guide decision-making.[56] In assessing the subsistence of copyright in recreative works (such as restorations), Ong persuasively argues

---

[50] (1924) 40 TLR 186.
[51] In *Interlego* (n39) 268 (Lord Oliver), as the case concerned an artistic work, the change needed to be visually significant. In *Sawkins v Hyperion Records* [2005] EWCA 565, [2005] 1 WLR 3281 changes to a musical work were sufficient to establish the originality of a derivative work because they impacted upon its playability.
[52] For example, a higher standard might be required of condensements than abridgements: *Macmillan v Cooper* (n50).
[53] *IPC Media v Highbury-Leisure Publishing* (n46) [9]; *Godfrey v Lees* [1995] EMLR 307 (Ch), 326; *Baigent v Random House Group* [2006] EWHC 719, [2006] EMLR 16; on Appeal [2007] EWCA Civ 247, [2008] EMLR 7 Lloyd LJ [106].
[54] Some have suggested that high-quality replicas of works of art may be protected by copyright: Laddie et al. [4.42]; Copinger et al. [3-133]; J Ginsburg, 'The Concept of Authorship in Comparative Copyright Law' (2002) 52 DePaul LRev 1063 cited with approval in *Sawkins v Hyperion* (n51) (Jacob LJ [83]). Also: *Elisha Qimron v Hershel Shanks* [1993] 7 EIPR D-157 (Israeli SC).
[55] D Nimmer, 'Copyright in the Dead Sea Scrolls: Authorship and Originality' (2001) 38 Houston LRev 1, 159: 'Copyright protection arises only for works that express an intent to produce something personal or subjective'; Ginsburg (n54).
[56] *Infopaq* (n36) might be interpreted in a more limited way, as merely requiring the availability of creative choices. However, this does not seem to fit well with subsequent cases, such as C-145/10 *Painer v Standard Verlags* [2012] ECDR 6, which required the stamp of the author's 'personal touch' on the work.

that the best approach is to focus on the *process* by which the derivative work has been created, rather than any visual change evident in the resulting work.[57] Although one might make a variety of policy-based arguments in favour of providing copyright protection for recreative works that would not equally apply in the context of Wikipedia, Ong does not confine his argument in this way. Rather, he makes the general point that the case law on derivative works tends to be unduly concerned with the character of the end-product, arguing that a determination of the existence of a new original work ought to extend beyond this to take into account the process by which it has been made.[58] The example of Wikipedia supports his argument as copyright law's static conception of a work appears to make it ill-adapted to Wikipedia's dynamic, process-orientated model of creativity.

We have seen that iterative processes of creativity have been accommodated within copyright's notion of the work on occasions where the precise identification of the moment or moments in which an original copyright work comes into existence is of less practical importance, for example, when copyright is owned by the same person(s). In such cases, drafts might be conceptualised as steps along a process which will end with a final work, although such a work might have been incomplete in the mind of the author at the time the drafts were made.[59] If sufficient labour and skill to establish originality can be shown at some point in that process, then determining the exact point in time at which there is a work might only become important for questions rarely of relevance in a dispute, such as the duration of copyright.

In *MacMillan Publishers v Thomas Reed Publications*, for example, the High Court was willing to consider a sequence of chartlets in successive editions of a nautical almanac all together.[60] The court was influenced by the fact that although the chartlets were the result of the efforts of a number of different people, any copyright subsisting in them was owned by the plaintiff.[61] Despite the attractive possibility of considering a series of versions together as the relevant original literary work which appears to arise from this case, as Wikipedia contributors retain their

---

[57] B Ong, 'Originality from Copying: Fitting Recreative Works into the Copyright Universe' (2010) 2 IPQ 165.

[58] Ong, ibid, focuses on giving weight to the intellectual skill, labour and judgement involved in creating many such works rather than relying upon policy arguments in favour of granting copyright protection to recreative works.

[59] Copinger et al. [3-06].

[60] [1993] FSR 455, also cited in *Biotrading v Biohit* (n45) 395 (Robert Walker J).

[61] Ibid, 464. Although it might not always be necessary to identify the precise draft which is the protected work, a Claimant should be required to demonstrate there is relevant authorship, see: *Telstra v Phone Directories* [2010] FCAFC 149 (Full Fed. Ct. of Australia).

copyright interests, barring joint authorship (which is considered in the next section), there is no similar unified ownership solution that would unite the rights of contributors in a series of versions of a Wikipedia page the way the court was able to do in that case.

Where a dispute involves the adjudication of rights between different contributors to different versions of a work over time, it is usually resolved by determining whether there has been a 'material change' (although it is difficult to predict what sort of change would suffice) so that the resulting work might be redefined as something new: an object of authorship as opposed to a copy.[62] In this way, determinations of the contours of a work can tend to slip into an analysis of the sufficiency of any relevant authorial input, which as the next section considers, is a part of the joint authorship test which proves to be problematic in the context of Wikipedia. Whether the best approach to the case law on derivative works is to focus on the injection of the author's subjectivity or the process of their creation, it seems clear that the current case law is a doctrinal maze, which makes it extremely difficult to understand how a multi-authored dynamic work like Wikipedia fits within copyright's concept of the work.

The collaboration of different people by small increments, working autonomously, over a significant period of time, does not fit easily within the confines of copyright law's idea of the work. This is exacerbated by the fact that Wikipedia allows many potential authors to be involved at different points in the creative process. Some argue that the CJEU's reasoning in *Infopaq* fractures the traditional notion of the copyright work in suggesting that parts of a work could be sufficiently original to be protected in their own right (where by the choice, sequence and combination of those words the author expresses his creativity in an original manner so as to achieve a result which is an intellectual creation).[63] Although fragmenting the work in this way might, at first, appear to better accommodate the creative process on Wikipedia by allowing each contributor the copyright in his or her specific contribution, this approach seems very artificial and is still likely to result in significant legal uncertainty as to the contours of a work.[64] It also appears to be at

---

[62] This distinction between the original and a copy tends to break down in the digital environment. This is a point which has been used to argue that copyright law is not well-adapted to the challenges of the digital age, for example: JP Barlow, 'The Economy of Ideas: Selling Wine without Bottles on the Global Net' <www.eff.org/pages/selling-wine-without-bottles-economy-mind-global-net>.

[63] *Infopaq* (n36) [47]; B Sherman, 'What Is a Copyright Work?' (2011) 12(1) Theoretical Inquiries in Law 99, 115.

[64] This is because, as will be argued in what follows, the kind of input which is required for a contributor to be considered an author remains uncertain.

odds with judicial statements about the necessity of objectively determining the boundaries of the work, lest copyright become a 'legal millefeuilles' allowing a claimant to try to claim multiple layers of protection by asserting that small parts of a work are independent works, thus making it easier to establish that an infringer has copied a substantial part.[65] Considering parts of Wikipedia pages to be independent works also does little to accommodate pages which cannot be easily divided as they have been heavily edited by large numbers of people. Thus, the fundamental conception of a copyright work as a fixed object which is (or might be) completed is poorly adapted to Wikipedia's creative process which results in works that do not have such neatly defined contours.

Further complications arise when considering Wikipedia as a whole. For the purposes of the CDPA, Wikipedia is probably a database rather than a compilation.[66] A database is defined as a 'collection of independent works, data or other materials which – (a) are arranged in a systematic or methodical way, and (b) are individually accessible by electronic or other means'.[67] These criteria are not explained in the CDPA or the Database Directive that lead to their implementation. Case law and commentary provide some guidance and suggest that the term 'database' ought to be construed broadly.[68] Wikipedia is a 'collection of independent works' because Wikipedia pages are 'separable from one another without their informative, literary, artistic, musical or other value being affected'.[69] Wikipedia pages are also 'individually accessible'

---

[65] *IPC Media v Highbury-Leisure* (n46) [23] (Laddie J) approved in *Coffey v Warner/Chappell Music* [2005] EWHC 449 (Ch) [10] (Blackburne J).

[66] The wording of s3(1)(a) suggests that where a work is both a database and a compilation it should only be treated as a database. The sui generis database right is beyond the scope of this book and has been considered elsewhere: J Lipton, 'Wikipedia and the European Union Database Directive' (2010) 26 Santa Clara Computer & Technology LJ 631; J Phillips, 'Authorship, Ownership and Wikiship: Copyright in the Twenty-First Century' (2008) 3 (12) JIPLP 788.

[67] s3A(1).

[68] E Derclaye, 'The Court of Justice Interprets the Database Sui Generis Right for the first time' (2005) 30(3) Eur LR 420; E Derclaye, 'Database Sui Generis Right: What Is a Substantial Investment? A Tentative Definition' (2005) 36(1) Intl Rev of Intellectual Property and Competition L 2; E Derclaye, 'Databases Sui Generis Right: Should We Adopt the Spin Off Theory?' (2004) 26(9) EIPR 402; E Derclaye, 'Do Sections 3 and 3A of the CDPA Violate the Database Directive? A Closer Look at the Definition of a Database in the UK and Its Compatibility with European Law' (2002) 24(10) EIPR 466; E Derclaye, 'What Is a Database? A Critical Analysis of the Definition of a Database in the European Database Directive and Suggestions for an International Definition' (2002) 5(6) JWIP 981. See Case C-444/02 *Fixtures Marketing v Organismos Prognostikon Agonon Podosfairou* [2004] ECR-I10549 [19]–[21]; C-545/07 *Apis-Hirstovich v Ladorka* [2009] ECR I-1627 [69].

[69] *Fixtures Marketing* ibid [29].

via a search function.[70] Derclaye suggests that the criterion of arrangement in a 'systematic or methodical way' is probably a fairly low standard, which should be read broadly so as to exclude only haphazard collections.[71] The existence of some structure to the data so that it might be organised after the application of a search programme, for example, would be sufficient.[72] Wikipedia satisfies this requirement because its software indexes and stores pages in a database.

As Wikipedia is constantly being updated, it might be difficult to determine when, and if, changes made to it over time result in a new database. In *British Horseracing Board v William Hill*, a database of horse racing details updated by around 800,000 changes a year was held to be a single database in a constant state of refinement.[73] Wikipedia is likely to be considered similarly.

Although Wikipedia as a whole is almost certainly a database, it is probably not sufficiently original as it currently operates. To meet this requirement it must constitute the author's own intellectual creation by reason of the *selection* and *arrangement* of its contents.[74] Reviewing, flagging and editing Wikipedia pages to ensure compliance with Wikipedia's editorial policies would probably be seen as a contribution to the *creation* of content (rather than its selection or arrangement). If Wikipedia became more controlled and its administrators took a more active role in the organisation of pages, it might meet the relevant standard. In that case (assuming the requirements for joint authorship are met), these administrators would own any copyright subsisting in Wikipedia as a database.[75]

---

[70] This threshold requirement is probably not high: Derclaye, 'Do Sections 3 and 3A of the CDPA Violate the Database Directive?' (n68) 469; Laddie et al. [30.23].
[71] (n70) 468.
[72] *Fixtures Marketing* (n68) [30]: 'while it is not necessary for the systematic or methodical arrangement to be physically apparent ... that condition implies that the collection should be contained in a fixed base, of some sort, and include technical means ... or other means, such as an index, a table of contents, or a particular plan or method of classification, to allow the retrieval of any independent material contained within it' (in the Opinion of Advocate General Stix-Hackl this is to 'ensure that only planned collections of data are covered' [40]).
[73] [2001] EWCA 1268, [2001] RPC 31 [71]–[73]. This approach was supported by AG Stix-Hackl's opinion in C-203/02 *British Horseracing Board v William Hill* [2004] ECR I-10415 [148]–[151] in which he described constantly updated databases as dynamic databases providing a rolling right (the CJEU did not specifically consider this point). Also *Beechwood House Publishing t/a Binley's v Guardian Products* [2010] EWPCC 12 [63]-[64].
[74] C-604/10 *Football Dataco v Yahoo! UK* [2012] ECDR 10.
[75] Administrators are contributing Wikipedia members of long-standing who ought not to be confused with the Wikimedia Foundation that owns and runs the website (but does not control its content). Lipton (n66) 647 argues that the Wikimedia Foundation is also unlikely to own any database rights subsisting in Wikipedia following *British Horseracing Board* (n73).

As it stands, however, relatively little effort is expended by individual contributors and administrators in this respect. Indeed, the value of Wikipedia and much of the reason for its success lies in its lack of explicit structure and the ability of contributors to easily link pages on the fly. This is despite the fact that, as Wikipedia has grown, efforts have increased to organise and structure it into categories and to identify which parts need to be improved or are yet to be written.

In summary, although it seems unlikely, at present, that copyright subsists in Wikipedia as a whole as a database, it is likely that copyright would subsist in individual Wikipedia pages as literary works. It is impossible to predict, however, how a court might construe the contours of such works. This uncertainty also complicates the task of determining which contributors would be considered authors of these works from a copyright point of view.

3.2.2 Are Wikipedia Contributors Copyright Authors?

Assuming that a given Wikipedia page is an original literary work, in most circumstances it would have multiple potential authors. For a Wikipedia contributor to be a joint author under the CDPA he or she must have:

(i) made a significant contribution of the right kind;
(ii) in pursuance of some common design or collaboration; and
(iii) his or her contribution must not be distinct.[76]

Although most contributions to Wikipedia pages will satisfy the last criterion, it is by no means clear that the others would be met. As has been argued in Chapter 2, the case law on joint authorship only provides limited guidance and is often specific to a particular set of facts.

In order to satisfy the first criterion, the contributor must have contributed some of the creative choices (or skill, labour and judgement) that makes the work original in the sense required by the CDPA. The contribution must be of the *right kind*, that is, in relation to the expression of the work and not just the ideas.[77] A joint author of a literary work must share some responsibility for what appears on the page, which has been explained as 'something which approximates to penmanship'.[78] This can often be a fine point.[79] In *Fylde Microsystems v Key Radio Systems*, a technician who tested and debugged software was

---

[76] s10(1); *Godfrey v Lees* (n53) 325–328; *Ray v Classic* (n40) 636; *Hadley v Kemp* [1999] EMLR 589. See 2.2.
[77] *Donoghue v Allied Newspapers* [1938] 1 Ch 106 (Ch).
[78] *Cala Homes v Alfred McAlpine Homes* [1995] EWHC 7, [1995] FSR 818; *Ray v Classic FM* (n40) 636 (Lightman J).
[79] Bently et al. 127–128. Compare *Hadley v Kemp* (n76) and *Stuart v Barrett* [1994] EMLR 449.

not a joint author of that software, despite the fact that the contributions made were extensive, technically sophisticated and involved the expenditure of considerable time and effort. This was because the technician's work was more akin to proof-reading than authorship.[80] Following this reasoning, many valuable Wikipedia contributors would not qualify as joint authors, for instance, when making minor edits, participating in dispute resolution procedures, developing bots, or creating and enforcing community policy. Similarly, some of these activities might be seen as taking place too early or too late in the creative process; or they might fall foul of the idea/expression dichotomy if they appear remote from the fixation of the work.[81]

In addition to contributing the right kind of skill and labour, the contribution must also be *significant*. In *Fisher v Brooker*, Blackburne J considered this to mean 'more than merely trivial'.[82] If this is an accurate formulation of the standard, although fairly low, it may still exclude the activities of a large number of contributors who only make very small contributions to individual pages. I have argued that whether or not a contribution is significant is a question of fact that depends upon the circumstances of the case.[83] If significance is a qualitative requirement, it is difficult to predict how it might apply to contributions to Wikipedia, especially given the lack of guidance from the case law.[84] If a restrictive approach (such as the pragmatic instrumental approach) is taken it is likely that most valuable contributors to Wikipedia would not be considered joint authors, failing the authorship limb of the test.[85] Worse still, if control is indicative of an authorial contribution then Wikipedia pages risk being considered author-less.

Section 10(1) requires that a work of joint authorship be 'produced through the collaboration of two or more authors', which has been

---

[80] [1998] FSR 449 (Ch) Laddie J stated, rather ambiguously, that section 10 'does not turn someone who is not an author into an author' suggesting, perhaps, that authorship requires more than the investment of skill, time and effort relied upon by the defendant in that case.

[81] Many of these activities resemble what Hacon J termed 'secondary skills' in *Martin v Kogan* [2017] EWHC 2927 (IPEC) [51]. He suggests the case law sets high bar in respect of such contributions. See further: 2.2.3.

[82] [2006] EWHC 3239, [2007] FSR 255 [46]. In that case Blackburne J considered the relevant contribution to be 'on any view substantial' [98]. Although the case was partially reversed on appeal ([2008] EWCA Civ 287), the Court of Appeal considering it to be an 'extremely unusual case' [34], it was again reversed by the House of Lords ([2009] UKHL 41). The trial judge's ruling on joint authorship was not challenged in either appeal.

[83] *Stuart v Barrett* (n79); 2.2.3 and 2.4.   [84] See 2.3.2.

[85] This is not inevitable as there are cases in which a more inclusive approach appears to have been taken, e.g., *Godfrey v Lees* (n53), *Stuart v Barrett* (n79), *Bamgboye v Reed* [2002] EWHC 2922, [2004] 5 EMLR 61, *Brown v Mcasso* [2005] FSR 846 (EWPCC).

described in the case law as 'joint labouring in furtherance of a common design'.[86] The fact that Wikipedia contributors, who usually will not have met, contribute incrementally and apparently independently, might seem to indicate a lack of collaboration. Yet, the Court of Appeal, in *Beckingham v Hodgens* held that a 'common design' did require proof of common intention to share joint authorship.[87] In Chapter 2, I argued that this should be construed to mean that there is no need for a specific intention, in a narrow sense, to be a joint author for the purposes of copyright law. Still, collaboration clearly implies a general intention to work together. When assessed in the light of creative reality, it is apparent that most Wikipedia contributors satisfy this requirement as discussion pages, consensus-driven policy measures and the Wikipedia community culture support the existence of a common design. The longer a contributor has participated and the more involved they have been as a member of the Wikipedia community, the more likely this argument is to be persuasive. Where multiple potential rights holders are involved, however, there is a tendency for courts to prefer to find separate layers of copyright wherever possible. If concerned to reduce the number of authors for pragmatic instrumental reasons, a court may be tempted to find an absence of collaboration, fracturing the creative process into many stages; thus, conceiving of Wikipedia pages as a series of derivative works rather than a joint work.[88] *Martin v Kogan* provides an example of such an approach, as the court appeared to consider collaboration to require cooperative acts by the authors in relation to each draft.[89]

Chon, writing in the US context, argues that in determining the authorship of digital creations, judges ought to favour an objective determination with reference to the existing expectations of the relevant internet subculture.[90] She suggests inferring the intention to be a joint author from the fact that an 'individual author voluntarily created his or her work in response to a call for participation that emphasised interactivity'.[91] Wikipedia's sharing culture might indicate that

---

[86] *Levy v Rutley* (1871) LR 6 CP 523 (Court of Common Pleas) 529 (Keating J).

[87] [2003] EWCA Civ 143, [2003] EMLR 18 [52]. Cf. L Zemer, *The Idea of Authorship in Copyright* (Ashgate 2007) 217 arguing that despite this decision UK courts tend to silently embrace a requirement for the intention to co-author to some extent. See also Ginsburg (n54).

[88] Many Wikipedia pages would then appear as tens or even hundreds of derivative works, few of which would be sufficiently different from the previous version to constitute a new copyright work.

[89] (n81) [25] (Hacon J): 'cooperative acts by the authors at the time the copyright was created, which led to its creation'.

[90] Chon (n38) 271.

[91] Ibid, 272 considering joint authorship from a US standpoint, where intention is specifically required: Copyright Act 1976 (US), s101.

contributors lack the intent to joint author specifically required in US copyright law. This argument, however, ignores the fact that copyright licences preserve the ownership interests of contributors.[92] In the UK this problem probably does not arise as any such argument relies upon the narrow interpretation of intention that I argue was rejected in *Beckingham v Hodgens*.

The purpose of the common design limb is to provide a way of distinguishing cases involving successive derivative works (each with different authors) from works of joint authorship (where many authors together contribute to a common project). Considering Wikipedia in isolation from its social norms, it might seem that each contributor potentially creates a new derivative work when making a small change to a Wikipedia page and that it would be in rare cases that such a contributor would bring about enough of a material change for that version to be sufficiently original. I have argued, however, that it makes more sense to think of Wikipedia as a series of drafts of a final work that may never come into existence.[93] This contention is supported by the existence of social norms (embodied, for example, in Wikipedia's consensually developed policies) which establish collaboration amongst the majority of Wikipedia contributors. Although contributors will vary in the extent to which they are familiar with, and subscribe to, Wikipedia's social norms, a contributor's response to the general invitation to the public to participate in the free Wikipedia encyclopaedia project ought to be enough to raise a presumption that the contributor is collaborating in the relevant sense.

One might then consider a Wikipedia page at any particular point in time and, with the aid of Wikipedia's history pages, identify which users have contributed to the written expression on the page as it existed at that moment taking into consideration its previous versions, as the court did in *MacMillan v Thomas Reed*. It would remain a difficult task to determine which, if any, have made a significant contribution of the right kind so as to count as joint authors and thus owners of any copyright that might subsist in that page. In Chapter 8, I present an inclusive, contextual approach to the application of the joint authorship test,

---

[92] Although contributors agree not to exercise some of their ownership rights. See 3.3.
[93] This may not be as problematic as it might initially seem. In an infringement claim a Wikipedia page might be considered at the moment at which infringement is alleged, in light of its previous versions. Of course, as a practical matter, litigation is very unlikely to arise as contributors agree to copyleft licences which permit most uses of Wikipedia pages and there are many disincentives to making an infringement claim (cost of proceedings, uncertainty as to legal entitlements, etc.).

which provides a framework for undertaking this task. Specifically, I suggest that the common design of the contributors ought to take on a more prominent role in the application of the joint authorship test and that the significance of a contributor's contribution ought to be assessed in light of the common design from which the joint work arises.

In summary, on the basis of current case law it seems at most uncertain, and at least unlikely, that some Wikipedia contributors would be considered to be joint authors of individual pages to which they have contributed. If this were established, the joint authors would hold their copyright interests as tenants in common so that although one author might sue in relation to an infringement, all joint authors would be required to grant any licence to reproduce a part of it.[94] This would present obvious logistical issues for Wikipedia's creative model in the absence of copyleft licences.

3.3 Copyleft Licences and the Ambivalent Role of Copyright Law

Copyleft licensing is commonplace on the internet as a response to the breadth of scope and perceived uncertainty of copyright restrictions on the reproduction of works.[95] Licences are used as a means for authors to opt-out of the automatic operation of copyright protection so as to authorise the copying of their works in advance in certain circumstances. The origin of copyleft licensing lies with the Free/Libre/Open Source Software movement, which adopted licences to enhance the development of a free collaborative exchange by software developers. Creative Commons then expanded upon this idea by producing a variety of tailor-made licences which are designed to cover many different works in which copyright might subsist and which are made available online for anyone to use.[96] For many commentators copyleft licences have a political significance. Gonzalez, for example, notes that the Free Software Foundation's General Public Licence reads as a mixture of legal contract and ideological manifesto[97] and Lessig presents

---

[94] See, further, 8.6.1.
[95] LP Loren, 'Building a Reliable Semicommons of Creative Works: Enforcement of Creative Commons Licenses and Limited Abandonment of Copyright' (2007) 14 George Mason LRev 271, 273.
[96] L Lessig, *The Future of Ideas: The Fate of the Commons in a Connected World* (Vintage Books 2002); <www.creativecommons.org>.
[97] AG Gonzalez, 'Viral Contracts or Unenforceable Documents? Contractual Validity of Copyleft Licences' (2004) 26(8) EIPR 331, 333. The preamble to the GPL has been

Creative Commons as the only ethical way possible for exercising copyright.[98]

On Wikipedia, copyleft licences police the interaction between copyright law's notion of authorship (implying ownership and control) and Wikipedia's own notion of collective creativity (the donation of creative efforts to a community project). Most content on Wikipedia is co-licensed under the Creative Commons Attribution-Sharealike 3.0 Unported Licence ('CC-BY-SA')[99] and the GNU Free Documentation Licence ('GFDL').[100] These licences allow anyone to copy or modify text on Wikipedia as long as they:
- credit the authors (by including a hyperlink/URL to the original Wikipedia page or by providing a list of all authors which may be filtered to exclude very small or irrelevant contributions);
- re-licence any modifications or additions under the CC-BY-SA or later versions[101];
- indicate if modifications or additions have been made to the original; and
- include a licensing notice stating that the work is released under CC-BY-SA and either a hyperlink/URL to the text of the license, or a copy of the licence.[102]

There is no requirement that reuse be for non-commercial purposes.[103]

Although copyleft licences are becoming extremely prevalent, there have been surprisingly few cases considering their validity.[104] In *Jacobsen v Katzer* the US Court of Appeals (Fed Ct) held that copyleft

---

described as reading like a 'declaration of independence': M O'Sullivan, 'The Pluralistic, Evolutionary, Quasi Legal Role of the GNU General Public Licence in Free/Libre/Open Source Software (FLOSS)' (2004) 26(8) EIPR 340, 341; or as the Free Software Movement's 'constitution': R Gomulkiewicz, 'General Public License 3.0: Hacking the Free Software Movement's Constitution' (2006) 42(4) Houston LRev 1015.

[98] L Lessig, *Free Culture: How Big Media Uses Technology and the Law to Lock Down Culture and Control Creativity* (Penguin Press, 2004). S Dusollier, 'The Master's Tools v The Master's House: Creative Commons v Copyright' (2005) 29 CJLA 271, 287: Creative Commons tends to see the commons as a 'principle, a religion or morality'.

[99] <en.wikipedia.org/wiki/Wikipedia:Text_of_Creative_Commons_Attribution-ShareAlike_3.0_Unported_License>.

[100] <en.wikipedia.org/wiki/Wikipedia:Text_of_the_GNU_Free_Documentation_License>.

[101] The validity of this provision is unclear: Gonzalez (n97).

[102] <en.wikipedia.org/wiki/Wikipedia:Copyrights>.

[103] It is likely, however, that the successful commercial exploitation of reproductions would detrimentally affect Wikipedia's ethic of sharing.

[104] For a useful outline of many of the cases to date, see Corbett (n4) and A Metzger and S Hennigs, 'License Contracts, Free Software and Creative Commons' Commons' in M Schauer and B Verschraegen (eds) *General Reports of the XIXth Congress of the International Academy of Comparative Law, Ius Comparatum – Global Studies in Comparative Law* (Springer 2017) Vol 24, 405.

licences are enforceable as contracts.[105] Although convincing arguments might be still made either way,[106] it seems likely that UK courts would treat copyleft licences as bare licences, not contracts, due to the apparent lack of consideration.[107] The US court in *Jacobsen v Katzer* located the reciprocity required for consideration in the advantages associated with the increased distribution facilitated by copyleft licenses and the conditions they impose on re-use (i.e., attribution). These arguments, however, may not be persuasive to a UK court given that the conditions of re-use require little more than the moral rights granted to authors by the CDPA and given that increased (free) distribution is not always advantageous per se.[108] On this view, copyleft licences operate as a defence to a claim of copyright infringement rather than as a foundation for an action for breach of contract, so that if a licence condition is not met, the only legal effect would be that the permission granted by the licence would cease to be effective.

The symbolic association of copyleft licences with the ideals of the free software and Creative Commons communities gives them a key role in constituting Wikipedia's culture of sharing, which may be more significant than their role as legal instruments.[109] In the context of Wikipedia, copyleft licences appear to operate as a type of customary law which relies primarily on the effect of social pressures for its moral force.[110] Copyleft licences rely upon property rights granted by copyright law but seek to exercise them differently. Despite their intention to create a copyright-

[105] 535 F 3d 1373 (Fed Cir, 2008); R Gomulkiewicz, 'Conditions and Covenants in License Contracts: Tales from a Test of the Artistic License' (2009) 17(3) Texas Intellectual Property LJ 335; J Wacha, 'Taking the Case: Is the GPL Enforceable?' (2005) 21 Santa Clara Computer & High-Technology LJ 451, 481; W Reynolds and J Moringello, 'Survey of the Law of Cyberspace: Electronic Contracting Cases 2008–2009' (2009) 65 The Business Lawyer available at: <ssrn.com/abstract=1437162>.

[106] Loren (n95) 312–313; Gomulkiewicz (n105) 346 criticises the concept of a bare licence as an artefact; M Henley, 'Jacobsen v Katzer and Kamind Associates – an English legal perspective' (2009) 1(1) IFOSS L Rev 41.

[107] P Johnson, '"Dedicating" Copyright to the Public Domain' (2008) 71(4) MLR 587; E Moglen, 'Free Software Matters: Enforcing the GPL, I' <emoglen.law.columbia.edu/publications/lu-12.pdf>; L McDonagh, 'Copyright, Contract and FOSS' in N Shemtov and I Walden (eds) *Free and Open Source Software* (OUP 2013) 69, 90. In civil law countries, where there is no requirement for consideration, these licences may be enforceable as contracts: McDonagh 98–99; T Dysart, 'Author-Protective Rules and Alternative Licences: A Review of the Dutch Copyright Contract Act' (2015) 37(9) EIPR 601, 602.

[108] The former argument might not be as strong in the case of Wikipedia as would be for copyleft licences more generally, given the exception to the attribution and integrity rights in relation to literary works made for inclusion in an encyclopaedia (s79(6)(b), s 81(4)(b)). On the difference between UK and US approaches to consideration: McDonagh ibid.

[109] O'Sullivan (n84) 345.

[110] K Bowrey, *Law and Internet Cultures* (CUP 2005) 95 argues it makes more sense to think of them as evidencing a relationship of trust, rather than a commercial relationship.

free zone for creativity,[111] copyleft licences necessarily rely upon the continuing validity of copyright law as a source of legal standards.[112] In this way, they have been seen as playing the game of copyright, not attempting to abolish it.[113] Reliance on property language and concepts in copyleft licences may undermine the goal of facilitating a sharing or 'free culture'[114] and the share-alike provision seems to make contractual rights more like property rights, as they resemble rights against the world that run with the work.[115] The community spirit which motivates many regular contributors to Wikipedia is built upon a shared understanding (embodied in the copyleft licences) that contributions are donated and not for profit. This assumption actually subtly reinforces copyright law's proprietary notion of authorship, because the grant of permission to reuse or modify a contribution is premised on the assumption that the contribution is valuable and might be owned in a copyright sense.

Copyleft licences might also tend to expand the perception of what can be protected by copyright law. The use of these licences raises a presumption in the minds of those encountering the works to which they are attached, that copyright subsists in those works and that it is necessary to observe the conditions of the licence to reproduce them.[116] As this chapter has argued, in the case of Wikipedia, the extent to which copyright subsists and might be enforced, is uncertain. In addition, users might not be aware that uses of the work covered by fair dealing defences need not comply with the licence conditions (as the licence is likely to operate, at most, as a defence to a claim of copyright infringement).[117] The copyleft licence used by Wikipedia attempts to expand the rights of contributors in some respects, for example, by providing for strong attribution rights and requiring creators of derivative works to re-license their works under the same licence.[118] Yet many, if not most, contributors to Wikipedia who must be attributed as authors under the licence will likely not be 'authors' who would have this right in light of the joint authorship case law. The attribution of contributors provides a locus for credit which might be gained within the Wikipedia

---

[111] M Fox, T Ciro and N Duncan, 'Creative Commons: An Alternative, Web-Based Copyright System' (2005) 16(6) Entertainment LRev 111, 116.
[112] J Boyle, 'Second Enclosure Movement and the Construction of the Public Domain' (2003) 66 Law and Contemporary Problems 33, 64–66.
[113] Dusollier (n98) 278.
[114] For example, references to a 'Commons Deed'. On the use of property metaphors in copyright more generally: M Rose, 'Copyright and Its Metaphors' (2002) 50 UCLA LRev 1.
[115] Dusollier (n98) 284.   [116] Corbett (n4) 527.
[117] Ibid. This point is highlighted in the most recent version of the CC-BY-SA used on Wikipedia.
[118] It seems unlikely that this provision is legally valid, but even if it were, it would be unenforceable against third parties: Gonzalez (n97).

community; it demonstrates one's belonging to a community that presents itself as altruistic to outsiders; and attribution might have an intrinsic value to the contributor. In this way copyleft licences help construct and allow for legal recognition of an alternative notion of authorship which is better adapted to the Wikipedia community: modifying the incidents and rewards of authorship and broadening the category of contributors who might be beneficiaries of this alternative conception of authorship.

Dusollier has suggested that it may be possible for the widespread use of copyleft licences, over time, to re-signify the meaning of authorship in the digital context.[119] She argues that caution is warranted in relation to the increasingly widespread use of such instruments which institutionalise a process which requires individual creators to give up benefits to which they may be entitled under copyright law, especially where this is done via licences which have been criticised as overbroad and inflexible.[120] Others have argued that copyleft licences are actually empowering, giving authors back their long-lost autonomy.[121] Yet, it is difficult to see how an author is empowered by giving away copyright entitlements – especially when this is done via a standard form which has been devised by a third party. In the case of Wikipedia, copyleft licences do not offer much authorial control as a contributor must agree to the version of the licence the community has adopted as a condition of participation. Dusollier argues that copyleft licensing is more concerned with user rights and free access to culture than it is with creators' rights. She criticises the social forces at play in copyleft licensing, arguing that they aim to make free access to works the politically correct way for creators to exercise their rights. She compares them to other social constructions which can operate to undervalue labour,[122] arguing that the narrative of a gift society (the sharing culture) risks rendering the work done by authors invisible.[123]

Furthermore, copyleft licences are not a complete substitute for copyright law because they do not have the benefits of being produced through a legislative process which involves the balancing of interests and public policy considerations.[124] There is a tendency to present copyleft

---

[119] Dusollier (n98) 286.
[120] Copyleft licences are difficult, if not impossible, to amend: R Gomulkiewicz, 'Open Source License Proliferation: Helpful Diversity or Hopeless Confusion?' (2009) 30 Washington UJ of L and Policy 261.
[121] N Elkin-Koren, 'What Contracts Cannot Do: The Limits of Private Ordering in Facilitating a Creative Commons' (2005) 74 Fordham LRev 375, 386.
[122] Dusollier (n98) 288.
[123] Ibid; 293, 289. She argues that authors must give free and informed consent for others to use their works, which includes freedom from social construction.
[124] Although this point might be made about all contracts, it seems particularly relevant here given the ideological aims of the copyleft movement.

licences as the 'people's response' to the perception that copyright law is out of step with the norms and expectations which have developed in the new digital environment. Yet, these licences are not produced by any sort of participatory process and do not reflect customs that have emerged over time – rather, they have been developed to reflect the will of strong norm entrepreneurs (e.g. Creative Commons).[125] In addition, the standardised form of these licences reinforces a licensing culture which some corporations have used to enforce strong proprietary control and restrict user rights (e.g., the use of End-User Licensing Agreements in the software industry).

Despite the potential for the widespread use of copyleft licences to slowly devalue the concept of authorship that copyright law aims to protect, the benefit of their use in the context of Wikipedia probably outweighs any potential detriment. This is because copyleft licences allow for a space to be carved out from the application of copyright law. This facilitates the survival of, and even nourishes, the unique means of collective authorship that thrives on Wikipedia. Not only do they appear to remove copyright law obstacles which might impede or chill creativity, but their terms also allow Wikipedians to shape their own notion of authorship to fit the inclusive, sharing, collaborative culture that is the reason for Wikipedia's success.

3.4 Insights for Copyright Law

Corbett argues that copyright law is poorly suited to the new types of creativity enabled by modern digital technology because it is not aligned with community norms and expectations.[126] Wikipedia provides a useful lens through which to examine this contention. Wikipedia does not fit neatly within copyright law's principles of subsistence. Indeed, it appears to challenge some of the notions at the heart of copyright law's conception of authorship. For instance, must a 'work' be an object capable of being finished? Which sort, and how much, labour, skill or judgement counts as 'authorship'? How do the rules on derivative works apply in situations where the reader is invited to interact with a work and become a creator? Is such a reader/creator 'collaborating' with other (previous and future) contributors to the same project? In practice, copyleft licences alleviate uncertainty in the application of copyright law by limiting potential claims of copyright infringement which might otherwise impede Wikipedia's day-to-day

---

[125] F Marrella and S Yoo, 'Is Open Source Software the New Lex Mercatoria?' (2006–2007) 47 Virginia J of International L 807.
[126] Corbett (n4).

operation. In fact, Wikipedia's culture of sharing both relies upon, and is partly constituted by, copyleft licences. Nevertheless, the legal effect and the general desirability of copyleft licences still remain unclear.

Authorship and ownership are not intertwined on Wikipedia in the same way that they are in copyright law. Wikipedia attempts to separate creativity from ownership in the name of a greater good: the Wikipedia project and its ethic of sharing. The phenomenal success of Wikipedia seems to undermine instrumental economic justifications for copyright law as necessary to incentivise creativity.[127] Contributors participate in Wikipedia willingly and appear to derive some personal, albeit non-monetary, benefit from their participation. In so doing they are not alone – many other creators (magicians, chefs, comedians, etc.) do not rely upon copyright law's incentives.[128] Although Dusollier argues that the prevalence of sharing economies facilitated by copyleft licences might undervalue the work of authors, it would be stretching her argument too far to suggest that copyright law ought to regulate all forms of creativity which might be conceived of in societal or cultural terms as authorial. Instead, her argument is a reminder of the need for copyright to remain an important source of good authorship standards that establish a presumption that authors are entitled to the pecuniary (as well as reputational benefits) from their creative activities.

Some suggest that creativity on Wikipedia is not 'authorship' and, therefore, that it might be the sort of creativity that copyright ought not to concern itself with.[129] Indeed, Wikipedia's contributors seem to have no desire for copyright law to directly apply to their activities, agreeing to copyleft licences which limit the restrictions copyright law might impose upon Wikipedia's creative model.[130] Yet, from whatever angle that you look at it, Wikipedia is exactly the sort of creation that the CDPA seeks to regulate. It is a literary work and it is clearly a product of authorship (it is created by many people who have made creative or intellectual choices that are evident in the expression). The problem is not that Wikipedia is not a work of authorship, but rather that copyright law's concepts are not currently applied with enough attention to the context in which creativity occurs. Aspects of Wikipedia's creative process make it ill-served by a restrictive, acontextual approach to the application of the joint authorship test. These include: the fact that many contributors make very small contributions, some of which might be too early or too late in the creative

---

[127] Elkin-Koren (n3) makes this point more generally in relation to what she terms social production. Also D Zimmerman, 'Copyright as Incentives: Did We Just Imagine That?' (2011) 12(1) Theoretical Inquiries in Law 29.
[128] See the literature on intellectual property's negative spaces referred to in Chapter 1, n65.
[129] Sunstein (n26) 153.   [130] Albeit retaining the moral right to attribution.

process or may fall foul of the idea/expression dichotomy – especially where it is restrictively applied (these may not be 'significant contributions of the right kind'); contributors, who may not have met one another, work incrementally and apparently independently (there may not be 'collaboration'); and Wikipedia is a perpetual work in progress (so it is difficult to determine the scope of the 'work').

The shadow of copyright law still casts itself over the norms which operate to create and regulate the alternative system of self-regulated creativity on Wikipedia.[131] The fact that copyleft licences rely upon copyright law for their effectiveness and as a source of standards should not be under-estimated. The Wikipedia community taps into some of the values of copyright's notion of authorship, whilst discarding others. Crucially, contributors retain any copyright in their contributions, and in choosing to forgo many of the benefits that that copyright interest might entail in the name of the Wikipedia project, they help constitute the sharing norms which sustain this loose-knit network of contributors. Although some contribute to Wikipedia just for fun or because they find it intellectually stimulating, many contribute out of a sense of altruism, because they value interaction with the Wikipedia community or because they wish to build a reputation within that community. In these situations, contributors may value the fact that however great or small, their contributions are acknowledged in the history pages and whenever any part of the page is reproduced pursuant to the copyleft licence.

If new forms of creativity, like Wikipedia, ought to be considered by copyright law as amounting to 'authorship', as I think they should be, the question arises as to what sorts of accommodations ought to be made for this fluid, interactive and participatory model of creativity. This book argues for a *contextual* approach to the application of the joint authorship test that places more emphasis on the collaboration limb of the test. In the context of Wikipedia, this means appreciating that there is collaboration present amongst contributors who are united by their response to a call for participation in the Wikipedia project. This is more likely to be the case, the more integrated contributors are in the Wikipedia community. This avoids the unreal conceptualisation of Wikipedia as a series of derivative works, none of which may contain enough of a material alteration to be considered original.[132] A contextual approach to the joint authorship test also means taking the common design of contributors

---

[131] R Coombe, *The Cultural Life of Intellectual Properties: Authorship, Appropriation and the Law* (Duke UP 1998).

[132] In the unlikely event of an infringement action, a Wikipedia page might be considered at the moment of infringement in light of its previous versions, similarly to the approach taken in *MacMillan Publishers v Thomas Reed Publications* (n60).

into account when determining whether a contributor has made a significant contribution of the right kind. This means that contributions that are viewed as important in the context of the common design will not be immediately excluded for not appearing significant on the face of the final form of the work. In this light those who enforce community policy might not be so easily dismissed as having not made an authorial contribution.[133]

This leads into the second aspect of my argument, which is that an *inclusive* approach should be taken to the application of the joint authorship test. In most cases it will be impossible to isolate only one or two contributors and consider them to be the sole authors of a Wikipedia page, particularly in light of the lack of control which contributors have in respect of their contributions. If a high standard were required for people to be considered joint authors, this might lead to the view that Wikipedia has no authors, which, in turn, would lead to a significant mismatch between copyright law and creative reality. There ought to be some limits, however, as ultimately authorship is a legal question (the requirement for a contribution of the *right kind* excludes contributions of mere ideas and trivial/de minimis contributions, etc.). The value of a legal standard of authorship, independent of community norms, is explored in later case studies.

Wikipedia demonstrates that private ordering can be very successfully used to regulate authorship issues (including issues relating to copyright ownership). Whilst there are good reasons to be sceptical about copyleft licences, they do have an important role to play on Wikipedia in providing a space which allows for this unique type of creativity to flourish.[134] Although the availability of private ordering mechanisms has been crucial in allowing Wikipedia to implement a notion of authorship that is tailor-made to the project, there remains an important role for copyright law. Copyright law provides an important source of default good authorship standards. These standards make it possible to constitute the sharing norms that Wikipedia depends upon for its success. As the example of Wikipedia indicates, critics have been justified in expressing concern that copyright law may not be well-adapted to Web 2.0 collaborations. Yet, I have suggested that this might not necessarily entail a crisis for copyright law. Instead, I argue that if copyright law is to retain its relevance and

---

[133] Community sustaining activities are significant contributions in the context of Wikipedia, although they may not be contributions of the right kind unless they involve a de minimis contribution of creative choices evident in the protected expression.
[134] They also allow Wikipedia to avoid copyright rules on joint ownership which are not well-adapted to large group collaboration. See 8.6.1.

credibility as a source of standards it must be clarified and brought closer in line to community norms and expectations.[135]

These observations do not just relate to the modern digital environment. The next chapter considers a case study of collective authorship that carries on a tradition which is ancient in origin, but which still thrives today: Australian Indigenous art. The case study of Australian Indigenous art provides additional insights about the limitations of the current approach to the application of the joint authorship test (particularly in relation to the application of the idea/expression dichotomy) and reveals more of the disadvantages of relying upon private ordering to remedy the gap between copyright law and creative reality in cases of collective authorship.

---

[135] Corbett (n4).

4   Australian Indigenous Art

The limitations of the current approach to the joint authorship test are also apparent outside the context of new forms of digital collaboration. This chapter presents a case study of collective authorship with ancient roots: Australian Indigenous art. I focus on Indigenous art produced in accordance with customary law that Indigenous communities consider to be a product of communal authorship. Although there is no UK case law on the application of the joint authorship test to works of collective authorship, Australian courts have had the occasion to consider, and reject, a claim of communal authorship in respect of Indigenous art. The definition of a work of joint authorship in Australian copyright law is virtually identical to that in the CDPA. Section 10 of the Copyright Act 1968 (Cth) defines a work of joint authorship as 'a work that has been produced by the collaboration of two or more authors and in which the contribution of each author is not separate from the contribution of the other author or the contributions of the other authors'. The similarity is unsurprising, given both pieces of legislation are based upon the UK Copyright Act 1911 and preceding UK law. Although the distance between UK and Australian copyright law has increased over time, when the cases considered in this chapter were decided, the Australian case law on joint authorship was sufficiently similar to that in the UK to provide a useful comparison for the purposes of this book.[1]

---

[1] The Australian definition requires a joint author's contribution to be not 'separate' (as the UK's previous 1956 Act did), rather than not 'distinct'. UK case law has tended to assume that the change of wording in the CDPA had no material effect, see Chapter 2, n92. In recent times, Australian courts have increased their emphasis on authorship when deciding copyright cases. This has included explicitly distancing the originality requirement from low, sweat of the brow iterations of that standard and linking it more closely to intellectual input (*IceTV Pty Ltd v Nine Network Australia Pty Ltd* [2009] HCA 14, (2009) 239 CLR 458). This potentially brings the Australian originality requirement closer to the intellectual creation standard. Another trend is the insistence on proof of authorship to establish subsistence (*Telstra Corporation Ltd v Phone Directories Co Pty Ltd* [2010] FCA 44; appeal dismissed by Full Court [2010] FCAFC 149, special leave to appeal to the High Court of Australia refused 8 September 2011 [2011] HCA Trans 248). Also, recent cases

In *Bulun Bulun v R & T Textiles*, the Federal Court of Australia struggled to find a way to protect an Indigenous community's interests in art within the bounds of copyright, because of the apparent difficulty establishing that these amount to *authorship* interests.[2] Indeed, one of the most significant challenges in providing effective protection of Indigenous cultural expressions is accommodating them within existing legal regimes for the protection of cultural property, such as copyright law. In this chapter, I argue that copyright law's difficulties in recognising Indigenous community interests in art stems from the influence of historically-located, culturally-specific understandings of authorship; and a preference for a restrictive approach (finding few joint authors) to the application of the joint authorship test. In the absence of copyright protection, Indigenous communities must rely on contracts and a patchwork of other legal doctrines, which only provide partial protection. Ultimately, Indigenous cultural expressions and traditional knowledge would be best protected by a sui generis regime that might be better adapted to this task. Nevertheless, I argue that the joint authorship test is probably more flexible than *Bulun Bulun* might suggest.

In the first section of this chapter, I consider the dynamics involved in the creation of Indigenous art and I provide some background to the issue of the protection of Indigenous cultural expressions in Australia. The second section considers a number of cases in which Indigenous people have sought to use copyright law to protect their interests in art. I analyse the main conceptual challenges that prevented the Federal Court of Australia in *Bulun Bulun* from recognising Indigenous communal authorship of an artwork. The third section considers some of the other ways in which Indigenous people have sought to have their interests in their cultural property protected. In this context, private ordering and market-based measures have provided limited assistance because of the inequality of bargaining power that arises from the disadvantaged socio-economic position of many Indigenous artists and their communities. The final section of this chapter suggests some insights for copyright law that arise from this case study, which supports the call for a more flexible, contextual approach to the application of the joint authorship test.

---

appear to have given greater prominence to the collaboration limb of the joint authorship test than appears to be the case in the UK, for example, *Acohs Pty Ltd v Ucorp Pty Ltd* [2010] FCA 577 [57]–[59], approved [2012] FCAFC 16; *Fairfax Media Publications Pty Ltd v Reed International Books Australia Pty Ltd* [2010] FCA 984 [85]–[101]; *Primary Healthcare Ltd v Federal Commissioner of Taxation* [2010] FCA 419 [121].

[2] (1998) 86 FCR 244.

4.1 Indigenous Art

The first part of this section considers the dynamics of the authorship of Indigenous art, including the meaning and consequences of authorship in Indigenous communities.[3] It is worth noting at the outset that a different analysis might apply to the work of many contemporary urban Indigenous artists which is not produced in accordance with, and regulated by, Indigenous customary law. Although there is a danger of adopting a definition of 'traditional' Indigenous art which is too static, there are important policy reasons to treat art produced in accordance with Indigenous customary law as a special case. This sort of art provides an example of collective authorship because it is communal in origin. The second part of this section outlines the social, cultural and political significance of the problem of protecting Indigenous art which provides contextual background for the judicial decisions on the subsistence of copyright in Indigenous art that are considered in the following section.

4.1.1 Authorship Dynamics: Building and Sustaining Cultural Identity

Indigenous art often has a spiritual or religious significance because it depicts and invokes an ancestral past, or 'Dreaming'. For Indigenous communities, the Dreamtime is a period when ancestral spirit beings emerged from the ground to transform the earth and determine the form of social life.[4] These ancestral beings are seen to have moved aside, often merging into land forms, yet retaining the power to intervene in the life of man. Certain pre-existing designs are seen as artistic manifestations of ancestral beings or aspects of ritual knowledge associated with the Dreamtime.[5] Although there is a great diversity of Indigenous cultures and legal systems in Australia they tend to share

---

[3] W Wendland, 'Intellectual Property, Traditional Knowledge and Folklore: WIPO's Exploratory Program – Part 1' (2002) International Review of Intellectual Property and Competition L 485, 491 objects to the use of the word 'traditional' as it seems to imply a quality of stasis that does not adequately account for the dynamic nature of Indigenous culture. Wendland (495) stresses that the important issue is not necessarily identifying the precise ambit of terms like 'traditional knowledge', but rather delineating the terms upon which they will be protected. It is in this spirit, and for practical reasons, that I use the word 'traditional' here and I adopt the term 'Indigenous cultural expressions' when referring to the debate more generally.

[4] D Ellison, 'Unauthorised Reproduction of Traditional Aboriginal Art' (1994) 17 UNSWLJ 327, 330–331; See also R Sackville, 'Legal Protection of Indigenous Culture in Australia' (2003) 11(2) Cardozo J of International and Comparative L 711, 714–715.

[5] Ibid.

relatively consistent principles governing the ownership and control of ritual knowledge and cultural expressions.[6]

According to Indigenous customary law, pre-existing designs ought not to be changed. It is believed that the designs' efficacy in activating ancestral power is impaired if they are modified too far beyond socially accepted norms.[7] Only certain designated persons (determined by descent, apprenticeship and initiation) have the right to depict pre-existing designs, which are considered to be owned by the relevant Indigenous community, as a whole. Indigenous art is integral to the social fabric of 'traditional' Indigenous communities, because the transmission of Indigenous cultural heritage is an essential part of it.[8] Art often provides the framework for ordering the hierarchy of relationships between people, ancestors, ritual knowledge and the land. Thus, paintings might have a dual aspect of representing relationships between things as well as being integral to constituting those relationships.[9] Once objects of cultural expression are removed from their context, they often cease to have meaning, and if appropriated or disrespected, their sacred nature might be lost.[10]

Authorship (of art) has a number of potential values within Indigenous communities governed by customary law. It is often an act of religious significance expressing and maintaining a relationship to the land.[11] It is primarily a way of transmitting and preserving culture, but the sale of certain artworks can also provide a valuable source of income for the artist and his or her community.[12] The authorship of art promotes community cohesion and helps socialise young members into a particular worldview.[13] This is because Indigenous artists must often undergo an

---

[6] T Janke and P Dawson, 'New Tracks: Indigenous Knowledge and Cultural Expression and the Australian Intellectual Property System' (Terri Janke and Company Pty Ltd, 2012) (<www.ipaustralia.gov.au/sites/g/files/net856/f/submission_-_terri_janke_and_company_ip_lawyers.pdf>) 6–7.
[7] Ibid.
[8] L Behrendt, C Cunneen, T Libesman, *Indigenous Legal Relations in Australia* (OUP 2009) 210.
[9] H Morphy, *Ancestral Connections: Art and an Aboriginal System of Knowledge* (U of Chicago P, 1991).
[10] A Diver, '"A Just War": Protecting Indigenous Cultural Property' (2004) 6(4) Indigenous L Bulletin 7.
[11] Morphy (n9). The sort of Indigenous art that is not of spiritual significance, e.g., the result of children playing, is not relevant for this book's purposes.
[12] See the testimony of Indigenous artist John Bulun Bulun in *Bulun Bulun v Nejlam Investments* (unreported, Fed. Ct. of Australia, Darwin 1989) and C Golvan 'Aboriginal Art and the Protection of Indigenous Cultural Rights' (1992) 14(7) EIPR 227, 228.
[13] Morphy (n9).

initiation period of apprenticeship, learning particular artistic techniques and discovering the meaning of certain designs and motifs. The artist is also a custodian of cultural knowledge; as such, he or she is responsible to the community for the appropriate use of the sacred knowledge embodied in the artwork. This can include subsequent uses of the original and any copies which are made of it, irrespective of whether those copies have been authorised by the artist.[14]

In Indigenous communities, the value of individual authorship is inextricably linked to community values and norms (such as the hierarchy of access to particular cultural meanings). During the period of apprenticeship, elders pass on the secret information needed to enable the artist to paint the artwork, as well as teaching the appropriate techniques for depicting ritual knowledge. Only then is the artist given the permission to depict certain aspects of the ritual knowledge that belongs to his or her tribe. Although a painting results from an individual's hand, from an Indigenous point of view the whole community is involved in its creation. The artist is merely a delegate of the tribe and a custodian of ritual knowledge, but it is the community as a whole who have created it in the relevant sense. Thus, the resulting artwork is seen as owned by the community as a whole, as the ritual knowledge depicted in it belongs to, and is controlled by, the community (as represented by elders).

The communal values of authorship for Indigenous communities contrast with the Western art market values of authorship, which tend to relate to authenticity – a value which attaches strongly to an artist as an individual (albeit as an Indigenous individual). This authenticity value is more easily accommodated by copyright law than communal values of authorship, because copyright law defines authorship in terms of origination. We have seen that origination has a tendency to be linked to the mechanical act of fixing a work in a material form.[15] The incompatibility of these two notions of authorship is evident in recent controversies about the authenticity of paintings, which include substantial unattributed contributions from family members of the named Indigenous artist 'author'.[16]

---

[14] This was acknowledged by the Federal Court of Australia in *Milpurrurru v Indofurn* (1994) 54 FCR 240, 246, where von Doussa J made an award of damages for 'cultural harm' as compensation to Indigenous artists for the stigma, humiliation and punishment that they were likely to suffer within their communities as a result of the unauthorised and offensive reproduction of their artworks.

[15] This may particularly be the case in Australia: E Adeney, 'Authorship and Fixation in Copyright Law: A Comparative Comment' (2011) 35 Melbourne University LRev 677.

[16] E Burns Coleman, *Aboriginal Art, Identity and Appropriation* (Ashgate 2005) 84–85.

4.1.2 Background to the Issue of Protecting Indigenous Cultural Expressions

The apparent gap in legal protection available for Indigenous artists has been a topical issue in Australia for many years.[17] At the same time, the legal protection of traditional knowledge and Indigenous cultural expressions are issues that have featured prominently on the international intellectual property agenda.[18] In both the national and the international context, this debate has been significantly affected by historical factors, such as colonialisation, and social justice concerns. On the international level, however, the protagonists are different. As the debate takes place been states, the issue of empowering indigenous groups within states which are reluctant to take measures to protect their cultural expressions tends to be elided. Despite this difference, the international and national debates feed into one another. Some commentators characterise this dispute as being one of the developed world's ideas of intangible property (embodied in current intellectual property law) versus the developing world's (or Indigenous) concepts of intangible property.[19] Indeed, under the current intellectual property status quo, developed countries

---

[17] The problem of Indigenous art 'rip-offs' in the souvenir market has been considered in a number of reports, e.g., *Stopping the Rip-Offs: Intellectual Property Protection for Aboriginal and Torres Strait Islander Peoples* <www.ag.gov.au/Publications/Pages/Stoppingtheripoffs October1994.aspx> (Australian Federal Government, October 1994); T Janke, *Our Culture: Our Future – Report on Australian Indigenous Cultural and Intellectual Property Rights* (Michael Frankel & Co and Terri Janke, 1998); and in the media: 'The 7.30 Report', ABC, 19 August 2010 <www.abc.net.au/7.30/content/2010/s2988038.htm>. It has been estimated that 80% of Indigenous souvenirs sold in Australian tourist shops are fakes: J Hobbs, 'The $200m industry of cheap fakes ripping off Indigenous artists', *Brisbane Times*, 24 March 2018, <www.brisbanetimes.com.au/entertainment/art-and-des ign/the-200m-industry-of-cheap-fakes-ripping-off-indigenous-artists-20180324-p4z63m .html>. In 2010, there was a controversy over a sculpture featuring unauthorised and offensive depictions of Wandjina spirits that was eventually removed following an action under planning regulations by the Blue Mountains City Council (R Ayres, 'The Wandjina case illustrates the lack of protection for Indigenous Culture', *Art+Law*, Issue 3, September 2010); and another concerning costumes worn by Russian ice skaters performing an 'Aboriginal dance' at the Russian National Figure Skating Championships (B Manton, 'Russian Ice Dancers Should Re-think their Routine' *Sydney Morning Herald*, 21 January 2010 <www.smh.com.au/opinion/politics/russian-ice-dancers-should-rethink-their-routine-20100121-mnwj.html>). More recently, Chanel faced criticism for selling a branded boomerang accessory (E Hunt, 'Chanel's $2,000 boomerang criticised for "humiliating" Indigenous Australian culture', *The Guardian*, 16 May 2018, <www .theguardian.com/fashion/2017/may/16/chanels-2000-boomerang-criticised-for-humiliat ing-indigenous-australian-culture>).

[18] In October 2000, for example, the WIPO General Assembly established an Intergovernmental Committee on Intellectual Property and Genetic Resources, Traditional Knowledge and Folklore.

[19] The characterisation of such interests as property is not entirely uncontroversial: Diver (n10).

do seem to benefit more in economic terms than developing countries.[20] Current intellectual property law can thus be seen as a product of dominant social and economic forces which have shaped modes of (cultural) production.[21] A central question in the debate on Indigenous cultural expressions is whether 'cultural rights' in the broadest sense are rival to intellectual property rights or essentially the same thing. Are such rights necessarily constructed in opposition to traditionally 'authored' works or should they be incorporated into the copyright fold? These questions reverberate throughout this chapter, as they do through the Australian case law considered in the next section.

Indigenous art is of great economic and cultural significance in Australia. The Indigenous art market has been valued at around 300 million AUD each year,[22] with some years reporting an annual growth in value of between 40 to 50%.[23] Indigenous art is also important because it can create a 'window of recognition' between white and black Australia, since the whole country can share a collective sense of pride in it.[24] The overall benefits of Australian Indigenous art are difficult to quantify. They include:

> Pride, self esteem, maintenance of culture, transmission of culture, intergenerational learning, meaningful activity, purposeful life, creative achievement, recognition from peers; recognition from national and international art media, provision of much of our nation's 'corporate identity'; provision of 'Australia's greatest cultural export' ...[25]

Unfortunately, Indigenous Australians are very rarely the main financial beneficiaries of their art.[26] Furthermore, there are widespread problems

---

[20] Some argue that a strong intellectual property regime will stimulate creativity for developing countries in the long term. It is, however, by no means clear that such a regime would promote creativity and development to a greater extent than allowing free copying.

[21] Behrendt, Cunneen and Libesman (n8) 224; C Craig, *Copyright, Communication and Culture: Towards a Relational Theory of Copyright Law* (Edward Elgar 2011) 12–13.

[22] T Janke, *Beyond Guarding Ground: A Vision for a National Indigenous Cultural Authority* (Terri Janke & Co, 2009) 6. The Australian Senate Standing Committee on Environment, Communications, Information Technology and the Arts, *Indigenous Art – Securing the Future: Australia's Indigenous Visual Arts and Craft Sector* (June 2007) ('Senate Report') placed it around $200–300 million, noting the dearth of available statistics. There has been a significant downturn in the Australian art market since the Global Financial Crisis, exacerbated by changes to the rules governing pension funds in 2010. This appears to have hit the Indigenous art market particularly hard: K Hamann, 'Indigenous Australian art market suffering substantial decline', 9 August 2013, transcript of ABC Radio report available at: <www.abc.net.au/pm/content/2013/s3822279.htm>; M Maneker, 'How the Australian Government Shattered Its Art Market', *Art Market Monitor*, 27 July 2016, available at: <www.artmarketmonitor.com/2016/06/27/how-the-australian-govt-shattered-its-art-market>.

[23] Senate Report, ibid 13.   [24] Golvan (n12) 227.

[25] Submission from Ms Christine Godden quoted in the Senate Report (n22) 15.

[26] According to the Senate Report, ibid 13–14, this was one probable explanation of evidence of the massive growth in the value of the industry combined with no

of unauthorised reproductions and uses of Indigenous art which have caused offence and cultural harm to Indigenous communities. The formal legal protection available for Indigenous cultural expressions is unclear and often seen to be inadequate. This issue has been the subject of a number of enquiries and public reports, most notably, the *Stopping the Rip-Offs: Intellectual Property Protection for Aboriginal and Torres Strait Islander Peoples* issues paper and the Janke and Frankell *Our Culture: Our Future* report.[27]

Indigenous people seek to have a number of different rights/interests enforced in respect of their cultural expressions. These include: the right to economic benefits from their commercialisation; the right to control their disclosure (including the right to keep certain things secret); the right to control their use and in particular to prevent derogatory, offensive and fallacious uses; the interest in their preservation and continuation (for identity/heritage reasons); the right to be acknowledged and attributed as their 'author'. Indigenous artists, communities, and their advocates, have sometimes struggled to enforce these rights/interests within the framework of existing legal regimes which provide protection to intangible property. This chapter focuses on copyright law – the regime which has often seemed best suited to address one of the most pressing problems in relation to Indigenous Australian art: unauthorised and/or offensive reproductions.

The issue of protecting Indigenous art cannot be separated from its social and historical context. The legacy of colonialisation, Indigenous people's historic experience of discrimination and injustice, the Indigenous struggle for self-determination and a sense of regret or responsibility for past wrongs felt by much of the white Australian community, are all interwoven into the social and cultural tapestry which forms the backdrop of judicial decisions and political debate on this subject.[28] In this context, improving protection for Indigenous cultural expressions is often seen as a matter of public importance, and part of an ongoing project of reconciliation between Indigenous people and the wider Australian community for the injustices of the past.[29]

---

commensurate expansion in the number of artists. This assumption was supported by evidence presented to the Senate inquiry.

[27] See n17. Other notable reports include: R Myer, *Report of the Contemporary Visual Arts and Crafts Inquiry* (2002) (Myer Report); T Janke, *Minding Culture: Case Studies on Intellectual Property and Traditional Cultural Expressions* (WIPO 2003); and *Beyond Guarding Ground* (n22).
[28] See further: Behrendt, Cunneen and Libesman (n8).
[29] 'Creative Nation', Commonwealth Cultural Policy Statement, October 1994, 67; C Hawkins, 'Stopping the Rip Offs: Protecting Aboriginal and Torres Strait Islander Cultural Expression' [1995] Aboriginal L Bulletin 3.

The process of reconciliation with the Indigenous peoples of Australia has been slow and fraught with difficulties.[30] The Australian legal system has proven limited in its ability to provide adequate and appropriate remedies for Indigenous Australians across a range of areas. The debate on the 'recognition' of Indigenous customary law, for example, always prioritises Australian law over Indigenous law.[31] The recognition of native title rights is also subject to a presumption that generally favours non-Indigenous land interests over Indigenous interests in land.[32] In addition, there are a number of practical problems which affect the ability of Indigenous people to take advantage of the legal protections which may already be available to them. One such example appears in the Arts Law Centre of Australia's newsletter:

> [we] advised one very senior artist in Arnhem Land who believed the document he signed (with a cross as he neither read nor wrote English) was a sale document for his painting. In actuality, the document also purported to assign all his copyright to a third party who produced photographic reproductions for online sale with no further royalty or payment.[33]

Indigenous Australians have sometimes been reluctant to bring legal claims, because of an historically fraught relationship with courts and the police, who have not always been perceived to be instruments of justice in their eyes.[34] This is exacerbated by the disadvantaged socio-economic position of many Indigenous artists. Although many of these issues are outside the scope of this chapter, they ought to be borne in mind when assessing the case law and, in particular, when assessing the adequacy of the current approach to determining the subsistence of copyright in Indigenous art.

---

[30] One step forward, such as the Australian Government's apology in 2008, is often followed by steps backwards, such as the failure to enact the Indigenous Communal Moral Rights Bill.

[31] C Graber, 'Aboriginal Self-Determination vs The Proprietisation of Traditional Culture: The Case of the Sacred Wanjina Sites' (2009) 13(2) Australian Indigenous LR 18.

[32] Behrendt, Cunneen and Libesman (n8) xiv.

[33] D Everard, 'Code of Conduct for Indigenous Art', *Art+Law*, June 2009, available at <www.artslaw.com.au/artlaw/archive/2009/09CodeOfConduct.asp>.

[34] For example: 'Report of the Royal Commission into Aboriginal Deaths in Custody', tabled in the Australian Federal Parliament on 9 May 1991 considered the underlying social, cultural and legal reasons for the disproportionately high rates of incarceration of Indigenous people. Chapter headings used in this report suggest some of the major issues, they include: the Legacy of History, Aboriginal Society Today, Relations with the Non-Aboriginal Community, The Harmful Use of Alcohol and Other Drugs, Schooling, Employment, Unemployment and Poverty, Housing and Infrastructure, Land Needs and Self-Determination.

4.2 Protecting Indigenous Art with Copyright

Establishing the subsistence of copyright in Indigenous cultural property presents a number of problems. Obstacles include the idea/expression dichotomy which might preclude protection for styles, motifs and themes; the requirement of originality;[35] the material form (fixation) requirement,[36] and the fact that copyright law struggles to give meaning to Indigenous notions of communal ownership and custodianship of particular cultural forms.[37] Body art, for example, might be too ephemeral to be protected.[38] Copyright law is also not an effective tool to protect ancient rock art, because the author or authors are generally unknown and any copyright-like protection will no longer subsist.[39]

This section considers a line of cases in which Indigenous artists and their communities have sought to use copyright law to protect their cultural expressions from unauthorised and offensive reproductions. These cases culminated with the Federal Court of Australia's decision in *Bulun Bulun v R & T Textiles*. This is an important case because it exemplifies the difficulties of accommodating Indigenous interests in art within copyright's conceptual framework.[40] *Bulun Bulun* concerned a claim by an Indigenous elder (as a representative of his community) that because an artwork was created in accordance with customary law, it was the product of 'communal' authorship and, as such, the court ought to recognise the community's interest in any copyright subsisting in the artwork. The Federal Court acknowledged the inadequacies of copyright law's provisions in this context. Constrained by the apparent limits of existing legal concepts, the court was unable to offer much effective relief, although it expressed its sympathy for this cause.

---

[35] Historically, there was a perception that there would be difficulty establishing the originality of Indigenous art depicting pre-existing clan-owned motifs. This concern has been put to rest following *Yumbulul v Reserve Bank of Australia* [1991] FCA 332, 21 IPR 481 and *Milpurrurru* (n14).

[36] Dances and stories might lack the material form required for copyright subsistence: E Adeney, 'Unfixed Works, Performers' Protection, and Beyond: Does the Australian Copyright Act Always Require Material Form?' (2009) IPQ 77 comparing UK and Australian law on this point.

[37] In addition, as already suggested, there are practical problems bringing claims and an imbalance in power relations.

[38] *Merchandising Corporation of America v Harpbond* [1983] FSR 32; *Creation Records v News Group Newspapers* [1997] EMLR 444 (Ch)

[39] On Indigenous rock art: 'Rock Art Revisited' in S Kleinart and M Neale, *The Oxford Companion to Aboriginal Art and Culture* (OUP 2000), Ch 5, 103. Ancient rock art will likely pre-date copyright legislation, which also now extinguishes any pre-existing common law copyright or similar customary right: 4.2.2.

[40] (1998) 86 FCR 244.

4.2.1 Cases Prior to Bulun Bulun

Before considering *Bulun Bulun* in detail it is worth considering some of the cases that laid the groundwork for that decision. Many early cases did not make it to court. In 1966, for example, the Reserve Bank of Australia was the subject of much public embarrassment for reproducing David Malangi's artwork (a bark painting entitled 'The Hunter') on the one dollar note without seeking his permission. The Bank had assumed the work to be of an 'anonymous and probably long dead artist'.[41] This case was settled with the artist receiving $1000, a fishing kit, and a silver medallion. In 1988, another widely publicised case involved the unauthorised reproduction of the artworks of fourteen Indigenous artists on T-shirts. This dispute was settled for a $150,000 payment, which the artists decided to share equally (irrespective of the number of infringing reproductions of each artwork) in accordance with their customary law.[42] This settlement provided hope that copyright law might prove a useful means of protecting Indigenous communities' interests in their art.

Further proceedings were brought against the Reserve Bank of Australia in *Yumbulul v Reserve Bank of Australia*. This dispute concerned the Reserve Bank's reproduction of Terry Yumbulul's 'Morning Star Pole' sculpture on the ten-dollar note with purported permission granted by the Aboriginal Artists Agency. Here, French J conceded the difficulties that arise in the interaction of traditional Indigenous culture and the Australian legal system relating to the protection of Indigenous art[43] concluding that Australia's copyright law might provide inadequate 'recognition of Aboriginal community claims to regulate the reproduction and use of works which are essentially communal in origin'.[44] He suggested that this matter ought to be dealt with by legislative intervention.[45] In this case, the court did not need to consider copyright issues directly, focusing instead on the validity and terms of licences that Yumbulul had granted the Aboriginal Artists Agency in respect of the work. The court was not persuaded by evidence which suggested that Mr Yumbulul had not fully understood the nature of the licences that he signed, although French J acknowledged that '... [i]t may be that greater care could have been taken in this case'.[46]

A subsequent case, *Milpurrurru v Indofurn*, concerned the importation of carpets which featured unauthorised reproductions of certain Indigenous artworks. In that case a great deal of evidence was presented concerning the regulation of art under customary law and the nature of

---

[41] Janke (n17) 8.
[42] *Bulun Bulun v Nejlam Investments* (n12). For more: C Golvan, 'Aboriginal Art and Copyright: The Case for Johnny Bulun Bulun' (1989) 11(10) EIPR 346.
[43] *Yumbulul* (n35) [1].   [44] Ibid, [21].   [45] Ibid, [2].   [46] Ibid, [21].

communal ownership under Indigenous customary law.[47] The Federal Court was not asked to recognise that the relevant Indigenous artworks, which depicted pre-existing clan-owned designs, were communally authored copyright works. Although copyright subsistence was ultimately admitted, the court specifically commented that copyright subsisted in the artworks because of the skill and judgement exercised by the particular artists in their interpretation of the designs.[48] At the time, this case was seen as a 'landmark in the protection of Indigenous culture'[49] because some earlier commentaries had characterised Indigenous artworks which featured traditional designs as non-original, since the actual form of such designs is so strictly determined (controlled) by customary law.[50]

Von Doussa J acknowledged the importance of the use of art by Indigenous communities as a means of recording stories of the Dreaming and for teaching future generations.[51] The cultural harm caused by the unauthorised and offensive reproductions of sacred images on the Defendant's carpets was indirectly recognised as the Defendants were required to pay additional damages (for flagrant infringement). This was justified on the basis of the stigma, humiliation and punishment that the three living artists were likely to suffer within their communities as they would be held responsible for the unauthorised and offensive reproductions (even though they had no knowledge of what had occurred, nor any control over it).[52]

Although the court in *Milpurrurru* did not explicitly uphold Indigenous customary law in relation to the ownership and appropriate treatment of the artwork, it did accommodate customary law within the scope of judicial discretion as permitted by court rules and procedures.[53] For example, the names of the deceased artists were not spoken in court in accordance with Indigenous customary law.[54] Furthermore, although the whole community could not be compensated for the devaluing of their cultural artefacts, the court made a collective award of damages (rather than individual awards to each Claimant), which would at least allow the

---

[47] (n14) 245–246.
[48] See von Doussa J's comments (n14) 248, although the subsistence of copyright in the artworks was eventually conceded by the carpet importers.
[49] Ms Bronwyn Bancroft, artist and chairperson of the National Indigenous Arts Advocacy Association: T Janke, 'The Carpet Case' (1995) 3(72) Aboriginal L Bulletin 36.
[50] Golvan (n12); *Milpurrurru* (n14) 247–248 noting that this had been previous perceived to be a problem, but considering that, '[a]lthough the artworks follow traditional Aboriginal form and are based on Dreaming themes, each artwork is one of intricate detail and complexity reflecting great skill and originality'.
[51] Ibid, 245.   [52] Ibid, 246, 277, 279 as permitted by Copyright Act 1968 (Cth) s115(4).
[53] Ibid, 243, 272–273.
[54] Ibid, 243. The deceased applicants were only referred to by name once for the purpose of ensuring that they were identified with certainty.

amount to be distributed amongst the artists equally according to custom.[55] This willingness to use judicial discretion to accommodate customary law might have seemed, at the time, like a first step towards the recognition of communal ownership of artistic works by Indigenous people within the Australian legal system.

4.2.2   Bulun Bulun

The Australian case law on copyright ownership and Indigenous art culminates with the Federal Court of Australia's 1998 decision in *Bulun Bulun*. This case concerned the importation and sale of printed clothing fabric which reproduced John Bulun Bulun's artistic work, 'Magpie Geese and Water Lilies at the Waterhole'.[56] As the Respondents admitted to infringing Bulun Bulun's copyright, the trial focused upon the allegations of the Second Applicant, George Milpurrurru, acting as a representative of the traditional Indigenous owners of the Ganalbingu country (Arnhem Land, Northern Territory), raising a number of claims in the alternative:

(i) that the relevant Indigenous community were equitable owners of the copyright subsisting in the artwork;[57]
(ii) that Mr Bulun Bulun held ownership of copyright in the artwork on trust for the community; or
(iii) that Mr Bulun Bulun's ownership of copyright in the artwork gave rise to fiduciary obligations in favour of the community.

At the heart of these claims was the fact that the artistic work incorporated sacred and important subject matter derived from the ritual knowledge of the Ganalbingu people that the artist was only able to reproduce because of certain rights granted by Indigenous customary law. Von Doussa J highlighted the significance of the case:

These proceedings represent another step by Aboriginal people to have communal title in their traditional ritual knowledge, and in particular in their artwork, recognised and protected by the Australian legal system. The inadequacies of statutory remedies under the *Copyright Act* as a means of protecting communal ownership have been noted in earlier decisions of this court: see [*Yumbulul* and

---

[55] Ibid, 272–273. The damage award was expressed in terms of an aggregate liability.
[56] (n2) 246.
[57] The Federal Minister for Aboriginal and Torres Strait Islander Affairs and the Attorney-General (NT) intervened to argue that this claim, in effect, involved an assertion of native title land rights over Ganalbingu country, which the court lacked the jurisdiction to determine in the absence of a proper application under the Native Title Act 1993 (Cth) s74. The interveners were significant because the respondent company was under administration and without them there would have been no contradictor.

Milpurrurru]⁵⁸ ... [t]he claim raises important and difficult issues regarding the protection of the interests of Indigenous people in their cultural heritage'.⁵⁹

Indeed, the court recognised the importance of the issues in dispute, in taking the unusual step of travelling to Arnhem Land to hear evidence from Indigenous elders and to inspect the site that was the subject of the artwork.⁶⁰

Von Doussa J explained that the claims were confined to the recognition of an equitable interest in the copyright subsisting in the artwork, for a number of reasons:

(a) Section 8 of the Copyright Act 1968 (Cth) precludes any copyright protection, except as provided by the Act. This provision was seen to remove the possibility that Indigenous customary law providing communal title to artwork could be recognised by the common law.

(b) Section 35(2), which provides that the author is the owner of any copyright subsisting in a work, was seen to preclude the notion of group authorship (except where copyright law's joint authorship test is satisfied).

(c) The case law on joint authorship was said to establish that it is not enough to supply the artistic idea for a work; instead, it envisaged a contribution of skill and labour to the production of the work itself. Von Doussa J clearly implies that these criteria are not satisfied in this case as he assumes that the community's contribution was only of unprotectable ideas.⁶¹

Von Doussa J and counsel for the parties were so convinced that the argument that the community might own a legal interest in copyright in the artwork had no possibility of success, despite a 'wide ranging search' for ways to establish this, that the statement of claim was amended to claim only equitable interests.⁶² This left the court with limited options.

The first claim was ultimately abandoned because the form in which it was originally stated appeared to imply that the community's interest

---

⁵⁸ *Bulun Bulun* (n2) 247. ⁵⁹ Ibid, 254.
⁶⁰ C Golvan, 'Aboriginal Art and Copyright: An Overview and Commentary Concerning Recent Developments' (1999) EIPR 549, 552.
⁶¹ *Bulun Bulun* (n2) 257–258 (von Doussa J) citing *Kenrick v Lawrence* (1890) 25 QBD 99 and *Fylde Microsystems v Key Radio Systems* [1998] FSR 449 (Ch).
⁶² *Bulun Bulun* (n2) 256–257. A lack of intention to create a trust was inferred from the sale of the artwork and retention of the proceeds by Mr Bulun Bulun, and the fact a reproduction had already been permitted in a book. The lack of certainty arose from evidence of Indigenous communal ownership that suggested that the beneficiaries of such a trust would be all present and future members of the clan.

in the artwork was an incident of native title to the land, but no application for native title had been made in the proper form.[63]

There could be no express trust in favour of the community because the facts did not establish evidence of an intention to create such a trust, and even if they had, the terms of any such trust would be likely to lack sufficient certainty.[64]

The court also considered a possibility that had been raised in argument that there might have been an express contract between the artist and the community. This also failed because there was no evidence of an intention to create legal relations because there was no suggestion of an 'express agreement of a contractual nature in which terms were agreed'.[65] Equally, a contract could not be implied, which is unsurprising given that the conditions required are directed towards upholding the reasonable expectations of parties to a transaction (as indeed is the law of contract).[66] The principles for implying a contract focus on factors such as business efficacy, which seem to be fundamentally at odds with the moral and deeply religious character of the relationship between an Indigenous artist and his or her community as expressed in the creation of art which embodies ritual knowledge.

Von Doussa J found it easier to establish the existence of a fiduciary duty, given the inherent adaptability of this legal category and its purpose to remedy harms that arise in situations where a special relationship of trust and confidence exists between parties. Von Doussa J held that Bulun Bulun owed a fiduciary duty to his community which arose from the nature of the ownership of artistic works amongst the Ganalbingu people, noting the grant of permission by representatives of the community to paint certain designs is 'predicated on the trust and confidence which those granting permission have in the artist'.[67] In holding that a fiduciary duty exists in these circumstances von Doussa J affirmed that the community's interest in 'the protection of [their] ritual knowledge from

---

[63] Native Title Act 1993 (Cth) s74 allows for the recognition of continuing Indigenous ownership of certain sorts of land. It is unfortunate that the court did not consider the possibility that intellectual property rights might arise as an incident of native title rights. Subsequent cases have foreclosed this possibility, citing von Doussa J's comments that recognising such rights would fracture a skeletal principle of the common law in *Bulun Bulun* (n 2) 256, see: *Western Australia v Ward* [2002] HCA 28, (2002) 213 CLR 1 [59], [60], [644]; in dissent [580] (Kirby J); *Neowarra v Western Australia* [2003] FCA 1402 following *Ward* and rejecting a claim that a native title right existed to use, maintain, protect and prevent the misuse of cultural knowledge (specifically, sacred painting and ceremonies) of the Wanjina-Wunggurr community in relation to a native title land claim. See further: Graber (n31).

[64] Ibid, 259.   [65] Ibid, 262–263.

[66] See: *BP Refinery (Westernport) v Hastings Shire Council* (1977) 180 CLR 266, 283. Although von Doussa J noted that there has been some success adopting the contract approach in Ghana: *Bulun Bulun*, ibid 263.

[67] Ibid, 261–262.

exploitation which is contrary to their law ... is deserving of the protection of the Australian legal system'.[68]

The content of this fiduciary duty, however, was held to be very narrow: merely requiring the artist to act in the interests of the community in relation to the artwork, so as to preserve the integrity of their culture and ritual knowledge.[69] This duty would not prevent the artist from pursuing his own interest to a certain degree, for example, by selling the artwork for profit. In this case the duty did not extend further than to oblige Bulun Bulun to sue infringers of copyright in the work, a duty which he had satisfied.[70] The existence of this fiduciary duty 'without more' was held to be insufficient to vest an equitable interest in the ownership of the copyright in the Ganalbingu people.[71] The fiduciary duty would only give rise to a constructive trust in the most extreme of circumstances – in order to allow the community to bring an action to enforce the copyright interest in the work in the artist's absence.

4.2.3 Bulun Bulun's *Limited Legacy*

Bulun Bulun was seen by many as a beacon of hope for the protection of Indigenous cultural expressions and has been the subject of much comment. Largely, this interest has been stoked by the Federal Court's recognition of the significance of Indigenous cultural expressions to Australia in general (not just Indigenous communities) and its admission that it is desirable to protect such expressions from misuse and unauthorised exploitation. Although *Bulun Bulun* might be seen as a symbolic judicial gesture of good faith, ultimately von Doussa J underlined that the problem is one which the legislature ought to resolve.[72] Indeed, the importance of *Bulun Bulun* has often been overstated.[73] The decision is of little precedential value, given that it is likely to be restricted to its facts and it largely ignores the social realities of the production and exploitation of Indigenous art.[74] The problem of widespread unauthorised and offensive commercial exploitation of Indigenous cultural expressions is unlikely to be ameliorated by the narrow fiduciary duty created in *Bulun Bulun*, as Indigenous artists are rarely unwilling to protect their community's interest in artwork

---

[68] Ibid, 263.   [69] Ibid, 262.   [70] Ibid, 263.   [71] Ibid.
[72] Ibid, 247 (von Doussa J) refers to the 'inadequacy of statutory remedies'.
[73] E Mackay, 'Indigenous Traditional Knowledge, Copyright and Art – Shortcomings in Protection and an Alternative Approach' (2009) 32(1) UNSWLJ 1, 6.
[74] M Rimmer, 'The Bangarra Dance Theatre: Copyright Law and Indigenous Culture' (2000) 9(2) Griffith L Rev 274, 278.

produced according to customary law.⁷⁵ Instead, the problem is the recognition of that interest in Australian law.

Bulun Bulun demonstrates an apparent lack of flexibility in copyright law's concepts of subsistence, which suggests that copyright law is ill-adapted to protect an Indigenous community's interests in its cultural expressions. And, unfortunately, there are unlikely to be more cases testing the limits of copyright protection in this respect. Aside from the practical problems of access to the court system, there seems little reason for Indigenous communities to take the financial risk of bringing another copyright claim for protection of their interests in art, since *Bulun Bulun* appears to categorise Indigenous communal ownership of artwork (and the various rights this ownership entails under customary law) as something that is fundamentally different from, and which cannot be contained within, copyright law's notion of joint authorship.

In several places in the judgement, von Doussa J characterises the Indigenous community's ideas of authorship as fundamentally different to copyright law's concept of authorship. For example, the claim for recognition of a connection between the creation of artistic works and land ownership was seen to risk fracturing a skeletal principle of the legal system (the separate recognition of real property and intangible property).⁷⁶ Similarly, it was considered contrary to established legal principle for the common law to recognise *communal* title.⁷⁷ The judgement involves an odd characterisation of Indigenous communal ownership under customary law, presented in one part of the judgement as analogous to copyright (so as to be extinguished by s8); while in another part, it is something fundamentally different to copyright (so much so, that recognising it would fracture a skeletal part of the legal system).

The issue of sovereignty features as a strong undercurrent throughout the decision. Von Doussa J affirms previous case law which limits the application of Indigenous customary law to those outside of the relevant Indigenous community. He holds that Indigenous customary law is only relevant as part of the factual matrix of a case, rather than as an independent source of obligations for third parties.⁷⁸ Yet, Indigenous customary law seems to have had no material impact on the assessment of the

---

⁷⁵ MacKay (n73) 6; K Weatherall, 'Culture, Autonomy and Djulibinyamurr: Individual and Community in the Construction of Rights to Traditional Designs' (2001) 64 MLR 215, 221–222 argues that *Bulun Bulun* will only ever have a limited practical effect because it is response-based and prohibitively expensive.

⁷⁶ *Bulun Bulun* (n2) 256.   ⁷⁷ Ibid, 257.

⁷⁸ Ibid, 262, 248 noting that the court in *Milpurrurru* (n14) took the consequences of unauthorised reproductions of artistic works under Indigenous customary law into account when determining the quantum of damages to award.

relevant factual matrix of the community's copyright claim, given the arguably pre-emptive dismissal of the possibility of joint authorship.

The court's failure to even attempt to apply the joint authorship test might be explained by what some have criticised as a judicial tendency to focus upon fixation, that is, how the material form of a copyright work comes into existence. In the previous chapter, I referred to Burton Ong's argument that courts, faced with derivative works, likewise emphasise the ultimate form which a work takes rather than the process by which it is created,[79] which might, for example, deny copyright protection for works such as art restorations.[80] In this way, the originality test sometimes appears to privilege contributions which are easily observed in the material form of the copyright work. We have seen that this characteristic affects the joint authorship test, because originality provides the yardstick for 'authorship' and feeds in to the assessment of whether a contributor has made the right kind of contribution to obtain a copyright interest.

Determining which sorts of contributions count becomes more difficult the greater the number of contributors, so the joint authorship test particularly struggles to come to terms with creations involving the contributions of large numbers of contributors.[81] This is exacerbated by the tendency to apply stricter requirements of authorship as a way to reduce the number of potential joint owners of copyright subsisting in the work (the pragmatic instrumental approach). In Chapter 2, I observed that one strategy to concentrate authorship is to locate it with the contributor who is most proximate to the reduction of the work to material form.[82] The tendency to conflate authorship with responsibility for the fixation of the work (which should be distinguishable from the protected expression) appears even more evident in recent Australian case law.[83]

---

[79] B Ong, 'Originality from Copyright Fitting Recreative Works into the Copyright Universe' (2010) IPQ 165.

[80] There are cases which suggest that this might not be the case: *Sawkins v Hyperion Records* [2005] EWCA Civ 565, [2005] 1 WLR 3281. Cf. *Bridgeman Art Library v Corel* 36 FSupp 2d 191 (SDNY 1999).

[81] D Simone, 'Copyright or Copyleft? Wikipedia as a Turning Point for Authorship' (2014) 25(1) Kings LJ 102; D Simone, 'Recalibrating the Joint Authorship Test: Insights from Scientific Collaborations' (2013) 26(1) IPJ 111.

[82] This was observed in the UK context (for example: *Brighton v Jones* [2004] EWHC 1157, *Robin Ray v Classic FM* [1998] FSR 622 (Ch), *Donoghue v Allied Newspapers* [1938] 1 Ch 106 (Ch) and in the US (*Garcia v Google* 786 F3d 733 (9th Cir, 2015) (en banc), see Tehranian J, 'Sex, Drones & Videotape: Rethinking Copyright's Authorship-Fixation Conflation in the Age of Performance' (2017) 68 Hastings LJ 1319.

[83] Adeney (n16) discusses the conception of authorship emerging from the High Court of Australia's decision in *IceTV* (n1) (Gummow, Hayne and Heydon JJ) [98]: the author is 'the person who brings the copyright work into existence in its material form'; *Telstra v Phone Directories* (n1) (Gordon J) [20] and *Primary Health Care* (n1) [37]. She attributes this, in part, to a misreading of UK law and also to the wording in s22 and s32 of the Copyright Act

The application of the joint authorship test, however, is by no means as clear cut as von Doussa J seems to suggest. First, the test's application depends upon the particular facts in issue. This means not only a significant degree of uncertainty as to the outcome of a case, but it also that previous cases do not foreclose the possibility of finding joint authorship in new circumstances. It is precisely this flexibility which I argue allows the test to adapt to the wide range of creative forms. Second, the joint authorship test struggles to precisely calibrate the necessary connection between a contributor and their creation for 'authorship' due to judicial concern that copyright law ought to be seen to be aesthetically neutral. This tends to preclude the explicit use of creativity, aesthetic quality, authorial intent, audience impact, or any other value-specific criterion linked to the work's genre, etc., in determining authorship. Instead, judges have attempted to use a number of metrics that might appear more objective to locate the author of the work.

In the UK context, we have seen that control has sometimes served as a proxy for authorship. On other occasions, contributions have been labelled as irrelevant to the creative process because they are too small, or of the wrong kind, or made too early or too late. Sometimes a contributor's skill, labour or judgement is not considered to be of the right kind where it appears relatively remote to the fixation of the work. I have argued, however, that reference to aesthetic criteria is inescapable in determinations of joint authorship. Aesthetic value judgements are inherent in construing the scope of the creative process, in determining the relative significance of different contributions and in drawing the line between mere ideas and protected expression.[84] Treating these matters as 'objective characteristics' tends to make copyright law more amenable to creative contributions which reflect traditional modes of cultural production (that might seem more self-evidently authorial) and less adaptable to contributions which fall outside the romantic author model.

Nonetheless, some cases show the flexibility to accommodate a more nuanced and contextual approach.[85] *Cala Homes v Alfred McAlpine Homes*, the classic case on joint authorship, suggests that the joint authorship test might be able to accommodate communal authorship of the type

1968 (Cth) which make reference to a work being 'made' only when it is reduced to material form.
[84] See 2.2.
[85] This might be to reflect creative realities (*Cala Homes v Alfred McAlpine Homes* [1995] EWHC 7, [1995] FSR 818) or to accommodate considerations of public policy (*Sawkins v Hyperion* (n80); *Interlego v Tyco Industries* [1989] AC 217).

that occurred in *Bulun Bulun*.[86] The reader will recall this case involved drawings made by draftsmen to precise specifications given by the design director of a company that designed and built homes. In holding the design director to be a joint author along with the draftsmen – the court emphasised that authorship required more than penmanship.[87] Contribution of the concept, the provision of precise specifications and ongoing control over the creative process was held to be sufficient to establish joint authorship. There are evident parallels between an Indigenous elder (acting on behalf of the tribe) and the design director in that case. Indeed, the former will often exercise even greater control. In the case of Indigenous art, ritual knowledge provides the source for the 'concept', the apprenticeship of the artist provides him or her with 'precise specifications' in relation to the execution of the artwork, and customary law provides at least as significant a means of exercising artistic control as a contract between designer and draftsmen.

Von Doussa J held that the common law could not recognise Indigenous customary law provisions on communal ownership, because section 8 of the Australian Copyright Act 1968 (Cth) provides that copyright law is 'entirely a creature of statute'. Yet, as Bowrey observes, he also assumed that the meaning of joint authorship was limited by doctrines drawn from precedent which cannot be found in the Act (e.g., the idea/expression dichotomy and the 'authorship' requirement).[88] As Indigenous communal authorship had not been considered in any previous case law, these doctrines might have been applied in a different and more accommodating manner, especially since the joint authorship test ought to be applied in a factually specific way.[89] Indeed, from the Indigenous point of view the painting was clearly a collaborative endeavour.[90]

In dismissing the Indigenous community's contribution as unprotectable 'ideas', von Doussa J's judgement belies the notorious slipperiness of the idea/expression boundary.[91] Bowrey notes that from an Indigenous

---

[86] Ibid, approved in *Milwell Pty Ltd v Olympic Amusements Pty Ltd* [1999] FCA 63 (Full Fed. Ct. of Australia) [33]. It is odd that *Cala Homes* is not referred to in the judgement, which relies on *Kenrick v Lawrence* (n61) as authority for the proposition that a person who contributes only an artistic idea is not a joint author, although the facts of *Cala Homes* more closely resembled this claim.

[87] n85, 835.

[88] K Bowrey, 'The Outer Limits of Copyright Law – Where Law Meets Philosophy and Culture' (2001) 12 L and Critique 75, 81.

[89] This is especially the case given the broad conception of relevant contributions to a work of joint authorship accepted by Laddie J in *Cala Homes* (n85) 835–836 (cf. the subsequent narrow reading of these comments in *Ray v Classic* (n82) 363). See p 41.

[90] Bowrey (n88) 81.

[91] P Masiyakurima, 'The Futility of the Idea/Expression Dichotomy in UK Copyright Law' [2007] 38 IIC 548.

point of view, ritual knowledge (recast as an idea) is inseparable from the artwork (conceived of as the expression of that idea). She argues that by imposing an interpretation which focusses only on Bulun Bulun's direct contributions, displacing the contributions of Bulun Bulun's ancestors and the ongoing role of contemporary Indigenous elders to the artistic work (as embodied in ritual knowledge), the court effectively constructed an entirely new work, which obliterates the significance of the original artwork from an Indigenous point of view.[92] The court deploys a conception of authorship that imports temporal and mechanical divisions into the creative process which seem to separate 'idea' from 'expression'; and which in this case, led the judge to suggest that the community had not made the right kind of contribution at the right moment in time, to be considered 'authors'.[93] Bowrey argues that underlying the court's reasoning is a commitment to established liberal values which privilege certain interests and certain legal subjects over others.[94] Thus, the judgement demonstrates a discursive gap between copyright law's notion of authorship and Indigenous conceptions of authorship.

Ostensibly judges claim to be applying copyright law's rules of subsistence in an aesthetically neutral manner, but the application of these rules necessarily involves making value judgements about who is entitled to credit as an author, making it a decision which has a hidden political dimension.[95] Bowrey contrasts von Doussa J's approach with the more accommodating approach that has often been taken in cases involving new technologies.[96] In *Sega Enterprises v Galaxy Electronics*, for example, a video game was held to be sufficiently 'embodied' to be a 'cinematographic film' as the possible sequences of 3D images existed in the minds of the designers and in various 2D models – despite the fact that sequences of images did not actually materialise until the game was played by a user. A similarly creative interpretation of the material form required for copyright subsistence, might have been applied to the

---

[92] Bowrey (n88) 82.   [93] Ibid, 81.   [94] Ibid.
[95] On how copyright law's ostensibly neutral principles might operate to reinforce existing power structures: J Tehranian, 'Copyright's Male Gaze: Authorship and Inequality in a Panoptic World' (2018) 41 (2) Harvard J of L and Gender 343; C Craig 'Reconstructing the Author-Self: Some Feminist Lessons for Copyright Law' (2007) 15(2) J of Gender Social Policy and the Law 207; S Vaidhyanathan, *Copyrights and Copywrongs: The Rise of Intellectual Property and How It Threatens Creativity* (NYU Press 2001), Ch 4.
[96] Bowrey (n88) 78 cites *Kalamazoo v Compact Business Systems* (1983) 5 IPR 213 (blank accounting forms held to constitute a 'literary work') and *Sega Enterprises v Galaxy Electronics* (1996) 35 IPR 161, (1997) 37 IPR 462 (video games were a 'cinematographic film') attributing the judicial approach in these cases to a 'legal infatuation with serving the perceived needs of actors in the so-called information economy'.

Ganalbingu community's claim: their ritual knowledge existed in their minds alongside an anticipation that the knowledge would be embodied in an artwork created under authorisation in a way that allowed community elders to significantly influence the content of the artwork (as executed by the artist). Arguably *Sega* may have been incorrectly decided or may be incomparable to the facts of *Bulun Bulun*.[97] Yet, Bowrey's analysis still raises interesting questions about copyright law's notions of authorship and joint authorship, which appear to privilege certain legal subjects over others, as the rules for establishing the subsistence of copyright are malleable allowing judges to expand the scope (and the beneficiaries) of protection where there appear to be good reasons for doing so.[98]

I have argued that the reason that the joint authorship test is flexible is to permit it to adapt to a variety of different creative contexts.[99] In the case of Indigenous art which incorporates ritual knowledge and has been created with permission pursuant to Indigenous customary law, the authorial contribution of the community is directly reflected in the protected expression of the artwork – by the control over the subject matter, style, depiction of encoded meanings, and through the transfer of skill and ritual knowledge in the initiation and apprenticeship of the artist. The significance of the Indigenous community's role is reflected in the requirement under customary law for artists to consult and obtain approval from elders in relation to the creation and subsequent uses of the work. Furthermore, there are good reasons to recognise that Indigenous communities' interest in art made in accordance with customary law amounts to an authorship interest as this: (a) recognises the social reality for Indigenous artists; (b) allows Indigenous

[97] In *Stevens v Kabushiki Kaisha Sony Computer Entertainment* [2005] HCA 54, 224 CLR 193 [86] (Gleeson CJ, Gummow, Hayne and Heydon JJ) ' ... amicus curiae rightly pointed to difficulties to which that case gives rise' although neither side challenged *Sega*. *Sega* was distinguished in *Aristocrat Leisure Industries v Pacific Gaming* [2000] FCA 1273 [67] but the principle that intellectual property legislation must be liberally interpreted, especially in the case of video games, was approved. A liberal approach was also taken in *Milwell v Olympic Amusements* (n86) [21]–[22], where joint authorship was granted to mathematicians whose extensive and complex work on prize scales used for coin operated draw poker video games was a substantial intellectual contribution that partly shaped the output, even if they did not contribute to the reduction of the prizes to material form.
[98] Bowrey (n88) 95 argues that the 'reinvention' of copyright concepts need not be confined to the accommodation of new technologies to the benefit of investors in those technologies. See: *Sawkins v Hyperion* (n80). Similarly, in the UK context, in *Hadley v Kemp* [1999] EMLR 589 (Ch) 639 where the dominant author was obvious the court took a very flexible approach to the idea/expression dichotomy, considering it sufficient that the musical works in question had already been fixed in Gary Kemp's 'musical consciousness' before rehearsals and the recording of the band members' performances.
[99] It is flexible because its application depends upon the facts of the case. The parts of the test which are questions of fact are also best understood in light of the specific creative context: 2.4, 8.4.1 and 8.5.

communities recognition for their valuable contributions; and (c) gives those communities (together with the artist) the ability to better control and manage artworks, which in a very real sense, are seen as communally authored.[100]

4.3 Other Solutions for the Protection of Indigenous Cultural Expressions

After *Bulun Bulun*, scholars have tended to agree that protection for Indigenous communities' interests in their art stretches copyright law beyond its conceptual limits.[101] Indigenous people are left to fill the gap with a patchwork of other legal doctrines, such as judicial discretion in relation to the award of damages,[102] fiduciary duties,[103] breach of confidence,[104] planning legislation,[105] heritage protection law,[106] contract[107] and consumer protection law.[108] Most scholars now agree

---

[100] Practical concerns that if such an approach were adopted, it would be difficult to identify all the Indigenous joint authors of a work are surmountable. Although it must be proven that a work is a product of human authorship, it is not necessary to identify the exact identity of the authors: *Telstra v Phone Directories* (n1). Shared Indigenous native land title is currently administered collectively. Representative bodies that might pursue copyright claims on behalf of Indigenous groups already exist – there are 120 autonomous local Aboriginal Land Title Councils governed by Boards elected by local Indigenous community members which collectively manage a range of community services. The Pitjanjara Council, for example, successfully obtained an injunction restrain the disclosure of its ritual knowledge in *Foster v Mountford* [1976] 29 FLR 233.

[101] Mackay (n73); K Bowrey, 'Alternative IP?: Indigenous Protocols, Copyleft and New Juridifications of Customary Practices' (2006) 6 Macquarie LJ 65; D Burkitt, 'Copyrighting Culture – The History and Cultural Specificity of the Western Model of Copyright' (2001) IPQ 146. Although K Bowrey, 'Economic Rights, Culture Claims and a Culture of Piracy in the Indigenous Art Market: What Should We Expect from the Western Legal System?' (2009) 13(2) Australian Indigenous LRev 43–44 notes the 'peculiar thing is this: much of the perception that mainstream intellectual property rights are limited is based only on conjecture... there are in fact few limits in recognising "collective" or "collaborative" labour in any commercial context'.

[102] *Milpurrurru* (n14).

[103] *Bulun Bulun* (n2); J Gibson, 'Justice of Precedent, Justice of Equity: Equitable Protection and Remedies for Indigenous Intellectual Property' (2001) 6(4) Australian Indigenous L Reporter 1.

[104] *Foster v Mountford* (n100); *Aboriginal Sacred Sites Protection Authority v Maurice; Re the Warumbingu Land Claim* (1986) 10 FCR 104.

[105] See n17 and Ayres (n17).

[106] D Ritter, 'Trashing Heritage: Dilemmas of Rights and Power in the Operation of Western Australia's Heritage Legislation' (2003) 23 Studies in Western Australian History 195.

[107] See Rimmer (n74).

[108] *Australian Competition and Consumer Commission v Australian Dreamtime Creations* [2009] FCA 1545; *Australian Competition and Consumer Commission v Nooravi* [2008] FCA 2021. Consumer protection law is most effective in relation to uses in the marketplace that are deceptive (i.e., explicit, false claims that a work is authentic Indigenous art).

that the issue of protecting Indigenous cultural expressions, with all its complexities, is probably best addressed with a sui generis legislative scheme that can incorporate a balancing of policy concerns. In the meantime, private ordering mechanisms can provide a flexible 'bottom up' solution. However, these tend to be most effective for those already motivated to protect Indigenous cultural expressions and they may be compromised by power imbalances. Given the social and cultural disadvantages that many Indigenous communities face, measures which rely on market forces, including collective trade marks; or private bargaining power, such as contract, are likely to enjoy limited success. To date, legislative attempts to improve protection for Indigenous artists have either addressed only a small part of the problem (e.g., resale royalties legislation[109]); or have fallen off the legislative agenda (e.g., the Communal Moral Rights Bill[110] and the Competition and Consumer Amendment (Exploitation of Indigenous Culture) Bill[111]).

In this section, I assess four of the best candidates for a non-copyright-based solution to the problem of protecting Indigenous cultural expressions: protocols/codes of conduct; collective/certification trade marks; contracts; and sui generis legislation.

4.3.1 Protocols and Codes of Conduct

Protocols and codes of conduct might be useful in enhancing the protection of Indigenous cultural expressions.[112] They encourage good practice in commercial dealings in reproductions of Indigenous cultural expressions and often provide informal dispute resolution mechanisms.[113] Over the previous years a number of such protocols have been developed by arts organisations.[114] In October 2009, both the Australian Federal government,

---

[109] The Resale Royalty Right for Visual Artists Act 2009 (Cth) only applies in limited circumstances and excludes private sales.
[110] An exposure draft of the Copyright Amendment (Indigenous Communal Moral Rights) Bill (Cth) was circulated in 2003. The introduction of the bill was postponed ostensibly until 2006, however, it has still not been reintroduced.
[111] This bill was introduced as a private member's bill on 13 February 2017. It dropped off the legislative agenda in September of the same year.
[112] Janke (n22) 26.
[113] Informal dispute resolution mechanisms are considered inappropriate in situations involving significant imbalances of power: G Clark and I Davies, 'Mediation – When is it not an appropriate dispute resolution process?' (1992) 3(2) Australian Dispute Resolution J 70, 78–79; R Field, 'Mediation and the art of power (im)balancing' (1996) 12 *QUTLJ* 264, 266–267; D Eliades, 'Power in mediation – some reflections' (1999) 2(1) ADR Bulletin 4, 6.
[114] Melbourne City Council developed a code of conduct for galleries and retailers of Indigenous art: 'Code of Practice for Galleries and Retailers of Indigenous Art' <www .melbourne.vic.gov.au> 23 December 2008. Protocols have also been developed by the

and State and Territory governments endorsed the Indigenous Australian Art Commercial Code of Conduct.[115] Although protocols and codes of conduct can be helpful in raising awareness of the issues, their effectiveness is undermined by the fact that they are voluntary and there are limited provisions to ensure compliance (ie the publication of non-compliant members' names online). These measures are likely to be most effective in relation to parties already interested in, and committed to, compliance. Even where this is not the case, the disadvantaged socio-economic position of many Indigenous artists may make it difficult for them to negotiate the inclusion of such protocols in contracts for the sale or other use of their art.[116]

4.3.2 Collective/Certification Trade Marks

Certification and collective trade mark registration schemes are intended to promote the collective interests of groups of traders.[117] The success of using these schemes to protect Indigenous art is ultimately dependent upon how well and how widely such marks are implemented, regulated and policed.[118] In 1999, based upon a recommendation of the *Our Culture: Our Future* report,[119] the National Indigenous Arts Advocacy Association ('NIAAA') introduced an Indigenous Label of Authenticity.[120] However, the Label of Authenticity suffered from a number of practical problems: delays in implementing the scheme,[121] overly strict registration requirements,[122] a failure to adequately publicise

---

Australia Council for the Arts, 'Publications' <www.australiacouncil.gov.au>; Screen Australia, 'Indigenous Filming Protocol' <www.afc.gov.au/filminginaustralia/indigproto/fiapage9.aspx>; and SBS, 'The Greater Perspective – Protocol and Guidelines for the Production of Film and Television on Aboriginal and Torres Strait Islander Communities' (2nd edn, 1997).

[115] <www.indigenousartcode.org>. The Code was a key recommendation of the Senate Report (n22) which revealed widespread endemic patterns of unscrupulous commercial behaviour by dealers within the Indigenous arts industry.

[116] MacKay (n73) 20 argues that one context in which protocols might be effective is where government or other funding grants are made conditional on compliance with the protocol.

[117] Trade Marks Act 1995 (Cth) s162, s169; Janke (n22) 23.

[118] L Wiseman, 'The Protection of Indigenous Art and Culture in Australia: The Labels of Authenticity' (2001) EIPR 14, 25.

[119] Janke (n17) 198; S McCausland, 'Protecting Communal Interests in Indigenous Artworks after the Bulun Bulun Case' (1999) 4(22) Indigenous L Bulletin 4 suggests that notices might also be put on artwork in order to deter unauthorised reproductions.

[120] <www.culture.com.au/exhibition/niaaa/labelqa.htm>.

[121] M Rimmer, 'Australian Icons: Authenticity Marks and Identity Politics' 2004(3) Indigenous LJ 139.

[122] 75% of the initial applications failed to have sufficient supporting documentation (the applicant's Aboriginality had to be attested to in writing with the common seal of two Indigenous organisations): Rimmer, ibid, 156.

the scheme, and quality control issues in the administration of the scheme.[123] Fundamentally, the scheme failed to gain the widespread acceptance of the Indigenous community it was intended to protect, since its requirement to prove 'authenticity' was considered insulting and inappropriate.[124] In 2002, the Australia Council suspended the NIAAA's funding, thereby rendering the label of authenticity scheme practically defunct.[125] Some suggest that trade marks for individual Indigenous art centres might be more successful and help to empower local communities (if accompanied with the proper administrative infrastructure).[126] The usefulness of such marks is limited, however, because they depend upon the market: consumers must understand the significance of the mark and be motivated to buy the authorised/genuine products bearing the mark. In the souvenir market, where problems of unauthorised and offensive reproductions of Indigenous art are rife, consumers are likely to be more concerned with price, than provenance.

4.3.3 Contract

Organisations, such as the Arts Law Centre of Australia, have not only developed model contracts and licensing agreements, but also provide free or low cost legal advice to Indigenous people to help them to negotiate suitable contractual arrangements.[127] The Bangarra Dance troupe illustrates that Indigenous cultural interests may be protected well via contract law.[128] The troupe reached a private agreement with the Munyarrun clan, granting it permission to reproduce themes from the clan's particular traditional dances and songs in its own performance. The agreement recognised Munyarrun clan copyright ownership of the dances and songs, set out a fee payment structure for use of the material, and established guidelines to ensure that the troupe's use is a respectful treatment of the cultural property. Yet, this is probably an exceptional case.[129] Further, insofar as such agreements intend to circumvent and modify the scope of copyright law there are real questions as to their

---

[123] Ibid, 164.
[124] Ibid, 262. The scheme also failed to adequately distinguish between Indigenous groups.
[125] Ibid, 160–161. This was associated with concerns related to poor governance and management of NIAAA and the fact that it did not include regional representation.
[126] Ibid, 165. A number of regional arts centres successfully use registered trade marks, e.g., Desart.
[127] As recommended in Janke (n22) 24. For example, Arts Laws provide a free sample Indigenous Art Centre and Gallery Consignment Agreement: <www.artslaw.com.au/Indigenous/IndigenousArtistAndArtCentreAgreement.asp>.
[128] Rimmer (n74).   [129] Ibid, 274.

enforceability.¹³⁰ Similar arrangements are unlikely to be replicated by less scrupulous parties that do not share the troupe's motivation to respect Indigenous culture. Contracts offer the benefit of promoting self-determination, allowing for more management and negotiation at the local level.¹³¹ The downside is that contracts cannot be enforced against third parties and might also lead to suboptimal results where there is unequal bargaining power (a key issue in this context).¹³²

4.3.4 Sui Generis Legislation

MacKay argues that sui generis legislation might meet the 'urgent need to reshape the conceptual landscape'.¹³³ Sui generis legislation could be specifically tailored to fit the needs of Indigenous artists and their communities; for example, providing more scope for non-Western concepts such as communal ownership, reflecting the unimportance of originality or novelty, and taking into consideration the intergenerational nature of Indigenous cultural property. It might also extend to a broader range of subject matter not protected by conventional intellectual property law, providing a more holistic approach to protecting Indigenous cultural expressions and traditional knowledge.¹³⁴ Additionally, sui generis legislation could incorporate a role for Indigenous communities' customary law. It is imperative that any new legislation should be drafted not just to ensure preservation of Indigenous culture, but also to promote its continuation. Although a sui generis system has the potential to empower Indigenous people and promote self-determination, these benefits are only likely to be achieved if Indigenous communities are integral in the drafting and implementation of such a scheme.

A sui generis solution is not wholly uncontroversial. Although few dispute that Indigenous artists need and deserve special protection, some have argued that sui generis regulation might merely serve to further

---

[130] Rimmer, ibid, cites Netanel's concerns over contracts which seek to circumvent copyright law provisions in the digital context: N Netanel, 'Copyright and Democratic Civil Society' (1996) 106 Yale LR 283, 305–306, 382–385.

[131] Bowrey (n101) 75 argues that private ordering allows one to capture the voice of a community instead of presuming to speak for it, as legislation might. Cf. P Drahos with J Braithwaite, *Information Feudalism: Who Owns the Knowledge Economy?* (Routledge 2002); also S Sell, *Private Power, Public Law: The Globalisation of Intellectual Property Rights* (CUP 2003).

[132] MacKay (n73) 21. This is supported by the Arts Law Centre of Australia's experiences (p108) and *Yumbulul* (p110).

[133] Ibid, 10.

[134] T Lopez Romero, '*Sui Generis* Systems for the Protection of Traditional Knowledge' (2005) 6 International Law: Revista Colombiana de Derecho Internacional 301–339.

marginalise Indigenous people and their cultural interests.[135] As a 'top down' approach, the concern is that such a scheme risks being perceived as lacking legitimacy and may thus prove ineffective in practice.[136] This risk could be addressed by ensuring extensive and broad consultation with Indigenous artists and their communities.[137] Furthermore, any sui generis regime must be complementary to the current legal system, not constructed in opposition to it.[138] Unfortunately, there has been very little investigation of the potential details and scope of a sui generis approach in Australia to date.[139]

4.4 Insights for Copyright Law

This chapter has exposed tensions between the reality of authorship in Indigenous communities and the conception of authorship which copyright law employs. For Indigenous communities, the process of creating art is essential to the preservation and continuation of their cultural identity; it is also an act that establishes and reinforces the creator's place within the social structure of the community. The author is merely a temporary custodian of that part of the ritual knowledge which he or she is allowed to depict. The author is responsible to the community for ensuring appropriate and respectful use of that knowledge both in their own artwork, and in relation to subsequent uses of the artwork by others. The ritual knowledge is understood to be owned by the community as a whole, although entrusted to certain elders and initiated artists for safekeeping, preservation and continuation.

There is a mismatch between the 'identifying' function of authorship as an indicator of the origin of the work in a specific sense linked to its material form or fixation (a Western notion reflected in copyright law); and the 'identity' function of authorship as an indicator of status within, and belonging to, a particular community (an Indigenous notion). In Indigenous communities, authorship encapsulates a strong responsibility value which corresponds to the idea of cultural custodianship.

[135] Bowrey (n101) 88.
[136] On the methodological issue of speaking 'for' Indigenous people: K Bowrey and J Anderson, 'The Politics of Global Information Sharing: Whose Cultural Agendas Are Being Advanced?' (2009) 18 Social and Legal Studies 479.
[137] Consultation is also vital to ensure that any such legislation suits the needs of the many different Indigenous groups which exist across Australia.
[138] MacKay (n73) 26 citing M Dodson and O Barr, 'Breaking the Deadlock: Developing and Indigenous Response to Protecting Indigenous Traditional Knowledge' (2007) 11(2) Australian Indigenous LR 19, 23.
[139] This is surprising given that such legislation has been successfully adopted elsewhere, for example, the Pacific Model Law (Model for the Protection of Traditional Knowledge and Expressions of Culture 2002).

The case law demonstrates some capacity within the Australian legal system to take this value into account, for example, in the damages award for culturally-based harm in *Milpurrurru* and in the fiduciary duty recognised in *Bulun Bulun*. Yet, courts seem unwilling to recognise the flipside of Indigenous authorial responsibility: the controlling influence of community norms (as embodied in customary law) over the creative process, particularly in claims against those outside of the relevant Indigenous community. This might be inferred from the extremely narrow scope of the fiduciary duty in *Bulun Bulun*. But, I argued that attributing weight to contextual factors which elucidate creative realities (such as community norms) is essential to the proper application of the joint authorship test in cases involving collective authorship.

Bowrey views *Bulun Bulun* as a lost opportunity to formulate copyright values in cultural terms.[140] A less cursory application of the joint authorship test might have revealed a number of areas in which Indigenous customary law could have valuably contributed to the relevant factual matrix. Von Doussa J's judgement is cast in an aesthetically neutral light, appearing to apply copyright law's rules of subsistence in a way that might seem free of value judgements external to those legal principles. Yet, we have seen that when he employed vague (open) concepts like the idea/expression dichotomy, he may have been influenced by cultural preconceptions about who is eligible for the 'author' label, resulting in a short-sighted focus on the individual(s) having direct responsibility for the physical material form of the work.

Indeed, it is a lack of analytical clarity about the way in which the joint authorship test is applied which makes it vulnerable to the influence of ingrained, unquestioned cultural pre-conceptions. This is particularly likely to affect the assessment of whether a putative author has made a significant contribution of the right kind. Judicial insistence on aesthetic neutrality in decision-making hides the inherently political dimension of copyright law cases in which judges must decide which subjects are 'authors' and what comprises an 'artistic work'.

Bulun Bulun reveals a perception of Indigenous communal authorship as something that is fundamentally different from, and even potentially threatening to, copyright's own conceptions of authorship and joint authorship.[141] Undeniably, Indigenous cultural expressions *are* different from traditional copyright subject matter in many ways: they are seen as the object of communal rather than individual rights; although they might evolve over time, they are generally not concerned with originality or

---

[140] Bowrey (n88) 82.
[141] Hence, von Doussa J's resort to principles of equity in *Bulun Bulun* (n2).

novelty. It is for these reasons that some argue that it simply does not make sense to conceive of Indigenous interests in their cultural expressions in terms of 'property' at all.[142] From this angle, Indigenous people appear to be caught in a difficult situation: in trying to fit their cultural property into Western categories they may gain partial protection, however, by attempting to conform to dominant notions of ownership, Indigenous people risk displacing their own cultural identity.[143] This argument might be countered by asserting the empowering potential of 'authorship' from the point of view of democratic participation and cultural self-determination.

Recognising an Indigenous community's interest in art created in accordance with customary law not only recognises reality from an Indigenous perspective, it also allows Indigenous communities to more effectively control the uses of their cultural artefacts. Whether or not copyright law provides the best means for protecting Indigenous cultural expressions is a complex question, which cannot be adequately addressed within the context of this book. It might suffice to say that copyright law alone is not best-equipped to deal with this issue, although it might do more to protect Indigenous art than the Federal Court of Australia's decision in *Bulun Bulun* would suggest. Ultimately, the best solution is likely to be a comprehensive sui generis approach, which deals with all the interests that Indigenous people seek to protect, and which recognises differences within and between Indigenous communities.[144]

For the purposes of this book, this case study illuminates concepts of authorship and joint authorship in copyright law by providing a clearer view of their limitations along with glimpses of potential possibilities. Whether or not one accepts the influence of the romantic author trope upon copyright law, it is apparent that copyright law envisages creativity as primarily as an activity of individuals rather than groups of creators. Apart from joint authorship (which has often been restrictively interpreted) group creativity is only dealt with explicitly in the context of employment (where the employer presumptively owns copyright) or of a compilation or collective work (where those who select and arrange contributions own the copyright in the whole work, while those who contribute distinct parts may own the copyright in those parts). This limited accommodation for group creativity may

---

[142] Diver (n10) citing *Bulun Bulun* (n2) and *Yumbulul* (n35) as authorities for this proposition.
[143] Ibid.
[144] There may still be 200 Indigenous legal systems in operation in Australia: Dodson and Barr (n138) 25.

have contributed to von Doussa J's reluctance to admit the possibility of communal authorship in *Bulun Bulun*.

A commitment to aesthetic neutrality has sometimes led judges to elide many considerations that relate to the context of creativity – focusing upon input (skill/labour/judgement) directly related to the act of fixation, rather evident contribution to the intangible expression of the work. This chapter has attempted to reveal how an ostensibly aesthetically neutral approach might actually mask conceptions of authorship which reflect bias arising from economic, historical, social and cultural hierarchies of power and influence.

Courts have shown willingness to take Indigenous customary law into account in procedural aspects, e.g., when assessing damages or structuring hearings. Yet, Indigenous customary law remains a significant, untapped resource for answering questions of fact in the application of the joint authorship test. Putting the *Bulun Bulun* decision to one side, I have shown how applying the joint authorship test in a more contextual manner would allow for recognition of all important intellectual or creative contributions to a work which are directly reflected in its expression, irrespective of whether they also involve a mechanical/physical contribution to its ultimate material form. In doing so, I proffer the possibility of re-imagining the concepts of authorship and joint authorship in copyright in a way which might be better adapted to the dynamics of creativity recognisable across a wide range of collaborative endeavours whether created using cutting edge technology or following ancient customary practice. In the next chapter, I test this hypothesis further by considering a very different type of collective authorship: scientific collaborations.

5 Scientific Collaborations

Collaboration is becoming an increasingly important, and in some areas an indispensable, feature of modern science. As the list of authors' names for scientific journal articles seem to grow ever longer, practices of authorial attribution face increasing criticism for inflating or diluting two traditional values of authorship in science: credit and responsibility. This chapter focuses on two disciplines which share a particularly strong imperative for scientific collaboration: biomedical science and particle physics. These are both fields in which it has become virtually impossible to make any significant advance without invoking cooperation between a variety of specialists and technicians. These disciplines also provide an interesting point of comparison, as each has adopted a different solution to the problem of allocating authorship in respect of the fruits of collaborative work. Copyright law may be able to learn from the benefits and limitations of these solutions.

The chapter begins with an introduction to the context of scientific authorship.[1] I consider the important functions of authorship within science's reputational economy (as a locus for credit and responsibility) and how these functions are challenged by the attribution practices of large collaborations. The second section of this chapter contrasts two different scientific communities' approaches to the problem of regulating authorship. Particle physics collaborations' inclusive approach to authorship seems to have been more successful than biomedical journals' attempts to isolate dominant authorial contributions. The third section briefly considers the subsistence of copyright in journal articles which report the research of large scientific collaborations and comments on the little case law on scientific authorship and copyright.

---

[1] This chapter considers authorship by reference to common practices of authorial attribution on scientific journal articles; for other views of the 'author' in science, see: H Rheinberger, '"Discourses of Circumstance": A Note on the Author in Science' in M Biagioli and P Galison (eds) *Scientific Authorship: Credit and Intellectual Property in Science* (Routledge 2003) 309, 311.

The case law suggests both the value, and the potential dangers, of incorporating social norms in copyright decisions. The final section suggests insights that this case study offers for copyright law, arguing that the special characteristics of large scientific collaborations provide additional support for an inclusive, contextual approach to the application of the joint authorship test.

5.1 Authorship Dynamics: Constructing Authority

This section considers the dynamics of authorship in science. I begin by looking at the norms that govern science and the role of authorship in science's reputation economy as a locus for credit and responsibility. Authorship has an important role in the process of establishing the authority of a scientific claim. The traditional notion of authorship in science was very individualistic, with the contributions of technicians and other less powerful players generally hidden and unacknowledged. I consider how the collectivisation of modern science has disrupted this traditional notion of scientific authorship.

Historians and sociologists of science have done much to clarify the prevailing concept of authorship in the sciences and to track its transformation.[2] Although attribution practices vary between disciplines, the scientific community shares some common assumptions about the essential features of scientific authorship.[3] Science aims to be useful by producing knowledge about nature.[4] Scientific authorship is best understood as a step in an epistemological process that establishes the authority, or truthfulness, of a scientific claim and, by extension, its author.[5] Such authority is established by the scientific community's own adherence to the conventions which it has established as the proper basis for trusting a claim. Robert Merton famously identified the norms which embody the normal expectations of the scientific community,[6] viz:

---

[2] Biagioli and Galison (n1) provides a set of interdisciplinary perspectives on this question.
[3] M Biagioli, 'Rights or Rewards? Changing Frameworks of Scientific Authorship' in Biagioli and Galison (n1) 260, 274.
[4] J Ziman, *Of One Mind: The Collectivisation of Science* (American Institute of Physics Press 1995) 239.
[5] J Ziman, *Science in Civil Society* (Imprint Academic 2007) 7; E Garfield, 'Giving Credit Only Where It Is Due: The Problem of Defining Authorship' (1995) 9(19) The Scientist 13.
[6] RK Merton, *The Sociology of Science: Theoretical and Empirical Investigations* (Chicago UP 1973) 310. These norms are now widely accepted: D Burk, 'Research Misconduct: Deviance, Due Process, and the Disestablishment of Science' (1995) 3 George Mason U Independent LRev 305, 310.

(i) **C**ommunalism (discoveries should be freely shared with the scientific community)[7];
(ii) **U**niversalism (impersonal and objective criteria should be used to evaluate claims);
(iii) **D**isinterestedness (scientists should subordinate their own biases and interests to the advancement of knowledge);
(iv) **O**rganised **S**cepticism (a new claim should not be accepted into the canon of scientific knowledge until it has been subjected to systematic scrutiny and validation); and
(v) originality (scientists should investigate novel and unanswered questions).[8]

Collectively referred to as CUDOS, this moniker serves as a fitting allusion to the role that these norms play in establishing the criteria for recognition, which is valuable within science's reputational economy.[9] Works of scientific authorship demonstrate compliance with these norms and with the scientific method.[10] This helps establish their claims as nonfictional and hence authoritative. Both the presentation and evaluation of scientific claims depend upon trust.[11] Trust is, thus, indispensable for the growth of scientific knowledge.[12]

In the eyes of the scientific community, an author is not viewed as the originator of a particular claim about nature. Rather, the author is the person who uncovered it – that is, the person who first hypothesised, tested, identified and verified the claim. The element of originality or novelty which the scientific community values relates to the selection of the problem and/or the methodological approach taken in investigating it. In contrast to copyright law, science tends to value creativity or effort expended in relation to the ideas/content embodied in a work, rather than

---

[7] The original term used by Merton was 'communism'. However, he later adopted the term 'communalism', which is now commonly used by modern sociologists of science: e.g., J Ziman, *Real Science: What It Is, and What It Means* (CUP 2000) 33. See also K Strandburg, 'User Innovator Community Norms: At the Boundary Between Academic and Industry Research' (2009) 77 Fordham LRev 101.

[8] Merton's original list did not include originality. Originality may be less important than the other norms given that it is also seen as good scientific practice to retest a claim. The meaning of this term in the context of science is explained below.

[9] The acronym alludes to the importance of adhering to these norms for retaining one's reputation and attaining the recognition of one's peers within the scientific community.

[10] This term is surprisingly slippery: the exact content of the 'scientific method' is not uncontroversial and some even claim that it does not exist. S Shapin, 'How to Be Antiscientific' in JA Labinger and H Collins (eds) *The One Culture? A Conversation about Science* (Chicago UP 2001) 99.

[11] S Shapin, *A Social History of Truth: Civility and Science in Seventeenth-Century England* (Chicago UP, 1994); J Pila, 'Authorship and E-science: Balancing Epistemological Trust and Skepticism in the Digital Age' (2009) 23 Social Epistemology 1.

[12] B Barber, 'Trust in Science' (1987) 25(1/2) Minerva 123; Shapin ibid.

effort relating to their expression in literary form. Despite this, considerable attention is paid to the presentation of scientific claims. Scientific writing is usually cast in emotionally-neutral, passively-phrased authoritative tones.[13] The pinnacle of scientific writing is impersonal, brief, clear, precise and direct.[14] This is because a scientific claim is most likely to be accepted by the scientific community when it is framed as an objective statement about nature and not as the scientist's opinion.[15]

Sociologists and historians of science locate the primary motivation for authorship in science in the benefits that it brings within the context of the reputation, or gift economy, of academic science.[16] This gift economy is a system of exchange premised on reciprocity, reputation and responsibility.[17] Publication is beneficial for scientists in two ways: (i) it is a marker of achievement and thus often linked to funding, promotion and professional opportunities; and (ii) it allows a scientist to build a reputation which is beneficial per se and may also lead to tangible benefits.[18] Responsibility is the flipside of the credit value of authorship within the scientific community. It requires good faith and scientific rigor. The author is held responsible, in particular, for adhering to the requirements of the scientific method and other ethical obligations (reflecting the crucial role that trust plays within the scientific community).[19]

The scientific gift economy is constructed in direct opposition to the market economy.[20] So, a scientific author's credibility, for example, is undermined if they seem to be primarily motivated by monetary concerns.[21] Equally, information which must be kept secret for it to have value in the commercial market, might need to be made public for it to be valuable in the reputation market.[22]

---

[13] C Bazerman, 'Emerging Perspectives on the Many Dimensions of Scientific Discourse' in JS Martin and R Veel (eds) *Reading Science: Critical Functional Perspectives on Discourses of Science* (Routledge 1988) 15.

[14] I Valiela, *Doing Science: Design, Analysis, and Communication of Scientific Research* (OUP 2001) 108, 127.

[15] Ziman (n4) 188.

[16] Biagioli (n3); C McSherry, 'Uncommon Controversies: Legal Mediations of Gift and Market Models of Authorship' in Biagioli and Galison (n1) 225.

[17] McSherry ibid.

[18] Biagioli (n3) 266 claims that scientific authorship is more about 'reward' than it is about 'rights'.

[19] Valiela (n14) 274; Shapin (n11) Ch 1. This responsibility includes not exaggerating or falsifying results; not negligently failing to control the appropriate variables; and avoiding potential conflicts of issues or other ethical violations. Thus, responsibility is more about 'playing by the rules' than it is about accountability for the truthfulness of a particular claim about nature.

[20] McSherry (n16).   [21] Indeed, such conflicts of interest are seen as unethical.

[22] Ziman (n4) 333.

By situating scientific authorship outside the realm of the marketplace, an air of neutrality and, thus credibility, is established.[23] Yet, there is a tension between market forces and the gift economy. Inevitably, scientists are influenced by monetary concerns, not least because they must earn a living, find funding for their studies and pursue inventions which might prove economically valuable.[24] McSherry sees authorship as the primary site for this tension between the gift economy and the market economy models in science.[25]

The traditional narrative of science is very individualistic.[26] The history of science is replete with stories of extraordinary pioneers who resemble the romantic author.[27] In the early years of science, scientific knowledge seemed to grow by accretion as a result of the activities of these observers and thinkers. Yet, although an individual generally stood behind a scientific claim,[28] science has always been a collective undertaking in some sense, developing cumulatively as a result of interactive processes such as peer review.[29] Indeed, the idea of the scientist as a lonely seeker after the truth is often historically inaccurate. Even great scientists relied on artisans, craftsmen and laboratory technicians.[30] The extensive contributions of such helpers were often dismissed as mere routine labour and rendered virtually invisible on surviving documentation of their work.[31] One explanation for this is the tendency for scientific authorship to gravitate to persons with institutional authority. Thus, Shapin argues that Robert Boyle was the scientific author of his

---

[23] McSherry (n16) 227 citing M Walshok, *Knowledge without Boundaries: What America's Research Universities Can Do for the Economy, the Workplace, and the Community* (Jossey-Bass 1995) 191.

[24] See R Eisenberg, 'Proprietary Rights and the Norms of Science in Biotechnology Research' (1987) 97 Yale LJ 177.

[25] McSherry (n16) 245 noting that 'one of the things that helps authorship mediate gift and market economies is the shared assumption that the two models do not share important assumptions'.

[26] Ziman (n4) 133.

[27] For example: S Shapin and S Schaffer, *Leviathan and the Air-Pump: Hobbes, Boyle, and The Experimental Life* (Princeton UP 1985).

[28] Shapin (n11): these individuals were usually 'gentlemen' thought to be bound by a code of personal honour, which, along with their financial independence, was seen to guarantee the trustworthiness of their claims.

[29] Ziman (n4) 98; NS Steinberg, 'Regulation of Scientific Misconduct in Federally Funded Research' (2000) 10 South California Interdisciplinary LJ 39, 43; A Warwick, '"A very hard nut to crack" or Making Sense of Maxwell's *Treatise on Electricity and Magnetism* in Mid-Victorian Cambridge' in Biagioli and Galison (n1) 133 offers the example of a technically difficult textbook, which, by the inclusion of many Cambridge mathematicians' attempts to understand and clarify it for their students in the second edition, became an increasingly interactive, collective product.

[30] MW Jackson, 'Can Artisans Be Scientific Authors? The Unique Case of Fraunhofer's Artisanal Optics and the German Republic of Letters' in Biagioli and Galison (n1) 113.

[31] S Shapin, 'The Invisible Technician' (1989) 77 American Scientist 554.

papers, despite the considerable input of technicians (such as Denis Papin who actually ran the experiments and even wrote up results), because it was Boyle who had authority over the investigations in the sense of taking responsibility for them. He had control over the workplace and work agenda, as well as the final decision on the content and form of the work.[32]

As scientific research is increasingly done by large-scale collaborations, science's traditional individualistic narrative is being openly challenged.[33] In modern scientific collaborations, the fact that it is difficult to identify a Boyle-like figure with overall authority or control over research projects, makes it even more difficult to render invisible the work of multiple expert contributors. This has had consequences for science's concept of authorship and its role in establishing the authority (and trustworthiness) of scientific claims.

Over the last decades, there has been a rapid shift in focus for science from autonomous basic research towards more directed commercial research. While some call this the rise of 'Big Science',[34] Ziman refers to it as 'collectivization':[35] 'scientists [now] have to work in teams, hunt in packs and share the use of many expensive instruments'.[36] Large collaborative projects such as NASA, the CERN collaborations, or the Human Genome Project are becoming an indispensable part of modern science. Typically, these collaborations depend upon the contributions of scientists from a range of different disciplines and a variety of supporting personnel (technicians, statisticians, managers, software developers etc). It is the need to acknowledge and reward such a diverse range of contributors to such projects that has resulted in ever-extending lists of 'authors' on the front of journal articles,[37] perhaps more akin to film end credits.[38]

---

[32] Ibid, 560.

[33] W Vesterman, 'The Death of the Scientific Author: Multiple Authorship in Scientific Papers' (2002) 8 Common Knowledge 439; Ziman (n4) 241–242.

[34] This is a term that has been attributed to AM Weinburg in 'Impact of Large-Scale Science on the United States' (1961) 134 (3473) Science 161. It is usually used to describe changes which occurred around World War II as scientific progress increasingly came to rely upon large-scale projects funded by national governments or groups of governments.

[35] Ziman (n4) 242 argues that science is being collectivized in two senses: (1) scientists are increasingly being forced to work together to achieve a 'collective effect'; (2) science is increasingly under the control of collectives such as government agencies and large industrial corporations.

[36] Ziman (n4) 241.

[37] 'The ATLAS Experiment at the CERN Large Hadron Collider', for example, published in the Journal of Instrumentation listed 2926 authors from 169 research institutions. P Davis, 'An Authorship Accelerator' dated 8 December 2008 <scholarlykitchen.sspnet.org/2008/12/08/hep-authorship>.

[38] T Conley 'End Credits' in Biagioli and Galison (n1) 360.

This fragmentation of authorship has disrupted the reputational economy of science.[39] Currently, identification as an author on a scientific article may imply one of a number of different connections to it. Authorial credit simply indicates that an individual has made some kind of contribution at some point in the process, be it designing the study, carrying out experiments, providing funding, supervising the project, designing software or other equipment used, collecting or analysing data, or providing technical assistance. Interpersonal relationships also affect decisions about the attribution of authorship. Senior scientists wield more influence than their junior colleagues in deciding authorship issues.[40] Controversially, authorship may be attributed based upon highly tenuous connections to the project. For example, a senior colleague may have their name added to the list simply to boost the chances of securing publication.[41] A survey of scientific publications between 1981 and 1990 revealed the world's 20 most prolific scientists averaged one new article every 3.9 days.[42] It seems evident from this figure that these individuals could not have made a significant contribution to all the papers on which their name appeared.[43] Aside from any copyright-based concerns, this has repercussions for the credit and responsibility values attached to authorship in science.[44]

Authorship norms vary between different parts of the scientific community, reflecting local structural dynamics and power relations.[45] Different journals also establish specific guidelines on attribution practice.[46] Scientific readers draw inferences about a particular author's contribution from their position within the list of authors. In many scientific disciplines, it is common for the person who has been most directly involved in the project and taken responsibility for its writing up to be listed first, whereas the supervisor, or person who obtained the funding for the study, would be named last. While typically, these two positions are the most prestigious, both attribution of authorship and the order of

---

[39] Biagioli (n3).
[40] AG Mainous III, MA Bowen, JS Zoller, 'The Importance of Interpersonal Relationship Factors in Decisions Regarding Authorship' (2002) 34 Family Medicine 462, 467.
[41] This contribution might be characterized as putting one's reputation on the line.
[42] Valiela (n14) 136.
[43] It appears to be common for scientists to be listed as authors on papers that they have not even read: J Birnholtz, 'When Authorship Isn't Enough: Lessons from CERN on the Implications of Formal and Informal Credit Attribution Mechanisms in Collaborative Research' (2008) 11(1) J of Electronic Publishing <dx.doi.org/10.3998/3336451 .0011.105>.
[44] And, more fundamentally, for the trust upon which science depends.
[45] T Scott, 'Changing Authorship System Might Be Counterproductive' (1997) 315 British Medical J 744.
[46] Rheinberger (n1) 310.

authors may vary from discipline to discipline, from institution to institution, and even from project to project. The answer to the question 'who is the author?' also depends, to some extent, upon the identity of the party posing it. Whilst journal editors are keen to define a locus of responsibility for published work, researchers may have more pragmatic concerns of just 'getting the job done'. Authorship may be used as a cost-free incentive to ensure busy people's participation.[47] Adopting a hierarchically-ordered list of authors is a notion that is alien to copyright and the attribution right alike. Indeed, copyright law tends to assume all authorial contributions have equal weight,[48] except in cases where factual circumstances rebut this inference.[49]

Despite being an issue of great practical significance, the correlation between authorship, professional recognition, and financial benefit is not easily measured.[50] As author lists grow longer, it becomes increasingly difficult to assess the contributions of each person named.[51] This has led to a suspicion that credit is being inflated while responsibility is becoming impermissibly diffuse. Rennie, Yank and Emanuel conceptualise scientific authorship as a coin featuring a positive 'credit' value on one side and a negative 'responsibility' value as its obverse.[52] While these values might be assumed to balance as a zero-sum game, in practice they suggest that as the number of authors increases, the responsibility levied on each author diminishes faster than the credit gained, separating the two sides of the coin from each other.[53] While intuitively it seems fair that those sharing the reputational benefits of scientific authorship must also accept their

---

[47] R Phillips, 'Researchers' Objective Is to Get the Job Done' (1997) 315 British Medical J 747.
[48] *Godfrey v Lees* [1995] EMLR 307, 329: there is a presumption that joint authorship gives rise to joint ownership in equal shares.
[49] For example: *Bamgboye v Reed* [2002] EWHC 2922 [42]; *Fisher v Brooker* [2009] UKHL 41. Even where joint owners hold unequal shares due to unequal authorial contributions (thus being entitled to different shares of royalties, etc.), they all have an equal right to control uses of the work and to any moral rights. See: 8.6.1.
[50] For this reason, alphabetical order has been criticized as resulting in winners and losers on arbitrary grounds. Ziman (n4) 372; Valiela (n14) 135 cites a similar solution: 'Order of authorship was decided from the outcome of a game of croquet played on the grounds of CCCC College'.
[51] Davis (n37).
[52] D Rennie, V Yank and L Emanuel, 'When Authorship Fails: A Proposal to Make Contributors Accountable' (1997) 278 JAMA 579, 580.
[53] Biagioli (n33) 263–264 agrees that concerns relating to the inflation of credit may be less well-founded than concerns relating to responsibility. M Biagioli, 'Documents of Documents: Scientists' Names and Scientific Claims' in Annelise Riles (ed) *Documents: Artifacts of Modern Knowledge* (U of Michigan Press 2006) 129, 149. Cf. S Seymore, 'How Does My Work Become Our Work? Dilution of Authorship in Scientific Papers, and the Need for the Academy to Obey Copyright Law' (2006) 12 Richmond J of L & Tech 11; Vesterman (n33).

share of responsibilities, this idea unravels in the context of many large-scale collaborative projects. Here, there may be good reason to credit valuable contributors who could not fairly be asked to bear responsibility for the project a whole and its published scientific claims.

5.2 Regulating Scientific Authorship with Private Ordering

Mario Biagioli has explored the different ways in which the attribution practices of biomedical science and particle physics collaborations have challenged the conventional notion of scientific authorship.[54] In the biomedical field, concern surrounding the diffuse nature of responsibility within large collaborations has led to calls for stricter control of authorial attribution. Particle physics collaborations, by contrast, seem more concerned to recognise valuable contributors, leading to an expanded notion of authorship. This section revisits Biagioli's comparison to ascertain whether either of these divergent experiences might illuminate the conceptualisation of joint authorship in copyright law.

5.2.1 Biomedical Science Collaborations: An Authorship Crisis

The challenges of allocating authorship in large scientific biomedical collaborations have been so acute that there is a perception of an authorship crisis. In part, this reflects the disruption wrought by long author lists which undermine the traditionally-recognised authority, or responsibility, value of authorship. In this section, I argue that the reactive strategy adopted by many biomedical journals, to restrict authorship claims, has achieved only limited success because it is not adapted to the realities of large-scale collaboration. Despite being motivated by the worthy aim of identifying those who can be held scientifically responsible for an article, this approach has tended to see the 'author' label gravitate instead to those holding most institutional authority. The section ends by considering Sean Seymore's argument that scientific attribution practices ought to yield to (US) copyright norms.

As we have seen, in the field of modern biomedical science, it is now virtually impossible for an individual to possess enough knowledge across fields to make a significant advance.[55] Attribution practices resulting in long author lists on articles reporting the research of large biomedical collaborations, however, have become associated with a number of high-profile incidents of scientific misconduct, which in turn, has spawned fears of

---

[54] Biagioli (n3).
[55] RC Dreyfuss, 'Collaborative Research: Conflicts on Authorship, Ownership and Accountability' (2000) 53 Vanderbilt LRev 1161, 1171.

a crisis in authorship.[56] Scientists and journal editors have become concerned that the credit value of authorship in large collaborations is becoming inflated and the responsibility value is becoming impermissibly diffuse – disrupting science's reputation economy and undermining the trust on which science depends. Some authorship practices which are now seen as inappropriate include:

(i) *Gift or guest authorship:* adding the name of a person who has contributed little to the publication. This might be to acknowledge earlier influence on the primary author's career; to make the paper appear more authoritative; or to increase its chances of publication. It may even be done to acknowledge someone who has provided access to facilities, data or funding. In some cases the gift author may not even be aware of their listing as an author.[57]

(ii) *Coercion authorship:* superiors who have had little or no direct involvement in the research request to be listed as an author – the importance of maintaining good working relationships may make it difficult to refuse such a request.[58]

(iii) *Mutual support authorship:* authors agree to put each other's names on papers where no direct contribution is made, e.g., to 'pad' their curriculum vitae.

(iv) *Ghost authorship:* a significant contributor to the work is not acknowledged as an author. This may be done to make the report appear independent from that person or their organisation,[59] or may involve junior researchers whose contributions are not acknowledged by their superiors.[60] Scientific authorship here is under-inclusive in copyright law terms. The previous examples, by contrast, are over-inclusive from a copyright point of view.

[56] R Epstein, 'Academic Fraud Today: Its Social Causes and Institutional Responses' (2010) 21 Stanford L & Policy Rev 135; Steinberg (n29).
[57] R Bhopal et al., 'The Vexed Question of Authorship: Views of Researchers in a British Medical Faculty' (1997) 314 (7086) British Medical J 1009: A study of 66 staff of a University medical faculty revealed that although gift authorship was perceived as unethical it was seen as common practice and, indeed, seemed to be encouraged by academic reward systems. 64% of respondents had experienced difficulties with authorship, the most common being denial of authorship in circumstances when the respondent felt authorship was merited.
[58] Providing access to equipment, providing materials or being a head of department may be contributions relied upon by people making such claims: L Claxton, 'Scientific Authorship Part 2: History, Recurring Issues, Practices, and Guidelines' (2005) 589 Mutation Research 31, 35.
[59] S Stern and T Lemmens, 'Legal Remedies for Medical Ghostwriting: Imposing Fraud Liability on Guest Authors of Ghostwritten Articles' (2011) 8(8) PLoS Med e1001070; A Matheson, 'How Industry Uses the ICMJE Guidelines to Manipulate Authorship – And How They Should Be Revised' (2011) 8(8) PLoS Med 1001072.
[60] Claxton (n58) 36.

Ghost and guest authorship are particularly problematic, since both have been associated with cases of scientific misconduct, and even, fraud.[61] Fraudulent authors have typically sought prestigious co-authors to lend credibility to their papers. In the early 1980s, John Darsee was behind infamous articles which falsified a number of studies at Emory and Harvard Universities. Many of the articles concerned included prominent heads of department as co-authors. Although these scientists had not fabricated the published data, they were criticised for allowing their names to appear on work which they knew too little about.[62] The ensuing controversy revealed divergent attitudes to the social incidents of authorship, namely, whether the heads of department had acted appropriately and what sanctions, if any, ought to be imposed on them.

The pharmaceutical industry has also faced criticism for co-opting 'independent' senior scientists, either to add credibility to their own studies or to mask the commercial function of journal articles which are leveraged to help advertise particular products.[63] Positioning a well-known scientist as a first author in biomedical publications is a prevalent tactic adopted by industry to convey the impression that this prominent individual has instigated or controlled the study and endorses the results.[64] Even if the content of the study is legitimate, this practice poses a serious problem for scientists who rely upon authorship indicating the true origin of an article in order to judge the information it conveys.[65] The trust upon which science depends may accordingly be undermined.

Several groups have introduced guidelines to address this crisis in authorship.[66] The guidelines produced by the International Committee of Medical Journal Editors ('ICMJE') are the most widely accepted.[67] They are quite prescriptive, requiring that each name listed in the by-line

---

[61] Stern and Lemmens (n59); AJ Fugh-Berman, 'The Haunting of Medical Journals: How Ghostwriting Sold "HRT"' (2010) 7(9) PLoS Med e1000335: 'the pharmaceutical company Wyeth used ghostwritten articles to mitigate the perceived risks of breast cancer associated with HT, to defend the unsupported cardiovascular "benefits" of HT, and to promote off-label, unproven uses of HT'; L McHenry, 'Of Sophists and Spin-Doctors: Industry-Sponsored Ghostwriting and the Crisis of Academic Medicine' (2010) 8(1) Journalology 129.

[62] J Smith, 'Gift Authorship: A Poisoned Chalice?' (1994) 309 British Medical J 1456.

[63] Matheson (n59); S Sismondo, 'Ghosts in the Machine: Publication Planning in the Medical Sciences' (2009) 39 Social Studies of Science 171.

[64] Matheson, ibid. [65] Ibid.

[66] Claxton (n58) 38–43. These include: the UK Organization Committee on Publication Ethics (COPE), the National Institutes of Health, University of Pennsylvania, University of California at San Francisco, the American Chemical Society, the American Statistical Society, and the Danish Committee on Scientific Dishonesty. See: Rennie, Yank and Emanuel (n52) 584.

[67] Garfield (n5).

refers to a person who *not only* takes full responsibility for the contents of the entire article, *but also* made a substantial contribution to: (i) the conception and design, or the analysis and interpretation of data; (ii) the drafting the article, or revising it critically for important intellectual content; and (iii) who has also given final approval of the version to be published (the 'triple-lock formula').[68] This approach is designed to reduce the number of contributors who might be named as authors. It attempts to single out those particular types of contributions that might together count as authorial because they ensure that authors are adequately involved in the instigation, control, and writing up of a study so as to be properly held responsible for the article.[69] Thus the guidelines aim to ensure that authorship is granted only to those who are best placed to ensure compliance with science's norms and assume authority for the article's claims.

To date, the ICMJE guidelines appear to have had only limited success.[70] This seems to be because they are insensitive to the fact that collaborative work often necessitates a division of labour. It might not be possible for any one person to have sufficient expertise fully to understand – and be fairly held responsible – for every part of a complex collaborative study. They also overlook the exigencies of large scientific collaborations, where the reward of authorship is required in order to secure the participation of busy people or as quid pro quo for funding or access to equipment.[71] The fact that the formula invariably excludes statisticians has been a particular cause for concern, since their role of interpreting data is vital for the rest of the team to understand the significance of the results.[72]

Matheson contends that pharmaceutical industry strategies 'play' the ICMJE guidelines to boost the credibility of their publications by exaggerating the apparent contributions of some academic authors, while downplaying the contributions of employed commercial

[68] 'Uniform requirements for Manuscripts Submitted to Biomedical Journals' (1997) 277 JAMA 928. Participation solely in the acquisition of funding or data collection, and general supervision of the group will not be sufficient to establish authorship.
[69] In this way the guidelines seem to echo historical practices which seemed to 'erase' the contributions of technicians as discussed in the previous section, see Shapin (n31).
[70] PC Gøtzsche et al., 'Ghost Authorship in Industry-Initiated Randomised Trials' (2007) 4 PLoS Med e535; E Wager, 'Authors, Ghosts, Damned Lies, and Statisticians' (2007) 4(1) PLoS Med e34; A Hudson Jones, 'Can Authorship Policies Help Prevent Scientific Misconduct? What Role for Scientific Societies?' (2003) 9 Science and Engineering Ethics 243.
[71] Claxton (n58) 35; R Horton, 'The Signature of Responsibility' (1997) 350 Lancet 5–6.
[72] Wager (n70); RA Parker and NA Bergman, 'Criteria for Authorship for Statisticians in Medical Papers' (1998) 17(20) Statistics in Medicine 2289.

writers.⁷³ This is achieved by a somewhat selective interpretation of the 'triple-lock' formula since it is permissible to name an academic as an author, provided he or she contributes either to the design of a study or data analysis, makes some revisions to the manuscript, and approves the final version. Equally, even if industry representatives undertake most of the design, data collection, analysis, and writing, if the role of final approval is allocated to an academic, then the guidelines disqualify the industrial representatives from authorship. It seems odd from a copyright standpoint to deny authorship to a person who has penned an article simply because he or she was not involved in certain other aspects of the study it reports.

Part of the challenge in tackling such strategic nominal compliance with the ICMJE guidelines is that doing so might open a Pandora's box. These practices mirror other practices which are widely tolerated and, in some quarters, are considered entirely appropriate.⁷⁴ Laboratory directors, departmental chairs and supervisors frequently expect to be included in the list of authors based solely on their institutional position.⁷⁵ All too often, attribution of authorship reflects power relations. Tales of senior professors who insist on being named as an author on all of the papers of junior colleagues are apparently not apocryphal⁷⁶ and the supervisor/student relationship has been at the heart of numerous legal disputes relating to the appropriate allocation of credit for scientific work.⁷⁷ As a practical matter, the most senior scientist involved in a research project typically has the final say over who is listed as an author, and in what order the names appear irrespective of whether they have been directly involved in writing up the final report. By stressing the importance of final approval, the ICMJE guidelines tend to reinforce these underlying power dynamics.

Sean Seymore suggests that the crisis of authorship might be eased by realigning scientific practices of attributing authorship with (US) copyright law norms.⁷⁸ Although the UK joint authorship test operates differently to the US test, much of his argument still translates in the UK context. Seymore identifies the source of issues surrounding the dilution

---

⁷³ Matheson (n59).   ⁷⁴ Stern and Lemmens (n59).
⁷⁵ PC Gøtzsche et al., 'What Should Be Done to Tackle Ghostwriting in the Medical Literature?' (2009) 6(2) PLoS Med e1000023.
⁷⁶ Ziman (n4) 372.
⁷⁷ *Chou v University of Chicago* 254 F3d 1347, 1361 (Fed Cir 2001); *Johnson v Schmitz* 119 FSupp 2d 90, 91 (D Conn 2000); M Astala, 'Comment, Wronged by a Professor? Breach of Fiduciary Duty as a Remedy in Intellectual Property Infringement Case' (2003) 3 Houston Bus & Tax LJ 31.
⁷⁸ Seymore (n53) [27] argues that scientific misconduct might subside if science professors were taught basic intellectual property law.

or inflation of authorship credit primarily with the expanding number of names in the middle of an article by-line, i.e., individuals most likely to have contributed (mere) labour (carrying out experiments or collecting data), as well as gift or coercion authors (those providing at best de minimis contributions). He endorses US copyright law's joint authorship test because it seems to link authorship to creativity (rather than mere labour) and prioritises contributions which focus on the planning, writing and reviewing of an article.[79] Here, however, Seymore may overstate the level of intellectual input that the US standard requires, as it is generally accepted that many fairly mundane works might be sufficiently original.[80]

Seymore also approves, in particular, of the application of the joint authorship test in a way that deliberates aims to minimise the number of authors of collaborative work.[81] Seymore therefore suggests that the ICMJE guidelines are a welcome step towards sector acceptance of US copyright norms. Yet we have seen that the way in which pharmaceutical companies have interpreted these guidelines demonstrates that they might be both under-inclusive and over-inclusive from a copyright point of view. They are under-inclusive insofar as they deny authorship to a contributor who was entirely responsible for writing an article for want of involvement in some aspect of the study's design or the interpretation of data, or because responsibility for final approval of the published version falls beyond their designated role. The guidelines are over-inclusive insofar as they enable someone who was only tangentially involved in the study and approved the final text to claim authorship, even though they may have only made a few editorial changes to that text.

Seymore, however, fails to engage with scholarly criticisms that US copyright law is poorly adapted to the challenges of determining the authorship of highly collaborative work (a criticism also familiar in the UK context). It is also doubtful that deference to copyright norms will resolve issues of scientific misconduct. Although this approach may well reduce the number of credited authors, copyright law might not always select the most appropriate contributors from science's point of view to establish the authority and trustworthiness of the article. After all,

---

[79] Ibid, [29]-[32].
[80] In the US, originality requires some 'creative spark': *Feist Publications Inc v Rural Telephone Service Co* 499 US 340 (USSC, 1991).Whilst this standard has often been thought to be higher than the UK's traditional skill, labour and judgement formulation because it requires some (albeit minimal) creativity, it is likely to be closer to the post-*Infopaq* approach to originality. See: 2.1.
[81] The current US approach is even more restrictive than any UK court has taken to date, but is similarly motivated by pragmatic, instrumental concerns (albeit of a slightly different nature): see 2.5.3 and 8.6.2. Also, M LaFrance, 'Authorship, Dominance, and the Captive Collaborator: Preserving the Rights of Joint Authors' (2001) 50 Emory LJ 193.

copyright authorship primarily relates to the origin of the expression of a work, and not ethical responsibility to the scientific community for its content. The role of scientific authorship in constructing authority would be undermined if authorship became detached from those who should assume responsibility for the process of making the claims of scientific significance in the article. More fundamentally, this approach ignores the reason for the increase in named authors (the globalisation of science and the growing need to co-operate across large teams) and it is by no means clear that it provides the correct incentives to ensure an optimum number of new scientific publications. Many of the contributors whose work is considered to be invaluable within particular scientific collaborations would likely fail even the comparatively more inclusive UK joint authorship test (as it currently appears to be applied).[82] That said, Seymore's appeal to copyright norms does highlight the potential role of copyright law as a source of good authorship standards. In particular, copyright law might provide a benchmark minimum standard for determining authorship based upon responsibility for the creation of the expression of a work, although it is not a panacea for the authorship crisis in the biomedical sciences. The value of copyright's authorship standards will be considered in more detail in Chapters 7 and 8.[83]

5.2.2 Particle Physics Collaborations: The Bureaucratisation of Authorship

Particle physics collaborations have been far more successful than their biomedical science counterparts at dealing with attribution issues. Large group collaboration is virtually unavoidable in the particle/high energy physics community. CERN, for example, is run by 20 European member states and includes scientists from 608 institutions and universities. Half of the world's particle physicists will have undertaken research at CERN at some point in their career.[84] Particle physics collaborations tend to adopt a corporate approach to credit, responsibility and the attribution of authorship. They have adopted a bureaucratic structure and produce standardised authorship protocols that prioritise overall coherence of the collaboration over the recognition of specific, individual contributions.[85] Indeed, owing to the heterogeneity of such collaborations, it may well be true that when the collaboration 'speaks' it says something that no one

---

[82] This might be because their contributions: are not directly reflected in the expression; are not the product of activities that copyright law considers 'authorial'; or because they are distinct. A Stokes, 'Authorship, Collaboration and Copyright a View from the UK' (2002) Entertainment LRev 121. See 5.3 and 2.2.
[83] Particularly 7.5 and 8.2.   [84] <public.web.cern.ch/public/en/About/Global-en.html>.
[85] P Galison, 'The Collective Author' in Biagioli and Galison (n1) 329, 332; Ziman (n4).

individual could say from first-hand knowledge.[86] Issues of responsibility are managed collectively through the use of internal review processes.

The Collider Detector at Fermilab ('CDF') Collaboration is a typical example. It has a standard alphabetic author list which appears on all publications. Criteria for inclusion on the list are established in guidelines developed by a committee. Authorship is conceptualised in terms of credit for accumulated labour dedicated to the common endeavour: for, without all the contributors no research could have been done.[87] It is perfectly possible, therefore, for a person to be listed as an author of a publication even though it was written whilst they were on a leave of absence. Prior to publication, once a draft of an article has received preliminarily approval by a publication committee, it is posted to an internal webpage. All members of the collaboration have the opportunity to comment on the draft, and then a revised 'final' version is posted. Those contributors who appear on the Standard Author List may withdraw their own name if they are unsatisfied with the article's final form. This leads to an interesting result: an article with fewer names appears to be less credible than an article with more names. This contrasts with the biomedical sciences, where more author names suggests a dilution of responsibility, and therefore, less credibility.[88] Adopting a slightly different approach, the Stanford Linear Detector ('SLD') Collaboration's authorship policies varied depending upon the scope of the target audience for the publication and the knowledge claim made within it.[89] Conference proceedings, for example, were to be attributed to 'The SLD Collaboration, presented by a particular person' with all of the SLD authors named in a footnote; whereas the authorship of internal memoranda was left as a matter for the writers to decide.

Acronyms, such as 'CERN' or 'SLD Collaboration', appear on publications operating like brand names in the sense that they perform an origin and a quality indicating function, acting as a placeholder for the underlying contributions of many individuals.[90] This is reminiscent of historical practices in respect of large group projects in which individual scientific contributions were likewise gathered together under the name of a 'sacralised' individual which represented the group.[91] In 1960s, for example, the largest hydrogen

---

[86] Galison ibid, 352.   [87] Biagioli (n3) 270; Birnholtz (n43).   [88] Biagioli (n3) 273.
[89] Galison (n85) 333–334.
[90] On the trade mark function of authorship: J Ginsburg, 'The Author's Name as a Trade Mark: A Perverse Perspective on the Moral Right of "Paternity"?' (2005) 23 Cardozo Arts and Entertainment LJ 379; G Lastowska, 'The Trade Mark Function of Authorship' (2005) 85 Boston U LRev 1171.
[91] H Gusterson, 'The Death of the Authors of Death: Prestige and Creativity among Nuclear Weapons Scientists' in Biagioli and Galison (n1) 281, 282 gives the example of the atomic bomb which was credited to Robert Oppenheimer despite the key roles of a number of other scientists.

bubble chamber collaboration at the Lawrence Berkeley Laboratory was referred to as the 'Alvarez Group'. Here, Luis Alvarez was seen as having ultimate responsibility for the work because he took all the decisions about which results to publish, and all funding for the group passed by him.[92] Particle physics collaborations have adopted this model, although they now use consensus-based decision-making processes to establish the authority of the group in respect of the claims that it makes. Despite not being the name of an individual scientist, collective nouns such as 'The ATLAS Collaboration' or 'CERN' convey equally relevant information about the source of publications and who takes responsibility for their content. The internal processes which determine authorship and produce/review articles before publication are crucial to establishing this 'corporate' identity based upon a model of collaboration which has a mind of its own. These procedures play an important role in establishing the authority of the authors over the article's claims (thus maintaining trust), since long alphabetical lists of author names in and of themselves convey little information on responsibility.

Particle physics collaborations seem adaptable to corporate solutions to the problem of authorship, because this is a field with a strong community culture: scientists are often located in the same place or share a piece of equipment. The same solution is unlikely to work in the biomedical sciences, where the membership of collaborations tends to fluctuate over time according to the requirements of the specific task undertaken. Cohesion is also less likely to develop between scientists collaborating on a clinical trial who may never have met, might be located in different places, and might even be competing for funding. In biomedical science, authorship is part of a perpetual struggle for professional advancement, whereas in the small cohesive particle physics community it is more just a 'fact of life'.[93] This is not to suggest that attribution of authorship is never controversial. Rather, that for individuals working in particle physics the focus may be more on being noticed in informal settings than on their publication record.[94]

In adopting this model, particle physics communities have not only redefined the role of authorship within the reputational economy, but have also experienced an evolution in attribution norms towards a more expansive view of what counts as authorship and a procedural means for collectively establishing responsibility or authority. Particle physics collaborations have been more successful at regulating authorship of their outputs than biomedical journals, because they have been able to develop a framework of processes which are better adapted to the different way that large collaborations author articles.

[92] Galison (n85) 329–330.   [93] Biagioli (n3) 272.   [94] Birnholtz (n43).

5.3 The Application of Copyright Law

Before considering whether the experiences of biomedical science and particle physics collaborations might offer insights for UK copyright law, it is useful to consider how copyright law's subsistence rules are likely to apply to journal articles which report the research of large-scale scientific collaborations.

For the purposes of the CDPA, a scientific journal article will almost always be considered an original literary work, but it is a more complicated task to determine which of the many contributors to a large collaborative study will be considered joint authors. As discussed in Chapter 2, it is difficult enough to predict how the test will apply to cases with a less than a handful of putative authors. Nevertheless, it is possible to provide some general observations.

First, trivial contributions are unlikely to qualify for joint authorship because they are not *significant* (at least a low quantitative, and probably a higher qualitative standard). In addition, many contributors will not have made contributions of the *right kind*. This would tend to exclude many preparatory contributions preceding the article which are not reflected in the expression of the work, including contribution of 'ideas'[95] and activities which are not of an 'authorship-type', including the generation of facts and data.[96] Thus, contributions relating to planning, controlling and directing experiments; carrying out experiments; securing funding; data-analysis and interpretation; providing access to samples or equipment; designing software or machines used in experiments; proof-reading papers; etc., may all be insufficient. Such contributions might only be relevant where accompanied by more than a trivial contribution to the expression of the work, although there is little guidance in the case law on this point. The narrow approach to the idea/expression dichotomy in *Ray v Classic FM* is particularly unforgiving in the scientific environment, as it would seem to characterise scientifically important contributions (for example, the design of a study) as either a contribution of unprotectable ideas[97] or a contribution made too early in the creative process to count as an authorial one.[98] Thus, the authorship limb of the joint authorship test is likely to exclude a large number of contributors who are currently named as authors on many scientific publications.[99]

---

[95] *Anya v Wu* [2004] EWHC 386 (Ch), [2004] EWCA Civ 755.
[96] *Donoghue v Allied Newspapers* [1938] 1 Ch 106; *Brighton v Jones* [2004] EWHC 1157, [2005] FSR 288; *Fylde Microsystems v Key Radio Systems* [1998] FSR 449 (Ch).
[97] [1998] FSR 622 (Ch), cf. *Cala Homes v Alfred McAlpine Homes* [1995] EWHC 7.
[98] Analogous to *Donoghue v Allied Newspapers* [1938] 1 Ch 106 (Ch).
[99] Being listed as an author will, however, create a rebuttable presumption of authorship: s104(2).

For the purposes of UK copyright law, authorship does not vest merely from an agreement to be an author.[100] Those who have made no intellectual contribution to the journal article will certainly be excluded. This excludes guest and gift authors, as well as contributors who have left particle physics collaborations, but are attributed authorship nevertheless, according to protocols which recognise important past contributions or dedication to the project's general aims. Conversely, joint authorship might be available to ghost authors and commercial scientists who have made authorial contributions but who are not listed as authors for 'political' reasons.

There are two types of likely candidates for authorship under the pragmatic instrumental approach. The prime candidate is the person(s) responsible for the actual writing of the article – most likely a junior scientist. This may require one to exclude many contributors whose contributions are significant to the content of the article, such as those who designed and supervised the study, those who provided the content for different parts of the article including crucial aspects such as data analysis and those who checked it. The second is the person(s) who supervised the study and had most control over the research process – most likely a senior scientist. Yet, that person is often unlikely to have made much of a direct contribution to the form of the writing or even its content. Both choices seem wrong in principle as they tend to divorce authorship from the creation of the protected *expression*. The first requires a myopic focus on the process of fixation, and the second grants authorship to the most powerful player. In addition, this approach requires an adjudication which ignores the many people who have made contributions which have added-value to, and shaped, the expression of the work. The failure of biomedical collaborations to reduce the number of authors of a scientific article by focusing only on dominant contributors is a lesson in the ineffectiveness of such a restrictive approach.

We should not overlook that joint authorship only arises if the relevant qualifying contributions are *not distinct*. This may exclude authors of accompanying diagrams, charts or tables (although they might have separate a copyright interest in them).[101] We have seen that the requirement for *collaboration* is not generally particularly demanding, as it does

---

[100] Copinger et al. [4.01], [4.38] citing *Levy v Rutley* (1871) LR 6 CP 523, 531 and *Wiseman v George Weidenfeld* [1985] FSR 525, 529 (where the point was accepted on all sides).
[101] Assuming that they are original, which is not usually an exacting requirement. In *Carlos v Javier and Maria Cruz* [2002] ECDR 23 (Madrid CA, 12th Section), for example, it was held that originality will not be denied to a diagram merely because the concepts represented in it are commonly known, or are regularly described in, textbooks.

not require proof of a specific intention to be a joint author.[102] Compliance with the social norms that govern the authorial group might indicate that a contributor is part of a collaborative endeavour, i.e., that they share a common design. Even if a 'gift' or 'guest' author were able to satisfy the authorship limb of the test (which is unlikely), they would still be denied joint authorship as they might not be seen to be collaborating. Sometimes courts have employed this requirement more strictly – seeking out cooperative acts temporarily proximate to the specific draft of a work in question.[103] This interpretation would prove problematic for large collaborations working on lengthy projects where membership of the collaboration varies over time as the project enters different phases.

I have suggested that a restrictive approach to the joint authorship test may make it difficult to apply in a way that seems credible in light of the creative realities of a scientific collaboration. In addition, the presumption of authorship which arises where one's name is on the work (s104 (2)) is likely to be misleading when applied in cases of collective authorship in science, as the lists of authors on articles are often both over-inclusive and under-inclusive from a copyright law point of view.[104] Although the presumption may go some way towards indirectly incorporating the authorial norms of particular scientific communities in the determination of copyright disputes, it provides no room to accommodate the different hierarchies of authorial importance communicated to a scientific reader by the order in which authors are listed (and is ultimately rebuttable).

There are few cases on the subsistence and ownership of copyright in scientific journal articles.[105] This is likely to be due to the importance of authorship in science's reputational or gift economy, which is constructed in opposition to the market economy. The right to royalties and control ensured by copyright, for example, seems to clash with scientific norms

---

[102] *Beckingham v Hodgens* [2003] EWCA Civ 143, [2003] EMLR 18.
[103] *Martin v Kogan* [2017] EWHC 2927 (IPEC) [25] (Hacon J).
[104] Even though this presumption might be easily displaced where there has been no contribution to the expression whatsoever, it may tip the evidentiary scales in favour of named authors in unclear cases.
[105] There was a misconceived joint authorship claim in relation to the Defendant's failure to credit the Claimant as the source of a scientific idea in their article in *Anya v Wu* (n95). In that case a joint authorship claim would have probably failed in any case due to a lack of collaboration. Disputes which implicate issues of authorship in science have tended to concern access to data or samples; defamation (*Noah v Shuba* [1991] FSR 14 (Ch)); failure to attribute a source (*Anya v Wu*); misleading claims/fraud; or employment issues (e.g., unfair dismissal following an authorship dispute). See: Dreyfuss (n55). In the US, there are some cases which have found that a fiduciary duty exists between students and supervising academics: *Chou* (n77); *Johnson v Schmitz* (n77).

which encourage open dissemination and economic disinterest. The attribution of authorship lies right at the point of tension between market and reputation economies, as aside from implying copyright ownership, authorship influences the allocation of credit for scientific work.[106] On occasion, particularly where the stakes in the reputational economy are high, scientists have turned to courts to resolve attribution issues.[107]

False attribution of scientific authorship was at the heart of *Weissmann v Freeman*, a high-profile US copyright dispute.[108] I shall devote some attention to this case notwithstanding the material differences between UK and US copyright law, because it demonstrates how the judicial characterisation of the context of creativity can prove pivotal when the joint authorship test is applied to a factual scenario.

Prior to the dispute in issue, Drs Heidi Weissmann and Leonard Freeman had worked together for many years undertaking research in the field of iminodiacetic acid. They had co-authored many articles and had devised a 'syllabus' (an article reviewing the state of the art in the field) together. For some years, the two produced an annual update of the syllabus. But then Weissmann published a version ('P-1') which she admitted was based on the previous joint efforts. Freeman subsequently reproduced P-1 under his own name without seeking Weissmann's permission. A key question was whether P-1 was a work of joint authorship (which they both owned copyright in) or an original derivative work solely owned by Weissmann. The trial and appeals courts took significantly different views of the context, which influenced their assessment of each scientist's contributions to P-1.

Judge Pollack, at trial, construed P-1 as a 'stock piece' in evolution, and therefore, a work of joint authorship owned by both scientists. He was influenced by the pre-existing professional relationship between the two scientists. He noted Freeman's senior position and emphasised that Weissmann's career had developed under Freeman's 'supervision, guidance and control'.[109] Judge Pollack observed that as 'principal

---

[106] McSherry (n16) 245.
[107] In *Noah v Shuba* (n105) 33, for example, an epidemiologist initiated legal proceedings in relation to a magazine article which reproduced a portion of his work adding to it in a misleading manner, which seemed to suggest that he approved of certain products. In awarding damages for false attribution of authorship in respect of the added sentences, the court took into account the ' ... author's interests in his reputation and integrity of his work'. A perception of unfair attribution contributed to the dispute and tragic events in *Fabrikant c. Swamy* (2011) QCCS 1385 (Superior Court of Quebec, Canada).
[108] Trial judgement: *Weissmann v Freeman* 684 FSupp 1248 (SDNY 1988). Appeal: *Weissmann v Freeman*, 868 F2d 1313 (2nd Cir 1989). See also: McSherry (n16) 68.
[109] More than half the judgement was dedicated to background and the relationship between the parties.

investigator', Freeman was frequently responsible for the experiments that they had both participated in, even though Weissmann typically did most of the 'writing up'.[110] Judge Pollack upheld Freeman's joint authorship claim because of his role in providing the authority for their joint work – focusing on his contribution to the ideas of scientific significance evidenced in the syllabus, rather than on the origin of its expression.[111] Judge Pollack went as far as accepting Freeman's view as expert opinion on the originality of the syllabus, while (surprisingly) dismissing Weissmann's arguments on this point as 'merely echo[ing] legal language found in the reported cases'.[112]

The Court of Appeals reversed this decision by a 2-1 majority, holding that P-1 was an original work solely authored by Weissmann and finding that Freeman's reproduction of it infringed Weissmann's copyright. Whilst Judge Pollack had characterised the dispute as an 'uncommon controversy', Judge Cardamone of the Court of Appeals identified the case as 'the paradigm of the problems that arise when a long relationship between accomplished professor and brilliant assistant comes to an end'.[113] Here, Judge Cardamone acknowledged Weissmann's efforts to break away from her role as Freeman's apprentice so that she might develop her own approach. In this context, their previous collaboration was seen to exemplify science's slow evolutionary development in which innovations are necessarily based on pre-existing, often joint works.[114] In Judge Cardamone's assessment, Freeman had not made a relevant contribution to P-1 and there was no intention for joint-authorship (a relevant aspect of the US joint authorship test). Further, in determining that the defence of fair use was not available, Judge Cardamone considered that in attributing authorship to himself, Freeman stood to gain something which, while 'ill-measured in dollars' had value within the scientific community as a means to influence professional advancement.[115]

In an attempt to reach a decision that took into account the peculiar context of scientific authorship, the trial judge was unduly influenced by the power dynamics which have often given senior scientists control over the attribution of authorship.[116] Judge Cardamone's reasoning in the appeal decision seems preferable because it incorporates a nuanced understanding of scientific authorship, whilst still remaining attentive to copyright law principles. For copyright, authorship is a question of law

---

[110] *Weissmann v Freeman* (trial, n108) 1253–1254 notes that Freeman's name 'lent authority' to Weissmann's work.
[111] Ibid, 1256. [112] Ibid, 1257. [113] *Weissmann v Freeman* (appeal, n108) 1315.
[114] Ibid, 1319. [115] Ibid, 1324.
[116] (trial, n108) 1252, Judge Pollack even discussed Freeman's conduct first, 'in the order of seniority'.

and not a matter of agreement amongst the parties.[117] The heart of copyright's concept of authorship is the idea that authorship is about more than who lends authority to a work – it relates to the origin of the protected expression.[118] In this respect, copyright might provide a bulwark against power imbalances within authorial communities, a particular issue in science where authorship is associated with authority and tends to gravitate upwards. This is not to say that judges ought not to take into account social norms in determining authorship, but merely that it is inappropriate to defer completely to such norms.[119]

Weissmann v Freeman provides a warning of the dangers of uncritically adopting community norms governing the attribution of authorship.[120] The previous two sections have shown how the values of authorship in modern scientific collaborations can be complex, varying from group to group, evolving over time, and even being contested within particular groups.[121] This case demonstrates how easily such norms are misconstrued. Yet, even where properly identified, social norms might enshrine power dynamics that risk distorting copyright's core notion of the author as the originator of expression protected as a copyright work. *Weissmann v Freeman* also provides an example of the value of retaining a legal notion of authorship in copyright law that is independent of community norms. It would have been difficult for Weissmann to obtain any redress within the scientific community. Indeed, during the dispute she was dismissed from her post, while Freeman was promoted.[122]

Although the reputation economy of science tends to operate in opposition to the market economy, scientists still depend upon copyright. Publications are necessary to secure jobs, funding, and promotions; and journals rely on the copyright subsisting in articles to be able to market their publications.[123] The attribution of authorship on articles also establishes a locus for credit and responsibility for scientific claims. In this context, copyright might have an important norm-setting role in

---

[117] Stokes (n82) 124.
[118] Similarly, copyright authorship is about more than who 'signs off' a work. See, Ginsburg (n90) discussing the dispute between Alexandre Dumas and his ghostwriter, August Maquet, as dramatized in the play *Signé Dumas* by Cyril Gely and Eric Rouquette.
[119] J Rothman, 'The Questionable Use of Custom in Intellectual Property' (2007) 93 Virginia LRev 1899, 1899 warns of the dangers of deferring to custom. See 8.2.
[120] Ibid.   [121] Biagioli (n3).
[122] R Kaufman, 'After 5 Years, Heated Controversy Persists in Science Copyright Case', *The Scientist*, 14 September 1992 at: <www.the-scientist.com/?articles.view/articleNo/12483/title/After-5-Years-Heated-Controversy-Persists-In-Science-Copyright-Case>.
[123] Scientists also benefit from broad circulation of their work to their peers in reputable journals: Birnholtz (n43).

establishing a legally enforceable minimum standard for authorship which, in most jurisdictions, also entails a moral right of attribution.[124]

5.4 Insights for Copyright Law

This section considers the insights this case study of scientific collaborations might offer for copyright law. First, such collaborations demonstrate the importance of the non-economic benefits of authorship. Second, they provide examples of imperfect solutions that copyright ought not to import wholesale because: (i) the ICMJE guidelines are generally under-inclusive, (ii) particle physics approaches are generally over-inclusive, and (iii) social norms ought to be considered, yet approached with caution. Copyright law has an important role to play as a source of good authorship standards, even though this is likely to be insufficient in itself to solve the perceived authorship crisis in the biomedical sciences. In the previous section I suggested that it might be difficult to apply the joint authorship test to collective authorship in science, particularly if the restrictive pragmatic instrumental approach is taken. In this section I argue that there is enough flexibility within the joint authorship test to take into account the special characteristics of large collaborations, as demonstrated in this chapter, yet leaving copyright's core notion of authorship intact.

The example of scientific authorship also demonstrates another creative community that attaches importance to the non-economic consequences of authorship. This raises broader questions about common incentive-based justifications for copyright's economic rights, which others have considered elsewhere.[125] The label of 'author' has an intrinsic value within the scientific community which is worth more than the possibility of recouping royalties. Indeed, participation in a collaborative project might be contingent upon prior agreement to receive authorship credit and accurate credit is something scientists may be willing to go to court to protect.[126] The importance of the attribution of authorship, independent of any copyright-based economic rights, reinforces the desirability of keeping the concepts of authorship and ownership separate. Equally, the importance of the non-economic consequences of authorship for scientists undermines one of the key assumptions of the pragmatic instrumental approach: that streamlining exploitation of the copyright interest is more important than ensuring that creators are recognised as authors. Indeed,

---

[124] Pila (n11); Dreyfuss (n56).
[125] The literature on intellectual property's negative spaces helpfully summarised by E Rosenblatt, 'A theory of IP's Negative Space' (2011) 34(3) Columbia J of L and the Arts 317. See also Chapter 1, n65.
[126] e.g., *Weissmann v Freeman* (n108), *Anya v Wu* (n95).

all of the cases discussed in which disputes concerning the authorship of scientific articles have reached the courts appear to have been motivated by the desire to ensure accurate attribution of a work, rather than to recoup lost royalties.[127] Thus, the moral rights granted to authors can be just as important to creators as their economic rights.

The processes by which large scientific collaborations create articles differ significantly from the romantic author model. A great level of organisation is required, and a division of labour is essential. The efforts of a number of highly specialised individuals, with considerable autonomy in relation to their own tasks, are coordinated with a view to achieving a common goal. The specialised knowledge and skills of contributors means that in a real sense the final product could not exist without most, if not all, of them. Few, if any, contributors have the expertise to be held responsible for the work as a whole, but many are incentivised to contribute by the prospect of authorship credit. The ICMJE guidelines, which restrict authorship claims to dominant contributors, respond poorly to this creative model. These guidelines allow authorship to gravitate towards those with institutional authority, while downplaying the contributions of junior scientists. The particle physics approach is better adapted to the way that large groups create. Its inclusive, non-hierarchical attribution practices reward many contributors and internal consensus-based processes allow for the collective management of responsibility. The downside of this approach is that it results in long author lists which convey inadequate information concerning the origin of an article and tends to divorce authorship from expression. It would not be appropriate for copyright to adopt either of these approaches, because both clash with copyright's core notion of authorship as understood in terms of the origin of the protected expression.

Yet, whilst it is important to maintain a core independent legal notion of authorship in copyright law, this concept ought to be applied in a way that takes into account the peculiar nature of large group collaboration. Despite the hazards of incorporating social norms, it is important that copyright law remains connected to creative communities' own understandings about authorship in order to maintain its credibility as an important tool for encouraging and regulating creativity.[128] *Weissmann v Freeman* demonstrates the value of an independent legal standard of authorship, which can be implemented in a way that is sensitive to the context of creativity. All too frequently, copyright's joint authorship test is

---

[127] *Weissmann v Freeman* (n108); *Noah v Shuba* (n105); *Anya v Wu* (n95).
[128] L Bently, 'Authorship of Popular Music in UK Copyright Law' (2009) 12(2) Information Communication & Society 179; A Barron, 'Copyright and the Claims of Art' (2002) 4 IPQ 368.

applied with an impoverished understanding of collaboration which assumes an integrated, monolithic notion of authorship that lacks the sophistication needed for determining authorship in large collaborations, which typically hinge upon a division of labour. The pragmatic instrumental approach is difficult to apply, as it is hard to identify one or two dominant authors. Attempts to do so are likely to reinforce power dynamics which are already thought to be unsatisfactory in science because they divorce authorship from the relevant aspects of the act of creation.

I would suggest that the joint authorship test is already equipped with tools which might be employed to gauge the value of contributions to large collaborative projects for copyright purposes in a contextual way. In applying the joint authorship test, judges have tended to treat the requirement that a contribution be 'significant' and the requirement that it be of the 'right kind' together.[129] This has created uncertainty as to the both the content and role of this limb of the test. Despite their flaws, social norms might provide a useful metric for determining which contributions are considered to be 'significant' within the context of a particular collaborative project. This would require a qualitative enquiry (that incorporates contextual considerations), and one which is distinct to the enquiry as to the 'kind' of contribution (which ought to remain grounded in the copyright (legal) notion of authorship). The requirement for a common design, not comprehensively elaborated in UK case law, might provide a conceptual apparatus to capture the different nature of creative processes in large collaborations. In this way, a collaboration's common design might provide a helpful benchmark in determining whether a contribution to a joint project is 'significant'. In the context of science, for example, the design of a study in accordance with the scientific method, the interpretation of results or even the correction of a major error, are very likely to be 'significant' contributions to the expression.

Most cases on joint authorship turn upon judicial characterisation of the contributions, particularly, whether a putative author has made the right kind of contribution.[130] For these purposes, many preparatory contributions and the contribution of ideas tend not to count.[131] This might suggest that many valuable contributors to scientific collaborations, such as those involved in planning, controlling, and directing experiments; carrying out experiments; designing software or machines used in experiments; and proof-reading papers, do not make the right kind of contributions. Yet, as argued in the previous chapter, the *expression* of the

---

[129] See 2.2.3.
[130] *Hadley v Kemp* [1999] EMLR 589 (Ch); *Beckingham v Hodgens* [2002] EWHC 2143 (Ch), [2002] EMLR 45, (n102); *Bamgboye v Reed* (n49).
[131] *Robin Ray v Classic FM* [1998] FSR 622 (Ch); 4.4.

work ought not to be conflated with its *fixation*.[132] Nonetheless some recent case law has seemed to take a more restrictive approach, privileging contributions to fixation over less tangible contributions to the expression.[133] The example of scientific collaborations, however, indicates the need to take a flexible approach to expression that takes into account the necessity of divisions of labour in large collaborations.[134] Other case law supports this approach. Laddie J in *Cala Homes* locates authorship thus:

It is both the words or lines and the skill and effort involved in creating, selecting or gathering together the detailed concepts, data or emotions which those words or lines have fixed in some tangible form which is protected.[135]

This broad conception of the protected expression would enable many more of the scientists involved in the process of creating and formulating the content of an article to be considered joint authors of that article, although it would still exclude contributions which may not be evident in the expression, e.g., data collection, making equipment, running experiments and obtaining funding. Although copyright law ought to be wary of granting authorship to those who have no more than 'signed' a work, lending their authority to it, authorship may be found when this is combined with control over the creative process that results in a contribution evident in the protected expression.[136]

The requirement that a contribution be of the right kind has been used as a way of enforcing copyright's core notion of authorship.[137] In this way, the joint authorship test might avoid the pitfalls of particle physics collaborations' over-inclusive approach by filtering contributions through copyright's core notion of authorship, which favours intellectual/creative contributions over mechanical ones and focuses on contributions to the expression (which I have argued ought to be broadly construed). Courts have sometimes tended to adopt a restrictive interpretation of the joint authorship test, favouring those contributors who appear dominant to the

---

[132] *Cala Homes v Alfred McAlpine Homes* [1995] EWHC 7, [1995] FSR 818 and *Ray v Classic* ibid

[133] *Ray v Classic* ibid 636 (Lightman J describing the facts in *Cala Homes* as exceptional); *Martin v Kogan* (n103). See also discussion at p 41–42.

[134] L Zemer, 'Contribution and Collaborations in Joint Authorship: Too Many Misconceptions' (2006) 1(4) JIPLP 283 also argues for such an approach.

[135] *Cala Homes* (n132) 835. See also *Heptulla v Orient Longman* [1989] 1 FSR 598 (HC of India); *Donoghue v Allied Newspapers* (n96).

[136] *Hadley v Kemp* (n130).

[137] E.g., *Fylde Microsystems* (n96), in which a technician who tested and debugged software was not a joint author of that software because his work was more akin to proof-reading than authorship.

exclusion of other contributors.[138] This resembles the approach taken by biomedical journals in selecting a few authors who appear worthier than others. This strategy is poorly adapted to the way in which large collaborations work together to create. The temptation to reduce the number of authors might be explained by instrumental concerns that arise from joint ownership – one of the potential consequences of joint authorship. Yet, authorship is a question that is conceptually distinct from ownership. Designations of authorship also usually entail moral rights, which have consequences that are quite separate from copyright's economic rights.

Although the conventional notion of scientific authorship differs from copyright law's concept of authorship, both are challenged by the activities of large collaborations. This chapter has suggested that the ways in which scientific communities have responded to the authorship challenges posed by large-scale collaboration might offer insights for copyright law. I have argued that the joint authorship test ought to be applied with an appreciation that large group authorship is a special kind of authorship. This requires proper account of the process of collaboration, not just an attempt to identify a small number of dominant contributors. As collaborations grow in size, there is a necessary division of labour. Even when a collaboration is hierarchically organized, often no one contributor may be held responsible for its creative products. For these reasons, the joint authorship test ought to be sensitive to the relative importance of contributions within the particular context of a collaboration.

It is also important that the joint authorship test does not merely reproduce power relations but tells us something about who is responsible for the creation of the expression of a work. For copyright, authorship ought to remain a question of law and not an empty vessel to be filled unquestioningly by external conceptions of authorship that might be unstable and contested within a creative community. Yet, the joint authorship test is flexible enough to allow it to be more sensitive to the creative processes of large collaborations than might commonly be thought. The joint authorship test, for example, might better allocate authorship within large collaborations by: (i) taking an expansive, qualitative view of which contributions are 'significant' with reference to the joint project (the common design of contributors); and balancing this by (ii) applying the restrictive filter of copyright's core understanding of authorship.[139]

---

[138] E.g., *Hadley v Kemp* (n130); *Brighton v Jones* (n96).   [139] See 2.1.

6 Film

Films are perhaps the archetypal example of collective authorship, as they tend to be a product of the efforts of a large number of specialised contributors. Unlike the other case studies considered in this book, the authorship of films has been specifically addressed by the CDPA. Films are treated as works of joint authorship,[1] with the producer and the principal director taken to be their authors.[2] The designation of two specific contributors as authors has been adopted, in part, as a response to the high risk, high investment nature of the film business. In this context, there appear to be good reasons to concentrate copyright ownership. But is the statutory designation of authorship to two particular contributors an effective solution to the problem of determining the authorship of works created by a large collaboration?

The legislative approach mirrors the film industry's historical tendency to hold one or two powerful players, often the director and/or producer, 'responsible' for a film. Yet, this view of authorship has constantly been under siege from different interest groups.[3] Recent trends in this industry and in film scholarship are for a more inclusive notion of authorship in line with the reality of the film-making process. Economic control of a film tends to be streamlined through the assignment of rights by contributors via contract. Film authorship, however, is publicly presented as diffuse – dispersed across long credits that make it impossible to tell exactly where authorship begins or ends.[4] The industry uses this ambiguity about authorship strategically as a way of encouraging

---

[1] Unless the producer and the principal director are the same person: s10.   [2] s9(2)(ab).
[3] P Decherney, *Hollywood's Copyright Wars: From Edison to the Internet* (Columbia UP 2012) 90.
[4] Screen credit is part way between a designation of authorship and mere acknowledgement. Contributors have a vested interest in preserving this ambiguity. This can be seen in the longstanding resistance by screenwriters and others to the use of possessory credits (e.g., 'film by ... '), which seem to definitively locate film authorship solely with a dominant contributor: C Fisk, 'The Role of Private Intellectual Property Rights in Markets for Labor and Ideas: Screen Credit and the Writers Guild of America, 1938–2000' (2012) 32 Berkeley J of Employment and Labour L 215, 256–258.

contributors – by showing that, great or small, their contributions matter. In this way, as with two of the previous case studies, the economic and reputational incidents of authorship are separated.[5] Contracts, as well as being a vehicle to concentrate and redistribute copyright ownership in the production company, have an important role to play when it comes to the non-economic consequences of authorship, including attribution.

Although the provisions on film copyright were intended to facilitate determinations of the authorship of a film, the reality is far more complex.[6] Courts have held that in some cases films might also be dramatic works whose authorship is determined in the usual way according to the joint authorship test.[7] Thus, film is not insulated from the problems of applying the joint authorship test to works of collective authorship discussed in previous chapters. Matters are further complicated by the fact that there may also be many different layers of copyright or underlying rights embodied in some films (each with potentially different authors). Indeed, perhaps counter-intuitively, a restrictive approach to the authorship of a film as a whole may increase pressure on judges to recognise copyright in underlying works in order to provide remedies to creators.[8] Film differs from the previous case studies in providing an example of a way to deal with the potential complexity of collective authorship outside the bounds of the joint authorship test – with numerous, distinct layers of copyright in its components.

This chapter begins with an overview of the contested nature of film authorship; the pragmatic use of authorship credit in the film industry and the trend towards a more inclusive approach. The second section considers the complex layers of copyright that might subsist in a feature film and the different rules that are used to determine the authorship of each layer. The third section looks at the use of private ordering solutions to resolve authorship questions and, in particular, the role of collective action in strengthening the bargaining power of groups of contributors. The final section considers the insights for copyright law that arise from this case study. Although the term 'film' in the CDPA might encompass works of a diverse nature (e.g., amateur video, news reports, footage of sporting events, surveillance footage), in this chapter I focus on commercial feature films, because they are the clearest examples of collective authorship.

---

[5] Chapters 3 (Wikipedia) and 5 (scientific collaborations).
[6] 'Report of the Board of Trade Copyright Committee' (Her Majesty's Stationery Company, October 1952) Cmd 8662 ('Gregory Report') 37.
[7] *Norowzian v Arks (No 2)* [2000] FSR 363 (CA).
[8] This may seem counter-intuitive given that a restrictive approach to the joint authorship test tends to be motivated by a desire to reduce the number of creators with copyright interests in the same subject matter (2.3.2).

Film   161

6.1   Authorship Dynamics: The Pragmatic Value of Authorship

In this section, I consider the authorship dynamics at play in the film industry. Dominant views about the authorship of films have remained under siege as the film industry has grown and as power has shifted between different industry players. Historically, authorship of a film was seen as residing with the most powerful industry players, typically producers or directors. In modern times, the industry/social understanding of authorship is more ambiguous, covering shifting sands and often employed pragmatically in the promotion of films. Authorship is atomised or fragmented in film credits for pragmatic reasons: to encourage and reward a broad range of contributors. Although film credits are notoriously long, they are not meaningless. In fact, credit is a matter of great importance to industry players.[9]

Feature film production shares a number of characteristics with the other case studies of collective authorship. Generally, a large number of individuals are involved in making a film, requiring a division of labour that is organised hierarchically.[10] Most contributors have very specialised skills. They might include producers, directors, cinematographers, scriptwriters, actors, composers, visual effects technicians, set designers, costume designers, managers, microphone operators, location scouts, and many more. The types of contributions made to a film vary and include creative contributions, technical support, management, promotional work, logistics, funding, etc. Many contributors have a significant amount of control and autonomy over decisions within their sphere of responsibility. Most contributors work collaboratively with other contributors.[11] Some players have an important role in giving feedback and approving or contesting the contributions of others. The actions of contributors are guided by industry practices, instructions from senior players, their own aesthetic sensibilities, their view of the common project, and their skills base.[12]

Film production, by its very nature, resists traditional romantic notions of authorship.[13] In a real sense, a film could not be made without the

---

[9] C Fisk, 'Credit Where It's Due: The Law and Norms of Attribution' (2006) 95 Georgetown LJ 49, 80, 109.
[10] J Naremore 'Authorship' in T Miller and R Stam (eds) *A Companion to Film Theory* (Blackwell Publishing 2005) describes film creation as a mix of industrialised, technical, theatrical and artisanal practices.
[11] The screenplay, for example, is a highly collaborative undertaking that might evince the contributions of a number of key players: P Bloore, *Managing Creativity and Script Development in the Film Industry* (Routledge 2013) 10.
[12] Bloore (n11) 10 describes film production as an 'industrial collaboration of different creative and commercial agendas'.
[13] A Notaro, 'Technology in Search of an Artist: Questions of Auteurism/Authorship and the Contemporary Cinematic Experience' (2006) 57 The Velvet Light Trap 86, 87.

contributions of many individuals. Yet, historically, authorship of a film was often associated with one of the few powerful players, either producers, studios or directors.[14] These contributors exert significant control over the film-making process, particularly, the authority to determine how far other contributors may exercise their own creative freedom, and even to replace one contributor with another. The producer's and the studio's claim to authorship is generally justified by their financial investment in, and overall control of, the film making process and personnel.[15] The director's claim tends to be based on their control over the creative aspects of the process such as the positioning of cameras, directing the actors, etc.[16] Although the precise amount of control exercised by these figures varies from production to production, their position has allowed them to plausibly claim responsibility for a film's success.

Most other contributors are credited in a way that more closely resembles acknowledgements than authorial by-lines. Screen credits are governed by complicated rules negotiated by the various talent guilds.[17] The extent to which other contributors are considered authors is obfuscated because film credits do not indicate where authorship begins or ends.[18] This ambiguity is deliberate and strategic. It allows a wide range of contributors to be rewarded and acknowledged.[19] In screen credits, authorship is atomised: a contributor is credited for their specific contribution.[20] In respect of authorial works, copyright has a mechanism for recognising that contributors might have different shares of responsibility for the creation of a work, in the possibility that joint authors might

---

[14] Decherney (n3) 89.
[15] FJ Dougherty, 'Not a Spike Lee Joint? Issues in the Authorship of Motion Pictures Under US Copyright Law' (2001) 49 UCLA LRev 225, 282–284, 311–313.
[16] Ibid.
[17] The US talent guilds are the most prominent in the industry, but there are also talent guilds/unions involved in collective bargaining in relation to issues of credit and working conditions in many other countries, for example, The Actors' Guild of Great Britain, the Guild of British Camera Technicians, the Media Entertainment and Arts Alliance (Australia and New Zealand), Alliance of Canadian Cinema, Television and Radio Artists, the International Federation of Actors. Not all countries have guild agreements, for example, Germany: A Datta, 'Collective bargaining agreements in the film industry: US guild agreements for Germany?' (2013) 2(1) Berkeley J of Entertainment and Sports L 200.
[18] Decherney (n3) 90: 'Hollywood authorship exists as a spectrum – one that is constantly in flux and always under siege'. The most significant contributors (the producer, the director, major actors, the screenwriter, the composer, etc.) are often mentioned in opening credits as well as in closing credits.
[19] Although those listed in the opening credits and at the beginning of the closing credits are often considered to have made contributions of a more authorial-type, than those listed towards the end of the closing credits.
[20] They might also be celebrated for their particular contribution in award ceremonies and trade magazines.

be entitled to unequal shares of ownership of the copyright subsisting in their joint work.[21] Yet, in the case of film copyright, the designation of joint authorship to the producer and the principal director appears to preclude the possibility of such a nuanced approach to authorship.[22]

A possessory authorship credit to the director is often a powerful tool in the marketing of a film, as in: 'A Stanley Kubrick Film' (*The Shining*) or 'A film by Quentin Tarantino' (*Pulp Fiction*), for example.[23] This sort of credit has a role akin to a trade mark in that it suggests something about the quality or character of a film to potential theatregoers.[24] 'A Steven Spielberg film' such as *Jurassic Park*, for example, might be expected to have spectacular special effects. The value of leaving the question of film authorship undetermined is so significant that these sorts of possessory credits have long been resisted by other stakeholders, particularly writers.[25] Indeed, possessory credits are the exception and not the rule when it comes to film credits.

In contrast to some of the other case studies, film production is usually characterised by high costs and high risks.[26] This affects aspects of the creative process. Preferred locations for filming and producing films change from year to year according to the availability of favourable regulatory regimes. Hollywood's studio structure facilitates the funding of films and mitigates the risks of film production. Studios can rely on a few high profit earning films or 'tent-poles' to finance the majority of films.[27] In the UK, commercial film production is dominated by independent film productions which usually require funding to be amassed from a variety of public and private sources.[28] These sorts of productions rely on a delicate

---

[21] Based on the quantity and the quality of their contributions to the work, see p44, n172. There are no provisions, however, for a particular order in the attribution of authorship.
[22] Although where a film is also a dramatic work such an approach might be implemented (within the bounds of the joint authorship test).
[23] A Martin, 'Possessory Credit' (2004) 45 (1) Framework 95. The possessory credit does not always refer to director: for example, as in 'Tim Burton's *The Nightmare Before Christmas*' (Tim Burton was a writer and producer, not the director). Possessory credits have also sometimes been used to refer to the writer of a work upon which a film is based, for example, 'Bram Stoker's *Dracula*'.
[24] On the importance of the label of 'author' outside the copyright context, see p68. This author function is also recognised in film studies as scholars might, for example, study the characteristics of the body of a work of a particular director.
[25] Dougherty (n15) 293; Fisk (n4).
[26] Film production in the UK is precarious and often unprofitable: R Murphy, 'Postscript: A Short History of British Cinema' in R Murphy (ed) *The British Cinema Book* (3rd edn, Palgrave Macmillan 2009) 417, 423.
[27] J Garon, 'Content, Control, and the Socially Networked Film' (2010) 48 U of Louisville LRev 771, 777–778.
[28] A significant proportion of film funding comes from government schemes and the distribution of Lotto funds. The BFI website provides information about available funding: <www.bfi.org.uk/film-industry>. See also: 'A Future for British Film: It Begins with the Audience ... ', Film Policy Review, Department for Culture Media

coordination of interests,[29] and even critically successful independent production companies can face chronic financial difficulties.[30] Where a number of different companies are involved in financing and distributing a film, rights management can be a complex affair.[31]

As risk is such a dominant feature of the industry, studios and production companies generally seek ownership of all intellectual property rights that might arise as a result of their investment.[32] Production companies consolidate their ownership of rights through contracts with all the various contributors to ensure they are unimpeded in their exploitation of the final product – so they are best-placed to recoup their investment. The need to streamline distribution was an important factor in the reforms which lead to the designation of the producer (and later also the director) as the author of a film in the CDPA.[33]

Since the first moving pictures, views on film authorship have been influenced by power struggles between different categories of contributors to determine the content of copyright law with respect to film.[34] The effective lobbying of groups representing the interests of producers and directors (rather than principled argument) might also go some way to explaining the special protection they are awarded under the CDPA.[35]

and Sport, 2012, 40. On the use of subsidies to promote creativity (instead of intellectual property rights): S Breyer, 'The Uneasy Case for Copyright: A Study of Books, Photocopies and Computer Programs' (1970) 84(2) Harvard LRev 281; J Love and T Hubbard 'The Big Idea: Prizes to Stimulate R&D for New Medicines' (2007) 82 Chicago-Kent LRev 1519. Different concerns relate to the production of short films, which can often be produced on a shoe-string budget.

[29] Channel 4, BBC Films and the UK Film Council generally support films only as partners in complicated co-production deals that sometimes take years to set up: R Murphy, ' Postscript: A Short History of British Cinema' in R Murphy (ed) *The British Cinema Book* (3rd ed, Palgrave Macmillan 2009) 423.

[30] J Barnett, 'Hollywood Deals: Soft Contracts for Hard Markets' (2015) 64 Duke Law Journal 605, 615.

[31] Complicated arrangements to share revenues from distribution can result in disputes, see M Rimmer, 'Heretic: Copyright Law and Dramatic Works' (2002) 2(1) QUT LRev 131, 137–139.

[32] Report from the Commission to the Council, the European Parliament and the Economic and Social Committee on the question of authorship of cinematographic or audiovisual works in the Community of 6 December 2002, COM (2002) 691.

[33] P Kamina, *Film Copyright in the European Union* (2nd ed CUP 2016) 149. Bently et al. 129.

[34] Rimmer (n31); Decherney (n3) 7–10, 89.

[35] This has been much discussed in the US context, e.g., T McFarlin, 'An Idea of Authorship: Orson Welles, *The War of the Worlds* Copyright, and Why We Should Recognize Idea-Contributors as Joint Authors' (2016) 66(3) Case Western LRev 701, 751 at n182. In the US context, the strategies and battles of different individuals seeking to promote their interests has also shaped the evolution of the case law, see: O Bracha, 'How Did Film Become Property? Copyright and the Early American Film Industry' in B Sherman and L Wiseman, *Copyright and the Challenge of the New* (Wolters Kluwer 2012) 141, 143.

Film

Although the provisions on film authorship appear to favour the producer, production companies still appear cautious of placing sole reliance upon copyright law, with all its uncertainties, to regulate issues relating to the authorship and ownership of copyright in films. Decherney carefully outlines how US film studios have used contract to stay one step ahead of copyright law.[36] Film production companies' reliance on contract may suggest that copyright law's provisions have little practical effect, yet, as I argue in 6.3, copyright law is an important source of default standards.[37] These standards are particularly important for those in weaker bargaining positions as they may help them to gain recognition and fair remuneration for their contributions.[38] The provisions of copyright law not only create a prima facie entitlement which is a favourable starting point for contractual negotiations, they also provide an underlying system of regulation of the incidents of authorship. Copyright law's regulatory role is significant, because contracts can never predict all eventualities, particularly in the early stages of a project when greater flexibility is needed.[39]

In the marketplace and in the eyes of the general public, film authorship has tended to be linked to financial clout and/or control of the creative process. As the film industry has transformed over time, different players have enjoyed prominence as authors. When films were originally sold on the basis of the novelty of the technology, it was the devisors of that technology, such as Thomas Edison, who were seen as the most important figures in the film industry.[40] Between the 1920s and 1940s, at the height of the production of studio films by the 'majors' or the 'big five' Hollywood studios,[41] certain corporate executives assumed an 'impresario' role and became highly visible as the 'face' of the studio. At that time, screenwriters and other contributors were paid employees of studios on long-term contracts and so were seen more as delegates than authors.[42] As auteur theory

---

[36] Decherney (n3) 99–101. Although he discusses this in the US context, UK production companies also tend to rely heavily on contracts rather than copyright law's default rules.

[37] On the significance of legal rules in providing bargaining endowments, see: R Mnookin and L Korhauser, 'Bargaining in the Shadow of the Law: The Case of Divorce' (1979) 88 Yale LRev 950, 968.

[38] Kamina (n33) 34. This is a more favourable outcome than granting them non waivable rights, as it still allows for the consolidation of copyright ownership (via contract) in the hands of the more powerful player, who is likely to best placed to ensure the most effective exploitation of the work. Contributors have an incentive to enter into such contracts, because most cannot exploit their copyright interest separately, see p193.

[39] Often much is left to an oral agreement or handshake at these stages and with 'key talent': Barnett (n30).

[40] Decherney (n3) Ch 1.

[41] From 1928 to 1949 these were Loew's/MGM, Paramount, Fox (which became 20th Century-Fox after a merger in 1935), Warner Bros and RKO.

[42] J Schwab, 'Audiovisual Works and the Work for Hire Doctrine in the Internet Age' (2011) 35 Columbia JL and the Arts 141, 147.

came to prominence in the 1950s, the role of the director received greater appreciation, fuelled by directors, such as Alfred Hitchcock, who developed a signature style.[43]

Since its early days, film production has also been closely linked to the cult of celebrity. In some situations celebrity names are promoted in a way that implies quasi-authorship. The 'star system' particularly encouraged credit to gravitate towards those celebrities which brought attention to films. Star power served as a bargaining chip, used to negotiate credit for the actor as an 'executive producer'. Credit is so significant that actors (and other contributors) might accept less remuneration for a better credit.[44] Investment in a film might be shored up by securing a commitment from a famous actor having an established track record for attracting large audience figures. Whilst it is true that one might garner some information about the likely quality of a film based upon the names of certain actors – such as Charlie Chaplin,[45] Tom Cruise, or Anthony Hopkins – star names are generally employed somewhat cynically for their ability to assure 'bums on seats'. Sometimes stars may be held responsible for box office flops,[46] unless they can successfully distance themselves from unpopular films, e.g., by arguing that they had not endorsed the end product.[47] It is rare, however, for a star to be seen as responsible as an author of the overall film in the same way studios or directors might be (unless they also had some involvement in producing, writing or directing it).

In the film industry, groups compete for status. Yet, no one is clearly *the* author of a film. Those viewed as artists have tended to be granted more prestige than those who are considered technicians or craftsmen.[48] After the dissolution of the studio system in the 1950s, contributors tended not

---

[43] P Watson, 'Cinematic Authorship and the Film Auteur' in J Nelmes (ed) *Introduction to Film Studies* (5th ed, Routledge 2012) 142, 148–152.
[44] On the value of screen credit, citing instances of this being recognised by courts accepting the evidence of film experts: R Davenport, 'Screen Credit in the Entertainment Industry' (1990) 10 Loyola Entertainment LJ 129, 148; SK Judge, 'Giving Credit Where Credit Is Due: The Unusual Use of Arbitration in Determining Screenwriting Credits' (1997)13 Ohio State J on Dispute Resolution 221, 229–230.
[45] Charlie Chaplin was presented as a romantic author figure in his times: Decherney (n3) 67–76.
[46] C Rosen, '"Transcendence" is a Real Bad Flop for Johnny Depp', *The Huffington Post*, 21 April 2014 <www.huffingtonpost.com/2014/04/21/johnny-depp-transcendence-flop s_n_5184999.html>; G Macnab, 'Johnny Depp's New Film Transcendence is Yet Another Expensive Flop – So Has The Star Lost His Mojo?' *The Independent*, 30 April 2014.
[47] For example, K Finbow, 'Nicole Kidman: "I had no control over Grace of Monaco"', *Digital Spy*, 27 May 2014.
[48] M Salokannel, 'Film Authorship in the Changing Audio-Visual Environment' in B Sherman and A Strowel, *Of Authors and Origins* (Clarendon Press 1994) 57.

to be employed, but rather contracted to work on a film-by-film basis.[49] This led to an improvement in status for 'creative' contributors, partly because they appeared more like authors than those who made mechanical or technical contributions.[50] Ever since, contributors' attempts to vie for more control, remuneration, and credit have tended to be linked to claims of responsibility for important creative elements in a film. Less powerful contributors have also begun drawing attention to the creative aspects of their work in an attempt to improve their status. The Screen Writers Guild, for example, have tended to stress the creative nature of writers' contributions as part of their bargaining to improve the terms of collective agreements.[51] Those arguing for an improvement in conditions for visual effects artists emphasise their influence on the overall aesthetic of the film.[52] Thus, authorship (understood as responsibility for the creative content of the work) is used as a tool to improve a contributor's bargaining position with more powerful industry players.

Authorship remains a greatly disputed issue in film studies today. It is not necessary to give a comprehensive account of film scholarship here, but suffice to make the following points. Early philosophy of film struggled with the question of whether film could be recognised as an art form.[53] As a popular cultural form, cinema appeared too vulgar to be considered on the same level as opera, theatre or poetry.[54] The idea of the director as *auteur* was first suggested by François Truffaut, who became one of the central directors in the French New Wave.[55] He argued that the only films worth valorising as 'art' were those in which the director had direct control over production and screen writing as well as in relation to the actors' performances.[56] His ideas were picked up by film theorist

[49] Schwab (n42) 147.   [50] Decherney (n3) 89–90.   [51] Ibid.
[52] E Rome, 'Oscars: Visual Effects Artists Protest Outside Dolby Theatre' *Entertainment Weekly*, 25 Feb 2013 <insidemovies.ew.com/2013/02/25/oscars-visual-effects-protest-life-of-pi> cites Bill Westenhofer's comments in support of fellow striking visual effects artists: 'Visual effects is not just a commodity that's being done by people pushing buttons ... *Life of Pi* shows that we're artists not just technicians'. Also, Paul Evans, Assistant National Secretary, Broadcasting Entertainment Cinematograph and Theatre Union: 'This goes to the heart of the contribution creative workers make to film. Imagine the *Planet of the Apes* without the apes, or the *Jungle Book* with no jungle, and it's clear what we're talking about' cited in 'BECTU seeks screen credits for all VFX artists' (10 July 2017) <www.bectu.org.uk/news/2731>.
[53] T Wartenberg, 'Philosophy of Film' in EN Zalta (ed) *The Stanford Encyclopedia of Philosophy* (2014) <plato.stanford.edu/archives/fall2014/entries/film/>. Copyright law has similarly struggled with whether to treat film as an authorial or entrepreneurial work, see 6.2.
[54] Ibid.
[55] Ibid. Truffaut's manifesto 'A Certain Tendency of the French Cinema' published in *Cahiers du Cinéma* January 1954 (No 31) translated and reproduced in BK Grant (ed), *Auteurs and Authorship: A Film Reader* (Blackwell 2008) 9.
[56] Wartenberg (n53).

Andrew Sarris and auteur theory grew in importance within the context of film studies.[57] Limiting the number of 'authors' of a film made it look less like a product of technicians and more like a work of art, the product of a romantic author: the director. By adopting literature's romantic author trope as the dominant paradigm for understanding film, theorists paved the way for the acceptance of film as a respectable art and this allowed for the growth of film studies as a discipline.[58]

Auteur theory has since been largely discredited because of its neglect of other important contributions to a film.[59] The interpretative strategies used to restrict the number of authors have also been exposed as artificial and highly constructed.[60] Yet, auteurism succeeded in cementing the authorial role of the director in public understanding.[61] Now, a director's reputation might sell a film almost as effectively as the reputation of its stars.[62] It also profoundly affected Hollywood's view of its own past.[63] Auteurism is not universally accepted in the film community, now being primarily perceived as a marketing tool.[64] Instead, film-making is widely acknowledged both in the industry and more generally, to be a cooperative, collaborative activity.[65]

The vast majority of contemporary film scholarship now favours an inclusive approach in which multiple authorship is embraced as a better model than auteurism.[66] Although discussion of individual directors'

---

[57] In 1962 Andrew Sarris called the approach, referred to as *la politique des auteurs*, the auteur theory: A Sarris, 'Notes on the Auteur Theory in 1962' in Grant, ibid, 35. See also A Astruc, 'The Birth of the Avant Garde: Le Caméra Stylo', *L'Écran français* (30 March 1948).

[58] Naremore (n10) 10–11.

[59] It was thought to have distorted the way that films were understood. Wartenberg (n53) describes the theory as 'clearly flawed'. See also: Martin (n23). Arguing for authorship to be located with the screenwriter, rather than the director: D Kipen, *The Schreiber Theory: A Radical Rewrite of American Film History* (Melville House 2006).

[60] B Gaut, 'Film Authorship and Collaboration' in R Allen and M Smith (eds) *Film Theory and Philosophy* (OUP 1997) 149.

[61] Fisk (n4) 257, 276 describes it (in addition to the US work for hire doctrine), as a threat to screenwriters.

[62] Notaro (n13) 87.   [63] Naremore (n10) 16.

[64] Watson (n43) 157–161 discusses Quentin Tarantino as a contemporary case of auteurism (within the context of an overall argument in favour of a pragmatic approach to film authorship).

[65] Rimmer (n31) 135–136. Acceptance speeches at film awards ceremonies, for example, usually acknowledge the valuable contributions of many others and stress the collaborative nature of film production.

[66] Gaut (n60) 149; P Livingston, 'Cinematic Authorship' in Allen and Smith (n60) 132; P Livingston, *Art and Intention* (OUP 2005); P Livingston, 'On Authorship and Collaboration' (2011) 69(2) J of Aesthetics and Art Criticism 221; P Sellors, 'Collective Authorship in Film' (2007) 65 J of Aesthetics and Art Criticism 263; S Bacharach and D Tollefsen, '*We* Did It: From Mere Contributors to Coauthors' (2010) 68(1) J of Aesthetics and Art Criticism 23; S Bacharach and D Tollefsen, 'We

styles remains a relevant project, contemporary film scholarship pays more attention to the context in which films are produced (influenced by cultural studies and semiotic analysis). The debate on film authorship remains a lively topic, however, in aesthetics where the focus is on how to conceptualise the authorial group responsible for creating a film.[67] Thus, an inclusive approach to determining the authorship of a film is most in line with the way in which the process of creating a film is now generally understood by film industry participants, film scholars and the general public.[68]

6.2 The Subsistence of Copyright

In this section, I argue that copyright law fails to provide adequate means of determining the authorship of a film because it struggles to conceptualise the subject matter of protection.[69] From one angle, a film is an industrial product – a recording best treated as an entrepreneurial work;[70] from another, it is a highly creative work best treated as an authorial work. The current hybrid treatment of films in UK copyright law reflects this ambiguity. In so doing, it eschews the certainty that the introduction of (first fixation) film copyright was expected to provide. I argue that the recognition of additional layers of copyright flows from the imperative to protect creators who would otherwise be excluded due to the CDPA's narrow view of film joint authorship. I begin by briefly introducing the history of copyright protection for film. Then, I consider the potential complexity of underlying copyright interests in a film (6.2.2). The next sections look at the subsistence of copyright in a film as a first fixation (6.2.3), and as a dramatic work (6.2.4). I end this section by reviewing some recent US cases which have taken a restrictive approach to film authorship and which demonstrate the pitfalls of pragmatic instrumental reasoning in this context (6.2.5).

Did It Again: A Reply to Livingston' (2011) 69(2) J of Aesthetics and Art Criticism 225; DH Hick, 'Authorship, Co-Authorship, and Multiple Authorship' (2014) 72(2) J of Aesthetics and Art Criticism 147.

[67] Ibid. Whether by the intentional contribution of artistically relevant features (Gaut); according to various types of shared intention (Livingston, Sellors); by membership of an artistic group that shares a joint commitment (Bacharach & Tollefsen); or in terms of responsibility for the form of the expression (Hick).

[68] See 8.2 on the limits of incorporating social norms in legal decision-making.

[69] Copyright law also struggles to define the boundaries of the literary work(s) on Wikipedia, see 3.2.1.

[70] Barnett (n30) 7: 'A Hollywood studio ... is primarily a vehicle for coordinating the inputs required to assemble a film project and financing, promoting and distributing films produced by internal production divisions and independent production entities'.

6.2.1 A Brief Historical Note

The way that UK copyright law has dealt with film has evolved over time. The 1911 Act (the first major piece of UK copyright legislation since film was invented), provided that the individual frames of a film could be protected as photographs. In addition, a dramatic work was expressly defined to include 'any cinematograph production where the arrangement or acting form or the combination of incidents represented give the work an original character'.[71] In 1952, the Gregory Report recommended instead that film be protected as a distinct type of work, in large part owing to the practical worry that too many people might claim authorship of a film, resulting in a complexity of claims.[72] The Report considered that films (as a whole) bore more resemblance to industrial products than they did to authorial works.[73] The text reveals that this view was motivated by an instrumental concern about the multiplicity of claims which might result from categorising a cinematographic film as an authorial work, and rested upon the underlying assumption that many component contributions to a film would still be protected separately as authorial works.[74] The perceived complexity of film as a collective product led to the Report's recommendation of a fixation-only form of protection for the film as a whole. Accordingly, the 1956 Act which followed protected cinematograph films as a first fixation, entrepreneurial-type work and explicitly removed any protection for film as an authorial work. Copyright was owned by the 'maker', being the person by whom the arrangements necessary for the making of the film were undertaken (now the 'producer' in the CDPA), but the Act was silent on the question of film authorship.[75] When the CDPA was enacted in 1988, the producer was designated as the sole author of a film, but later as compromise concession to Europe, the director was also considered to be an author.[76] Thus, the historical tendency was to prefer to treat films as industrial products, awarding copyright ownership to the entrepreneur who took initiative, invested in, and took charge of, the project. In this way the law

---

[71] 1911 Act s35(1). Before then, individual frames of a film could be protected as a series of photographs under the Fine Arts Copyright Act 1862 and the dramatic content of a film could potentially be protected under the Dramatic Copyright Act 1833.
[72] Gregory Report (n6) 37.
[73] Ibid 34 for this reason a relatively short duration of protection was recommended. On the tension between technical and creative contributions to film and its effect on the question of film authorship: Salokannel (n48). At the time the 1956 Act was implemented auteur theory was only beginning to come into prominence (see n57).
[74] Gregory Report (n6) 33, 36–37.   [75] 1956 Act s3(4), s13(10).
[76] Copyright and Related Rights Regulation 1996 implemented the Term Directive, Art 2, bringing the UK closer to the continental approach which already recognised the creative contribution of the director as authorial.

was shaped to fit industry practice at the time, rather than existing copyright principles on creative subject matter.[77]

Parts of the Gregory Report appear to recognise that films are the product of creative collaboration.[78] There is something counter-intuitive in then denying authorial copyright protection to films simply on the basis that they have too many potential authors.[79] This tension between two conceptions of a film (as an industrial product, but also as a creative work) might explain the hybrid protection that films enjoy today that includes thin protection of the fixation only ('film' copyright); but also protection of the cinematographic work as an authorial work (a 'dramatic work').[80] Film copyright reflects a historical view of film as a craft and the policy concern to reward investment. However, the true complexity of film authorship is reflected by judicial development of the law in the acknowledgement that a film might be a dramatic work (likely to have many authors); and in the recognition that individual contributions might constitute separately protectable copyright works. I argue that this is a response to the evidently authorial characteristics of most films and the underlying imperative in copyright law to protect creators.

6.2.2 Explaining the Complexity of Film Copyright

Unpacking the subsistence of copyright in film is a complicated matter. There are likely to be a number of overlapping copyright interests, as different contributors make separate component copyright works which make up the final product.[81] Indeed, Kamina perceives the crux of the problem to be the diverse nature of the contributions which go towards making a film, rather than just the large number of contributors.[82] These contributions may be made at different points in the production process

---

[77] M Handler, 'Continuing Problems with Film Copyright' in F Macmillan (ed) *New Directions in Copyright Law* (Edward Elgar 2007) Vol 6, 173, 177. In the Gregory Report the choice to view film as an industrial product was partly explained by the fact that no *single* creator of a film could be found. This comment appears to confirm the fears of some scholars of the undue influence of the romantic notion of authorship; see 2.4.
[78] Gregory Report (n6) 33: 'The manufacture ... of cinematograph films undoubtedly calls into play a variety of skills, in part technical, in part artistic ... film has called forth in its production a measure of artistic skill'.
[79] Gregory Report (n6) 37.
[80] The distinction is probably best understood by reference to the 1956 Act's distinction between (authorial) 'works' and 'other subject matter' (entrepreneurial works), see Bently et al. 36, 118–119, 128–130.
[81] Most textbooks agree on this point, e.g., Cornish et al. [11-11]; Bently et al. 68 (scenic effects and costumes, if artistic works, will have separate copyright). It was also assumed by the Gregory Report (n6) 33, 36–37 and underlies its recommendation for a fixation only form of copyright protection for film.
[82] Kamina (n33) 141. *Lucasfilm v Ainsworth* [2008] EWHC 1878, [2009] FSR 103.

and may potentially encompass the whole spectrum of types of work protected by copyright. Some may exist autonomously, being capable of exploitation independently of the film (e.g., props and costumes); whereas others may be inseparable from the film (e.g., editing). Some autonomous elements will not be protected by copyright, as they do not fall within any of the categories for copyright works (e.g., *mise-en-scène*). In the UK, fictional characters will not be afforded separate copyright protection,[83] although drawings of cartoon characters in an animated film may be protected as artistic works.[84] Makeup may not be protectable because it is not an artistic work and/or may lack adequate permanency.[85] But copyright may vest in accompanying music as a musical work and also as a sound recording.[86] The actors are likely to have performance rights in respect of their performances.[87] The screenplay is an underlying dramatic work and the final film might be considered to be a derivative (dramatic) work of that screenplay.[88]

Prior to *Lucasfilm v Ainsworth*, there was a general assumption that sets, costumes and props would often be protectable as artistic works.[89] In *Shelley Films v Rex Features*, the question of whether copyright subsisted in costumes and prostheses as works of artistic craftsmanship was considered a serious issue to be tried and it was held plainly arguable that copyright could subsist in a film set as a work of artistic craftsmanship.[90] In *Creation Records*, Lloyd J could 'readily accept that a film set does involve craftsmanship', distinguishing it from an assembly of '*objets trouvés*', but he stopped short of commenting on whether it might have the requisite artistic quality to be protected.[91] Establishing the subsistence of copyright in components of a film as artistic works (whether as

---

[83] Kamina (n33) 112 summarises the authorities: *Kelly v Cinema Houses Ltd* [1928–35] MCC 362 (Maugham J 368) (cf. dicta of May LJ in *O'Neill v Paramount* [1983] CAT 235). This might be contrasted to the position in the US (*Nichols v Universal Pictures* 45 F2d 119 (2nd Cir, 1930)) and on the continent (Kamina 112–113).

[84] *King Features Syndicate v O and M Kleeman* [1941] AC 417 (HL) (Popeye); *Mirage Studios v Counter-Feat Clothing* [1991] FSR 145 (Ch) (Teenage Mutant Ninja Turtles).

[85] *Merchandising Corporation of America v Harpbond* [1983] FSR 32 (CA).

[86] The latter is a fixation only form of protection more akin to a neighbouring right than to copyright (s5A).

[87] CDPA, Pt II.

[88] It is unlikely to be seen as a literary work given that this category of work explicitly excludes anything that might be considered a dramatic work (s3(1)). A storyboard is also an artistic work that derives from the script.

[89] Kamina (n33) 111; most textbooks assume this to be the case: n81. Cf. *Lucasfilm* (n82).

[90] [1994] EMLR 134, 143 (Mann QC sitting as Deputy High Court Judge): 'In principle this would seem correct [that copyright can subsist in a film set as a work of artistic craftsmanship] since, if the set is imaginatively conceived and implemented overall as a work of artistic craftsmanship, it cannot matter that it happens to be made up of numerous, perhaps many thousands, of components in some of which, when considered separately, copyright might not exist, provided the effect and intent overall is artistic.'

[91] As a work of artistic craftsmanship: s4(1)(c); [1997] EMLR 444, 449.

works of artistic craftsmanship or as sculptures) may now be more difficult. In *Lucasfilm*, at first instance, Mann J found that a Stormtrooper helmet from the *Star Wars* films was plainly a work of craftsmanship, but held that it was not artistic.[92] For similar reasons, to be further discussed, the helmet was not protectable as a sculpture either. There may be an argument that the careful arrangement of a set is a protectable compilation (but possibly not collage).[93] Although a compilation is a type of literary work (which might not seem the most natural characterisation of a film set), this interpretation is plausible given the definition of a literary work as including anything that is written, spoken or sung.[94] In the CDPA, 'writing' is defined very broadly to include 'any form of notation or code, whether by hand or otherwise and regardless of the method by which, or medium in or on which, it is recorded'.[95]

The reasoning adopted in *Lucasfilm* might lead one to conclude that props and costumes will only be classified as artistic works in rare cases. At first instance, Mann J set out a series of guidelines for determining whether, or not, a work is sculpture.[96] He concluded that the Stormtrooper helmet was not a sculpture because it had a utilitarian, rather than an artistic purpose. The Supreme Court agreed with Mann J's reasoning that although the helmet had contributed to the artistic effect of the finished film, it was merely a utilitarian step in the production process – the 'work of art' was the film itself.[97] Nonetheless the Supreme

---

[92] *Lucasfilm* (n82); the issue was not considered on appeal: *Lucasfilm v Ainsworth* [2009] EWCA Civ 1328, [2010] Ch 503.
[93] s3(1)(a), s4(1)(a). In *Football Association Premier League v Panini UK* [2004] FSR 1 (CA) [25] it was suggested that an album of stickers of football players might be a compilation. In *Creation Records* (n91) the arrangement of a scene was held to be too ephemeral to constitute a collage. The court also thought that the placement of objects (without any sticking or gluing, etc., to hold them in place) precluded finding it to be a collage. The court did not consider whether the scene might be protected as a compilation. It might be necessary, however, to take a broader view of CDPA's categories of work following Case C-5/08 *Infopaq Intl v Danske Dagblades Forening* [2009] ECR I-6569, in which the CJEU implies that all that is required for copyright subsistence is that the work be the author's intellectual creation, see above p 24 n47 and p 26 n70.
[94] s3(1).
[95] This argument could not extend to the musical score because a literary work is defined as excluding musical works. An editor's selection and arrangement of the scenes is also unlikely to be able to be a compilation because it is not relevantly written in any notation or code.
[96] Accepted on appeal by the Court of Appeal (n92) and Supreme Court (*Lucasfilm v Ainsworth* [2011] UKSC 39, [2012] 1 AC 208). It is not entirely clear which guidelines were most persuasive in the instant case as Mann J simply sets them out and then moves to his conclusion that the sculpture lacked artistic purpose: (n82) [121].
[97] (n82) [121]; ibid, [44]. J Pila, 'The "Star Wars" Copyright Claim: An Ambivalent View of the Empire' (2012) LQR 15, 17 argues that the court's approach was correct insofar as the multi-factor test focused on the intent of the creator and the view of society with respect to the nature of the creation, but that the suggestion that objects created as a step in *any* production process would not be artistic works is more problematic.

Court appeared to express some hesitation in accepting the trial judge's findings, acknowledging the 'imagination that went into the concept' of the helmets.[98] Thus, *Lucasfilm* might possibly leave space for the separate protection of highly imaginative and artistic props, sets, or costumes as artistic works which satisfy Mann J's guidelines.[99]

In contrast to the helmet, Mann J had considered that the preliminary paintings on which the Stormtrooper costumes were based might be artistic works.[100] Given this finding, it is difficult to understand why the helmet was a utilitarian object (on the basis that it was merely a step in the production process), as the arguably the same logic would apply to the paintings.[101] Whilst it is true that a helmet usually has a functional purpose (protecting the head), the main purpose of this specific helmet was not functional – it was to suggest various qualities of the character of a Stormtrooper.[102] A key difference between the helmet and the preliminary paintings may be that the helmet was made to be incorporated into the final product (the film), whilst the paintings were clearly distinct works, which did not appear in the final film. Indeed, the reasoning adopted by the trial judge (approved by the Supreme Court) seems to suggest that any artistic purpose in relation to the helmet was somehow nullified or subsumed in the film.[103] Thus, it appears that the helmet was thought to lack *independent* artistic purpose simply because it formed a component of a joint work.[104] If copyright law's imperative to incentivise and reward creators is to be taken seriously, surely the corollary of refusing to recognise a separate copyright interest subsisting

---

[98] Ibid. Even Mann J, at first instance, had accepted that the helmet was one of the most abiding images of the film.

[99] The guidelines are set out in *Lucasfilm* (n82) [118]–[119]. The most significant factor being the purpose of the work (it must be for visual appeal).

[100] They were considered to be original graphic works. This appears to have been conceded by Mr Ainsworth (n82) [89]. By extension, this suggests that storyboards might be protected as artistic works.

[101] A strange result, as noted in A Hobson, 'Imperial Stormtroopers, Art Works, and Copyright Defences' (2009) 4(1) JIPLP 16.

[102] The creator's aesthetic purposes in making the Stormtrooper helmet seems to be acknowledged in the Supreme Court's reasoning that a replica helmet in a twentieth century war film would be even less likely to be a sculpture (n92) [44].

[103] 'While it was intended to express something, that was for utilitarian purposes. While it has an interest as an object, and while it was intended to express an idea, it was not conceived, or created, with the intention that it should do so other than as part of character portrayal in the film ... it lacks artistic purpose' (trial) (n82) [121] (Mann J). 'But it was the *Star Wars* film that was the work of art that Mr Lucas and his companies created. The helmet was utilitarian in the sense that it was an element in the process of production of the film' (Supreme Court) (n96) [44] (Lord Walker and Lord Collins SCJJ) (Lord Phillips and Lady Hale concurring).

[104] In the sense that its purpose is intertwined with, and a part of, the artistic purpose of the film (to produce a particular aesthetic experience for the audience).

in 'imaginative' (i.e., creative) component parts of a film ought to be a broader approach to construing the authorship of the film as a whole.[105] This is not something that the court had the occasion to consider and, in any case, is very unlikely that the facts would have supported a claim to joint authorship of the film.[106] A more persuasive justification for the decision might be found in the Supreme Court's consideration of the need to preserve a graduated scheme of protection for three-dimensional objects in the CDPA, in which functional objects receive the lowest degree of protection.[107]

The Supreme Court suggested that highly imaginative props, costumes or sets might be protected as artistic works. This is now particularly likely to be the case post-*Infopaq*, as UK courts may now need to take a broader approach to the CDPA's categories, including artistic works.[108] Furthermore, there is a general preference to conceptualise of complex works as comprising multiple distinct layers of copyright works wherever possible ostensibly to simplify questions of multiple ownership.[109] This minimises the number of people who must together manage the exploitation of a jointly owned copyright work, but does not eliminate complexity as the result is many separately owned copyright works. The difficult issue of detangling rights in a film will be complicated even further if *Infopaq* is interpreted to meld the requirement of 'originality' with that of a 'work'; i.e., if any part of a work which

---

[105] Indeed, *Lucasfilm* follows the recognition that some films will also be dramatic works in *Norowzian v Arks (No 2)*. The Gregory Report (n6) 36–37 relied upon comparable reasoning (in the opposite sense) when it justified the narrow definition of film authorship which it proposed on the basis that many contributors to a film would have separate copyrights in the underlying works they had created.

[106] One might argue that as the visual appearance of the Stormtrooper is '[o]ne of the most abiding images' of this cult film, the question of whether person who created this look is a joint author of the film as a dramatic work merits serious consideration (n82) [2]. The facts of the case, however, present difficulties when it comes to establishing a claim to joint authorship of the film Ainsworth's behalf (the uniform was closely based on pre-existing designs by other contributors, George Lucas retained a high degree of creative control and Ainsworth did not initially know that the helmet was to be used in a film). On the joint authorship of film as a dramatic work: 6.2.4.

[107] (n92) [48]. Although the theory of functionality upon which the court relies remains somewhat obscure.

[108] Indeed, it is surprising that the Supreme Court did not explicitly consider the impact of CJEU case law in its decision: Pila (n97) 16.

[109] M Spence, *Intellectual Property* (OUP 2007) 96 noting this results in fewer joint authorship cases in the UK than in countries such as the US, France and Belgium. Cornish et al. [11-04] arguing for a cumulative rather than an exclusive approach to applying the CDPA's categories of works and in this regard preferring the approach in *Anacon v Environmental Research* [1994] FSR 359 (Ch) (Jacobs J) and *Sandman v Panasonic* [1998] FSR 651 (Ch) (Pumfrey J), to the approach in *Electronic Techniques v Critchley* [1997] FSR 401, 413 (Ch) (Laddie J).

contains an expression of the author's own intellectual creation may be *separately* protected.[110] On this view, each particular scene of a film (or any of its component parts) might be separate works as long as they are the result of creative choices/appropriate skill, labour and judgement. Such an approach would be at odds with UK cases that have stressed the necessity of objectively determining the scope of the work, on the basis that copyright is not a 'legal millefeuilles'.[111] In Chapter 3, I argued that fracturing the 'work' in this way is problematic in the context of Wikipedia and the same appears true here for film.[112]

In addition to the potential complexity of underlying rights in component parts of a film; many films (as a whole) are likely to enjoy dual protection.[113] The recording (fixation) is protected by film copyright and cinematographic films may also qualify for protection as dramatic works. The next two subsections consider the authorship of both these types of work.

6.2.3 Film as a First Fixation

Film copyright is a mechanical-type of copyright that subsists in a recording of images and sound.[114] Copyright is acquired by the act of first recording, irrespective of any personal labour or skill.[115] Copyright will subsist in the film recording, provided that it is not simply copied.[116] The definition of a film is broad, and includes a 'recording on any medium from which a moving image may by any means be produced'.[117] *Spelling Goldberg v BPC Publishing* identified three characteristics of film: (i) it is a sequence of images; (ii) recorded on material; (iii) capable of being shown as a moving picture.[118] The soundtrack is treated as part of the film, but this does not affect any copyright subsisting in it separately as a sound

---

[110] There are good reasons to prefer AG Wathelet's view that there are additional requirements for a 'work': Case C – 310/17 *Levola Hengelo* ECLI:EU:C:2018:618.
[111] Thus Claimants might not try to claim many layers of protection by asserting that small parts of a work are independent works, thus making it easier to establish that an infringer has copied a substantial part of the work: *IPC Media v Highbury-Leisure Publishing* [2004] EWHC 2985, [2005] FSR 20 [23] (Laddie J), approved in *Coffey v Warner/Chappell Music* [2005] EWHC 449 (Ch), [2005] FSR 34 (Ch) [10] (Blackburne J).
[112] p83–84.
[113] L Bently and B Sherman, *Intellectual Property Law* (OUP 2009) 60 consider that they occupy a space between authorial and entrepreneurial works. The Rental and Related Rights Directive and the Term Directive also distinguish between 'cinematographic works' and related rights in mere fixations, called 'films' or 'videograms'.
[114] *Norowzian v Arks (No 1)* [1998] FSR 394 (Ch).
[115] s5B(4); Laddie et al. [3.100], 125.
[116] This means that it must not be reprographically copied from another film. [117] s5B.
[118] [1981] RPC 283.

Film

recording.[119] Although film copyright arises easily without the requirement of an original/authorial contribution, it subsists only in the fixation and, therefore, is only infringed by literal copying (taking the actual images/sounds recorded in the film).[120] Consequently, a copyright film is not infringed by unauthorised acts such as transcribing it, performing it as a play, or even reshooting it scene-by-scene (although these acts may infringe copyright in any underlying works, e.g., the screenplay). A film is presumed to be a work of joint authorship, with its authors deemed to be the producer and the principal director.[121]

The producer is defined as the 'person by whom the arrangements necessary for making the film are undertaken'.[122] Thus, the producer is not the person who makes the recording in the literal sense of holding the capturing camera. Rather, it is direct organisational control over the process of production which is material – meaning the producer is the person who organises, coordinates and controls the production of the work.[123] This definition is significant because it excludes an investor (which may be a financial institution) from being deemed an author automatically – arguably 'making arrangements necessary for the making of the film' implies some additional input. While it may not be enough simply to commission a film, or to finance it, these contributions are potentially relevant when combined with other contributions.[124] There is no definition of 'principal director', but this is likely to be the person who has creative control over the making of a film.[125] While turning on the specific facts, it will generally be straightforward to identify these figures in the case of feature films.[126] It is perhaps more problematic to locate the authors of films which arise

---

[119] s5B(2) and (5).
[120] *Norowzian v Arks (No 1)* (n114). Section 17(4) provides that the copying of a film includes 'making a photograph of the whole or any substantial part of any image forming part of the film' – so infringing use need not be as a 'moving image'. See: *Spelling Goldberg Productions v BPC Publishing* [1981] RPC 283 (CA) (a single frame); *Football Association Premier League v QC Leisure (No 2)* [2008] EWHC 1411 (Ch) (four frames of a video stream not a substantial part); *R v Higgs* [2008] EWCA 1324, [2009] 1 WLR 73 [9] (Jacob LJ) (obiter, a single frame 'probably' infringement). There is no adaptation right in relation to film (s21(1)).
[121] Unless these are the same person: s9(2)(ab). [122] s178.
[123] *Adventure Films v Tully* [1993] EMLR 376.
[124] *Beggars Banquet v Carlton* [1993] EMLR 349; *Century Communications v Mayfair Entertainment* [1993] EMLR 335. Thus a commissioner might be, but is not necessarily, considered an author.
[125] *Slater v Wimmer* [2012] EWPCC 7 [72]; Laddie et al. [7.41] suggest that the use of the word 'principal' limits the scope for recognition of those who have made a lesser level of creative input to the film.
[126] *Slater v Wimmer* ibid [80].

in more ad hoc circumstances and thus lack natural candidates for the role of producer and director.[127]

In *Slater v Wimmer*, for example, adventurer Wimmer planned a skydive over Mount Everest, and arranged for Slater, a free-lance documentary-maker, to film it.[128] After the event, both parties used the footage without the consent of the other. Arrangements surrounding ownership of copyright in the film were sketchy, as there was no written agreement and the parties disagreed over the express term in their oral contract. The court was left to decide the matter according to the statutory rules on film authorship. Birss J held that Wimmer was the producer, as it was 'his project' – he had made all the arrangements for the dive to be filmed and had paid the costs of filming, including Slater's travel expenses. Slater was the principal director as 'he decided what to film and how to do it'. This included controlling the settings of the camera and choosing the relevant angles.[129]

The court did not imply any contractual terms requiring the transfer of intellectual property rights from director to producer. Although Wimmer had reimbursed Slater's expenses, he did not make any additional payment for his work as a cameraman. This was seen as indicative of a need for Slater to retain control over the footage, i.e., a copyright interest in the film.[130] The parties were held to own copyright in the film as tenants in common in equal shares.[131] This resulted in what Bonadio characterises as an 'unpleasant lock-in situation', since both director and producer must consent before either may exploit the film.[132] *Slater v Wimmer* illustrates that even the current simplified solution of deemed joint authorship of a film fails to eliminate obstacles to its exploitation. This lock-in situation may seem ironic, given that the default rules on film authorship were originally devised to avoid exactly such a situation.[133]

Slater v Wimmer also highlights that copyright authorship may have real economic value, which individual creators can use as a bargaining chip to ensure fair remuneration.[134] The reasoning in this decision makes clear that it was lack of remuneration for Slater's camera work which left the judge unpersuaded by arguments that a transfer of copyright should

---

[127] Handler (n77) 186–187. [128] (n125). [129] Ibid, [73]. [130] Ibid, [95].
[131] Ibid, [89].
[132] E Bonadio, 'Joint Ownership of Films in the Absence of Express Terms' (2012) 7(7) JIPLP 493.
[133] This would have been the case before the principal director was added as a statutory joint author (see 6.2.1). This situation is avoided in the US where each joint owner has the right to non-exclusively licence uses of the work without the consent of the other joint owners (subject to the obligation to account): MB Nimmer and D Nimmer, *Nimmer on Copyright* (Matthew Bender 2011) §6.10[A][1][a] or [3-36]. Alternative approaches to joint ownership are considered at 8.6.
[134] Kamina (n33) 34.

be implied. In this way, the decision elevates fairness over efficiency, providing an important reminder that it is creators (authors) who are at the centre of copyright law.[135]

As we have seen, the designation of the producer and the principal director as the authors of a film is explained by the need to limit the number of copyright owners to ensure that films might be exploited efficiently (without hold-ups) and investment recouped. Similar concerns underlie the treatment of employee works. In this case, however, the CDPA provides for presumptive employer ownership of copyright in works created by employees within the course of their employment,[136] whilst employees still remain recognised the *authors* of their works.[137] The more restrictive approach to film authorship might be explained by calls for certainty given the high-risk, large capital investment required for many films. But, it is just as likely to be explained by powerful lobbying for special protection by interested parties. Indeed, it is not clear that the current legal position supports certainty, given the complex layers of copyright interests that inevitably subsist in many films.[138]

The term of film copyright is calculated on the 'life plus 70 years' formula, but based upon the date of the death of the last of the following: the principal director; the author of the screenplay; the author of the dialogue; the composer of music specially created for, and used in, the film.[139] This is an unusual provision as copyright law generally adopts the author as the point of reference for the duration of protection and not all the contributors listed here are recognised as joint authors of film copyright.[140] Perhaps this provision is a tacit acknowledgement of the significant creative contributions made by these contributors.[141] In addition, although moral rights usually do not subsist in entrepreneurial works, the principal director of a film is granted certain moral rights which the producer does not

---

[135] *Slater v Wimmer* (n125) [90]. The recognition of the value of creative authorship might seem to sit uneasily here in relation to an entrepreneurial work – film copyright – which protects investment rather than creativity. But the inclusion of the principal director as an author is the result of European harmonisation that adopted the position of most Member States which recognise directors as authors on the basis of their creative contribution to a film. Thus, film copyright appears to be a hybrid between an entrepreneurial and an authorial work: Bently et al. 129.
[136] s11(2).
[137] The different treatment of film might relate to the moral rights consequences of authorship. But these have been modified in the case of employee works (s79(3), s82) and a similar solution could have been adopted for film.
[138] This may not have much of a practical impact, given that the film industry relies primarily upon contract to deal with issues of copyright ownership, 6.3.
[139] s13B. [140] And one recognised joint author – the producer – is omitted.
[141] This provision was added to implement the Term Directive, Art 2(2), which reflects the broader view of film authorship in some Member States.

enjoy.[142] This appears to recognise the creative role of the principal director (the producer is more of an orchestrator than a creator). These provisions on term and moral rights seem to inch towards statutory recognition of the creative contributions contained within a film, despite the fact that this tends to clash with the notion that film is an industrial product. The case law has gone much further, as the next section demonstrates.

6.2.4 Film as a Dramatic Work

Film copyright leaves any underlying rights intact. This preserves the possibility that a film may also be a dramatic work.[143] A dramatic work is described as including a work of dance or mime, but otherwise the statutory definition is open-ended.[144] Case law takes us further and has established that a dramatic work is a 'work of action, with or without words or music that is capable of being performed before an audience'.[145] There must be 'sufficient unity' to a dramatic work for it to be capable of being performed,[146] which is likely to exclude computer games,[147] news reels[148] and sports matches.[149] While a film might be a recording of a dramatic work, following *Norowzian v Arks (No 2)*, it might also be a dramatic work itself.[150] This is significant, because unauthorised *recreation* of a dramatic work is an infringing act, whereas this is not the case in relation to the film copyright.[151] The distinction between the two is best understood by reference to the facts of the case which established the principle.

Norowzian v Arks concerned a short film, 'Joy', made using a technique called jump-cutting which involves deleting some of the frames of the

---

[142] ss77, 80.
[143] T Rivers, 'Norowzian Revisited' (2000) EIPR 389 suggests this was probably not the intention of the legislature. On the debate about overlapping categories of works in film compare I Stamatoudi, '"Joy" for the Claimant: Can a Film Also be Protected as a Dramatic Work' (2000) 1 IPQ 117 and R Arnold, 'Joy: A Reply' (2001) 1 IPQ 10. Films which came into existence before the 1956 Act came into force were, and continue to be, dramatic works or photographs only.
[144] s3(1)(d).   [145] *Norowzian (No 2)* (n7) 367 (Nourse LJ).
[146] *Green v Broadcasting Corporation of New Zealand* [1989] 2 All ER 1056 (PC).
[147] *Nova Productions v Mazooma Games* [2006] EWHC 24 (Ch) [116] this point not challenged on appeal: [2007] EWCA Civ 219; [2007] RPC 25 [3].
[148] Laddie et al. [3.117], 137 also suggests that security footage may not be a dramatic work, although the 'latest 24 hour Internet shows' may be.
[149] Copinger et al. [3-39] consider that although a football match is not an intellectual creation (C-403/08 *Football Association Premier League v QC Leisure* [2012] 1 CMLR 29 [98]), a film of a sports event may be a dramatic work where it has been filmed in such a way as to increase its impact.
[150] Affirmed in *Dramatico Entertainment v British Sky Broadcasting* [2012] EWHC 268, [2012] RPC 27 [63].
[151] *Norowzian (No 1)* (n114).

film. While the film was based upon a recording of a person performing, it was then edited using this jump-cutting technique to create a sequence of movements which would be physically impossible to recreate by an actor.[152] The resulting film was the inspiration for a commercial which depicted a man dancing, with the same surreal effect, in front of a pint of Guinness. The commercial did not infringe the film copyright in 'Joy' because no part of it had been directly, reprographically reproduced. In *Norowzian v Arks (No 1)*, the first instance judge concluded that a film could not be a dramatic work per se, but it could record a dramatic work (although he did not think the 'dance' in Joy was a dramatic work, being incapable of performance).[153] In *Norowzian v Arks (No 2)*, the Court of Appeal disagreed finding that a film was capable of being a dramatic work per se,[154] since 'capable of being performed' included performance by artificial means, such as the screening of a film. In holding that the film itself was a dramatic work, the appellate judges differed in their reasoning.[155] Nourse LJ came to this conclusion in light of the Act's broad definition of a dramatic work, which he thought would often, although not always, include a film. Buxton LJ, on the other hand, considered the need to interpret the CDPA consistently with obligations under International copyright law. As the Berne Convention equates cinematographic works with other authorial works, he reasoned that they ought to be given the same level of protection.[156] This required all cinematographic works to fall within the Act's definition of a dramatic work, even in cases where the particular film did not appear to be a 'dramatic work' in the natural meaning of the term.

It seems likely that the conclusion in *Norowzian v Arks (No 2)* that a film might also be an authorial (dramatic) work was motivated, at least in part, by the need to find a means to recognise and reward creators, given the very thin protection which film copyright provides.[157] Thus, the court side-stepped the UK legislature's approach of treating film as an industrial product (with thin protection and concentrated authorship) and

---

[152] *Norowzian (No 2)* (n7).
[153] It is hard to make sense of this part of the reasoning, because it seems to imply that the underlying dramatic work embodied in the dance had somehow disappeared during the editing of the film. Rivers (n143).
[154] Stamatoudi (n143) criticises the decision, suggesting that a film ought not to be seen as a dramatic work per se. Cf. Arnold (n143).
[155] A film could also be a recording of a dramatic work. In this case there may have been a recording of the dance in the initial film or 'rushes', however, this was not relevant as the claim concerned the particular surreal 'dance' evident in the film. As a result of such extreme editing, the original dramatic work could no longer be said to be recorded in the film (n7) 210.
[156] See Arnold (n143).
[157] A Barron, 'The Legal Properties of Film' (2004) 67 MLR 177, 207 citing the judge's comment that Joy was a 'striking example of the film director's art'.

adopts an interpretation that better reflects creative reality.[158] This provides a more holistic protection than the only other tool available to the court to reward creative contributors: finding they created distinct underlying copyright works (see 6.2.2).[159]

The many films which are the product of editing for dramatic effect will almost certainly amount to dramatic works (a 'film dramatic work').[160] This is in addition to any other underlying dramatic works which the film might record, e.g., the screenplay. The case law on joint authorship makes it exceedingly difficult to predict who the joint authors of a film dramatic work might be.[151] This is reflected in the fact that the main copyright commentaries disagree. Copinger et al. consider authorship to be limited to those 'directly responsible for originating the action' which they suggest includes only the producer and director.[162] Laddie et al. agree that the director would be an author, but consider that in some cases the scriptwriter might also count, and in their view, the producer would not have an authorship claim.[163]

Most contributors to a film that is a dramatic work ought to satisfy the requirement for *collaboration* (or *common design*), unless they are engaged in purely ancillary activities.[164] Arguably, a scriptwriter might not share the relevant common design if the script was written independently and

---

[158] The Gregory Report appeared to consider a film to be a creative work greater than the sum of its parts, although the reforms it suggests do little to recognise this, (n6) 36: ' ... although the functions of actors, actresses, producers, directors, camera-men, creators of scenic effects and so on may be capable of separate analysis, the fact remains that each has little or no significance apart from that of the others and the resulting film itself is an entity which differs from the sum of its parts'.
[159] Nonetheless this approach fails to recognise the creativity of film in its entirety as an ensemble of contributions. Piecemeal protection appears to be the trend (despite *Lucasfilm* (n92)), as explained in many textbooks and the Gregory Report (n6) 37, see text at n105.
[160] This would exclude, for example, surveillance video. [161] Kamina (n33) 157–166.
[162] Copinger et al. [4-22], [4-34] suggest that the authors of the screenplay and any underlying works are not authors of the dramatic work – rather, they are authors of their separate literary or dramatic works.
[163] Laddie et al. [3.120], given the producer's lack of creative input. Laddie et al. also consider that a dramatic work must be a work of entertainment and would exclude from its definition aspects which are fluctuating and indefinite such as actors' performances ([3-44], [3.177]). This cannot be the correct reason for excluding actors from joint authorship of the dramatic work in the context of a film which provides a record of them (as opposed to theatre performances). A better reason would be that they are not a contribution of an authorship-type: *Brighton v Jones* [2004] EWHC 1157; *Hadley v Kemp* [1999] EMLR 589 (Ch) 646.
[164] *Beckingham v Hodgens* [2003] EWCA Civ 143, [2003] EMLR 18. Catering and logistics, for example, provide ancillary support and probably do not share the common design to create the work. A narrow interpretation of collaboration as requiring cooperative acts by all putative joint authors in respect of each draft as was required in *Martin v Kogan* [2017] EWHC 2927 (IPEC) [25] would be unworkable in the context of a film dramatic work which is likely to be assembled from multiple different parts made over a relatively long period of time.

before any concrete plan to make a film had been set in motion. In such a case, the scriptwriter would be the author of the script, but not a joint author of the resulting film dramatic work. Common design may also be lacking where contributors are contracted to provide discrete contributions (e.g., costumes or props) with little knowledge of their work's intended use. (In some cases, these may be protectable as separate works, see 6.2.2).

The requirement that a joint author's contribution must not be *distinct* rarely causes issues in the case law on joint authorship, but it is surprisingly difficult to pin down its meaning. A contribution is probably not distinct merely because it is identifiable or distinguishable. Instead, the question is more likely to relate to whether the work would be different in character without the contribution; or conversely, whether the contribution is dependent upon the rest of the work.[165] In other words, the contribution must be integral to the work.[166] The purpose of this part of the test is to distinguish between a collection of works by different authors (co-authorship); and a joint work, that is, a single work made by multiple authors. Thus, independent authors of individual encyclopaedia entries are not together joint authors of the encyclopaedia as a whole. Where a work is separately exploitable this might seem to suggest that it is distinct. But separate exploitability is probably not a requirement, which makes sense because it is contingent on market factors which may change over time.[167]

Whether or not a contribution is distinct is probably a question of fact and it would seem to make sense to assess this in light of creative realities. Yet, we have seen what appears to be a bias towards treating works separately whenever possible to avoid problems entailed by multiple authorship.[168] This results in the recognition of many layers of copyright protection, which does not avoid the concern that many right holders might hold-up exploitation (which must usually be dealt with via the doctrine of implied licences).[169] This jurisprudential tendency creates great uncertainty as to which contributions to a film are distinct and which form part of the joint work, which further complicates the task of determining the authorship of a film dramatic work.

---

[165] E.g., *Beckingham v Hodgens* [2002] EWHC 2143 (Ch), [2002] EMLR 45 where although the violin part of the song could be identified separately in terms of musical notation, it was not 'distinct' because the part was dependent upon what was already there. It would have sounded odd and lost its meaning on its own.
[166] *Fisher v Brooker* [2009] UKHL 41; [2009] 1 WLR 1764; [2009] ECDR 17.
[167] Kamina (n33) 156, 159 commenting on the 1956 Act.
[168] Certainly courts have preferred to treat preparatory work as separate from the final work: *Martin v Kogan* (n164), *Brighton v Jones* (n163).
[169] As was the case in *Brighton v Jones* ibid.

Kamina considers that those who contribute and arrange the music, the art director, and those who help design costumes, props, etc. would not be considered authors of a film dramatic work because their contributions are separate.[170] Similarly, the screenplay may be distinct from the film dramatic work.[171] Copinger et al. would exclude sets because they are static,[172] but would include sound, lighting effects, dialogue and acting directions.[173] If, as *Lucasfilm* suggests, costumes or props are not independent artistic works because they are a step in the production process of a film, one might assume that the corollary of this reasoning would be that such contributions are not 'distinct' from the film dramatic work (otherwise, potentially authorial work appears to vanish just because it forms part of a collective product). This interpretation, however, does not fit with the Supreme Court's view that props, costumes or sets which are highly imaginative might still be protected as (distinct) artistic works. In light of the foregoing it is clear that the bias towards protection as separate components potentially complicates the task of making sense of the joint work which is left. It is a mere skeleton which bears little resemblance to the work which audiences perceive and which creators believe themselves to be collaborating to create.[174]

Another considerable hurdle is the requirement that a joint author must make a significant contribution of the right kind. The case law provides some indication of the sorts of contributions which will *not* suffice. Most obviously, suggesting the concept or idea for a film is not a contribution of the right kind.[175] *Norowzian* establishes that an editing technique is an unprotectable idea, but this would probably not exclude film editors as they use a combination of techniques to create a particular dramatic feel. Contributions of investment alone (as may be the case for a producer), will not be sufficient as they are not evident in the expression. For similar reasons, certain pre-expressive contributions may not count, for example, design drawings for the set or costumes – although these may be separate artistic works. As 'interpretation' or 'performance' is not seen as an authorship-type contribution, this may

---

[170] Kamina (n33) 162–163.
[171] By analogy with *Chappell v Redwood Music* [1980] 2 All ER 817, [1981] RPC 337 (HL).
[172] (n149) [3-37], [3-84].
[173] [3-92]. Although, curiously, Copinger et al. do not appear to consider their creators likely to be joint authors of a film, perhaps on the basis that these are not significant contributions of the right kind (n162).
[174] It is also at odds with the usual objective approach to determining the boundaries or scope of a copyright work: see n111.
[175] *Tate v Fullbrook* [1908] 1 KB 821 (CA); *Donoghue v Allied Newspapers* [1938] 1 Ch 106 (Ch).

exclude the contributions of actors.[176] Similarly, 'proof-reading' is not an authorial contribution, even when a significant amount of time and effort is expended (as in *Fylde Microsystems v Key Radio Systems*).[177] This might exclude producers who suggest small changes or visual effects technicians who 'clean up' the film removing minor errors. In the case of a theatre production, there is precedent to suggest that the contribution of 'scenic effects' is not sufficient based on the need for certainty in the subject matter of a dramatic work. But these concerns may be less cogent in the context of film.[178]

It is much more difficult to identify *positively* those contributors who make a significant contribution of the right kind. Joint authors are those who originated the protectable elements of the dramatic work.[179] Thus, Copinger et al. suggest this implies contributing something of *dramatic* significance, but this is not easy to pin down and the open-ended statutory definition of 'dramatic work' offers little assistance to put flesh on the bones.[180] Drawing upon the similarities between film and photography may assist. An author makes a relevant contribution to a photograph when they make choices which relate to the subject's pose, the lighting, camera angle, framing, atmosphere and developing techniques, etc.[181] While all of these are relevant to film too, arguably the different medium requires an even broader approach that encompasses any choice that impacts the visual and emotive character of the action as portrayed.

---

[176] *Hadley v Kemp* (n163). Cf. D Free, 'Beckingham v Hodgens: The Session Musician's Claim to Music Copyright' (2005) 1(3) Entertainment and Sports LJ 93. A performance is not a separate copyright work, but an actor may have performance rights in relation to his or her performance; CDPA, Pt II.

[177] [1998] FSR 449 (Ch), although this case might be distinguished on the basis that it concerned a literary, rather than a dramatic, work.

[178] *Tate v Fullbrook* (n175) where the court's reasoning relied upon the requirement that the work be capable of being printed and published in the Dramatic Copyright Act 1833 and Copyright Act 1842. A similar result was found under the Copyright Act 1911 in *Tate v Thomas* [1921] 1 Ch 503 where contribution to scenic effects and stage 'business' were not of the right kind because they were not certain (additionally, suggesting a title and a few catch phrases were negligible contributions). Concerns related to certainty of the subject matter may not apply to film, which provides an accurate and stable recording of scenic effects. Still, there remains the possibility that a court might not consider these to be contributions of the right kind, as matters of theatrical presentation, see *Brighton v Jones* (n163).

[179] Rivers (n143) suggests it is unhelpful that most of the cases concern the very different context of the theatre.

[180] Ibid, (n149) [3-264], [3-388] gives the examples of choice of camera angle, lighting or editing.

[181] *Painer v Standard Verlags* [2012] ECDR 6 [91]. The composition of a photograph, combined with being at the right place at the right time, may also be sufficient: *Temple Island Collections Ltd v New English Teas Ltd* [2012] EWPCC1, [2012] FSR 9 [27].

Some suggests that a dramatic work requires a story.[182] The wording of the CDPA does not justify a requirement for a fully formed narrative, but might require at least some action which communicates a 'message' in a loose sense ('drama'[183]). On this view, the dramatic quality of a dramatic work might reside in the aesthetic aspects of work (its look, feel and sound) insofar as these elements are significant to the communication of a 'story' in the sense described. Thus, an editor who cuts shots together to create the dramatic feel and flow to the action of a film might be a joint author. Similarly, those responsible for the dialogue, acting directions and background music might potentially have a good claim. From this angle, it is difficult to understand why this would exclude the contribution of actors, whose performances certainly influence the emotive and visual character of the action.[184]

Although inevitably context-specific, on this view, the director, the editor, the cinematographer, the music director and even the screenwriter may have supportable claims to be joint authors of the final film dramatic work (assuming that their contributions are not distinct). Whether any other types of contributors count might be eligible for joint authorship is more uncertain. We have seen that a restrictive approach when applying the joint authorship test results in very few joint authors, and those who have heavily invested in the production have a strong incentive to argue for the concentration of the authorship of a dramatic work in their hands.[185]

Based upon the hierarchical organisational structure in film production, one might expect those with control over the creative process (the director or the producer) to argue that as dominant contributors, they ought to be the only authors of a film dramatic work. Yet, the analysis in 6.1 reveals that

---

[182] Kamina (n33) 74–80; Barron (n157) 204 argues that in this way the definition is affected by a bias towards commercial fiction cinema potentially excluding more experimental or avant-garde types of film. On this basis she suggests that stylistic or non-narrative elements might not form part of the protected dramatic work.

[183] *The Oxford English Dictionary* (<www.oed.com>) defines 'drama' as a 'composition in prose or verse, adapted to be acted upon a stage, in which a story is related by means of dialogue and action, and is represented with accompanying gesture, costume, and scenery, as in real life; a play' and a 'series of actions or course of events having a unity like that of a drama, and leading to a final catastrophe or consummation'. 'Dramatic' is defined as: 'Of, pertaining to, or connected with the, or a, drama; dealing with or employing the forms of the drama' and 'Characteristic of, or appropriate to, the drama; often connoting animated action or striking presentation, as in a play; theatrical'.

[184] For an argument for considering a wider range of collaborators (including actors) as authors of dramatic works in the case of theatre, see Rimmer (n31). Both Copinger et al. [3-94] and Laddie et al. [3.47] would exclude an actor's performance from the scope of a dramatic work.

[185] On the other hand, where strong contractual arrangements provide for the assignment of any copyright interest owned by film contributors, production companies may wish to argue that many contributors are authors so as to prolong the duration of copyright (seventy years from the death of the last surviving joint author): s12(2) and (8).

Film

such arguments are blind to the creative reality of film production in which many of the contributors do resemble copyright authors, given the degree of autonomy they enjoy in relation to the form of their contribution (even though their contribution, and their employment, may be subject to another's veto). I argue in this book that judges ought not to be persuaded by the pragmatic instrumental arguments powerful industry players might offer for the concentration of authorship in the hands of dominant/controlling contributors. The following section illustrates some of the pitfalls of this sort of pragmatic reasoning.

6.2.5 The Pitfalls of Pragmatic Reasoning

Although this book is primarily concerned with UK law, a brief digression to consider some recent US cases on the joint authorship of film may be instructive. These cases demonstrate the sort of reasoning which courts might adopt when influenced by pragmatic concerns about joint ownership. They show a restrictive approach, which tends to treat control as a proxy for authorship, taken to its logical conclusion.

In *Aalmuhammed v Lee*, Jefri Aalmuhammed claimed to be a joint author of *Malcolm X*, a film directed, produced and written by Spike Lee (with others).[186] Mr Aalmuhammed had assisted the actor Denzel Washington prepare for the film; reviewed the script suggesting extensive revisions to ensure historical accuracy; directed the actors on occasions; created two additional scenes; translated for subtitles; supplied his voice for voiceovers; edited parts of the film in post-production; and provided technical help in relation to the location. Although he had asked for a credit as a co-writer, he was actually listed as 'Islamic Technical Consultant' and his name appeared far down the list of credits. Judge Kleinfeld acknowledged that Mr Aalmuhammed had made substantial contributions but held, nevertheless, that he was not a joint author of the film.

In reaching this conclusion, the judge considered that the test for joint authorship should be applied strictly in respect of a highly collaborative work. Aside from the usual requirement of making an original (copyrightable) contribution, in his view, a joint author of a film must also have 'superintended' the work by exercising control.[187] Concerns surrounding the efficient exploitation of collaborative work permeate the judge's

---

[186] 202 F3d 1227 (9th Cir, 2000).
[187] Ibid, 1235. Judge Kleinfeld also considered other factors such as objective manifestations of shared intent to co-author and whether the audience appeal of the work turns upon the contributions such that the share of each in its success cannot be appraised; but he stressed that here, and in many cases, control will be the most important factor.

reasoning far more explicitly than anything that might be found in UK joint authorship case law.[188] In particular, Judge Kleinfeld worried that contributors might hold a film entrepreneur to ransom and thus that an expansive concept of authorship would risk discouraging film entrepreneurs from consulting with others for fear of losing control of 'their' work.[189] This line of reasoning led the judge to conclude that authorship of a film would generally be limited to someone towards the very top of the screen credits,[190] implying that a film might be authored by a single individual.[191]

Judge Kleinfeld's approach seems to falsely equate creative control with sole authorship, which – somewhat counter-intuitively – means that few of the most collaborative types of works would be likely to be considered joint works.[192] As Dougherty argues, this approach required the court to ignore the established meaning of a fundamental copyright concept: authorship.[193] Additionally, it was a missed opportunity to formulate a test for the authorship of joint works that fairly rewards contributors for their collaborative contributions.[194] This complex issue was completely avoided, by treating control as a proxy for authorship.

Dougherty points out that an authorship standard based on control (understood in terms of the ability to accept or reject a contribution) is particularly unhelpful in this context. While control is an important factor in determining whether there is a work-for-hire (a work created in the course of employment), it is largely irrelevant to authorship and particularly joint authorship.[195] Further, this approach gives rise to the possibility that a film might have no authors, since it is conceivable that the person or company with overall control makes no contribution to the creative expression.[196]

---

[188] On the influence of such considerations on US courts determining joint authorship claims: S Balganesh, 'Causing Copyright' (2017) 117(1) Columbia LRev 1, 41

[189] (n186) [27]–[28]. In the US the concern is the risk of licences being granted too readily, rather than to hold-ups (because a joint owner might licence a work without the permission of the other joint owners), see ch 2 n175 and n282.

[190] (n186) 1233: 'sometimes the producer, sometimes the director, possibly the star, or the screenwriter – someone who has artistic control'.

[191] Dougherty (n15) 277.

[192] Particularly where the creative process is hierarchically organised. M LaFrance, 'Authorship, Dominance, and the Captive Collaborator: Preserving the Rights of Joint Authors' (2001) 50 Emory LJ 193; S Balganesh, 'Unplanned Coauthorship' (2014) 100 (8) Virginia LRev 1683, 1738.

[193] Dougherty (n15) 275, stressing that authorship relates to a creative contribution to the protected expression.

[194] Dougherty, ibid, argues although the court aimed to increase certainty, departing from precedent in this manner actually creates greater uncertainty.

[195] Ibid, 279. Control may be an important factor, however, in distinguishing contributions to fixation from contributions to original expression (so a scribe/amanuensis, who lacks control over the content/expression of a work, is not its author). Cf. Balganesh (n188).

[196] Dougherty, ibid, 280. This may mean that commercial motion pictures would rarely be held to be joint works.

Dougherty argues that as the judge's concerns relate to issues of joint ownership, they should have been dealt with by reconsidering prevailing interpretations of the consequences of joint ownership (rather than by distorting the joint authorship test).[197] This argument is supported by the findings of this book.

A subsequent case, also from the Ninth Circuit, *Garcia v Google*, hints at some of the strange results that might follow in reaction to this restrictive view of joint authorship.[198] In the first appeal in that case, Judge Kozinski delivered the majority opinion holding that a claim that an actress had copyright in her performance in a short film was likely to succeed.[199] He did not impose the higher standard for authorship developed in *Aalmuhammed* because her claim was in respect of her performance as a separate copyright work and not in relation to the joint authorship of the film as a whole. She was held to have granted the producer an implied licence to reproduce her performance in the anticipated film, a licence that did not extend to its incorporation in the offensive short film that was in fact produced and which differed radically from anything that she could have imagined when cast.

The restrictive approach to the joint authorship test following *Aalmuhammed* would have meant that Garcia had no copyright interest in the film as a joint work (and thus could not request the takedown of the offensive film). Yet, the court was clearly persuaded that Garcia had made an authorial contribution to the film which ought to enable her some control over its subsequent uses. Recognising an additional layer of copyright protection subsisting in her performance, however, is an inadequate response that creates additional complexity and fails to fully capture the collaborative nature of film production.[200] This decision shows how restrictive approach to joint authorship that flies in the face of creative realities might persuade judges to fragment the copyright work in order to provide a remedy for creators.[201]

Judge Kozinski's opinion in *Garcia v Google* was widely criticised[202] and ultimately overturned by the Ninth Circuit sitting *en banc* ('*Garcia II*'[203]).

---

[197] Ibid 281, 306, 319.   [198] *Garcia v Google* 743 F3d 1258 (9th Cir, 2014).
[199] The amended opinion filed 11 July 2014 expresses this with greater equivocation at 11. Garcia's performance could be considered an original work because of the open-ended definition of a 'work of authorship' in the Copyright Act 1976 (US), s102(a).
[200] As argued above: 6.2.4.   [201] The same trend exists in the UK, see 6.2.2.
[202] J Dougherty, 'The Misapplication of "Mastermind": A Mutant Species of Work for Hire and the Mystery of Disappearing Copyrights' (2016) 39 Columbia J L & Arts 463; J Tehranian, 'Sex, Drones & Videotape: Rethinking Copyright's Authorship-Fixation Conflation in the Age of Performance' (2017) 68 Hastings LJ 1319, 1328 notes that twenty-three amicus curiae briefs were filed.
[203] 786 F 3d 733 (9th Cir 2015).

The majority opinion, delivered by Judge McKeown, did not consider that Garcia's performance constituted a separate copyright work. The court was persuaded by Google's argument that this would create a 'Swiss cheese' of copyrights in film with inevitable fragmentation obstructing the further uses of those works.[204] It was unconvinced that the doctrine of implied licences was sufficient to address these complications.[205] In response to this pragmatic concern, the decision presented a narrow view of authorship, suggesting that Garcia could not be an author of her performance because she had no control over its fixation.[206] In reaching this conclusion, the court relied upon its earlier ruling in *Aalmuhammed*, despite the fact that that case concerned a joint authorship claim, whereas Garcia claimed individual authorship of her specific contribution. In so doing, the court appeared to extend the control standard to works of individual authorship where these occur in the context of the production of a film.[207]

In his dissenting judgement, Judge Kozinski accused the majority of making a total mess of copyright law and undermining the rights it grants to creators.[208] He pointed out that the majority's argument that Garcia's performance was not a work rested on the fact that it was created to be part of a later-assembled film, which is contrary to established precedent in seeming to imply that Garcia's copyright disappeared into the film.[209] He expressed his grave concern that this result has the effect of distancing the rewards and incentives of copyright from their intended beneficiaries: creators.

A subsequent case, *16 Casa Duse v Merkin*, takes the control standard even further by combining the reasoning of *Aalmuhammed* and *Garcia II*.[210] The case concerned a director's claim to copyright in respect

---

[204] In the words of the court at 743: 'Treating every acting performance as an independent work would not only be a logistical and financial nightmare, it would turn a cast of thousands into a new mantra: a copyright of thousands'.
[205] Ibid, 743.
[206] In the US a copyright work must be fixed by and on the authority of the author: Copyright Act 1976 (US), s101. Tehranian (n202) 1325, 1344 notes that the author is not usually required to themselves record, or fix, the work and that this interpretation conflates authorship with fixation. For a critique of the role of fixation in conceiving of authorship in the common law: E Adeney, 'Authorship and Fixation in Copyright Law: A Comparative Comment' (2011) 35 Melbourne University LRev 677.
[207] (n203) 742.
[208] Ibid: 749, 751. Although concurring with the majority for other reasons, Judge Watford noted that 'much of what the majority says about copyright might be wrong' (at 747).
[209] Ibid, 750 citing *Effects Associates v Cohen* 908 F2d 555 (9th Cir 1990). Dougherty (n202) 466. This reasoning resembles the approach taken in *Lucasfilm v Ainsworth* (n82) and (n96) where a helmet created as part of a costume made for use in a film lacked independent artistic purpose apparently on the basis that it was merely a component of another 'work of art': the film (see n103).
[210] 791 F3d 247 (2d Cir, 2015). This dispute arose because no work for hire agreement had been made with the director.

of: (i) his contribution to the final version of a film; and (ii) raw footage created during the production process. The Court of Appeals for the Second Circuit held that the director's contribution to the film did not itself constitute an independent work protectable by copyright because he did not have control over its final form (following *Garcia II*).[211] The raw footage was considered to be an earlier version of the final film and the dominant player, the producer, was held to be its sole author based upon his 'superintendence' of the film (following *Aalmuhammed*).[212] In coming to this decision the court considered that it was the producer who had organised the production, hired staff and had decision-making authority with regard to agreements with third parties. These factors were considered more significant than the director's control over the creative aspects of the footage. By electing to vest authorship in the entrepreneur best-placed to exploit the creative work (the producer), the court denied the director *any* copyright interest in the fruit of his creative labours (either as an independent work or as part of a joint work).[213] This line of reasoning, thus, creates a situation with no safety valve for the recognition of important creative contributions to film, which is clearly contrary to copyright law's imperative to incentivise and reward authors.[214]

Unsurprisingly, the court's decision in *16 Casa Duse v Merkin* relied heavily on the same pragmatic instrumental reasoning which was evident in *Garcia II* and *Aalmuhammed*.[215] As Judge Kozinski argued in his dissent in *Garcia II*, and as this book argues, these instrumental concerns are overstated and in trying to address them the court ignores the important role of copyright in providing creative contributors with leverage in order to ensure optimal outcomes of private ordering.[216] Furthermore, as commentators have emphatically pointed out, the control test and the fiction of the dominant author bear no relation to the reality of the creative process of film-making.[217] This trio of decisions demonstrates the difficulties judges

[211] Ibid, 258. [212] Ibid, 260.
[213] A Casey and A Sawicki, 'The Problem of Creative Collaboration' (2017) 58 William and Mary LRev 1793, 1835.
[214] Tehranian (n202) 1357 noting that ' ... *Casa Duse* could be read as consonant with *Garcia II* in that it reaffirmed and extended *Garcia II*'s erosion of intellectual property rights that artists might have in the product of their creative labor'. It also completely circumvents the work for hire rules.
[215] *16 Casa Duse v Merkin* (n214) 258: 'Filmmaking is a collaborative process typically involving artistic contributions from large numbers of people ... If copyright subsisted separately in each of their contributions to the completed film, the copyright in the film itself, which is recognized by statute as a work of authorship, could be undermined by any number of individual claims.'
[216] (n203) 753.
[217] Dougherty (n202) 468 describes the control test as a mutant species of the work for hire doctrine. A Casey and A Sawicki, 'Copyright in Teams' (2013) 80 U of Chicago LRev 1683, 1720.

face when attempting to serve two contradictory purposes: efficient exploitation (apparently requiring a concentration of ownership) and incentivising a range of creative contributions without which there would be no work to exploit. They also provide a cautionary tale which illustrates that a restrictive application of the joint authorship test based on instrumental reasoning can tend to privilege entrepreneurs over creators,[218] in a way that risks distancing copyright not only from creative reality, but also from its fundamental goal to incentivise and reward creators.[219]

6.3 Private Ordering

In practice, the problems of determining the authorship of a film are usually offset by an employer's presumptive ownership of copyright in the works created by his or her employees, combined with use of contracts (express or implied) to transfer copyright ownership from creators to producers/exploiters.[220] The significant costs involved in the production and distribution of films means that it makes sense to concentrate ownership rights in this way.[221] Given the complexity of copyright interests that we have seen may subsist in a film, production companies rely upon contracts with all participating parties to ensure that ownership of all potentially copyright-protected contributions subsisting in a film are assigned over to them. Under the classic studio system that prevailed in Hollywood between the 1920s and late 1940s, all 'talent' was typically employed by a studio under a long-term contract. Now, contributors tend to be hired on a project by project basis as independent contractors rather than employees. This heightens the importance of copyright contracts, because production companies are not presumptive owners of copyright in the works created by those who they commission.[222]

Contracts have generally proved to be an effective tool for regulating ownership issues in relation to film which might explain the lack of

---

[218] Tehranian (n202) 1358–1359.
[219] Tehranian (n202) 1357, 1360, 1365. This controversial outcome has revived scholarly interest in the concept of authorship in US copyright law: Balganesh (n188); C Buccafusco, 'A Theory of Copyright Authorship' (2016) 102 Virginia LRev 1229; Casey and Sawicki (n213); Dougherty (n15) and (n202); Tehranian ibid.
[220] Dougherty (n15) 238, 317–318, 327–333; *Garcia II* (n203) 752. See further: 8.6.1.
[221] Schwab (n42) 149.
[222] G Poll, 'Harmonization of Film Copyright in Europe' (2002) 50 J of the Copyright Society of the USA 519, 532. In the UK commissioners will usually have an implied licence to use the work for the purpose for which it was commissioned: *Robin Ray v Classic FM* [1998] FSR 622 (Ch). In exceptional circumstances where it is necessary to ensure the business efficacy of a contract, a court may impose a constructive trust implying an equitable assignment of copyright to the commissioner: *Griggs v Evans* [2003] EWHC 2914 (Ch), [2004] FSR 31.

litigation in this area.[223] Indeed, in an opinion in 2002, the European Commission cited this as a key factor weighing against the need for further copyright harmonisation in relation to film.[224] The Commission stressed both the practical need to place rights in the hands of the producer and the importance of respecting the basic principles of author's rights protection (granting copyright to creators).[225] Contract law provides a way of satisfying both imperatives.

Uncertainty about the scope of copyright interests and potential conflict of laws issues (for transnational productions) motivate film producers to settle matters related to intellectual property ownership well in advance.[226] Contributors also have an incentive to agree to transfer ownership rights to producers because effective exploitation of the resulting work serves their interests too.[227] Contributors to a film will seldom be able to separately monetise their particular contribution and the film's success is likely to bring with it additional reputational benefits or new business opportunities.[228] This joint incentive to cooperate is often incorporated into film contract terms that link remuneration to a film's commercial success.

The default entitlement under copyright law is important because it assists creative contributors to gain recognition for their contributions and improves their bargaining position in other negotiations (in relation to employment conditions, remuneration, etc.).[229] Contributors might further strengthen their bargaining position through collection action.[230] There are guilds that represents most of the major 'creative' contributors to film: writers, production crew, actors, musicians, cinematographers, producers, directors, independent production companies, editors, etc. There are also craft guilds that represent location scouts, camera technicians, stunt action co-ordinators,

---

[223] G Dworkin, 'Authorship of Films and the European Commission Proposal for Harmonising the Term of Copyright' (1993) EIPR 151, 152; Bently et al. 129.

[224] Report on the question of authorship of cinematographic or audiovisual works in the Community (n32) 691: 'In practice, potential difficulties in exploitation of the works that arise due to the fact that there may be more than one author, are overcome by contractual arrangements.'

[225] Ibid, 4.

[226] EI Obergfell, 'No Need For Harmonising Film Copyright in Europe?' (2003) 4 European Legal Forum 199, 201 disagrees with the Commission's opinion that there is no need to harmonise film copyright provisions for this reason.

[227] Ibid, 200.

[228] Schwab (n42) 149. In *Effects Associates v Cohen* (n209) 559 the court recognised that special effects footage would not be particularly valuable on its own.

[229] Dworkin (n223) 153. In *Effects Associates v Cohen* (n209) 556–557 the court recognised the value of holding a copyright interest in forcing negotiations on issues of rights and price. The court held that in the absence of a contrary agreement, a company that created special effects footage retained a copyright interest in that footage even though it later became part of the film, rejecting an argument that 'moviemakers do lunch, not contracts'.

[230] Datta (n17) 205.

etc.[231] Collectively bargained agreements cover issues including working conditions, pay rates and credit. They reflect a compromise between production companies and other industry players. The guilds can wield significant muscle to protect their membership's interests,[232] including organising collective strike action, such as the highly publicised Writers Guild of America ('WGA') strike in 2008 concerning the calculation of residual payments for the reuse of writers' work in new media.[233]

The film case study shows how the financial and the reputational incidents of authorship are split.[234] Whilst studios/production companies have fought to retain control and ownership of copyright interests in a film, they have conceded to a complicated system of self-regulation of the associated authorship credit in negotiation with the guilds. This system permits some of the visible benefits of authorship to be shared more widely than copyright law might appear to allow.[235] Screen credit is valued because it can affect how much contributors get paid, influences future employment prospects and signals their level of regard within the community.[236] Fisk has undertaken a comprehensive analysis of the WGA process for determining authorship credit, as set out in their Screen Credits Manual, which is enlightening.[237] It is highly bureaucratic, although the process itself is determined democratically by the membership. She reports that the WGA 'treats authorship as an historical fact reflecting degrees of creative contribution to be deduced based on the significance of the various writers' work'.[238] The WGA rules seek to control the number of people that can be credited as a 'writer' so that term retains its reputational value and does not become too diluted.[239] Thus the WGA rules provide a valuable source of information, albeit not the only one, concerning the relative value of different writers' contributions.[240]

---

[231] For a list of film industry trade union bodies, see Copinger et al. [26-246].

[232] Fisk (n9) 13 argues that this is because they are fairly transparent, arise as a result of participatory processes, are fairly equitable and provide due process. The guild procedure does have its limits, as its effectiveness may be undermined by external powers as occurred with the blacklisting of certain writers during the Cold War: Fisk (n4) 231. On the usefulness and limitations of incorporating social norms in legal determinations: 8.1 and 8.2.

[233] More recently, the Screen Actors Guild members voted in favour of strike action in response to the refusal of employers to provide scale wages or residuals in relation to animated programs made for subscription-based streaming platforms: D McNary, 'SAG-AFTRA Members Approve TV Animation Strike Authorization' *Variety* (18 July 2018) <variety.com/2018/tv/news/sag-aftra-tv-animation-strike-1202877662>.

[234] As in the case of Wikipedia (Chapter 3) and scientific collaborations (Chapter 5).

[235] C Fisk, 'The Jurisdiction of the Writers Guild to Determine the Authorship of Movies and Television Programs' (2010) 48 English Language Notes 15 <ssrn.com/abstract=1694043> 8; Fisk (n4) 250.

[236] Fisk (n9). [237] Ibid, 7. [238] Ibid, 8.

[239] Dougherty (n15) 285, n322. The WGA also offers an arbitration service.

[240] Fisk (n9).

Overall, guild rules and procedures represent a workable trade-off between appropriate recognition for creative contributors and efficient exploitation for producers. This results from concentrating the financial and reputational rewards with those whose contributions are considered the most significant.[241] The self-government of credit via bureaucratic procedures somewhat resembles the practices of large particle physics collaborations (see 5.2.2). Similarly, the scheme results in a list of 'authors' which reflects those contributors who have had a substantial impact on the content and form of the work.[242] A crucial difference between the film and particle physics cases, is that the former seeks actively to limit the number of credited writers, a measure which has been adopted to enhance the status of 'writer' vis-a-vis 'director'.[243] This may result in a list that is under-inclusive from a copyright perspective.

Film studios rely on a mix of soft and hard contracts to govern relationships among the multiple parties that supply inputs to any film project.[244] Oral contracts are most frequently used with high-value talent such as actors and directors, even where large sums are at stake.[245] Unsigned 'deal memos' can be used as the basis of an oral contract, especially where it is necessary to act while an idea is still 'hot'.[246] Oral contracts might be used for a number of reasons. They are expedient in terms of time, and as the film industry is fairly close-knit, it avoids the implication of distrust which might surround a demand for signature on a written agreement particularly in relation to powerful individuals who may enjoy a great degree of clout while possessing a sensitive ego.[247] Oral contracts might also be relied upon out of habit, as parties are likely to defer to norms where it is too difficult or costly to work out whether an oral or written contract is best.[248] This explains why some contracts are not formalised, even where this might be relatively easily achieved.

Barnett provides an interesting analysis of the use of 'soft contracts' in Hollywood, which he describes as: 'a mix of legal and reputational governance situated between the standard alternatives of short-term contracting governed solely or primarily by law and repeat-play relationships

---

[241] Ibid, 11; (n4) 244.
[242] Fisk (n4) 218 gives the example of Robert Towne who won the Oscar and got sole credit for the screenplay for *Chinatown* even though the owner of the film had changed the ending to one that he had not written and did not want.
[243] Ibid, 244.   [244] Barnett (n30) explains the economic rationales for doing so.
[245] GM McLaughlin, 'Oral Contracts in the Entertainment Industry' (2001) 1(1) Virginia Sports and Entertainment LJ 101, 103, 118 noting that Charlton Heston did not sign a complete contract prior to filming 60 of his films.
[246] Ibid, 119, 126.   [247] Ibid, 127, 130.
[248] E Posner, 'Norms, Formalities, and the Statute of Frauds: A Comment' (1996) 144 U Pennsylvania LRev 1971, 1974.

governed solely or primarily by reputation'.[249] Parties use ambiguity as to whether a contract indeed exists strategically to manage the 'chicken-and-egg problem': a studio or outside investor may be unwilling to commit definitely until a star is signed up; while the star will not commit until finance has been secured; and the distributor will on come on board only once the star and investor have been contracted.[250] Studios work around this problem by employing time-limited option contracts which condition performance obligations on the occurrence of certain events; or by relying upon a mix of open-ended communications which constitute an 'unsigned deal'.[251] Soft contracts between studios, or other production entities, where there are few major players and high-value 'star' talent seem effective because of reputational sanctions for unreasonable behaviour.[252] In this context, where the same parties need to deal repeatedly with each other, a bad reputation might significantly damage a contributor's career.

Although the film industry manages authorship issues very well through a mixture of hard and soft contracts, there are limitations to private ordering. Contributors in weaker bargaining positions are not always able to adequately protect their interests. This is reflected by the establishment of collective bargaining organisations. The success and endurance of the guild system is a testament to the fact that there is a real need which they address.

6.4 Insights for Copyright Law

Private ordering has been very successful at regulating authorship in film. It has enabled a separation of the economic and reputational incidents of authorship. Both the success of private ordering and the importance of the non-economic (reputational) incidents of authorship demonstrate that many of the assumptions relied upon by what I have termed the pragmatic instrumental approach are mistaken.[253]

Private ordering can offer flexible tailor-made solutions, allowing for the allocation of rights and remuneration in a more context-sensitive way than copyright laws' default rules allow.[254] In the film industry, for

---

[249] Barnett (n30) 608 describes Hollywood's contracting practices as 'an efficient adaptation to an environment characterized by three salient features: high specification and enforcement costs, significant but limited reputational pressures, and high holdup risk and outcome uncertainty'.
[250] Ibid, 619.   [251] Ibid.   [252] McLaughlin (n245) 130.   [253] See further: 8.4.3.
[254] It also leaves this question to those best-placed to understand the nuance of the surrounding factual matrix.

example, authorship is dispersed in film credits in a graduated manner so as to incentivise and reward contributors in a proportionate fashion. Private ordering can also compensate, in part, for the uncertainty in the law. Copyright law, nonetheless, still plays an important normative role in providing good authorship standards.[255] It establishes the default position from which both sides must bargain, and thus, the shadow of the law inevitably shifts the dynamics in negotiations on issues of attribution (credit), remuneration and ownership.[256] As we saw in the conclusions to the preceding chapter, copyright law has the potential to play an important role of protecting the interests of creators who are in a weak bargaining position.

In the world of film, we have traced how authorship historically gravitated to powerful figures with control over the film-making process. This view of authorship is now largely discredited because electing a figurehead author ignores the important contributions of many others. In the film industry, guilds, particularly writers' guilds, oppose use of possessory credits; while in film studies, scholars have all but abandoned auteurism in favour of more inclusive approaches. Yet, copyright law's joint authorship test appears to continue to lean towards a restrictive approach. Such an approach provides non-dominant contributors with no support for their arguments to share in the benefits of authorship.

Copyright law should seek closer alignment with the creative reality of film authorship. This does not preclude the parties from achieving pragmatic solutions for coordinating the exploitation of a work through private ordering. The optimal role for copyright law is to establish default minimum standards.[257] These standards serve to reduce the distance between the bargaining positions of the relevant players. To be useful in regulating film authorship, however, copyright law's standards must relate to the reality of film authorship in a meaningful way.[258]

The legislative solution to the complex problem of determining the authorship of a film, primarily responds to the practical problem that film producers need ownership rights for commercial exploitation of a film. It

---

[255] Handler (n77) 182–192 on the importance of this role for copyright law in the context of film.
[256] Decherney (n3) discusses the impact that copyright law has had on business models in the US film industry over time.
[257] 2.1.
[258] This is not to say that copyright ought to defer to community standards. See further: 8.1 and 8.2

seeks to minimise disruption to commercial practices, seemingly with little regard to protecting *creators*.[259] Yet, as Michael Handler points out, there is little evidence that this approach actually reduces cost of managing rights for film exploitation.[260] In Chapter 1 I observed that copyright law stands accused of having a preoccupation with protecting disseminators of, and investors in, creative works, to the detriment of those who actually create them.[261] Film copyright seems to lend support to this accusation.

The pragmatic legislative approach of designating two contributors as the only authors of a film has failed to create the intended legal certainty.[262] This restrictive interpretation of the work, advocated in the Gregory Report as the antidote to collective authorship, has been by-passed by the court in *Norowzian* in light of the realities of film production. I argue that this has occurred, in part, because the legislative solution clashes with copyright law's imperative to protect creators. In response to this imperative, judges have located two safety valves: (i) recognition of independent copyright works in contributors' separate contributions; and (ii) treating many films as embodiments of dramatic works having an undisputed authorial quality and creative author(s). In light of the contextual approach to the joint authorship test which I argue for in this book, an appreciation of creative realities (including the presence and scope of any common design) should guide which valve is most appropriately deployed in respect of a particular contribution.

The copyright law position on film authorship might appear largely irrelevant, since the film industry seems to function successfully by placing reliance on contract,[263] yet sometimes contracts will not be agreed or their terms will be disputed (e.g., *Slater v Wimmer, Aalmuhammed, Garcia v Google* and *16 Casa Duse*). Copyright law still has an important role to play in acknowledging and rewarding creators in such cases. The predominant concern that unreasonable claims of joint authorship may be brought by relatively minor contributors seems best addressed by greater legal certainty which might be engendered by focusing debate on the quality and quantity of creative contributions required to merit the 'author' moniker.[264]

---

[259] Handler (n77) 177 describes film fixation copyright as a 'triumph of pragmatism'.
[260] As issues of authorship and ownership generally tend to be successfully managed with private ordering. Ibid 183.
[261] J Litman, 'Real Copyright Reform' (2010) 96(1) Iowa LRev 1.
[262] See the discussion of *Slater v Wimmer* (n125) at 6.2.3, although this may be an unusual case. I have argued that most of the uncertainty is due to the complexity of the morass of potential underlying works.
[263] Dworkin (n223) 151, 152.
[264] This reasoning is particularly compelling, since the current legislative solution may still result in hold-ups, e.g., *Slater v Wimmer* (n125), see p178.

Private ordering is not immune from power imbalances. Large motion picture companies are not known for their generosity to relatively minor participants in the film-making process; thus, it seems ill-advised to completely delegate private ordering to remedy all the defects in film copyright.[265] Although private ordering may be ameliorated by collective action and industry standards, these should be underpinned by copyright law which ensures a minimum standard of protection for creators. This reflexivity (between legal and industry standards) might be self-reinforcing, serving to improve the quality of private ordering and provide recourse for creators when no written agreement exists.

In sum, there has been a tension between two competing conceptions of film: (i) as an industrial product made under the organisation of a few entrepreneurs by organising the input of multiple contributors; and (ii) as a work of art based upon the artistic vision of one or two romantic authors/ auteurs. Increasingly, modern conceptions of film authorship in film studies and the film industry resist this false dichotomy. Yet, copyright law appears caught in the dichotomy, whilst being unsure which way to face: conceptualising film in part as an industrial product (the fixation); and in part as a work of art in the many potential layers of copyright protection for authorial contributions. Instead of striving to choose between these two conceptions, or attempting to face both ways at once, copyright law ought to take a third way. I argue that it should embrace an *inclusive, contextual* approach to determining the authorship of a film as a dramatic work.

The current pragmatic instrumental approach to the joint authorship test might tend to lead to authorship gravitating to the most powerful players, or those with the most control. In discussing how US case law concerning film authorship has developed following *Aalmuhammed*, I highlighted the dangers of using power/control as a proxy for authorship. Screenwriters, for instance, provide a very significant kind of creative input, yet notoriously lack any control.[266] Proper recognition that a film is actually *created* by a range of collaborators inputting a variety of skills (each with some autonomy in shaping the form of their contribution), and recognising these contributors as joint authors of that film is clearly preferable to the copyright thicket that results from attempts to accommodate their legitimate interests by creating new layers of copyright. In film, when applying the joint authorship test,

---

[265] Handler (n77); Dougherty (n15) 325. See, for example, the dispute in *Aalmuhammed v Lee* (n186) and the facts of *Slater v Wimmer* (n125).
[266] Dougherty (n15) 294.

the focus should be on the common design of the contributors. This would provide the best point of reference for determining whether a contribution is 'significant' enough to make the contributor a joint author; and also whether the contribution is 'distinct' (thus possibly a separate copyright work).

7 Characteristics of Collective Authorship and the Role of Copyright Law

This chapter draws together the insights from the case studies to reveal the core characteristics of collective authorship and to elucidate copyright law's role in regulating highly collaborative work. The chapter is split into five sections. The first section extracts the features of the creative process which makes collective authorship special, and distinguishes it from both individual authorship and collaboration involving only a few people. The second section explores the range of meanings which 'authorship' might have in different collective authorship groups. The third section identifies two significant gaps between copyright law's assumptions about authorship and the reality of collective authorship. The fourth section evaluates the private ordering mechanisms which collective authorship groups have adopted to bridge these gaps and the final section identifies the complex role that copyright law currently plays in the regulation of collective authorship.

7.1 The Nature of Collective Authorship

The special characteristics of collective authorship provide important insights about the nature of the collaborative process. The case studies demonstrate that collective authorship, by its very nature, differs from individual authorship and even some collaborations involving only a few people, in that it necessarily requires:
(i) a division of labour;
(ii) the sharing of responsibility for the intellectual content of a work among the contributors; and
(iii) social norms which regulate the creative process.[1]

This book argues that these unique characteristics should be taken into account when copyright law's joint authorship test is applied to a work of collective authorship.

---

[1] Here, 'social norms' is used in a broad sense to refer to the rules, standards and attitudes arising from community interactions, which govern and inform participants' behaviour and thoughts. See further: 8.1.

The first characteristic – a division of labour – arises from necessity owing to the numbers of individuals involved. Contributors to works of collective authorship often make highly-specialised, diverse contributions. This division of labour may be structured hierarchically, as is often the case for commercial feature films, or it may develop in an organic, ad hoc way as seen on Wikipedia. The division and distribution of tasks might be fluid (e.g., Wikipedia) or fixed, as in Indigenous communities, where an individual's contribution to an artistic work is restricted by factors such as descent, initiation and permission from elders. Although division of labour is inevitable whenever a work is created with more than one person's involvement, it is particularly significant for large groups. The way in which work is shared among contributors reveals much about how a group 'authors' a work.

As a result of the sheer number of collaborators, each usually enjoys significant autonomy in relation to the form of their own contribution. This is particularly likely to be the case where collaborators are highly specialised. It then proves impossible, or at least impractical, for one person to have 'hands-on' control over the activities of every contributor, as we saw in the film[2] and science[3] examples. In these cases, delegation of creative control is essential, at least to some degree, if contributors are to perform their roles effectively. Even where a strict hierarchy is in place, contributors – other than those undertaking simple mechanical tasks – are likely to enjoy significant freedom as to the final form their intellectual input takes. Directions 'from above' typically require interpretation, making personal choices (or 'originality' in copyright terms) inevitable in their implementation. This diffuses creative control throughout the body of contributors.

In the case studies, Wikipedia contributors have the greatest degree of autonomy over their creative efforts, since anyone can add, change or delete content from Wikipedia (although their contribution, in turn, can easily be reverted or changed by another contributor). Yet, even the Indigenous artists who, being bound to observe customary law, have their creative freedom most strictly curtailed retain scope to add their own personal touches.[4] This suggests that in large collaborations,

---

[2] For example, although a producer might express the desire that a costume reflect a particular aesthetic, the costume designer might take inspiration from a variety of sources and come up with costumes that reflect his or her view of how that aesthetic is best realised.

[3] The head of a scientific research project, for example, may not have the knowledge or expertise to understand the work of all its contributors. This means that he or she can only direct the activities of other contributors in a general sense and must leave a large measure of creative control in the hands of each contributor.

[4] Doubts about the originality of Indigenous art, in copyright terms, were laid to rest in: *Milpurrurru v Indofurn* (1994) 54 FCR 240 (Fed. Ct. of Australia).

Collective Authorship and the Role of Copyright Law   203

authorship is distributed widely, that is, many contributors make contributions of an authorship-type in the copyright sense. This remains true even where it is possible to identify some contributors – be it an elder, director, film producer or laboratory head – who have *more* control over the creative process than the rest. This second characteristic of collective authorship – many contributors share responsibility for the intellectual content of the work – would support an inclusive approach to determining the authorship of such works for copyright purposes.

Indeed, in contrast to the restrictive trend that emerges from some copyright cases,[5] we have seen that the idea that collaborative work might be 'authored' by a dominant individual because of their overarching influence on the creative process is now considered outmoded in most of the non-legal scholarship reviewed in this book.[6] Historians of science have revealed that valuable inputs from technicians were downplayed (their names erased from records of their work), while the groundbreaking work of the 'Alvarez group' was only possible because of the combined efforts of the many scientists united behind the name of the one 'sacralised' individual.[7] Neither practice sits well with the modern and inclusive attribution practices in science. Similarly, film theorists now typically regard auteurism as a fallacy that relied upon artificial strategies to 'prove' a director to be the sole author of a film, despite the myriad of other contributors who brought the director's instructions to life.[8] Most film theorists now conceptualise a film as a product of multiple authors, even though they may disagree on who those authors are. Although 'authorship' has different meanings for different creative groups and different academic disciplines, scholarship seems united in a trend away from the collapsing of authorship into singular romantic author figures. Yet, surprisingly few have advocated how – or indeed that – this (re-)conceptualisation should be translated into a reformed joint authorship test.[9]

The case studies reveal a third characteristic which results from the autonomy evident among collaborators in collective authorship groups: a mechanism must exist to coordinate group behaviour towards the collective goal. We have seen that such coordination problems tend to be solved by

---

[5] See 2.2.3 and 2.3.2.
[6] The seminal work Roland Barthes and Michel Foucault has had significant impact in this respect: R Barthes, 'The Death of the Author' in S Heath (trans) *Image, Music, Text* (Fontana, 1977) 142; M Foucault, 'What is an Author?' in D Bouchard (ed) *Language, Counter-Memory, Practice: Selected Essays and Interviews by Michel Foucault* (Cornell UP 1977).
[7] 5.1   [8] 6.1.
[9] 2.5.1. On the value of a closer alignment of copyright law to creative reality, see 2.5.4 and 8.1.

relying upon prevailing social norms within the particular creative community/subcommunity; or, where these are inadequate, developing new norms tailored to suit the collaboration. Wikipedia, for example, has developed norms which foster the community spirit needed to motivate contributors. Social norms often embody collaborators' shared views about the creative process.[10] They can operate to regulate attribution practices and they can establish the benefits (and attendant responsibilities) of authorship. In this way, social norms often reveal predominant views about what distinguishes a mere contributor (who might warrant acknowledgement) from an 'author' who can be held responsible for the work. Social norms, thus, provide a useful metric for assessing the value, or significance, of an individual's contribution within a particular creative context.

The way in which social norms regulate the creative process reveals an important aspect of the nature of a work of collective authorship. Although social norms vary substantially from collaboration to collaboration, as was evident from the differences between biomedical science and particle physics collaborations,[11] a common linking factor is that contributors do more than merely making an individual contribution to the work. By their actions and attitudes, they also have a role to play in creating, observing and enforcing the social norms which govern the creative process. Thus, a work of collective authorship is best conceptualised as greater than the sum of individual contributions[12]. In this manner, the dynamics of the creative process of a group are different from that adopted by an individual creator. Rarely is it accurate to conceive of collective authorship as involving many contributors acting as metaphorical arms, mechanically implementing one person's vision. A search to find the one (or few) controlling mind(s) to label as the work's 'authors' seems fundamentally to miss the point of how large groups work together to create a work of collective authorship.

7.2 The Meaning of Authorship for Each Collective Authorship Group

This section employs the case studies to enhance our understanding of what authorship means (how authorship is attributed and what this signifies) in the different cases of collective authorship. Four propositions emanate from this analysis:

---

[10] Norms have been described as the grammar of social interactions: C Bicchieri, *The Grammar of Society: The Nature and Dynamics of Social Norms* (CUP, 2006).
[11] 5.2.
[12] This maps onto the conception of a work of joint authorship assumed by the CDPA (2.2, p34).

1. Authorship has a different meaning in each collective authorship group;
2. Authorship signifies responsibility for the work according to community-specific criteria;
3. Authorship signals status within a particular community; and
4. Power dynamics can affect the attribution of authorship.

I consider each proposition in turn, highlighting its significance for copyright law.

7.2.1 Different Meanings of Authorship

Just as the dynamics of creativity differ in each case study, so too does the meaning of the 'author' label. This is because in each creative community, authorship has a different role to play according to that community's values. These values determine who is deemed to merit the title of author as well as the benefits and responsibilities that this status entails. The different meanings of authorship have been considered in some detail in the previous chapters, so in this section, it is sufficient to collate the findings.

In Chapter 3, I argued that the Wikipedia community has created a tailor-made concept of authorship suited to the project's needs. Authorship on Wikipedia is an inclusive and community-orientated notion founded on sharing. It is a dynamic concept that is defined in terms of participation in a project with altruistic goals. 'Good' Wikipedians (who adhere to its goals and policies) are rewarded whereas 'bad' contributors will (at best) find their contributions 'reverted' or (at worst) will be banned from contributing further.

Australian Indigenous communities understand authorship very differently.[13] Here, authorship of Indigenous art is an act of cultural and religious significance that expresses and maintains a community's relationship to the land, its culture and ancestors. Indigenous art serves to preserve, sustain and transmit important cultural beliefs and Indigenous artists act as custodians of this cultural knowledge. The ritual knowledge depicted in an artwork belongs to the community as whole. The artist, as a custodian of ritual knowledge, is held responsible for its use or potential misuse.[14]

In science, written publications are the main channel for the dissemination of findings amongst the scientific community, so that new claims may be evaluated, replicated and ultimately accepted into the canon of scientific knowledge.[15] Although the idea of the scientific author is open to different interpretations, what is common is that authorship carries

[13] 4.1.   [14] p 111.   [15] 5.1.

both a credit value, or mark of scientific achievement, and a responsibility value. An author must adhere to the requirements and ethical obligations of the scientific method or risk reputational harm. The responsibility value attached to a particular claim establishes its trustworthiness in support of science's epistemological aim to produce knowledge or 'truth'.

The concept of authorship in film has faced constant siege from different interest groups.[16] Historically, authorship tended to gravitate either to those who exercised the most creative control or to the entrepreneurs who financed the project. Now, authorship is more of a marketing tool having a brand-like 'quality' function. While actors' names might sometimes be used in a way which suggests quasi-authorship, typically it is the director and/or producer who will be held responsible for the overall film. Film authorship remains hotly contested, although the trend is towards a more inclusive approach. Recourse to listing contributions in film credits serves as a pragmatic compromise, bestowing the impression of an authorship hierarchy without fixing precise boundaries of the concept. These credits have significant reputational consequences within the industry.

When applying the joint authorship test a court should be aware that authorship has different meanings in different contexts and that attribution practices vary between collective authorship groups and over time.

7.2.2 Authorship Signifies Responsibility for the Work

Although authorship has different meanings in different creative contexts, it has a stable core feature: in every case study, authorship signifies responsibility for what is seen as meaningful in a work. The kinds of inputs that are valued depend upon the authorial group and tend to include many different types of contributions to the creative process.

In the case studies, the value of contributions tends to be assessed by reference to their role in the *creative process* rather than by reference to the final form of the work alone. For example, creative contributions to film are more highly valued than technical or mechanical contributions. Directors and producers have a special responsibility for the aesthetic content and success of a film as they are in a position to coordinate the efforts of many of the other participants. The value of a particular contribution to a scientific article is assessed by reference to the process-orientated requirements of the scientific method as well as the ongoing ethical requirements embodied in Merton's norms.[17] Wikipedia contributors are similarly assessed according to adherence to the project's own

[16] 6.1.   [17] Chapter 5, p 133.

policy norms, which have been crafted to reflect its aims.[18] Indigenous art forms part of the process of handing down cultural knowledge from one generation to the next. The artist is responsible for the faithful and respectful depiction of ritual knowledge in accordance with customary law. In each case, the final form has been shaped in accordance with the common design of the contributors. This collective focus on process highlights the shortcomings of attempting to assess the significance of a specific contribution to a collaborative work based upon the final artefact in isolation.

This focus on meaningful contribution to the creative process best fits with Laddie J's broad approach to the idea/expression dichotomy in *Cala Homes* (which prioritises the concepts and emotions embodied in the *content* of the protected expression, over the mechanical fixation of its final *form*). This broad approach is also a good fit for a key characteristic of collective authorship: shared responsibility for the creative content among many contributors. In Chapter 4, I argued that such an approach would have allowed for the recognition of the communal origin of the artwork in *Bulun Bulun*, as it was the community's contributions which made the artwork meaningful from an Indigenous point of view.[19]

In some case studies, the view that authorship signifies responsibility for the work has resulted in a gradation of authorship. On film credits, for example, producers and directors are usually listed first so they would, no doubt, count as authors; whereas, a contributor towards the end of the list (e.g., caterers, logistical support) would probably not count. We have seen how the film industry leverages this ambiguity to its advantage by designating responsibility for specific aspects of the production process, thereby avoiding selective distribution of the label 'author'.[20] In scientific collaborations, the order in which a contributor is listed in the by-line communicates information to the scientific reader about their importance and their role.[21] Although copyright has a mechanism for recognising

---

[18] Chapter 3, p 74–75.

[19] The contributions of the Indigenous community are evident in the expression of the artwork in the same way that the design director's contributions were evident in the drawings made by draftsmen in *Cala Homes v Alfred McAlpine Homes* [1995] EWHC 7, [1995] FSR 818. The court's narrow approach to the idea/expression dichotomy in *Bulun Bulun* might be the result of a cultural bias in favour of those contributors who most closely resemble the romantic author. See 4.2.3.

[20] Although those who make contributions which are recognised to be 'creative' tend to find it easier to establish that they are authors than those whose contributions are regarded as purely technical (6.1). The connection between authorship and creativity is reflected in the CDPA both in the definition of the author as the 'creator' of a work and also in the more generous scope of copyright awarded to authorial works as opposed to entrepreneurial works (2.1).

[21] 5.1.

different shares of responsibility as joint ownership might arise in unequal shares, there are no particular provisions relating to the order of attribution of authorship.

In sum, as the dynamics of authorship vary greatly, the case studies suggest that it would be inaccurate to evaluate a contributor's contribution in isolation from its context in a particular collaboration. This might be achieved by giving the collaboration limb a greater role in the application of the joint authorship test.[22] Further, a joint author's level of contribution should be reflected by deviating from the default presumption that joint authorship results in joint ownership in equal shares.

7.2.3   Authorship Signals Status within a Particular Community

In many contexts, authorship credit is used as a reward for accumulated labour to a particular project (for example, scientific collaborations, Wikipedia and film). The attribution of authorship is also used to signal belonging to, or an elevated status within, that community. This is evident most strongly in the case study of Indigenous art. The whole process of the creation of Indigenous artworks (including the apprenticeship and initiation of artists, etc.) promotes community cohesion and helps socialise young members of the group into a particular worldview. All members of the group have an ongoing connection to the artwork and artists have a special place in the hierarchy of access to cultural knowledge as custodians of ritual knowledge.

Authorship indicates belonging to a particular joint endeavour and is inextricably linked to community norms.[23] The reputational benefits of authorship within authorial communities are often valued more highly than copyright ownership. Indeed, in the context of collective authorship, authorship is sometimes consciously distanced from remuneration (Science, Wikipedia, Indigenous art) and from control (Wikipedia). This view of authorship contrasts starkly with the typical economic incentives-based view of copyright law that assumes authors are motivated by the ability to control reproductions of their works in order to recoup royalties (see 7.3). This aspect of collective authorship also reinforces the need to keep the concepts of authorship and ownership separate in copyright law, given the important ramifications of authorship in the CDPA other than copyright ownership, for example, the right to

---

[22] As argued at p 34.
[23] For example, positive contributions to Wikipedia can build the esteem of a particular contributor among the community of regular contributors; collectively, such contributions help constitute the culture of sharing which sustains Wikipedia (3.1). As to the value of norms in regulating collective authorship groups, see 7.1.

attribution. Furthermore, it provides an additional reason for an inclusive approach to the joint authorship test, as the reputational value of authorship credit might provide a more efficient incentive than those premised upon financial remuneration.[24]

7.2.4 Power Dynamics Affect the Attribution of Authorship

The case studies illustrate that the attribution of authorship in collective authorship groups may be influenced by power dynamics within those groups. In the context of biomedical science, there are ongoing controversies about inappropriate attribution practices, which tend to favour powerful players. Senior scientists and heads of laboratories often ask to be added to the list of authors on an article where they could not be reasonably considered responsible for the scientific work in it. Sometimes these figures are added without their knowledge as a way of increasing the likelihood of publication of the article. There are equivalent practices in film where authorship has historically tended to gravitate to the most powerful players such as the director (with creative control) or the producer (with financial might and possibly also creative control). The endurance of possessory credits, despite strong resistance from many film contributors, is a testament to the ability of powerful players (in this case directors) to claim more than their authorship share.

As demonstrated by the US case, *Weissmann v Freeman*, discussed in Chapter 5, copyright law has the potential to act as a bulwark against such power dynamics by ensuring that authorship is allocated based upon an appropriate kind of contribution that is evident in the expression of the work. In this way, copyright law can provide an independent authorship standard detached from the power dynamics that operate in collective authorship groups.[25] In the context of film (Chapter 6), I argued that copyright might provide an important default standard that weaker parties can use to improve their bargaining power in contractual negotiations and collective action in relation to authorship issues such as credit or remuneration. Thus, copyright law has an important role to play in supporting positive

---

[24] In addition, copyright law can have value to creators as a source of legally sanctioned authorship standards, which might be used to bolster claims for authorial recognition or greater remuneration.
[25] UK courts have similarly resisted simply adopting industry views on authorship out of concern that these may reflect power dynamics which unfairly deny authorship credit to less influential contributors: *Bamgboye v Reed* [2002] EWHC 2922, [2004] 5 EMLR 61 [79]; *Brown v Mcasso* [2005] FSR 846 (EWPCC) [44]; *Fisher v Brooker and Onward Music* [2006] EWHC 3239, [2007] FSR (12) 255 [45], [46], [60], [62].

social norms and undermining negative ones that may not be compatible with copyright law's core notion of authorship.[26]

7.3 The Gap between Copyright Law's Assumptions about Authorship and Creative Reality

There is a twofold gap between copyright law's assumptions about authorship and the creative reality of collective authorship. First, copyright law's assumptions about the motivations for authorship often do not correspond with the primary motivations for creation in cases of collective authorship. Second, the attribution and regulation of authorship is often nuanced and varies greatly in different creative contexts, whereas copyright law appears to take a standard one-size-fits-all approach to the regulation of authorship and its incidents. In this respect, collective authorship groups tend to take an inclusive approach, whereas there is a trend in some copyright cases towards a restrictive approach.

The fact that contributors to works of collective authorship are often motivated by intrinsic reasons suggests that an economic-incentive based view of copyright is incomplete. The primary motivation for creativity in the contexts of Wikipedia, science, and Indigenous art seems unrelated to concerns about royalties. Wikipedians contribute to Wikipedia for fun, out of boredom, for altruistic reasons, or because they might gain esteem within the community of regular contributors. In science, recognition by academic peers and reputational benefits are key motivating factors for authorship. Indeed, scientists may actively distance themselves from financial incentives because disinterestedness is one of the foundational norms of science. Although the sale of artwork can be an important lifeline for Indigenous communities, the creation of art is first, and foremost, a matter of religious and cultural significance. Even in the context of film, the most commercially significant case study, some contributors will accept less remuneration in return for a better credit (which has significant reputational value).

In some cases, a sharing economy is an important factor in motivating contributions.[27] The success of Wikipedia is often attributed to a sense of

---

[26] On the value of linking authorship to responsibility for the creative content of a work, rather than other more nebulous connections, see p 145.

[27] Sharing economies (also known as gift or reputation economies) often operate in opposition to the market economy (e.g., Wikipedia and science). The opposition between these two different systems of exchange, might also explain arguments that Indigenous peoples risk losing an important dimension of their traditional cultural expressions by trying to fit them into Western categories of protection for cultural property which are premised upon its commodification (4.4). On copyright law and the commodification of culture: A Barron, 'The Legal Properties of Film' (2004) 67 MLR 177; F MacMillan, 'The Cruel C: Copyright and Film' (2002) EIPR 483.

community that is sustained by many individual acts 'donated' to the shared project. Indigenous art is seen as cultural property belonging to the relevant Indigenous community and scientific articles are presented as 'gifts' to the scientific community.

Credit is highly valued because of the reputational benefits that it might bring. Contributors to works of collective authorship often value credit more than financial benefits or even control. The importance of credit is evident in the fact that particle physics collaborations tend to establish authorship protocols to govern how credit will be distributed before any measurements are taken. In the case of film, the possessory credit (which suggests that a particular person is *the* author) is widely seen as an illegitimate power grab, which undermines the sharing of authorship or quasi-authorship among many contributors in the otherwise extremely inclusive film credits. Similarly, scientific journals record much academic debate about which contributors in large collaborative projects deserve to be credited and the order in which they ought to be credited.

This suggests that there are good reasons to ensure that authorship and ownership are treated as distinct concepts in the CDPA. This is because authorship leads to moral rights (including a right to attribution) as well as economic rights.[28] The experience of collective authorship suggests that in determining who counts as an author it is better to ensure that enough creators can access the right of attribution, than to restrict authorship on the basis that this might streamline the economic exploitation of the work.[29] This is further supported by the fact that ownership issues tend to be successfully managed with private ordering (see 7.4).

This book forms part of the growing body of literature that suggests that the economic incentive justification for copyright law is incomplete.[30] The persuasiveness of the economic incentive theory is often thought undermined by the existence of fields in which creativity

---

[28] Only the latter might be assigned.
[29] The latter approach cannot be guaranteed to be truly effective, unless authors are reduced to one. In the case of some highly collaborative work, a restrictive approach might even result in an authorless work, see: FJ Dougherty, 'Not A Spike Lee Joint? Issues in the Authorship of Motion Pictures Under US Copyright Law' (2001) 49 UCLA LRev 225, 280.
[30] J Silbey, *The Eureka Myth: Creators, Innovators, and Everyday Intellectual Property* (Stanford Press 2014); D Zimmerman, 'Copyright as Incentives: Did We Just Imagine That?' (2011) 12 Theoretical Inquiries in L 29; N Elkin-Koren, 'Tailoring Copyright to Social Production' (2011) 12 Theoretical Inquiries in L 309; K Raustiala and C Sprigman, 'The Piracy Paradox: Innovation and Intellectual Property in Fashion Design' (2006) 92 Virginia LRev 1687, 1762–1765.

thrives despite an absence of intellectual property protection ('IP's negative spaces').[31] The case studies considered in this book provide a more direct challenge to the incentive theory, because they concern copyright law's heartland as they involve works that fall neatly within the copyright law's rules of subsistence. The case studies are also not confined to small creative niches, but rather concern activities of significant cultural and economic importance. In light of the limitations of this traditional economic incentive justification for copyright law, this book provides support to arguments for a re-examination of the influence of the 'incentive story' on copyright law and policy.[32]

The attribution of authorship is far more nuanced in creative communities than it appears to be in copyright law. Copyright tends to assume that authorship is a binary question: either you are an author or you are not. Yet for many collective authorship groups it is possible to have different degrees of authorship according to the significance of the contribution to the whole. In film and science, author lists or 'credits' tend to be long. In these contexts, the order in which contributors are listed is of great significance and affects the associated the reputational value. The current approach to the joint authorship test lacks an appropriate framework for taking these subtleties into account. Whereas copyright case law has often preferred a simplified, restrictive approach to determining joint authorship, collective authorship groups usually embrace more complex, inclusive methods. The copyleft licences which govern Wikipedia, for example, require attribution of all contributors (although filtering out trivial contributions is permitted).

The example of collective authorship demonstrates that copyright law seems disconnected both from common motivations for creativity and from the ways in which authorial groups value their own creative activities.[33] In light of this disconnect, it is unsurprising that most collective authorship groups turn to private ordering mechanisms to regulate their own creative practices.

---

[31] For example, the activities of magicians, chefs, comedians, etc. Rosenblatt (n12) provides an overview of the literature, drawing together common themes to construct a theory of IP's negative spaces. See also Chapter 1, n65.

[32] Zimmerman (n30) 58.

[33] This finding is supported by empirical scholarship: CJ Buccafusco, 'On the Legal Consequences of Sauces: Should Thomas Keller's Recipes Be Per Se Copyrightable?' (2007) 24 Cardozo Arts & Entertainment LJ 1121; D Oliar and C Sprigman, 'There's No Free Laugh (Anymore): The Emergence of Intellectual Property Norms and the Transformation of Stand-up Comedy' (2008) 94 Virginia LRev 1787; E Fauchart and EA von Hippel, 'Norm-Based Intellectual Property Systems: The Case of French Chefs' (2008) 19(2) Organization Science 187.

7.4 Bridging the Gap between Copyright Law and Creative Reality with Private Ordering

In this section I consider the private ordering mechanisms that collective authorship groups have adopted to bridge the gaps between copyright law and creative reality. Private ordering is a fairly broad term that can be understood as referring to a variety of regulatory mechanisms which do not originate from the state.[34] In the case studies, the attribution of authorship and its consequences have frequently been affected by such mechanisms. These have included: journal guidelines, contracts, collectively bargained agreements, protocols, codes of conduct, copyleft licences and social norms. In general, the attribution and consequences of authorship tend to be fairly successfully managed by collective authorship groups with private ordering mechanisms. This ought not to be surprising, as Ellickson and others have shown that people generally rely on norms and customs to govern their behaviour, rather than resort to law.[35]

I begin by considering the most successful examples of the regulation of authorship issues with private ordering, before turning to those that are less successful. This helps to identify the benefits and the limitations of private ordering as a mode of regulation. I then interrogate the assumption integral to the pragmatic instrumental approach, that groups of authors are unable to effectively arrange the exploitation of their work, and consider the role which copyright law might play to mitigate against the limitations of private ordering.

7.4.1 Successful Examples

The most successful examples of the regulation of authorship (and its incidents) with private ordering mechanisms in the case studies are Wikipedia, particle physics collaborations and film.

Copyleft licences are crucial to the success of Wikipedia, because they facilitate the highly iterative process of creation that it relies upon.[36] Each contributor, when submitting their contribution to the site, must agree to

---

[34] MJ Radin and RP Wagner, 'The Myth of Private Ordering: Rediscovering Legal Realism in Cyberspace' (1998) 73 Chicago-Kent LRev 1295 noting that many such mechanisms rely upon the law of property or the law of contract; S Schwarcz, 'Private Ordering' (2002) 97 Northwestern U LRev 319, 324.

[35] In his seminal work on the social norms that operate among farmers and ranchers in Shasta County, California, Ellickson suggested that legal theorists persistently overestimate the role of law in regulating conduct. R Ellickson, *Order without Law: How Neighbours Settle Disputes* (Harvard UP 1991) 137–138, 280–281. See also E Posner, *Law and Social Norms* (Harvard UP 2009).

[36] 3.3.

allow anyone to reproduce, change or delete their contribution for free at any time in the future. This provides subsequent contributors with a defence to potential future claims of copyright infringement in respect of previous contributors' contributions. Copyleft licences allow for the constant re-working or refactoring of Wikipedia pages in real time (without the need to pay royalties or ask for permission). The licences alleviate uncertainty about who might count as an author by treating all contributors equally. They allow the community to tap into some of the values of copyright law's notion of authorship whilst discarding others. They also provide for ways of attributing authorship that are adapted to the internet age.[37]

Copyleft licensing also plays a subtler role on Wikipedia. The association of copyleft licences with the Creative Commons movement and free software community bolsters the sharing ethic which motivates many Wikipedia contributors. This creates a community spirit that encourages more positive than negative contributions to Wikipedia. The role of copyleft licenses as an embodiment of Wikipedia's social norms is far more significant than their role as legal instruments. The most significant force governing the social incidents of authorship are these social norms, which are developed and implemented by regular contributors. Contributors create and enforce these norms when they engage in the behind-the-scenes parts of Wikipedia (for example, awarding each other 'barnstars', reverting the contributions of vandals, or participating in the resolution of disputes).

In the context of science, protocols developed by particle physics collaborations have been effective in regulating the complex authorship issues that arise in large collaborations.[38] These protocols enshrine mechanisms of ensuring group responsibility for the scientific content of collectively authored articles. Preliminary versions of articles, for example, may be posted on an internal webpage where all members of the collaboration may comment on them. Mechanisms for determining the attribution of authorship may vary depending upon the context; for example, attribution practices might differ in relation to journal articles and conference papers. These protocols have enabled particle physics communities to use credit liberally as a reward for accumulated labour, whilst ensuring that the group takes responsibility for the scientific content of articles. As these protocols are often determined before most of the research has been undertaken, they shape the expectations of all contributors who join the collaboration from the outset.

[37] For example, by including a hyperlink to the Wikipedia page concerned, see p 91.
[38] 5.2.2.

In the film industry, private ordering mechanisms have also tended to be very successful.[39] Most authorship and copyright ownership issues appear to be quite well managed with contracts. This is important given the high risk, high investment nature of the film business. The existence of guilds enables contributors to boost their bargaining power via collective action as well as improving the quality of contractual negotiations.[40] Indeed, collective bargaining by guilds has been a significant force in the negotiation of terms for members on issues of pay, conditions and credit in some sectors; whereas, those not represented by a guild, such as the visual effects sector, struggle to negotiate favourable terms. Soft contract measures (e.g., option agreements and unexecuted contracts) are also used to promote cooperation whilst maintaining flexibility. These place reliance upon the prevailing industry social norms and the possibility of reputational sanctions to maintain reasonable conduct by the parties.

7.4.2 Less Successful Examples

Private ordering has proved less successful in the regulation of authorship issues in the case of Indigenous art and biomedical science collaborations.

Within Indigenous communities, customary law is effective at regulating the creative process and the consequences of authorship. Yet, as customary law is not enforced by the Australian legal system, it is ineffective vis-à-vis outsiders. Most scholars agree that copyright law provides inadequate protection for the range of interests that Indigenous communities seek to protect in their artwork. Indigenous communities have sometimes turned to private ordering to attempt to address these gaps. Codes of conduct and protocols have only tended to be successful in regulating the conduct of those who are already motivated to respect Indigenous communities' interests. Additionally, contracts are of limited use because Indigenous artists are likely to be in a relatively weak bargaining position and even favourable contractual terms do not bind third parties.[41]

---

[39] 6.3.

[40] An interesting example of informal collective action in the context of theatre is the reported actions of the cast of the musical *Hamilton* who secured a profit-sharing agreement following an impassioned letter to the lead producer stressing their invaluable contributions in the shaping of the show during rehearsals: R Morgan, 'How *Hamilton*'s Cast Got Broadway's Best Deal', *Bloomberg*, 28 September 2016 <www.bloomberg.com/features/2016-hamilton-broadway-profit/>.

[41] 4.3. Attempts to adopt a collective trade mark have similarly been unsuccessful. Although the main reason that this scheme was abandoned was because it was poorly drafted and ineffectively publicised; it is unlikely that such a market-based solution would be effective, as consumers may not make the effort to seek out and pay more for genuine Indigenous art (particularly in the tourist market).

Biomedical journals have adopted guidelines, such as the ICMJE's triple-lock formula, that attempt to restrict the number of contributors who can be credited as authors on articles.[42] It is possible to surmise that these have proved largely unsuccessful, because they do not reflect the reality of collective authorship, for the reasons which have been explored already, based upon the necessary division of labour and resulting dispersion of 'creative' control. They tend to ignore the powerful value of authorship credit in facilitating collaboration, encouraging and rewarding contributors for participating in a joint project. The guidelines have lacked success because they have been imposed 'top down' with too little regard for the causes of credit inflation and without genuine consent from all those to whom they apply.[43] They can tend to reinforce, rather than alleviate, the power dynamics which may operate in biomedical collaborations. Junior contributors may be ill-placed to resist requests for 'guest authorship' from their seniors, and are more likely to be made a 'ghost author' on publications to which they have made substantial contributions.[44]

7.4.3 The Benefits and Limitations of Relying upon Private Ordering

The case studies demonstrate suggest that using private ordering mechanisms to regulate authorship has strengths and weaknesses. The most obvious benefits are flexibility and efficiency.[45] Private ordering might also have intrinsic benefits, such as promoting creators' autonomy, self-determination and liberty. There are limits to the desirability and effectiveness of private ordering mechanisms where there are imbalances of power; where they are imposed top-down on those who have not consented to them; and when there are public interests at stake. The analysis of private ordering in this section leads to a number of insights for copyright law: (i) private ordering is often a desirable way of regulating authorship; (ii) public structuring of private ordering (in the sense of legal constraints) is necessary to minimise the limitations of such mechanisms; and (iii) the general success of private ordering mechanisms in regulating issues related to the exploitation of collective authorship works suggests

---

[42] See 5.2.1.
[43] Private ordering is generally seen as undesirable where there is no genuine consent. This explains the existence of legislation restricting the use of contracts of adhesion and consumer protection law in general. See JH Reichman & JA Franklin, 'Privately Legislated Intellectual Property Rights: Reconciling Freedom of Contract with Public Good Uses of Information' (1999) 147(4) U of Pennsylvania LRev 875.
[44] Worse still, pharmaceutical companies may be able to undermine the spirit of the guidelines by selectively applying them; see p 142–143.
[45] M Lemley, 'Intellectual Property and Shrinkwrap Licenses' (1995) 68 Southern California LRev 1239 outlines the benefits of contract.

that the pragmatic instrumental approach is based upon flawed assumptions.

The most significant benefit of private ordering is that it provides flexibility and efficiency.[46] This includes the ability to adapt regulatory strategies over time and to changing circumstances. Particle physics collaborations, for example, each have their own protocols and committees to deal with authorship issues. Protocols might be amended, and committees might act, to adapt practices to changing circumstances. There are usually different rules of attribution for different contexts and dispute resolution procedures. Some methods of private ordering offer more flexibility than others. Copyleft licences, for example, adopt a fixed 'standard form' which may be difficult (or impossible) to amend, and lack interoperability with other similar licences.[47] Yet, it is worth remembering that I have argued that the primary role of copyleft licences is to support the social norms that govern creativity on Wikipedia (and those social norms are very flexible).[48]

Private ordering allows communities to tailor their responses to regulatory challenges.[49] In this way, private ordering might be better able to reflect the concerns of the relevant players, than judges and legislatures who have access to a much smaller regulatory tool box.[50] Public ordering is more restricted in its approach to regulatory challenges, especially where it needs to be generalisable as in the case of legislation.[51] The CDPA, for example, provides broad categories of works for which there is a single definition of authorship and a single joint authorship test.[52] Thus, although

---

[46] J Macey, 'Public and Private Ordering and the Production of Legitimate and Illegitimate Rules' (1997) 82 Cornell L Rev 1123; S Dusollier, 'Sharing Access to Intellectual Property Through Private Ordering' (2007) 82(3) Chicago-Kent LRev 1391 notes the use of private ordering to expand or change the operation of rights, which has been observed in the case of Wikipedia, see 3.3.

[47] RW Gomulkiewicz, 'Open Source License Proliferation: Helpful Diversity or Hopeless Confusion?' (2009) 30 Washington UJ of L and Policy 261.

[48] 3.3. On the usefulness of relying upon social norms to regulate behaviour: 8.1. Wikipedians have also developed numerous policies and guidelines for governing Wikipedia content as well as a range of dispute resolution procedures: 3.1.

[49] Dusollier (n46).

[50] W Fisher, 'Property and Contract on the Internet' (1998) 73 U Chicago-Kent LRev 1203, 1252.

[51] M Madison, 'Legal-ware: Contract and Copyright in the Digital Age' (1998) 67 Fordham LRev 1025, 1137.

[52] Whether or not the definition of authorship is truly unitary is up for debate. Some cases appear to suggest that the category of work affects the type of contribution required to count as an author, e.g., *Sawkins v Hyperion Records* [2005] EWCA 565, [2005] 1 WLR 3281; *Interlego v Tyco Industries* [1989] AC 217 (PC), etc. It is uncertain whether this will still be the case, as the current European jurisprudence seems to suggest a unitary definition of authorship following Case C-5/08 *Infopaq v Danske Dagblades Forening* [2009] ECR I-6569: see Chapter 2, n47 and n70. Yet, the type of work in question may still affect the sorts of choices which indicate that it is the author's own intellectual creation, see p 24, n47.

a literary work may be a novel, a scientific journal article, a page of Wikipedia, a computer program or a database, the same definition of 'work' and 'author' will apply to it. Private ordering allows for more varied conceptualisations of authorship and its consequences than the CDPA's one-size-fits-all regime. The case studies suggest that private ordering permits a very wide range of different approaches to regulating the attribution and the consequences of authorship. In this way, private ordering seems to support a greater diversity of creative models, some of which may be impeded by the ordinary operation of copyright law (e.g., Wikipedia). These models can provide lawmakers with a source of inspiration and, over time, they might provide valuable information on the merits of a range of different approaches to the regulation of creativity.[53]

In order for private ordering to work well, it appears that the interests of the relevant parties should be represented in the private ordering process. This can be seen from the unsuccessful top-down attempts of biomedical journals to change the attribution practices of large collaborations.[54] By involving members of the collaboration in decision-making, particle physics groups have been able to regulate authorship issues more successfully than biomedical journals.[55] Copyleft licences are successful at regulating authorship on Wikipedia even though they are a top-down regulatory mechanism which reflects the will of strong norm entrepreneurs (e.g., Creative Commons).[56] The crucial difference is that they are a good fit for supporting the social norms that govern authorship on the Wikipedia project and which arise from consensus-driven measures that are created, and consented to, by the community of regular contributors (and thus are adequately representative).[57] Additionally, they are egalitarian in so far as they do not favour one category of contributor over another.[58]

---

[53] On the value of allowing the flourishing of different normative networks: M Iljadica, *Copyright Beyond Law: Regulating Creativity in the Graffiti Subculture* (Hart Publishing 2016) 286.
[54] 5.2.1.   [55] 5.2.2.
[56] This may be changing as copyleft licences become increasingly prevalent and widely accepted in particular domains, such as self-publishing on the internet. F Marrella and CS Yoo, 'Is Open Source Software the New Lex Mercatoria?' (2006–7) 47 Virginia J of International L 807.
[57] This is a feature of norms which makes them amenable to incorporation in judicial decision-making: 8.2, 8.3.
[58] J Rothman, 'The Questionable Use of Custom in Intellectual Property' (2007) 93 Virginia LRev 1899, 1971 considers copyleft licences favourably because they have 'aspirational goals'. Others are concerned about their tendency to enshrine a view which might devalue authorship, making free access to works the politically correct way for an author to exercise his or her rights: S Dusollier, 'The Master's Tools v the Master's House: Creative Commons v Copyright' (2005) 29 Columbia J of L and Arts 271, 288 (comparing them to other social constructions which can operate to undervalue labour).

In some situations, the most efficient solution may be to allow groups to regulate authorship themselves via private ordering.[59] Indeed, much of the literature on social norms stresses their ability to ensure efficiency and welfare maximisation. Social norms and other forms of private ordering may reduce the cost of regulation in terms of capital and labour. The parties themselves are in the best position to evaluate the advantages of different regulatory arrangements. Private ordering, thus, increases the possibility of finding consensual solutions that reflect the preferences of all the parties.[60] In addition, private ordering allows for different standards of authorship in different contexts, which makes them flexible in a low-cost way.[61]

Proponents of private ordering (via social norms) claim that they are most effective at regulating tight-knit communities.[62] This may explain why particle physics collaborations have been more effective at regulating authorship issues than biomedical collaborations. Wikipedia is created by a large disparate group of volunteers located all over the world – yet, is also very successfully self-regulated. The architecture of the wiki software, active 'behind-the-scenes' areas and the use of automated tools to perform repetitive maintenance tasks are crucial in this respect because they provide tools to facilitate the development and enforcement of consensus-based policies in the absence of proximity between contributors. Perhaps, then, the key to successful governance via social norms is iterative transactions, rather than the presence of close-knit community.[63]

Private ordering, particularly contract, has sometimes been supported on the basis that it promotes individual liberty because it increases choice.[64] Private ordering is also thought to have the intrinsic benefits of promoting autonomy and self-determination.[65] This is most likely to be the case where self-regulation arises as a result of a fair, transparent, representative procedure agreed by consent.[66] Where the group

---

[59] Macey (n46) 1140.
[60] R Mnookin, 'Divorce Bargaining: The Limits on Private Ordering' 18(4) J of L Reform 1015, 1018.
[61] Fisher (n50) 1211–1212, 1237–1239. According to Mnookin, ibid, private ordering might avoid resort to litigation thus reducing public and private costs as well as minimising emotional upset (taking the example of divorce settlements).
[62] Ellickson (n35) 156–166.
[63] T Sagy, 'What's So Private About Private Ordering' (2011) 45(4) L and Society Rev 923 (arguing there is an important relationship between private ordering and social hierarchy).
[64] Mnookin (n60) 1018.
[65] K Bowrey, 'Alternative IP?: Indigenous Protocols, Copyleft and New Juridifications of Customary Practices' (2006) 6 Macquarie LJ 65.
[66] Mnookin (n60) 1019 argues that capacity is a limit to private ordering, given that it presupposes rational, well-informed, self-interested participants. The possibility of temporary diminished capacity or 'transactional incapacity' is discussed by R Eisenberg, 'The Bargain Principle and its Limits' (1982) 95 Harvard LRev 741, 763.

concerned is marginalised, it is sometimes seen as an especially desirable means of regulation, provided self-regulation bolsters self-determination.[67] Yet, private ordering has not proved an effective means for Indigenous communities to enforce their interests in art. This is because the application of customary law within an Indigenous community does nothing to promote self-determination in relation to the wider Australian community which does not support customary law with legal sanctions. This reveals another characteristic of private ordering: it is most effective when supported and structured by public ordering.[68]

Private ordering is highly susceptible to imbalances of power and other defects of the market.[69] This potentially limits the usefulness of relying on private ordering unless players are in a reasonably equal bargaining position.[70] Thus, Indigenous artists have found contracts to be a relatively unhelpful tool, given they tend to be in a weaker bargaining position than those with whom they are contracting. Different types of contributors to films have organised themselves in talent guilds to promote their interests and shape contractual negotiations on issues of pay, credit and working conditions. Collective bargaining is an effective way of ensuring solutions to the regulation of authorship issues that adequately reflect the interests of different parties, because it can help redress the imbalances of power between them. Law also has a significant role to play in redressing power imbalances to ensure that private ordering functions effectively.[71] There are many examples of legal rules that exist to shape private ordering in this way, for example, the *contra proferentum* rule in contract law,

---

[67] Private ordering may be seen to promote cultural autonomy: G Barzilai, *Communities and Law: Politics and Cultures of Legal Identities* (U of Michigan P 2003) 13.

[68] G Dinwoodie, 'Private Ordering and the Creation of International Copyright Norms: The Role of Public Structuring' (2004) 160 J of Institutional and Theoretical Economics 161.

[69] Mnookin (n60) 1017, 1024–1031 arguing that relative bargaining power is one reason to limit private ordering (the others being capacity concerns and externalities).

[70] In some situations, for a variety of reasons, people might not be thought to have the capacity to properly consent to private ordering: Mnookin (n60). There do appear to be cases involving Indigenous art where capacity to understand the full implications of a contract could be called into question – as may have been the case in *Yumbulul v Reserve Bank of Australia* [1991] FCA 332, 21 IPR 481 (Fed. Ct. of Australia); see p 110 and also Arts Laws' experiences, p 108. There are a number of examples of Indigenous artists selling their artwork in circumstances of undue influence or unconscionable conduct, see J Oster, 'Proposal for a Regulated Indigenous Art Industry' (2006) 6 (18) Indigenous L Bulletin 21.

[71] R Mnookin and L Korhauser, 'Bargaining in the Shadow of the Law: The Case of Divorce' (1979) 88 Yale LRev 950, 968 arguing that legal rules create bargaining endowments or 'bargaining chips'. This affects negotiations because it modifies the parties' best alternative to a negotiated agreement (BATNA). R Fisher and W Ury, *Getting to Yes: Negotiating Agreement without Giving In* (Houghton Mifflin 1981) 45 explain the role of the BATNA concept in negotiation.

equitable doctrines such as unconscionability, and consumer protection law.

Another well-recognised limit is that private ordering is indifferent to the interests of third party 'outsiders',[72] as well as important public interests.[73] Contract law shapes private ordering to constrain these potential limitations.[74] Thus, it imposes limits on the freedom to contract to promote economic public order (e.g., free competition) and protective public order (e.g., to protect weaker parties to transactions).[75] Similarly, fundamental rights often trump private ordering.[76] Private ordering might sometimes conflict with other important policy goals that are embodied in legislation.[77] The extent to which private ordering can be used to avoid copyright law's standards, for example, is a matter that has caused much scholarly debate.[78] On the question of authorship, the situation is relatively clear: authorship is ultimately a legal question, not a matter of agreement.[79] When it comes to determining the authorship of a copyright work, the CDPA provides a definition that embodies a balance of the policy goals that copyright law seeks to achieve: a contribution of creative or intellectual choices to the protected expression.[80]

Private ordering's indifference to outsiders[81] is not the only issue. Sometimes, it fails to represent the interests of all those to whom it applies.[82] For these reasons, despite the benefits of private ordering in terms of efficiency, dynamism and contextualism, there remains an important role for law in helping to address some of the limitations of

---

[72] Lemley (n45) 1285.
[73] N Elkin-Koren, 'What Contracts Cannot Do: The Limits of Private Ordering in Facilitating a Creative Commons' (2005) 74 Fordham LRev 375, 1197–1199; Mnookin (n60) 1017, 1031–1035.
[74] Mnookin ibid, 1031.
[75] L Guibault, *Copyright Limitations and Contracts: An Analysis of the Contractual Overridability of Limitations on Copyright* (Kluwer Law International 2002) 123.
[76] Guibault ibid.
[77] Mnookin (n60) 1016 stresses the importance of considering fairness and other societal considerations.
[78] E.g., Elkin Koren (n73); Madison (n51); Guibault (n75).
[79] This point is discussed in Copinger et al. [4-38]. See also *Samuelson v Producers Distributing* [1932] 1 Ch 201, (1932) 48 RPC 580, 586; *Wiseman v George Weidenfeld* [1985] FSR 525.
[80] See 2.1. Thus, for example, the requirement of a contribution to expression (rather than ideas) ensures a robust public domain; whilst the requirement for a contribution of creative choices ensures that the author has made a contribution to culture (in the words of B Kaplan, *Unhurried View of Copyright* (Columbia UP 1967) 46 'to make the copyright turnstile revolve, the author should have to deposit more than a penny').
[81] J Weinberg, 'ICANN and the Problem of Legitimacy' (2000) 50 Duke LJ 187, 191, 257. Schwarcz (n34) 324.
[82] A good example is contracts of adhesion: Radin and Wagner (n34) 1311–1313.

private ordering and in protecting important public interests.[83] Eric Posner argues that there is an important place for law in enhancing good social norms and undermining bad ones.[84] To this end, Catherine Fisk suggests that community practices on the attribution of authorship ought to be assessed in relation to six criteria: transparency, participation, equality, due process, efficiency and substantive fairness.[85]

Overall, issues relating to the ownership of copyright subsisting in a work of collective authorship generally appear to be successfully managed with private ordering. Most contributors to films, for example, sign contracts with the production company at the outset assigning their copyright interests. Powerful players sometimes use options and unexecuted contracts, relying upon social norms and default legal rules as a disincentive for unreasonable behaviour. This gives them increased flexibility and helps individuals manage the large risks involved in film projects. Some collective authorship groups are unconcerned with remuneration and thus are able to resolve ownership issues very easily. Wikipedians, for example, all agree to copyleft licences that remove any possibility of ownership conflicts, because they agree not to exercise their rights to control or remuneration as a condition of participation in the project.

Scientific authors often assign (or exclusively licence) their copyright interest to journal publishers as a condition of publication. This act concentrates ownership rights in a single entity. Even where this is not the case as, for example, with open source publishing, scientists are often happy to allow reproductions of their work because the reputational value of authorship increases on wide distribution. Royalties for individual scientific journal articles are likely to be negligible (or nil in the case of open source publishing). Conflicts on issues of copyright related remuneration are unlikely to arise because this conflicts with science's norm of disinterestedness. Disputes amongst scientific authors are far more likely to occur on matters relating to the attribution or false attribution of authorship than they are on ownership issues.[86] From these examples it appears clear that the issue of coordinating ownership and the exploitation of works is often not as problematic as the pragmatic instrumental approach assumes it to be.

---

[83] Radin and Wagner ibid 1317 stress the importance of a baseline of due process and public policy limits on contractual private ordering.
[84] Posner (n35).
[85] C Fisk, 'Credit Where It's Due: The Law and Norms of Attribution' (2006) 95 Georgetown LJ 49. These factors have much in common with the vectors that Rothman uses to assess whether a custom ought to be incorporated into a copyright decision: J Rothman, 'The Questionable Use of Custom in Intellectual Property' (2007) 93 Virginia LRev 1899; see, further, 8.2 and 8.3.
[86] *Noah v Shuba* [1991] FSR 14 (Ch); *Weissmann v Freeman* 684 FSupp 1248 (SDNY, 1988), 868 F2d 1313 (2nd Cir, 1989); *Anya v Wu* [2004] EWCA Civ 755.

Whilst private ordering can be a good way of bridging the gap between copyright law and creative reality, we have seen that private ordering is less effective where there are imbalances of power between parties and where there are broader public interests at stake. These limitations of private ordering indicate that there remains an important role for copyright. In particular, copyright can provide a source of authorship standards that are independent from imbalances of power within the creative authorship group. Copyright law's default standard can help shape private ordering to further important policy goals, particularly, copyright law's purposes to reward and incentivise *creators*. Therefore, there is an important role for copyright law in shaping private ordering.[87]

Private ordering and the law might interact in two main ways. First, private ordering might be within a range of valid alternative regulatory mechanisms that the law tolerates (or even upholds).[88] Second, private ordering may be taken into account in the application of legal rules, as part of the matrix of relevant facts. In this section, I have been mostly concerned with the first type of interaction, by considering how collective authorship groups use private mechanisms to tailor the legal provisions to meet their community's creative needs. For example, scientific collaborations and films have used private ordering mechanisms to encourage contributors by implementing a gradation of authorship credit, which provides for more possibilities than the CDPA's binary author/non-author approach to attribution. The private regulation of attribution in this way is permitted by copyright law in the sense that it is not prohibited.[89] It may even be upheld as a result of the operation of statutory presumptions on authorship.[90] This is a useful example of how the legal regime leaves space for parties to resolve certain issues in a manner that better suits their needs via private ordering. There is an important role for public ordering in shaping these private ordering mechanisms.[91] In relation to the gradation of authorship credit, copyright

---

[87] Private ordering often presupposes some public ordering: Radin and Wagner (n34) 1296; S Dusollier, 'The Master's Tools v the Master's House: Creative Commons v Copyright' (2005) 29 Columbia J of L and Arts 271; (n46).

[88] Or even actively encourages: Mnookin (n60) 1036 argues that the primary function of the legal system at the time of divorce is to *facilitate* private ordering.

[89] L Bently and L Biron, 'Discontinuities between legal conceptions of authorship and social practices: What, if anything, is to be done?' in M van Eechoud (ed) *The Work of Authorship* (Amsterdam UP 2014) 237.

[90] ss 104 and 105.

[91] Dinwoodie (n68); L Guibault, 'Wrapping Information in Contract: How Does it Affect the Public Domain?' in L Guibault and PB Hugenholtz (eds), *The Future of the Public Domain: Identifying the Commons in Information* (Kluwer Law International 2006) 87, 103 notes that public ordering governance regimes have an important symbolic role in that they embody the idea that certain activities are so important that they ought not to be

law provides a basic structure for private ordering practices by providing that certain contributors (in certain circumstances) have a legally enforceable right to be included (the attribution right where it is asserted); and certain people have the right to not be included (the right to object to false attribution). The next section of this chapter further considers the role of copyright law in collective authorship.

The following chapter considers the second way in which private and public ordering may be enmeshed. In that chapter I consider the extent to which social norms ought to be taken into account in the application of the joint authorship test. Social norms, it must be observed, are a form of private ordering. An important distinction ought to be made at this point. Although social norms might be evidenced by private ordering mechanisms, such as protocols or contracts; those mechanisms are not coterminous with the social norms. In the following chapter I suggest an inclusive, contextual approach to the application of the joint authorship test, which takes into account the social norms which operate to regulate creativity in cases of collective authorship. I also consider the limits of such an approach. But first, I review the complex role that copyright law currently plays in the regulation of collective authorship.

7.5 The Role of Copyright Law and Its Concepts

Copyright law forms part of the background upon which collective authorship groups organise their creative activities. Rosemary Coombe argues that law and culture relate to one another in an 'ongoing mutual rupturing'.[92] Indeed, culture also appears to influence law. Some have suggested that copyright law has been influenced by the literary trope of the romantic author. I have argued that copyright decisions necessarily involve aesthetic criteria and that judges are likely to be influenced by prevailing cultural values.[93] The opposite is also true, that is, that copyright law influences cultural practices. The example of collective authorship reveals that copyright law does not always affect cultural practices in straightforward ways. Copyright law can modify the bargaining positions of contributors in private ordering processes. Copyright law can provide a source of good authorship standards (although these might sometimes be reinterpreted). In other cases copyright's normative force is reshaped and

---

manifested purely in private transactions. Thus, she argues that privatisation regimes that undercut this symbolic role are presumptively offensive.

[92] R Coombe, 'Contingent Articulations: A Critical Cultural Studies of Law' in A Sarat and T Kearns (eds) *Law in the Domains of Culture* (University of Michigan Press 1998).

[93] 2.3.3. See Chapter 4 for a critique of the influence of Western notions of authorship in copyright decisions on Indigenous art.

repurposed in order to better suit the needs of the collective authorship group. Murray, Piper and Robertson suggest that intellectual property is often appealed to in creative communities in 'pragmatic ways, opportunistically and instrumentally'.[94] Their suggestion appears to be borne out in the case studies on collective authorship.

Copyright law is sometimes looked to for its expressive function, that is, its capacity to provide an authoritative pronouncement on authorship. The attribution of the label of 'author' in copyright law has significance for the public at large because intellectual property law can serve as a valuable source of default rules, policy and public interest safeguards.[95] Copyright law pronouncements on authorship have a symbolic meaning that can support or detract from certain contributors' abilities to assert that they are authors. Copyright law also provides an important default legal position that can help or hinder contributors in negotiations with other contributors as well as with investors or distributors.

Copyright law is clearly a matter of great importance in the film industry as a tool for investors to ensure that they can recoup their investments.[96] Production companies and other investors carve up the distribution and licensing rights to a film.[97] Indeed, Hollywood studios are probably best conceived of as intellectual property management companies rather than film producers. There is a preference for private ordering in the film industry due to the size of the investment involved in making a film and the 'tentpole' model of some film production businesses which rely on revenue from a few big successes to sustain a number of ongoing projects which may not make a profit.[98] Contributors generally sign contracts which involve the assignment of copyright in their contributions to the producer or production company even where they negotiate some share of resulting profits. Although there is a strong preference for the resolution of intellectual property issues via contract rather than in accordance with the default position provided by copyright law, the default legal position matters as it might offer important bargaining chips which can increase the bargaining power of contributors.[99]

---

[94] L Murray, S Tina Piper and K Robertson, *Putting Intellectual Property in Its Place: Rights Discourses, Creative Labor, and the Everyday* (OUP 2014) 14.

[95] J Pila, 'Authorship and e-Science: Balancing Epistemological Trust and Skepticism in the Digital Environment' (2009) 23 Social Epistemology 1; RC Dreyfuss, 'Collaborative Research: Conflicts on Authorship, Ownership and Accountability' (2000) 53 Vanderbilt LRev 1161; R Coombe *The Cultural Life of Intellectual Properties: Authorship, Appropriation and the Law* (Duke UP 1998), particularly the Introduction.

[96] 6.3.   [97] 6.3.   [98] p 163.

[99] The amount of lobbying on the question of film copyright (notwithstanding the prevalence of private ordering) attests to the value of default standards in boosting claims to authorship and ownership.

In bargaining, contributors stress the 'creative' nature of their contributions in order to strengthen their claims to remuneration or credit. Yet, interestingly, most of the language in the film industry tends to avoid use of the term *author*. The relevant textbooks speak of rights management, residuals and 'credits'.[100]

Even where copyright law is seen as irrelevant, or an obstacle to the joint project (e.g., Wikipedia), it has a valuable, but covert, role to play. Wikipedia's culture of sharing both relies upon, and is partly constituted by, copyleft licences. The fact that copyleft licences rely upon copyright law for their effectiveness and as a source of standards means that the shadow of copyright law still casts itself over the norms which operate to create and regulate this alternative system of self-regulated creativity. The Wikipedia community taps into some of the values of copyright's notion of authorship, whilst discarding others. Contributors retain copyright in their contributions and in choosing to forgo many of the benefits of that copyright interest in the name of the Wikipedia project they help constitute the sharing norms which sustain the community. Despite the fact that Wikipedia's model of creativity seems to resist copyright law's notion of authorship, Wikipedia affirms the importance of copyright law and significant resources are spent flagging and removing copyright infringing content. There is even a 'barnstar' available as a community reward for this activity. In some ways the fact that contributors are seen to be contributing something of value (both intrinsically valuable and recognised as copyrightable) bolsters Wikipedia's sharing economy.

In a sense, the indiscriminate use of copyleft licences has the effect of amplifying authorship, as every contributor purports to licence their 'rights' regardless of how great or small their contribution may be. Copyleft licences establish a presumption that subsequent contributors must follow its terms in order to copy or modify a contribution. This may not always be strictly true from a legal point of view.[101] More contributors enjoy the right to be attributed as authors under the terms of copyleft licences than they would under moral rights provisions. In this way, copyleft licences expand authorship rights in one sense (attribution), whilst contracting them in another (control).

---

[100] E.g., P Bloore, *The Screenplay Business: Managing Creativity and Script Development in the Film Industry* (Routledge 2012); G Doyle, *Understanding Media Economics* (2nd edn, Sage 2013); D Gray, *Setting up and Managing a Production Company* (Medialex Publications 2006).

[101] For example, at least in the UK, bare licences or copyleft licences likely operate only as a defence to a claim of copyright infringement, which will not arise for trivial contributions, since copyright will not subsist. See, further, 3.3.

Sean Seymore argues that the authorship crisis in the biomedical sciences might be addressed by realigning journal practices with (US) copyright norms, which would restrict the attribution of authorship to fewer contributors.[102] Yet in making this argument, he may overstate the usefulness of those standards. Seymore fails to engage with the scholarly critique that the joint authorship test is ill-equipped to deal with large-scale collaboration and he elides the potential mismatch between copyright and science's different concepts of authorship. The analysis in Chapter 5 shows that the authors that UK copyright law would select are unlikely to align with those who ought to be considered responsible for an article from a scientific point of view. This is even more likely if US copyright norms are appealed to given the highly restrictive approach to joint authorship which prevails in that context.[103] This provides an example of the tendency observed by Murray, Piper and Robertson, to refer to intellectual property standards in pragmatic, opportunistic and instrumental ways.[104]

Seymore's analysis does suggest an important basic component of copyright authorship which seems attractive. That is, the fact that copyright law identifies the author as the creator of the expression (content) of the work. In this way copyright law provides support for the normative view that those responsible for creating the work *qua* copyright work, are authors. The difficulties of establishing scientific responsibility are exacerbated as attribution is increasingly distanced from responsibility for the creation of the content of a work. Indeed, many of the most problematic practices involve the attribution of those who have had very little to do with the creation of the work (gift authorship, coercion authorship, mutual support authorship), or the failure to attribute those who were closely connected to its creation (ghost authorship). In this respect copyright law's notion of authorship might provide a good source of standards (although the scientific author and the copyright author will likely never perfectly align).

This appeal to copyright norms might appear surprising in the context of science, since the two appear to have little in common. Many of science's assumptions are opposite to those of copyright law. Copyright law assumes that authors want control over their works, which may allow them to extract royalties for uses of it. Science, on the contrary, values openness and economic disinterestedness. Yet, there is some convergence between these two worlds on the issue of authorship. Copyright is necessary for scientists to be able to publish their work in reputable journals.[105] Publication is important for science, and copyright facilitates this by allowing publishers

[102] See p 144. [103] 2.5.3. [104] Murray, Piper and Robertson (n94) 14.
[105] Cf. the open science movement which is gaining increasing momentum, particularly, in response to the perceived expensiveness of scientific publications and unfair commercial practices of some of the larger scientific publishers. See: A Swan, 'Open Access and the

to profit from publications without fear of free-riding. Whilst royalties might not be a relevant concern for scientists, the accurate attribution of authorship to the creators of the work is important because authorship is a locus for credit and responsibility within the scientific community.

Although copyright law has an important role to play as a source of good authorship standards, the dominant approach to the joint authorship test in the UK leaves it ill-equipped to play this role. In Chapter 1, I observed that many copyright scholars suggest that the joint authorship test might not be well-adapted to collective authorship. The analysis of all the case studies have borne this out, revealing that the pragmatic instrumental approach is based upon a number of incorrect assumptions about collective authorship and risks denying many genuine authors the rights to which they would otherwise be entitled under the CDPA. It is impossible to sensibly implement this approach in the context of scientific collaborations, as too many contributors who bear direct responsibility for the protected expression would be excluded. Similarly, there is great uncertainty as to who might be a joint author of a film dramatic work, which is compounded by the potential recognition of multiple underlying copyright works. The emphasis on the authorship limb at the expense of the collaboration limb, means that the joint authorship test lacks the tools to make sense of a work such as Wikipedia. Wikipedia pages risk being viewed in an unreal way as a series of derivative works (many of which will lack originality), instead of a joint work authored by many contributors with a common design.[106] Furthermore, we have seen that an acontextual approach to joint authorship caused the Federal Court of Australia in *Bulun Bulun* to elide the role of an Indigenous community in the creation of the expression of an artistic work.[107]

Although collective authorship groups are generally able to regulate authorship effectively with private ordering, there remains an important role for copyright law: (i) as a source of good authorship standards that are independent from the power dynamics which operate in creative communities; and (ii) as a method of promoting copyright's policy goals. In order to be able to effectively regulate collective authorship, the joint authorship test ought to be applied in a way that appreciates the nature of collective authorship and the context in which it occurs. This might go some way towards addressing the problem identified by Jessica Litman that although people tend to buy into copyright norms, they do not tend

---

Progress of Science' 95 American Scientist 198; L Guibault and C Angelopoulos, *Open Content Licensing: From Theory to Practice* (Amsterdam UP 2011), Ch 6.

[106] There are similar difficulties in construing the boundaries of the work in the case of film; see Chapter 6. A broader approach to the application of the joint authorship test to the dramatic work, might make it easier to avoid a thicket of underlying rights.

[107] 4.2.3 and 4.4.

to translate them into rules in the same way that the copyright statute provides.[108]

7.6 Summary

Analysis of the case studies has yielded insight into the nature of collective authorship, in particular:
- Collective authorship is a different process to individual authorship;
- There is a division of labour and responsibility for the creative, aesthetic or intellectual content of a work is shared among many contributors;
- Social norms have an important role to play in motivating and regulating authorship;
- Authorship has different meaning, and is attributed differently, in different contexts;
- Power dynamics can affect the attribution of authorship;
- Attribution is often more important to creators than royalties or control;
- Authorship issues are often successfully managed with private ordering mechanisms;
- There are limits to the desirability of relying on private ordering mechanisms alone; and
- Copyright law norms matter to creative communities (although perhaps not always in straightforward ways).

Based upon this insight, a number of factors ought to be borne in mind when applying the joint authorship test to cases of collective authorship. These are as follows:
  (i) Authorship has important ramifications for creators other than copyright ownership.
  (ii) The factually specific application of the joint authorship is a positive feature, rather than a defect, because it allows the test to be flexible to different creative contexts.
  (iii) The joint authorship test ought to be applied in a way that is sensitive to the creative context.
  (iv) Social norms provide an indispensable source of information about the creative process (particularly in relation to what contributors consider to be a valuable contribution and other shared assumptions).

---

[108] J Litman, 'Copyright Noncompliance (Or Why We Can't "Just Say Yes" to Licensing)' (1996) 29 NYU J of Intl L and Politics 237, 238. Litman writes in the US context, but it seems likely that this sentiment is reflected throughout the common law copyright world.

(v) An inclusive approach to the application of the joint authorship test reflects the creative realities of collective authorship better than the current pragmatic instrumental approach.
(vi) There are good reasons to be cautious about how social norms are taken into account in legal decision-making.
(vii) 'Authorship' in copyright law is an important legal standard that is independent from the power dynamics that operate in authorial groups.

In light of these points, the next chapter proposes an inclusive and contextual approach to the joint authorship test. In so doing, the chapter considers both the usefulness and the limitations of the social norms which apply in various creative communities as a resource for answering questions of fact which arise in the application of the joint authorship test.

8 An Inclusive, Contextual Approach to the Joint Authorship Test

Copyright law is said to be undergoing a credibility crisis, in that it seems disconnected from modern creative practices.[1] Anne Barron suggests that 'copyright discourse is perpetually haunted by the problem of reconciling the often conflicting demands of certainty and legitimacy'.[2] This book has shown this tension played out in the case law on joint authorship, which seems to falter on both accounts. The pragmatic instrumental approach sacrifices legitimacy for certainty. It concentrates authorship in the hands of a few dominant contributors in order to streamline exploitation of copyright works, and by doing so, it distances authorship from both its creative reality and copyright's own notion of an 'author'. The judicial preoccupation with aesthetic neutrality, on the other hand, is motivated by a legitimacy concern: that judges tend to lack the expertise to make aesthetic determinations. This preoccupation might explain the lack of analytical clarity evident in judicial decisions concerning joint authorship. (Although judicial reasoning rarely explicitly incorporates aesthetic criteria, it is likely that such criteria are being considered, but latently.) This in turn, makes it extremely difficult to predict how the joint authorship test might be applied to works of collective authorship (compromising certainty).

This book argues that copyright law has an important role to play in the regulation of collective authorship, but that it can only fulfil this role effectively if the creative realities of collective authorship are taken into account when the joint authorship test is applied. Fortunately, the joint authorship test already contains the tools and the inbuilt flexibility to do this.[3] With this in mind, I suggest a recalibration of the joint authorship test to restore the balance between the conflicting demands of certainty and legitimacy.

---

[1] N Elkin-Koren, 'Tailoring Copyright to Social Production' (2011) 12 Theoretical Inquiries in L 309, 310.
[2] A Barron, 'The Legal Properties of Film' (2004) 67 MLR 177, 204–205.
[3] To recap, a joint author must make a contribution: (i) that is not distinct, (ii) is in pursuance of a common design/collaboration, and (iii) constitutes a significant contribution of the right kind (2.2).

This chapter proposes an approach to the application of the joint authorship test that is *inclusive* (of all those who have made a significant contribution of creative choices or intellectual input to the protected expression) and *contextual* (in that it explicitly takes the context of creativity into account). I argue that this approach is best suited to copyright's purpose (to encourage and reward creativity) and more closely aligned with the realities of collective authorship.[4] The superficial allure of the simple solutions which the pragmatic instrumental approach appears to offer ought to be resisted. Instead, judges should be mindful of the social norms that apply within a particular collective authorship group. These social norms provide information which is likely to be highly pertinent when a court is required to determine whether there is 'collaboration' among contributors and who has made a 'significant' contribution (which is 'not distinct'). Social norms also provide judges with a useful reference point for assessing creative matters which mitigates against outcomes being influenced by their subjective judgements of aesthetic merit.

Yet, there are some dangers in uncritically incorporating social norms in judicial decision-making. Thus, I suggest a three-prong framework for filtering norms based on their certainty, representativeness, and policy implications. In addition, the joint authorship test requires that a contribution is of the 'right kind'. This provides an important safety mechanism that ensures that authorship is only granted to those who have made a more than de minimis creative or intellectual contribution to the protected *expression* (filtering out contributions solely of an investment or orchestration type and mere ideas).

This chapter begins by considering why social norms might be relevant to judicial decision-making in this context. I argue that judges should take social norms into account in their decisions for three reasons: (i) they provide important information about the facts of a case; (ii) the credibility of copyright depends upon its ability to correspond with, and reflect, reality in at least in a minimal sense; and (iii) people are more likely to obey copyright law where it appears to them to be fair and legitimate. The second section considers the limits of incorporating social norms in judicial decision-making. I argue that social norms should not be simply deferred to; rather, they should be carefully assessed. The third section suggests a framework for assessing when norms ought to be incorporated into judicial decision-making. The fourth section revisits three themes in the joint authorship case law set out in Chapter 2.[5] The fifth section

---

[4] Although this book is concerned with collective authorship, this approach is likely to be relevant to collaborations of all sizes where similar authorship dynamics exist among collaborators.

[5] 2.3.

proposes an inclusive, contextual approach to the application of the joint authorship test bearing in mind both the usefulness of incorporating social norms in copyright cases and the limitations that must be borne in mind. It provides some examples to elaborate on how this approach might work in practice. The penultimate section considers how this analysis of the joint authorship test interfaces with the law on the joint ownership of copyright interests. It evaluates the current legal position, draws upon some alternative approaches from US law and scholarship, and suggests some modest legislative amendments. The final section offers some concluding remarks and suggests avenues for future research.

8.1   The Relevance of Social Norms

Social norms have been studied extensively in the social sciences, particularly, by anthropologists, sociologists and economists.[6] The body of literature on law and social norms has been growing in recent times.[7] In the legal context, scholars have argued that the state might achieve certain regulatory outcomes more effectively by choosing to ignore, strengthen or undermine particular social norms.[8] Some, taking an optimistic view, argue that social norms offer a more efficient and flexible way of regulating behaviour than legal rules.[9] They also consider it important that legal rules uphold certain norms so as to fulfil parties' expectations or to promote their interests in autonomy.[10] Others are more pessimistic and highlight some of the dangers of placing reliance on social norms, including increased social costs or conflict with fundamental values, such as distributive justice. The two sides disagree on whether it is best for law to be imposed 'top-down' by the state or to grow from the bottom up by enforcing social norms.[11] Ultimately, the best approach is likely to depend upon the

---

[6] C Bicchieri & R Muldoon, 'Social Norms', *Stanford Encyclopaedia of Philosophy* <plato.stanford.edu/entries/social-norms>.

[7] Posner suggests that this scholarship grew out of the Legal Realist scholarship of the early 20th century. E Posner, 'Introduction' in E Posner (ed) *Social Norms, Nonlegal Sanctions, and the Law* (Edward Elgar 2007) ix. See Chapter 1, n34.

[8] Posner (n7). E Posner, 'Social Norms and Social Roles' (1996) 96 Columbia LRev 903, 907, 958–959.

[9] E Posner, *Law and Social Norms* (Harvard UP 2000); R Ellickson, *Order Without Law: How Neighbors Settle* Disputes (Harvard UP 1991) argues that social norms are welfare maximising.

[10] M Albertson Fineman, *The Autonomy Myth: A Theory of Dependency* (The New Press 2004); L Guibault, *Copyright Limitations and Contracts: An Analysis of the Contractual Overridability of Limitations on Copyright* (Kluwer Law International 2002); R Mnookin, 'Divorce Bargaining: The Limits on Private Ordering' 18(4) J of Law Reform 1015, 1018; G Barzilai *Communities and Law: Politics and Cultures of Legal Identities* (U of Michigan P 2003) 13.

[11] R Cooter, 'Normative Failure Theory of Law' (1997) 82 Cornell LRev 947.

particular issue being regulated. However, it can be said that even where a top-down approach is preferred, at least some understanding of the social norms that operate in a given community is essential in order to predict the likely effects of legal rules on that community.[12]

At first blush, copyright law might appear too standardised to accommodate the vast range of creative works which it regulates with a single definition of authorship and of joint authorship.[13] Here, the brevity of the definitions belies the degree of in-built flexibility since both tests must be applied having regard to the relevant facts of the case. In this light, it is paramount to establish the facts accurately. Yet, case law and scholarship[14] rarely pin down on the appropriate source of those 'facts' and the point(s) at which they ought to feed into the joint authorship test. This book proposes that social norms prevalent in collective authorship groups, provide the best source of information to answer the factual questions relevant to determining the authorship of copyright works, particularly those created by large groups. Here, 'social norms' is used in broad sense to refer to the rules, standards and attitudes arising from group interactions, which govern and inform participants' behaviour and thoughts.[15] Later in this chapter, I set out a framework for considering the usefulness and value of social norms when seeking answers to questions of fact that arise in the application of the joint authorship test.[16]

The case studies revealed that social norms tend to serve an important role in governing the creative process in cases of collective authorship.[17] These social norms emerge in response to coordination problems that arise as a result of many contributors engaging a creative process which necessitates a division of labour and the sharing of creative control.[18] Although some groups might set out to create norms, more often they are the

---

[12] E Posner, 'The Regulation of Groups: The Influence of Legal and Nonlegal Sanctions on Collective Action' (1996) 63 U of Chicago LRev 133, 193.

[13] On the possibility that social norms might alleviate the problem of a one-size-fits-all intellectual property regime: D Oliar and C Sprigman 'There's No Free Laugh (Anymore): The Emergence of Intellectual Property Norms and the Transformation of Stand-up Comedy' (2008) 94 Virginia LRev 1787, 1839-40.

[14] Much copyright scholarship remains similarly committed to the exclusion of aesthetic considerations from copyright decision-making on questions of authorship: J Cohen, 'Creativity and Culture in Copyright Theory' (2007) 40 U of California Davis LRev 1151. See, further, Chapter 2.

[15] See Bicchieri (n6). Sunstein (n8) 914 defines social norms as: 'social attitudes of approval and disapproval, specifying what ought to be done and what ought not to be done'. L Lessig, 'The Regulation of Social Meaning' (1995) U Chicago LRev 943, 951 observes that 'social meaning' provides a semiotic resource that members of a society or subculture can use to induce others to behave in a certain way; he defines social meanings as 'the semiotic content attached to various actions, or inactions, or statuses, within a particular context'.

[16] 8.3.   [17] 7.1.   [18] 7.1.

unexpected/unplanned result of individuals' interactions[19] or are drawn from external sources (e.g., predominant norms in a particular discipline or genre). Social norms provide a good source of information about the creative reality and shared assumptions of creators working on a particular project. By offering insights on how the project is understood by contributors, they provide information about whether (and which) contributors are *collaborating* (i.e., what is the ambit of the common design). They also provide information about the *significance*, or value, of a particular contribution to the project (in light of the common design of contributors).[20]

In copyright cases, judges have shown themselves willing to take some social norms into account in their decision-making, especially when determining aesthetic questions, for example, in determining authorship by reference to the musical or artistic, etc. character of a work[21] or when accepting evidence from musicologists (e.g., that performance is not part of a musical work).[22] Despite this, current copyright jurisprudence generally fails to engage *explicitly* with aesthetic values, owing to a judicial preoccupation with aesthetic neutrality.[23] I have argued that reference to aesthetic criteria when determining the authorship of a work does not necessary violate the principle that copyright protection ought not to depend upon a judge's own view of the aesthetic *merits* of a work. In fact, explicitly taking social norms into account may be the best way of ensuring that decisions are not dictated by a judge's subjective aesthetic preferences. Instead, a relevant creative community's views (objectively construed) ought to be the point of reference for aesthetic determinations.[24] This failure to engage with social norms directly and overtly has reduced the visibility of important contextual factors that support an inclusive definition of joint authorship. Additionally, it seems to enhance the appeal of the pragmatic instrumental approach which presents itself as yielding simple and efficient answers that appear to evade any nuanced evaluation of the significance of different contributions to collaborative work. This book argues that the pragmatic instrumental approach is rarely likely to lead to the right answer when it comes to determining the authorship of work created by large groups.

There are at least two other reasons to make reference to social norms in judicial reasoning. The first is that the credibility of copyright law

---

[19] Bicchieri and Muldoon (n6).
[20] This requirement ought to be a qualitative one: 2.2.3.
[21] E.g., *Sawkins v Hyperion Records* [2005] EWCA 565, [2005] 1 WLR 3281; *Interlego v Tyco Industries* [1989] AC 217 (PC). See further: Chapter 2.
[22] *Hadley v Kemp* [1999] EMLR 589 (Ch).
[23] 2.3.3. Making a similar point in the US context: RK Walker and B Depoorter, 'Unavoidable Aesthetic Judgments in Copyright Law: A Community of Practice Standard' (2015) 109(2) Northwestern University LRev 343.
[24] A framework for the incorporation of social norms is provided in 8.3.

depends on its ability to correspond, at least in a minimal sense, with social reality.[25] One might question how copyright law can claim to be the principal legal mechanism for the regulation of creativity if it is completely detached from the realities of creative communities.[26] Although the designation of authorship is rightly a legal question, any legal determination must relate, and seem relevant, to creative practice. Indeed, it is virtually impossible to make an appropriate decision on joint authorship without considering such factors. It is vital for the ongoing credibility of copyright law that these considerations are dealt with openly. This is also likely to enhance the clarity and quality of decision-making by inviting more explicit and thoughtful consideration of the value and usefulness of particular norms in joint authorship determinations.[27]

Secondly, as an instrumental matter, the public is more likely to obey laws that they consider to be fair and legitimate.[28] All law relies on a certain amount of self-enforcement and co-operation from the community to ensure its effectiveness in regulating behaviour.[29] Psychologists have found promoting self-compliance is more effective than deterrence factors.[30] The perceived *fairness* of a law appears to be the single most important factor in shaping compliance, including in the realm of intellectual property law.[31] A significant element of the perceived fairness of

---

[25] L Bently and L Biron, 'Discontinuities between legal conceptions of authorship and social practices: What, if anything, is to be done?' in M van Eechoud (ed) *The Work of Authorship* (Amsterdam UP 2014) 237 argue that realigning legal and social authorship norms is important for copyright law's legitimacy. Also: J Tehranian, 'Infringement Nation: Copyright Reform and the Law/Norm Gap' (2007) Utah LRev 537.

[26] Noting the likely negative impact on legal compliance arising from wide gaps between social norms and legal rules: C Jensen, 'The more things change, the more they stay the same: Copyright, digital technology, and social norms' (2003) 56 Stanford LRev 531.

[27] M Madison, 'Legal-ware: Contract and Copyright in the Digital Age' (1998) 67 Fordham LRev 1025, 1137–1138 argues that direct exposure of the legal system to community norms ensures that norms are reconciled with copyright policy, and with time, judicial decisions produce relatively stable bodies of rules that reflect community standards of fairness.

[28] Tom Tyler's work is very influential in this field, see especially: *Why People Obey the Law* (Princeton UP 2006).

[29] Tyler (n28) 271. Also, D Kahan, 'Gentle Nudges vs. Hard Shoves: Solving the Sticky Norms Problem (2000) 97 U of Chicago LRev 607 suggesting that authorities are reticent to enforce laws that depart significantly from social norms.

[30] Tyler (n28) 270. Some of the literature is outlined in: J Tankebe, 'Viewing Things Differently: The Dimensions of Public Perceptions of Police Legitimacy' (2013) 51 Criminology 103; T Tyler and J Jackson, 'Popular Legitimacy and the Exercise of Legal Authority: Motivating Compliance, Cooperation and Engagement' (2014) 20(1) Psychology Public Policy and L 78.

[31] Fairness is even more important than the likelihood of being caught or punished: Tyler ibid. T Tyler, 'Compliance with Intellectual Property Law: A Psychological Perspective' (1996) 29 International L and Politics 219, 227 recommends tapping into what the public feels to be fair in order to promote compliance. Noting that compliance is a significant copyright policy issue given the general proliferation of copying on the internet

copyright law is those who are seen to benefit from protection.³² Ensuring that copyright law protects 'authors' corresponds to common expectations and is a simple step towards promoting compliance. As Jessica Litman succinctly puts it (discussing copyright licensing), '[p]eople don't obey laws that they don't believe in'.³³ Inadequate, irrelevant and ostensibly unfair legal provisions are likely to be ignored or circumvented. The pragmatic instrumental approach discussed in Chapter 2 is likely to clash with what most contributors to works of collective authorship would consider 'fair'. Wikipedia, for example, has responded to this by adroitly side-stepping copyright's potentially restrictive and uncertain concept of authorship using copyleft licences.³⁴ Furthermore, granting authorship to a few dominant individuals while denying it to other valuable contributors disconnects authorship from the creation of the expression.³⁵ The ICMJE journal guidelines for biomedical collaborations provide an example of a regulatory strategy that seems to have been largely unsuccessful because it is disconnected from creative realities.³⁶ Where the law accords with public views about what is fair, it can also have an important symbolic function which, in turn, promotes compliance.³⁷

The perceived *legitimacy* of the law can also promote compliance.³⁸ Thus, people are more likely to obey laws that they believe serve

---

(219). See also J Litman, 'Copyright Noncompliance (or why we can't "just say yes" to licensing)' (1996) 29 International Law and Politics 237.

³² Hence the frequent appeals to the plight of the deserving author when lobbying for copyright reform, see: L Bently, 'R v. Author: From Death Penalty to Community Service' (2008) 32(1) Columbia J of L & the Arts 1.

³³ Litman (n31) 239; M Schultz, 'Fear and Norms and Rock & Roll: What Jambands Can Teach Us about Persuading People to Obey Copyright Law' (2009) Berkeley Technology LJ 651 also argues that copyright law ought to be realigned with social norms to promote compliance.

³⁴ 3.3.

³⁵ This clashes with the understanding, common in all the creative communities considered in the case studies, that authorship signifies responsibility for what is considered valuable about the work: 7.2.2.

³⁶ 5.2.1.

³⁷ Litman (n31) 237 points out that ' ... laws that we keep around for their symbolic power can only exercise that power to the extent that people know what the laws say'. Thus, it is also important to promote analytical clarity in judicial decision-making.

³⁸ Tyler (n31) 224 discusses two strategies which have proven to be more effective than deterrence in promoting compliance. These are based on legitimacy ('one's feelings that one ought to obey the law') and morality ('an individual's personal feelings about what is right or wrong'). Of the two, he suggests that a morality-based strategy is easier to implement given the recent decline in public respect for legal authorities (230). A similar trend is likely to exist in the UK: D Bloomfield, K Collins, C Fry and R Munton, 'Deliberation and Inclusion: Vehicles for Increasing Trust in UK Public Governance' (2001) 19 Environment and Planning C: Government and Policy 501, 508–509; C Pettie, P Seyd, P Whiteley, *Citizenship in Britain: Values, Participation and Democracy* (CUP 2004).

reasonable social purposes and that are not, for example, simply vehicles to create profits for special interest groups, such as large corporations.[39] This provides another good reason to favour an inclusive, contextual approach over a pragmatic instrumental one.[40] The latter approach risks unfairly advantaging powerful players, such as film producers, who already constitute special interest groups that have been able to use lobbying to secure greater protection of their interests.[41]

The concept of an author being a creator of protected expression is at the heart of copyright law's claims to legitimacy.[42] The pragmatic instrumental approach distances the beneficiaries of copyright protection from copyright law's *raison d'être*: to reward and encourage authors.[43] Thus, there is a good instrumental reason to ensure that copyright law's concept of authorship is in touch with creative realities (so as to appear fair to those to whom it applies), and reflects the underlying purpose of copyright law to incentivise and reward creators of protectable expression. This prioritises the legitimacy of copyright law, promotes compliance, and is fairer than resort to dubious authorship proxies which promise easy answers in factually complex scenarios.

8.2 The Dangers of Deferring to Social Norms

In the previous section, I argued that there are a number of good reasons for judges to take social norms into account in the application of the joint authorship test. Few, if any, theorists suggest that social norms and customary industry practices ought to be completely disregarded in legal decision-making, but there are three main reasons why most counsel the exercise of caution. First, it may be difficult to identify the content of social norms with certainty. Second, the content of a particular social norm might be cause for concern on the basis of its lack of efficiency,

---

[39] Tyler ibid, 233.
[40] The existing copyright literature on this point focuses on the need to recognise users' interests, not just the powerful interest groups that tend to influence the legislative process see Jensen (n26), Litman (n31).
[41] Jenson ibid, 540. As, ultimately, has been the case in the US where a restrictive approach to joint authorship has been taken to its logical extreme, see 2.5.3 and 6.2.5.
[42] W Cornish, 'The Author as Risk-Sharer' (2002) 26 Columbia J of L & the Arts 1, 12: copyright law derives most of its legal and moral force from the act of creating. See also RR Kwall, *The Soul of Creativity: Forging a Moral Rights Law for the US* (Stanford UP 2009) on the morality of copyright law.
[43] Some argue that copyright law is primarily a mechanism for disseminators, publishers and other intermediates to recoup their costs, thus, ensuring the widespread distribution of creative works (rather than their production). This view ignores the fact that both the letter and the spirit of the CDPA place the author before the disseminator. Thus, the conceptual divide between authorship and ownership, as discussed in Chapter 2.

desirability or fit with the law. Third, the incorporation of social norms in judicial decisions risks colonising independent legal standards.[44] In this section I consider how these three concerns relate to one another. This provides the necessary groundwork for the following section in which I propose a framework to aid a *careful* integration of social norms in the application of the joint authorship test.

One concern is that social norms might be insufficiently stable or reliable. This is most likely to be the case where the content of the norm is unclear or contested. The case study of science, for example, reveals how norms on attribution can vary over time, between and within disciplines.[45] Legal rules ought to satisfy certain minimum standards of clarity, openness and predictability.[46] This is particularly the case for copyright law, where the provisions on authorship provide the basis for the ownership of property rights. Social norms, similarly, should only feed into legal decision-making where the content of the norm is fairly certain, and the norm is widely accepted and stable in the creative context concerned. For example, the practice of routinely listing the head of a laboratory as an author of an article for a biomedical science journal, when that person has made no contribution to the research, is contested in that field.[47] This would counsel against feeding such a norm into the application of the joint authorship test. In contrast, naming those who are responsible for most of the writing up is a certain, widely accepted and stable norm in science.[48]

Some warn that efficiency, one the extolled virtues of social norms, is not universally applicable.[49] Yet, the perceived inefficiency of a norm does not diminish its value as a source of information about the realities of the creative process. Indeed, I have argued that social norms are relevant primarily for reasons other than their efficiency. Social norms reflect the attitudes, standards and rules that govern the behaviour of groups of creators. Taking these creativity realities into account might enhance the credibility of copyright law, which is valuable for intrinsic as well as instrumental reasons.

---

[44] J Rothman, 'The Questionable Use of Custom in Intellectual Property' (2007) 93 Virginia LRev 1899, 1908.
[45] 5.1
[46] J Raz, 'Rule of Law and its Virtue' in J Raz, *The Authority of Law: Essays on Law and Morality* (Clarendon Press 1979) 210.
[47] As evidenced by the response to the Darsee scandal and the introduction of authorship guidelines by biomedical journals in an attempt to resist these practices, see 5.2.1.
[48] The conflicting practice of pharmaceutical companies of omitting the name of a commercial writer to give an article the appearance of independence is controversial and not widely accepted, see 5.1 and 5.2.
[49] Rothman (n44); E Posner, 'Law, Economics and Inefficient Norms' (1996) 144 U Pennsylvania LRev 1697; A Katz, 'Taking Private Ordering Seriously' (1996) 144 U Pennsylvania LRev 1745, 1749.

Some argue that because social norms are not explicitly made or consented to, they do not represent the parties' *actual* expectations.[50] Social norms are likely to be least representative where there are imbalances of power within the relevant group. Norms which develop in these situations are unlikely to represent a fair balancing of the interests of all parties. Thus, an entrenched hierarchy in the film industry explains why producers and directors traditionally received authorship credit, whilst screenwriters did not.[51] There are good policy reasons not to incorporate unequal or unrepresentative social norms in legal decision-making.[52] Where a norm is stable and uncontested within an authorial group, it is more likely to be appropriately representative of those contributors.

Jennifer Rothman has provided a leading critique of the incorporation of social norms in US intellectual property decisions.[53] When considering the question of whether an unauthorised use of a copyright work might count as a 'fair use', Rothman is concerned that recourse to industry practices is unlikely take the public interest in to account, whereas this ought to weigh heavily in this analysis.[54] This reasoning seems sound, but the concerns underlying it are less pertinent to the question of joint authorship. In this scenario, it is the interests of different contributors that are being balanced as between themselves, with less of a role for public interest concerns. Still, even in this context a norm should be rejected where it conflicts with copyright law's purposes or other important policy goals.[55]

Questions which are essentially legal in nature ought to be answered independently of social norms, with judges guided by the policy and purposes of the CDPA instead. In 2.4 I argued that whether a putative joint author's contribution is of the *right kind* is a legal question, which requires independent judicial evaluation in light of the normative dimension of authorship. There is more room to incorporate social norms in answering the test's remaining factual questions. Social norms, thus, may be helpful when evaluating the significance of a contribution to a joint work or assessing whether contributors are working with a common design.[56]

---

[50] J Gardner, 'Some Types of Law' in D Edlin (ed) *Common Law Theory* (CUP 2007) 51; see also Bicchieri and Muldoon (n6).
[51] 6.1.
[52] On the importance of equality as a substantive value in a theory of justice, see, for example, E Chemerinsky, 'In Defense of Equality: A Reply to Professor Westen' (1983) 81 Michigan LRev 575, 585–591.
[53] Rothman (n44) 1908, 1902 is concerned that custom has 'tremendous influence on IP law'; also J Rothman, 'Copyright, Custom and Lessons from the Common Law' in S Balganesh (ed) *Intellectual Property and the Common Law* (CUP 2013) 230.
[54] Ibid, 1937, especially the interests of users of copyright works.
[55] One such policy goal might be substantive equality among contributors who qualify as authors.
[56] These ought to be treated as factual questions: 2.4.

Even Rothman, who is otherwise sceptical about the merits of incorporating norms in intellectual property decisions, sees them as valuable evidence of parties' intentions and standard industry practice.[57]

Authorship cannot be a purely legal enquiry. As the case studies demonstrate, authorship tests need to be able to adapt across industries, in very different contexts, and over time. It is this need for flexibility which supports recourse to social norms in answering the factual questions which arise. Nevertheless, not all social norms can provide appropriate answers to these questions. Theorists are right to caution away from incorporating norms which reflect a great inequality of bargaining power between parties,[58] which overlook third-party or policy interests, or run contrary to higher societal values. Thus, norms should be introduced into the judicial decision-making process to answer the right kind of questions, and then selected with care.

The next section provides a framework for assessing the desirability of norms, which is then used to define an inclusive, contextual approach to the joint authorship test in the sections that follow.

8.3 A Framework for Considering Social Norms

Although some of the literature on law and social norms is relatively recent, the idea that it is important for judges to have regard to customary practice is quite old. Indeed, recourse to custom as a source of legal rules is at the heart of the common law method.[59] From the early days of the common law, judges developed rules to consider whether it was appropriate to recognise custom as law.[60] According to Blackstone, a custom was a good candidate to be incorporated into the common law if it satisfied the following requirements: antiquity, continuing peaceable use, certainty, reasonableness, compulsoriness and consistency.[61] These requirements might be boiled down to two central concerns relating to the proof of the existence and the reasonableness of the custom.[62] These requirements intend to filter out the aspects of custom that are potentially arbitrary and burdensome to non-community members.[63] The need to

---

[57] Rothman (n44) 1937.
[58] ibid 1956. Although powerful interest groups may also affect the legislative process, Rothman considers that these groups have a more pronounced impact on custom which develops beyond the context of open debate and public commentary. See also: Posner (n49) 1709.
[59] Rothman (n53).
[60] A Loux 'The Persistence of the Ancient Regime: Custom, Utility and the Common Law in the Nineteenth Century' (1993) 79 Cornell LRev 183, 189.
[61] W Blackstone, *Commentaries*, Volume 1, 76-78.
[62] Loux (n60) 186. *Halsbury's Laws of England* (5th edn, LexisNexis 2012) Vol 32, 1(3)(i).
[63] H Smith, 'Community and Custom in Property' (2009) 10(1) Theoretical Inquiries in Law 5, 10.

ensure that illegitimate or undesirable customs do not spread and are not upheld by the law was recognised from these early days.[64]

My suggestion is not that courts ought to adopt social norms and enforce them as if they were legal rules.[65] Rather, social norms should serve as an important resource of contextual information that may help courts to answer questions of fact, when seeking to apply the joint authorship test.[66] Social norms reveal what contributors consider to be meaningful aspects of both the creative process and the resulting creative work. As part of the factual matrix at the time a work was created, thus, social norms are likely to elucidate on the existence and parameters of a common design, which contributions are significant, and possibly which are distinct. In this section, I suggest a three-prong framework to guide the incorporation of social norms in the application of the joint authorship test, which draws upon the limits to the incorporation of custom that the common law has recognised.[67] This framework addresses the three potential defects of social norms noted: their lack of certainty; the influence of power imbalances on their development; and the fact that they develop without regard for public interests and the interests of third parties. I suggest that the desirability of a social norm might be ascertained by considering: (i) its certainty, (ii) its representativeness, and (iii) the policy implications of adopting it. This framework requires proof that the social norm exists in a stable form and that it does not enshrine values that might be repugnant to the law's overall purposes.

Determining the existence and content of social norms ought to be primarily an objective undertaking. Walker and Depoorter have devised a methodology for assessing aesthetic matters in copyright cases which might be a useful resource.[68] They suggest courts begin by identifying the community of artistic practice that accurately reflects the aesthetic norms and traditions that informed the work, based upon evidence from the parties and expert witnesses. This evidence provides a baseline understanding of the relevant creative environment. Next, the court should adopt the perspective of a hypothetical member of the relevant community, and then ascertain which aspects of a work would be viewed as

---

[64] Ibid, 11.
[65] It makes sense to have particularly strict requirements for enforcing customary rules. A more tolerant approach can be taken when considering social norms as part of the relevant factual matrix of a case, as ultimately authorship is a legal question.
[66] Rothman (n44) 1968 argues that custom should be relevant only to questions about what the parties intended or what is generally done, and not those concerning answers to normative questions of what ought to be done.
[67] Rothman, ibid, suggests a 6-vector approach to guide the incorporation of custom in intellectual property decisions: certainty, motivation, representativeness, application of the custom (against whom), application of the custom (for what proposition), and implications of the custom. See also Rothman (n53).
[68] Walker and Depoorter (n23) 376–367.

aesthetically valuable from that perspective.[69] The authors liken their methodology to the reasonableness standard in torts, since it too is adaptable to changing circumstances, and seems to provide a standard that is responsive to artistic innovation without sacrificing consistency.[70] Such an approach, or one similar, might prove a useful way of discerning relevant social norms.[71] Given the unique characteristics of collective authorship, the relevant community of practice from which a norm might be discerned may sometimes be the specific collective authorship group (e.g., regular Wikipedia contributors), whereas at other times it will be the relevant sector or subsector of creative practice.

(i) Certainty

Identifying the relevant norm and dealing with changing norms may sometimes prove problematic, making the requirement for certainty an important limb of the proposed framework. Courts ought not to incorporate social norms into legal decisions unless they are identifiable, stable and widely accepted in the relevant creative sub-sector or group.[72] Indigenous customary law on the authorship of art would seem to satisfy the requirement of certainty,[73] whereas the ICMJE guidelines might not, because they lack widespread acceptance.[74] In recognition that social norms may change over time, when applying the joint authorship test, the relevant enquiry ought to relate to the social norms that existed at the time the work was created.[75] Proof of certainty provides a measure of transparency and stability, which attenuates concerns that the incorporation of social norms might potentially inject an element of arbitrariness to joint authorship cases.[76]

---

[69] Ibid, 349, calling this the 'Community of Practice' and acknowledging this standard's rough approximation to the hypothetical skilled addressee of patent law.

[70] On the value of the judicial employment of devices that allow the application of extra-legal standards, such as the reasonable person standard: J Gardner, 'The many faces of the reasonable person' (2015) 131 LQR 563.

[71] For reasons of simplicity and cost, courts might see no need to introduce an additional hypothetical person standard, and prefer to approach determining social norms as any other question of fact, taking into account a range of relevant evidence.

[72] Although it does not make much sense to impose a requirement of 'immemorial existence' in this context, the stability of the norm over time should be required. The length of time might depend on the characteristics of the creative industry in question.

[73] Australian courts have often accepted evidence on these matters in copyright cases, see 4.2.

[74] 5.2.1.

[75] For more complex cases of constant works in progress, such as Wikipedia pages, see the methodology based on the approach in *MacMillan Publishers v Thomas Reed Publications* [1993] FSR 455 (Ch) suggested above: p 82 and p 97.

[76] C Fisk, 'Credit Where It's Due: The Law and Norms of Attribution' (2006) 95 Georgetown LJ 49 considers these to be important characteristics of desirable private ordering regimes.

Although it might be argued that powerful parties will be best-placed to prove the existence of a social norm that favours their own position, this is no different than many other aspects of intellectual property disputes.[77] Expert evidence is already commonly adduced on issues of copyright subsistence (including authorship).[78] Judges are very accustomed to, and adept at, determining industry practice in other contexts, for example, in contract cases.[79] There is no reason to suppose that discovering the social norms that operate in creative communities will be any more challenging in this context than it is in others.[80] In any event, the importance of getting joint authorship 'right' is surely worth the price of any problems of proof that may arise from the explicit consideration of social norms. The case studies discussed in this book demonstrate that cost of an acontextual approach – a fundamental disconnect between copyright law and the reality of collective authorship – is likely to far outweigh any benefit.[81]

(ii)   Representativeness

The legitimacy of applying custom is at its greatest when applied to the very community that established it.[82] The common law has always held that customs should only apply to those who demonstrate consent to them. This requirement for consent might seem to underlie Blackstone's requirements for the custom's continuity, and existence since time immemorial; and that it be peaceable (undisputed) and compulsory.[83] In this sense, consent was a legal fiction, particularly given the requirement of the immemorial existence of the custom.[84] Social norms typically arise as an

---

[77] Rothman (n44) 1959, notes formal written statements of social norms, such as guidelines, are more likely to be developed by powerful players. While easy to produce in court, these may not always be an accurate reflection of actual practice.
[78] L Bently, 'Authorship of Popular Music in UK Copyright Law' (2009) 12(2) Information Communication & Society 179.
[79] S Carter, 'Custom, Adjudication and Petrushevsky's Watch: Some Notes from the Intellectual Property Front' (1992) 78 Virginia LRev 129, 130 (although expressing some scepticism about the court's expertise to undertake exercises of 'judicial anthropology').
[80] While there may be some uncertainty surrounding which social norms a court will consider relevant, this ought to be kept within tolerable limits with the 'certainty' limb of the proposed framework. Uncertainty might be expected to reduce as the body of case law in a particular creative sector builds. A valuable side effect of uncertainty is that it encourages the parties to use contracts to clarify such matters.
[81] See 2.2, 7.1 and 7.2.2.
[82] *Millar v Taylor* (1769) 4 Burr 2303, 2368 (Yates J): custom is '*lex loci*, the law of the place'. This attests to the value of applying social norms which govern collective authorship to contributors to the group project.
[83] Rothman (n53) 243–244.
[84] Loux (n60) 208. *Chapman v Smith* (1754) 2 Ves Sen 506, 510 (Lord Hardwicke LC) for legal purposes this date was fixed at the year 1189.

unplanned result of individuals' interactions.[85] Given this absence of active consent to a social norm, I prefer the term 'representativeness'. Under this second prong, I suggest that norms that are developed with the input and participation of contributors are to be preferred to top-down norms. Similarly, courts should hesitate to incorporate customs that clearly only serve one party's interest to the detriment of other interests.[86]

This part of the framework provides a bulwark against undesirable norms which can result from imbalances of power within creative communities. In the case study of scientific collaborations, it has been observed that power imbalances can have a negative impact on prevailing social norms. Thus, senior scientists can exert significant control over the attribution of authorship, in ways which distance authorship from the creation of the work and even those having scientific responsibility for it.[87] Likewise, some directors have used their superior bargaining power to obtain a possessory credit on a film which seems to imply they are its sole author despite the prevailing inclusive view of film authorship.[88] The literature on social norms supports the observation that power dynamics within groups can prevent community norms from being ideal in terms of efficiency and/or fairness.[89] The need to protect weaker parties is also recognised in many parts of the law and commentators have made similar suggestions in slightly different contexts.[90] Fisk, for example, suggests that attribution regimes ought to be assessed on the basis of equality, substantive fairness and participation,[91] and Rothman argues that before relying upon custom in an intellectual property context, judges must consider those to whom it would apply and the 'motivations' of a custom.[92] All of these factors are potentially relevant to the 'representativeness' of a social norm in the sense meant here. Collectively bargained agreements on screen credit and particle physics authorship protocols are examples of social norms that seem adequately representative.[93]

(iii) Policy Implications

It is essential for courts to take account of policy considerations when considering whether, or not, to incorporate a particular social norm. The requirement of reasonableness was considered to be one of the most important restrictions on the incorporation of custom into the common

---

[85] Bicchieri and Muldoon (n6) and Gardner (n50) 60–63 note that custom is not expressly or intentionally made.
[86] Rothman (n44) 1970–1974; Fisk (n76) 74–76.   [87] 5.2.1.   [88] See pp 163, 197.
[89] Smith (n63) 14.
[90] This might be seen, for example, in the *contra proferentem* rule in contract law or in the equitable doctrine of unconscionability.
[91] Fisk (n76) 74–76.   [92] Rothman (n44) 1970–1974.   [93] 5.2.2, 6.3.

law.[94] Even where a custom was widely accepted and long-standing, it was not appropriate for judges to defer to it as a proxy for what is reasonable.[95] A custom would be assessed for its substantive fairness and with regard to public interests. Social norms, likewise, develop without regard for the interests of third parties and other public policy concerns. The third prong of my framework provides a measure to assure the primacy of copyright law's policy goals and filter out particularly undesirable norms.[96] This requires some consideration of whether the adoption of a particular norm into law would yield objectively desirable end results.[97] This approach has the added benefit of allowing the incorporation of social norms to evolve in line with the standard setting function of copyright law.[98]

8.4 Revisiting the Critique of the Joint Authorship Test

Having outlined a framework for incorporating norms into the joint authorship test, and before suggesting a revised approach, I briefly recap the three themes observed in the current application of the test, as discussed in Chapter 2.[99]

8.4.1 Factual Specificity

In Chapter 2, I suggested that the factual specificity of the joint authorship test makes it very difficult to predict the outcome in any particular case, especially where no earlier cases have been decided based on a similar factual matrix.[100] Faced with the unique dynamics of creativity in collective authorship groups, the factually specific nature of the test is a positive attribute since it affords flexibility to adapt to a range of creative contexts. It is imperative, however, that the 'facts' are correctly understood. In this respect, the social norms which regulate creativity in collective authorship groups provide a good source of information about the creative process (provided their limitations are borne in mind).

8.4.2 The Preoccupation with Aesthetic Neutrality

I have also argued that judges' acute awareness of the copyright principle that outcomes should not turn on their own view of a work's aesthetic

---

[94] *Halsbury's Laws of England* (5th edn, Lexis Nexis 2012) Volume 32, 1(3)(iii)9.
[95] Rothman (n53) 244.   [96] Rothman (n44) 1977.   [97] Ibid, 1976.
[98] Ibid. Instead of being locked in by courts, an undesirable norm might evolve over time. A court's decision not to uphold an undesirable norm (or uphold a desirable one) might shape the evolution of norms over time.
[99] 2.3.   [100] 2.3.1.

merits has evolved into a preoccupation with aesthetic neutrality.[101] Yet, it seems almost impossible to determine (possible joint) authorship without some regard to aesthetic considerations, since the process necessarily requires the evaluation and weighing of various different contributions to the creative process. Given this, I argue that social norms might provide an invaluable resource which can be deployed to avoid decisions based upon a subjective assessment of aesthetic merits.

I have argued that creative communities are best-placed to understand the relative value of each contributor's contribution to the whole. By taking the social norms that operate in particular creative contexts into account, judges can define relevant aesthetic criteria which help establish joint authorship, whilst devolving any questions of aesthetic value to creative communities. Adopting social norms as a point of reference for aesthetic matters is likely to result in better quality decisions that more accurately reflect creative realities. Additionally, we have seen that an open, transparent, contextual approach may enhance the credibility of copyright law as a tool to encourage, reward and regulate creativity.[102] This may have the knock-on effect of enhancing compliance or at least, promoting increased analytical clarity in judicial decision-making.

8.4.3 The Pragmatic Instrumental Approach

The case studies suggest that adopting a pragmatic instrumental approach to the application of the joint authorship test is misguided, because divorces the test not only from copyright's core concept of authorship (arising from the act of creation of the protected expression), but also from the reality of collective authorship.

The pragmatic instrumental approach appears to impose a higher standard in the case of joint works than applies to individually-authored works. This approach undermines copyright law's goal to reward and incentivise *creators* of protected expression, because one or two contributors will receive too much (gaining all of the authorship credit), whilst many more will receive no authorship share at all. Worse still, authorship is likely to gravitate to the most powerful or dominant contributors with most control, who are generally already well-placed to protect their own interests via contract. The larger a collaboration, the more likely these contributors are to resemble orchestrators or investors, rather than creators. Although these figures are a vital part of the creative process, the

---

[101] 2.3.3. Cohen (n14) considers this anxiety is also reflected in copyright scholarship, leading to a preference for abstraction and a propensity to ignore the context of creativity.
[102] 8.1.

CDPA already protects their interests in appropriate circumstances via the specially adapted entrepreneurial copyrights (that belong to 'makers' rather than 'creators') and with the presumption that employers own copyright in works created by employees in the course of their employment.[103] Indeed, by distinguishing between makers (deemed authors) and creators (true authors), the provisions of the CDPA make it clear that an 'author' is different to an orchestrator or investor.[104] An approach to the joint authorship test which requires courts to distance themselves so far from the core meaning of 'authorship' is clearly problematic. Not only does such an approach result in too few authors, it also results in the wrong contributors being granted all, or too much, of an authorship share.

Additionally, under the current approach, authorship might also tend to gravitate to those most directly connected to the fixation or recording of the work. Yet copyright authorship relates to responsibility for the protected expression, not its fixation. The case studies demonstrate that the pragmatic instrumental approach divorces the joint authorship test from creative realities of collective authorship, which require creative control to be shared amongst a large number of contributors. Although many contributors may make a range of valuable contributions to the protected expression, far fewer will be involved in the fixation of the work. The pragmatic instrumental approach requires judges to construct a fiction about how a work is created in order to elevate the contributions of one or two individuals and deny the contributions of the other contributors. These legal fictions, based on down-stream instrumental concerns rather than legal principles, are likely to lead to unpredictability in the case law.[105]

The pragmatic instrumental approach is based on the assumption that multiple joint owners will struggle to exploit a work effectively. The case studies, however, indicate that this may not be a significant concern, as private ordering solutions seem to operate to good effect to regulate authorship issues, such as attribution, and copyright ownership. The Wikipedia community utilise creative commons licences that virtually eliminate the most common coordination problems which arise from multiple ownership, whilst still retaining the right to attribution, which is clearly important to its contributors.[106] These licences also provide for workable ways of implementing the attribution requirement in the digital environment.[107]

---

[103] Even here, there is provision for express terms to trump employer/investor rights (s11(2)).
[104] See 2.1. This is also clearly demonstrated in the case law: *Cummins v Bond* (1926) 1 Ch 167; *Shepherd v Conquest* (1956) 17 CB 427, 139 ER 1140, 1147; *Hatton v Kean* (1860) 26 LJCP 20, 25.
[105] 2.3.2. [106] 3.3.
[107] For example, it is considered sufficient acknowledgment to provide a hyperlink to the relevant page (see p91).

Contracts can be particularly valuable tools for resolving the ownership issues which might result in cases of multiple ownership, because they can be flexible and context-specific. Contracts can provide efficient, flexible solutions but they might also have intrinsic benefits, such as promoting autonomy and self-determination.[108] The film case study demonstrates that contracts are capable of regulating complex scenarios involving the copyright ownership of numerous works of multiple authorship.[109] In some other scenarios, ownership issues may be unlikely to arise in the first place, either because authors have no interest in controlling future uses of their work or because authorship has greatest value in a sharing economy (e.g., science and Wikipedia).[110]

The case study relating to Indigenous art highlights the limitations of private ordering. Contract law can only be relied upon to deal with ownership issues if the relevant parties first anticipate the difficulties and then actually take the step of entering into a contract.[111] They prove ineffective where there is no capacity to agree, where there are significant inequalities of bargaining power and where they give rise to additional societal costs.[112] Individual Indigenous artists may be ill-equipped to negotiate with business savvy art dealers and museums concerning the purchase or use of their work.[113] Equally, where authorship occurs in the context of a sharing economy, contributors may care little about issues of ownership. In all these cases, copyright law important because it is the source of the default rules.

Yet, as has been considered already, copyright rules will only be helpful in protecting authors' interests where they reflect creative realities. This book argues that this requires an inclusive approach to joint authorship, which remains faithful to the same core notion of authorship that exists for individually authored works. Such an approach more accurately reflects the reality of collective authorship,[114] and provides less powerful contributors with a bargaining chip to leverage, thereby improving the overall quality of contractual negotiations.[115] The film case study

---

[108] 7.4.3.   [109] 6.3.   [110] 3.1, 5.1.
[111] *Yumbulul v Reserve Bank of Australia* [1991] FCA 332, 21 IPR 481 (Fed. Ct. of Australia) seems to provide an example an Indigenous artist who may have not completely understood the ramifications of the contract he signed; see p 110.
[112] A contract is also limited to those who are parties to it and cannot affect the conduct of third parties.
[113] For a notable exception demonstrating the use of contract to ensure respectful uses of Indigenous ritual knowledge in accordance with customary law: M Rimmer, 'The Bangarra Dance Theatre: Copyright and Indigenous Culture' (2000) 9(2) Griffith LRev 274. See 4.3.3.
[114] 7.1. Collective authorship might require the input of a large number of often specialised contributors, only some of whom undertake completely mechanical, non-creative tasks.
[115] Dominant contributors are unlikely to need the bargaining help they receive from the application of the pragmatic instrumental approach: RC Dreyfuss, 'Collaborative

illustrates how certain players have sought recognition as 'authors' or 'creative' contributors as a means of improving their bargaining power in negotiations concerning remuneration and credit.[116] Indeed, scholars have argued, and the case studies reflect, the role of copyright law as a source of good standards as well as a way to improve one's bargaining position.

The pragmatic instrumental approach elides the concepts of authorship and ownership in an unhelpful way. By focusing solely on the economic consequences that a designation of joint authorship brings (joint ownership), the moral rights aspects of authorship appears to be overlooked. Yet, the right of attribution is particularly valued, at least in the creative communities considered,[117] and the integrity right will be valuable in contexts where a creator's reputation is at risk.[118] Authorship and ownership are conceptually distinct. I argue that complications that may arise in relation to joint ownership of copyright in works of collective authorship ought to be dealt with, if at all, in the law of joint ownership. Having proposed a recalibration of the joint authorship test below, I shall then consider the implications of this test for the law of joint ownership in the section that follows.

8.5 An Inclusive and Contextual Approach to the Joint Authorship Test

Based upon my evaluation of current UK jurisprudence, and integrating insights from the four case studies, I propose an approach to the application of the joint authorship test that is:
- adapted to the ways in which collective authorship groups work together to create (Chapter 7);
- sensitive to the relevance of social norms (8.1); but also
- mindful of the dangers of uncritically incorporating social norms (8.2).

What do the case studies reveal about how the joint authorship test might be applied to yield a *suitable* mechanism for determining the authorship of works of collective authorship? First, the test should be *inclusive*, rather than restrictive. As a minimum, satisfying the authorship requirement should not be stricter in the case of joint authorship than it is for individual authorship. Otherwise, the test fails to reflect the reality of collective authorship and promotes the interests of some contributors over others,

---

Research: Conflicts on Authorship, Ownership and Accountability' (2000) 53 Vanderbilt LRev 1161, 1207.
[116] p 167. On the importance of copyright as a source of standards: 2.5.4, 7.5.
[117] The importance of attribution within collective authorship groups raises the question of whether the current provisions on the right of attribution offer too little protection (particularly given the assertion requirement in s78).
[118] E.g., *Noah v Shuba* [1991] FSR 14 (Ch).

skewing the incentives and rewards which copyright protection provides. Secondly, the joint authorship test should be applied *contextually*. Authorship should be a flexible concept that can adapt to creative practices that change over time and that differ between creative communities. Contextuality is the best way to make a one-size-fits-all copyright regime operate in a credible way.[119]

Pursuant to s10 of the CDPA (and relevant case law) for joint authorship to arise, a contributor must:
(i) act in pursuance of some collaboration or common design,
(ii) by making a contribution that is not distinct; further,
(iii) his or her contribution must be significant; and
(iv) and it must count as a contribution of the right kind.

I have identified the first three questions as questions of fact and the final question as one of law. I have also argued that the statutory definition implies that a joint work involves authors working together to create a something that is greater than the sum of its parts.[120] This fundamental conception of joint authorship might serve to guide the implementation of the test.

In outline, an inclusive, contextual approach to the application of joint authorship test might be achieved in the following way. The common design of contributors will often be a convenient starting point, since this will shed light on the significance of a particular contribution. Prevailing social norms will be of relevance in relation to the questions of fact ((i)–(iii) above), as long as they satisfy the three-prong policy framework identified at 8.3 (certainty, representativeness and policy implications). Of those collaborators who have made significant, non-distinct contributions, only those contributors who satisfy the legal definition of authorship, having made a contribution of the 'right kind', might be considered joint authors. In the rest of this section, I explain this approach in further detail, offering examples of how it might work in practice.

I have argued that whether, or not, there is *collaboration* or a *common design* is best assessed with regard to the shared assumptions of the creators. Although there is no need to prove any subjective intention to share joint authorship,[121] the collaboration element of the test necessarily

---

[119] On the value of non-legal standards in judicial decision-making: J Gardner, 'The many faces of the reasonable person' (2015) 131 LQR 563. Gardner notes '[w]hen a social rule already coordinates well, the law may be hesitant to create a legal rule, which would inevitably draw different lines and might fail to gain social traction. Creating a legal rule in such a situation might even make coordination worse, by creating uncertainty over which of the two rules to use' (573–574).
[120] 2.2.   [121] *Beckingham v Hodgens* [2003] EWCA Civ 143, [2003] EMLR 18.

requires some intention to work together, since it is difficult to see how one might accidentally or unwittingly collaborate with another.[122] Social norms capture the shared assumptions and attitudes of contributors to creative works.[123] These assumptions are particularly relevant when they satisfy the requirements of the three-prong framework suggested at 8.3.

In Chapter 2, I observed that this stage of the joint authorship test has an important function because it distinguishes a joint work from a collection of separate works, or a series of derivative works.[124] On its face, the question of whether the highly iterative creative process evident on Wikipedia produces a series of derivative works or multiple joint works seems quite challenging, even to those well-versed in copyright law. But, an appreciation of the social norms which operate in this context makes the question significantly easier to answer. From this perspective, it is apparent that because the social norms establish collaboration amongst the regular contributors, Wikipedia pages are not a series of individually-authored derivative works, but a number of joint works.[125]

The requirement that a joint author make a contribution which is not *distinct* serves to distinguish between a collection of works by different authors (co-authorship); and a joint work, that is, a single work made by many authors together (joint authorship).[126] As this limb affects the scope/boundaries of the joint work, this should be objectively determined as a matter of fact. The assessment of whether a particular contribution is not distinct because it is integral to the work (in the sense that it is dependent upon that which is already there) should be made in the light of creative realities. This approach would result in less complexity than artificially identifying multiple layers of distinct and separately protectable copyright works.[127]

The assessment of whether a contributor has made a *significant* contribution is best determined in light of the common design of the specific collaboration concerned and relevant social norms. In Chapter 2, I argued that this is primarily a qualitative, rather than a quantitative question.[128] Although a qualitative approach opens up the possibility of subjective judgements of aesthetic merit seeping into decision-making, I

---

[122] 2.2.2.   [123] 7.1.   [124] 2.2.2   [125] See further, Chapter 3, p 89.
[126] On the difference between joint authorship and co-authorship: Copinger et al. [4–17], [4–44].
[127] Objectively discerning the boundaries of a copyright work avoids complex copyright 'millefeuilles': *IPC Media v Highbury-Leisure* (n53) [23] (Laddie J) approved in *Coffey v Warner/Chappell Music* [2005] EWHC 449 (Ch) [10] (Blackburne J). There is a risk of a contrary approach being taken in order to avoid multiple ownership of a joint work by attempting to fragment it into as many separately protectable component works as possible; discussed in the context of film: 6.2.2, 6.2.4.
[128] 2.2.3.

have argued that this risk can be mitigated by referencing social norms explicitly at this point.[129] This devolves the decision of the kinds of contributions which are significant to the social norms governing creativity in that particular context, i.e., the best resource of the relative value of contributions. This approach avoids the pitfalls and analytical obfuscation associated with an abstract or acontextual approach.[130] This is not to say that judges should simply adopt an authorial community's view of who is an author, but rather that, as social norms provide the backdrop for the collaborative venture, this is a resource which will assist courts to assess which contributions are meaningful and valuable contributions to the content of the work in the particular context. Instead of seeking those with dominant and/or controlling role, the enquiry should focus on identifying all who might be considered responsible for the protected expression based upon the value of their contributions in pursuit of the common design.

An inclusive, contextual approach entails a shift in emphasis from whether an individual contribution is 'authorial' in some conventional sense to one which hones in on the collaborative nature of the joint work. So, for example, in the context of a scientific collaboration: the design of a study in accordance with the established scientific method is likely to be a significant contribution in light of the common design of contributors to produce research that will be accepted as valid by the relevant scientific community.[131] Similarly, a statistician who analyses data from a scientific experiments might make a significant contribution to a journal article reporting the results of that study because this input is needed to translate the results into an intelligible form.[132] To take another example, a Wikipedia contributor might make a significant contribution to a Wikipedia page by editing a page to secure compliance with the Neutral Point of View policy.[133] Likewise, a contributor to a film who composes tense background music to accompany on screen action by building suspense is also likely to have made a significant contribution if the common design is to create a thriller.[134]

When it comes to considering whether the contribution is of the *right kind* (amounting to 'authorship'), then this needs to be done with an eye

---

[129] A more explicit approach makes it more difficult for unconscious aesthetic biases to creep into judicial reasoning, see 4.2.3 and 4.4.
[130] See 2.3.3. The 'elephant test' for artistic works (you know one when you see one) suggested by the Court of Appeal in *Lucasfilm v Ainsworth* [2009] EWCA Civ 1328 [77] exemplifies an acontextual approach, and met with scepticism from the Supreme Court: *Lucasfilm v Ainsworth* [2012] 1 AC 208 [47].
[131] The scientific method and Mertonian norms (5.1) are likely to pass the framework in 8.3.
[132] p 142 (the significance of the work of statisticians).   [133] p 74.   [134] pp 167, 182.

to the reality of creativity. But, the question is primarily a legal one.[135] A contribution of the right kind is a contribution amounting to copyright authorship, that is, a more than de minimis contribution of creative choices or intellectual input to the protected expression. I have argued that this authorship standard should be no higher for joint works than it is for individually authored works. As this is the normative stage in the analysis, the purposes of the CDPA and the limits of copyright protection need to be taken into account. Thus, courts ought to consider the idea/expression dichotomy and perhaps also characteristics of the category of work in question.[136] This basic legal test provides a second filter to safeguard that, regardless of any social norms, a contributor will only be a joint author if they have made a contribution of the 'right kind'. Thus, purely financial contributions will never suffice, nor will the contribution of mere ideas. Overall decision-making control will be insufficient unless coupled with creative choices or other intellectual input evident in the protected expression.[137] The case studies suggest that a restrictive approach to the idea/expression dichotomy – which looks at the fixation, rather than the protected expression – should be rejected. We have seen that works of collective authorship tend to arise from a diverse range of different creative inputs which form part of the protected expression, and few of these may be directly linked to the process of fixation.

In addition to ensuring that the purpose of copyright law is fulfilled and that other policy goals are served, there is another reason to retain a legal dimension to the joint authorship test: the question of authorship is too important to be subordinated to market forces. The legal dimension of the joint authorship test might provide protection for creators in weaker bargaining positions, such as junior scientists and film contributors.[138] Indeed, one central justification for the copyright regime itself is premised on the need to protect authors against those who would take advantage by free-riding on the back of their creative efforts. The scheme embodied in the CDPA, which assumes that authors will typically contract with publishers or other disseminators (assigning or licensing their copyright interest) and/or will grant licences to other users of their works, requires a minimum level of equality of bargaining power to operate. An inclusive

---

[135] Bently and Biron (n25) note that this is important because authorship forms the basis upon which property rights are granted.
[136] See further Chapter 2, n47 and n70.
[137] Although control over the creative process might sometimes be relevant to an assessment of the significance of a contribution (assuming it is accompanied by intellectual contributions evident in the protectable expression); it is unlikely to be relevant to whether a contribution is of the right kind.
[138] This value is inherent in the court's reasoning in *Slater v Wimmer* [2012] EWPCC 7; see also p 178.

An Inclusive, Contextual Approach to the Joint Authorship Test   255

default approach to the joint authorship test best serves this purpose. It incentivises the more powerful party to define issues of ownership at the outset by raising the cost of failing to do so. This inclusive outcome is what many film contributors have tried to achieve by establishing guilds. The guilds have the power to negotiate with producers on a more equal footing to arrive at collective agreements with more favourable terms than would be available to individual contributors.[139] An inclusive approach is also preferable even where there is no inequality of bargaining power, or where contributors are not concerned about the ownership of copyright, because it better reflects the reality of collective authorship.[140]

Adopting this inclusive, contextual approach to the joint authorship test might mean, for example, that a scientific author who deletes important inaccuracies in an article might count as an author.[141] This contribution is seen as significant according to the scientific community and it also counts as a contribution of creative choices or intellectual input to the protected expression (broadly construed).[142] Similarly, such an approach, may have allowed for the recognition of communal authorship in *Bulun Bulun*.[143] In light of customary law, there was a clear common design between *Bulun Bulun* and his community (as represented by its Elders): the transmission and preservation of sacred cultural knowledge. Viewed in the light of this common design, the contribution of the community was significant. The initiation and apprenticeship of an artist chosen as the community's delegate and custodian of ritual knowledge, as well as the expectation of ongoing control of the community over subsequent uses of the artwork attest this. In Chapter 4, the Federal Court of Australia's assumption that the Indigenous community had contributed only unprotectable ideas was re-examined. Once the context of creativity is considered, *Bulun Bulun* appears analogous to *Cala Homes* in which a design director was held to be a joint author of drawings made by the draftsmen under his direction.[144] Thus, although the Indigenous community did not contribute to the fixation of the work, it was arguable that they did contribute to the protected expression.

---

[139] 7.4.1, p 194, p 196.   [140] 7.1.
[141] This was the result reached in a case which came before the Polish Supreme Court (Case II CSK 527/10, 22 June 2010): T Targosz, 'Authorship By Deletion', *Kluwer Copyright Blog*, <kluwercopyrightblog.com/2011/11/02/authorship-by-deletion-supreme-court-june-22-2010-ii-csk-52710>, dated 2 November 2011.
[142] p 132–133.   [143] 4.2.
[144] p 119–120. Indeed, *Bulun Bulun* has been explained as a result of a bias toward traditional 'Western' modes of production. Thus, it fails to reflect the reality of the authorship of art in the Indigenous community concerned: K Bowrey, 'The Outer Limits of Copyright Law – Where Law Meets Philosophy and Culture' (2001) 12 L and Critique 75.

The three-prong framework and the legal requirement of authorship ensures that undesirable norms are not uncritically adopted into law. For example, the attribution practices that many have criticised in biomedical science would not be accepted because they are not stable and uncontested.[145] Furthermore, 'gift' or 'guest' authorship will not meet the legal requirement for a contribution of the right kind to the expression of the work. Instances of irrational discrimination will also fall foul of the final step of the framework: the implications of adopting the social norm.[146]

The common law's flexible, incremental and problem-based approach to law-making is ideally suitable for the implementation of a flexible context-sensitive approach to joint authorship. The lack of explicit European harmonisation of the law on authorship and joint authorship leaves adequate space for the adoption of the particular inclusive, contextual approach which I advocate here.

8.6 Alternative Approaches to Joint Ownership

It follows from the argument of this book that I consider any statutory amendment of the joint authorship test unnecessary and potentially undesirable.[147] The test in its current form is flexible enough to adapt to creative dynamics in wide range of different contexts.[148] This book has shown that contextuality is particularly important when allocating authorship in cases of collective authorship. Use of open-textured language for the joint authorship test is inevitable since it must apply to such a broad range of works. Any attempt to draw clearer lines or elaborate the test in more detail test risks depriving the law of this essential flexibility. Furthermore, the inclusive contextual approach advocated here does not lend itself well to detailed statutory language.[149] Statutory amendment might be more appropriate in respect of one important consequence of joint authorship – joint *ownership* of copyright.

This book has argued that an inclusive approach to the joint authorship test is both better suited to achieving the normative goals of copyright law

---

[145] 5.2.1.
[146] Social discrimination can affect attribution practices, see M Terrall, 'The Uses of Anonymity in the Age of Reason' in M Biagioli and P Galison (eds), *Scientific Authorship: Credit and Intellectual Property in Science* (Routledge 2003) 91.
[147] This advantage of the proposed approach is significant in light of the difficulties in achieving real legislative reform in the area of copyright due to the influence of established interest groups and lobbies.
[148] A context-sensitive methodology might also facilitate copyright law's ability to respond to a range of different impulses for creation.
[149] On the potential benefits of vagueness in the law: M Spence and T Endicott, 'Vagueness in the Scope of Copyright' (2005) 121 LQR 657.

and more closely aligned with creative reality in cases of collective authorship. I have also argued that it is wrong to assume that multiple ownership of copyright will always impede the exploitation of the work, as this is often well-governed by private ordering (which is preferable for a number of reasons[150]). An inclusive approach to the joint authorship test is likely to encourage private ordering further and may also improve its quality.[151] Nevertheless, circumstances will arise where private ordering breaks down and copyright law's default rules on joint ownership will prevail.[152] Although a thorough analysis of the law joint ownership, which evaluates all possible avenues for reform is beyond the scope of this book it is possible to make some general observations. In the next section, I outline the current approach to joint ownership in the UK, briefly review some alternatives, and suggest a modest legislative amendment to promote better group management of jointly owned copyright interests.

8.6.1 The Current Approach to Joint Ownership

Joint authors are the default first owners of the copyright interest that subsists in a joint work (absent a relationship of employment or an agreement to the contrary).[153] The CDPA does not make the nature of the relationship between joint owners explicit, but there has been a judicial preference to find that joint owners hold their copyright interests as tenants in common.[154] This is not a hard and fast rule, as a joint tenancy has been found where circumstances have warranted it.[155] Although the categories of tenancy in common and joint tenancy arise from general property law, courts have been mindful of the difference between copyright and tangible property. Thus, in *Lauri v Renad* joint owners were described as 'tenants in common of a peculiar kind' or 'part owners' – the court stressing that these

---

[150] 7.4.3.   [151] 7.5.   [152] These rules also influence contributors' bargaining power.
[153] s11(1), s10(3). Joint authors might also agree, in advance, to assign their copyright ownership to another party: s91. On joint ownership of intellectual property generally: D Marchese, 'Joint ownership of intellectual property' (1999) 21(7) EIPR 364.
[154] In *Lauri v Renad* [1892] 3 Ch 402 Kekewich J held that joint *authors* could only hold as tenants in common incorrectly assuming that *Powell v Head* (1879) 12 Ch D 686 was settled law on this point, see Laddie et al. [22.570], also: *Stuart v Barrett* [1994] EMLR 448; *Beckingham v Hodgens* [2002] EWHC 2143 (Ch), [2002] EMLR 45.
[155] *Mail Newspapers v Express Newspapers* [1987] FSR 90. The circumstances of the case were fairly unusual. A husband and wife who had together commissioned wedding photos owned copyright in them as joint tenants (rather than tenants in common) such that one passed away the other would have the right of survivorship and could grant an exclusive licence in respect of the work. Millett LJ, 96 considered that ' ... in tragic circumstances such as this it would be deplorable if the surviving husband were not in a position to authorise a newspaper to publish the photographs for the benefit of the family without other newspapers being free to do so ... '.

terms are used for ease of reference, rather than accuracy.[156] Historically, joint owners were usually presumed to own equal undivided shares of the copyright interest.[157] This presumption has been rebutted in a number of more recent cases which have found ownership in unequal shares based upon unequal contributions of joint authors.[158] In *Slater v Wimmer*, the court suggested that questions of whether joint owners are tenants in common or joint tenants, and whether they are entitled to equal or unequal shares are 'subject to the particular circumstances and to any agreement on the point'.[159] Courts, thus, enjoy a significant degree of flexibility in construing the legal relationship between joint owners. In light of arguments advanced in this book, the 'significance' of a joint author's contribution would seem likely to provide the best guide for determining their proper ownership share.[160]

The CDPA is far less flexible when it comes to the rights of joint owners to control uses of the joint work. In most situations they are required to act in unison.[161] So, although a joint owner might independently assign their ownership share, they may not dispose of the copyright interest in the work as a whole without the accord of all joint owners.[162] Similarly, grant of a licence requires the consent of all joint owners.[163] Therefore, each joint owner has a veto power in relation to the exploitation or use of

---

[156] *Lauri v Renad* (n154) 413.
[157] *Prior v Lansdowne Press Pty Ltd* [1977] FLR 59, [1977] RPC 511; *Stuart v Barrett* (n154); *Beckingham v Hodgens* (n154).
[158] E.g., *Bamgboye v Reed* [2002] EWHC 2922 [42] (ownership divided one third to two thirds); *Fisher v Brooker* [2009] UKHL 41 (Fisher's organ solo entitled him to 40 per cent ownership of the copyright in the song 'A Whiter Shade of Pale').
[159] (n138)[89].
[160] See 8.5. Creative communities have developed understandings about how to valourise creative contributions and it is already the case that creators may distribute royalties amongst themselves according to notions of equity: C Waelde, 'What is beyond the score?' in A Rahmatian (ed) *Concepts of Music and Copyright: How Music Perceives Itself and How Copyright Perceives Music* (Edward Elgar 2015) 23, 44–45.
[161] One joint owner can independently sue in relation to an infringement of copyright in the joint work, but they may have to account to the other owners: *Powell v Head* (n154), *Lauri v Renad* (n154), *Cala Homes v Alfred McAlpine Homes* [1995] EWHC 7, [1995] FSR 818, 836. It may be necessary to join the other joint owners as defendants and any damages recoverable are likely to be in respect of the joint owner's share only: *Prior v Lansdowne* (n157).
[162] *Powell v Head* (n154); *Cescinsky v Routledge* [1916] 2 KB 325.
[163] s16(2), s173(2). Interestingly, the authors of *Laws of Australia* (accessed via Westlaw Australia, stated to be current as of 13 October 2013) [23.1.6500] (in a context where there is no equivalent express legislative provision requiring all joint owners agree to licence) consider that the primary consideration ought to be the effect of the exercise of the exclusive right on the value of the economic property. Thus, they consider that a joint owner may independently reproduce or licence the work if this increases demand for the work. But, they might be prevented from doing so and called to account for any loss (as well as any profit) if their judgement is found defective.

An Inclusive, Contextual Approach to the Joint Authorship Test 259

the work regardless of relative value of their contribution to it (if they were a joint author).[164] In addition, since copyright law requires the consent of *all* joint owners for *anyone* to exercise one of the exclusive rights, each joint owner is in the same position as a third party when it comes to their own use of the work.[165] Although this question has received very little judicial consideration to date, the same rules appear to apply irrespective of whether joint ownership arose from joint authorship or by another means (e.g., assignment or testamentary disposition).[166] The CDPA now provides a significant obstacle to a court wishing to take a more permissive approach in respect of the actions of joint author-owners, as s173(2) states explicitly that references to one owner refer to all owners and that 'in particular, any requirement of the licence of the copyright owner requires the licence of all of them'.

Prior to the enactment of this section, there may have been more room for argument. Section 173(2) sought to codify principles previously derived in the case law from the rule of statutory interpretation that the singular includes the plural[167] (supported by an analysis of the concept of a tenancy in common and a consideration of policy issues[168]). Courts considered that general property law on tenancies in common could not be directly transposed into copyright law due its intangible subject matter.[169] A joint owner was not thought to be able to exercise any of copyright's exclusive rights independently, as this would place a joint owner at the mercy of other joint owners who might ruin its market value by offering licences too

---

[164] The problem of obtaining consent from joint owners who cannot be located will now be alleviated to some extent by the orphan works licensing scheme: <www.gov.uk/guidance/copyright-orphan-works>.

[165] This differs from the approach taken in patent law, where although all joint owners must agree to licence or assign a patent, each joint owner can independently make the invention: Patents Act 1977, s36. Cornish et al. suggest that the difference might be explained by the need to protect a copyright author against an entrepreneur when both have become co-owners ([13–21] (n77)).

[166] The vast majority of cases concerning the rights of joint owners concerned joint ownership arising other than by virtue of joint authorship. M Spence, 'Aspects of Co-Ownership' (1987) 5(2) Copyright Reporter 11 has argued that copyright ownership rules should not differ depending on how ownership arose on the basis that this 'would only lend greater confusion to an already complex area of the law'.

[167] The Interpretation Act 1978, s6(c) and Sch 2, [2]; CDPA s16(2). *Cescinsky v George Routledge* (n162) 329–330.

[168] *Powell v Head* (n154) 689–690 (Jessel MR): 'It is against the very essence of part-ownership or co-ownership that when there is a tenancy in common, one of the two can dispose of the right of the other, there being no partnership or other form of agency' (Also noting the special nature of the subject matter and considering it to be closer to incorporeal property than real property).

[169] *Cescinsky v George Routledge* (n162) 330 (Rowblatt J): 'In my opinion, the old common law rule as to the right of a co-owner to use the common property has no application to such property as copyright. It seems to me that a sole right of reproducing, although divisible as to title, must be indivisible as to exercise'.

cheaply.[170] Yet, very few of these cases concerning joint ownership arose in circumstances of joint authorship and none concern highly collaborative work. In light of the common law's flexibility as to the nature of the relationship between joint owners (and in the absence of the express statutory provision) a court may well have adopted a different approach, were such a case to have been considered.[171]

There are, however, advantages to granting each joint owner a strong right to control uses of the work. First, this provides certainty. Second, whilst it might not immediately seem fair to grant each joint owner an equal right to veto uses of the work (irrespective of the size their ownership share), if a joint work arising from joint authorship is best conceived of as something *greater* than the sum of its parts, then, it would not exist without *all* contributions. From this perspective, it seems proper that the law encourages all author-owners to agree to the exercise any of the exclusive rights.[172] But most importantly, a strong default position is also likely to encourage creators to arrive at private ordering solutions which best suit their needs. We have seen that private ordering allows creative communities to shape flexible and context-appropriate means of regulating authorship and that legal entitlements might enable individual or collective action to secure better bargains. Private ordering however, is just one of a number of tools which might help resolve problems of collective action.

Courts have implied licences and implied contractual terms at their disposal in appropriate circumstances as another means to ensure that multiple right holders do not provide an undue barrier to exploitation.[173] Where a contract exists, a licence to use might be implied when, as a matter

---

[170] Ibid.

[171] D Vaver, 'Venturing into Intellectual Property Jointly and Confidentially' (2012) 25(1) IPJ 11, 15–17 notes that the current rules on the ownership of intellectual property interests are not necessary incidents of the particular right concerned and that co-ownership appears to have been dealt with as an after-thought. He comments, 'The ethos of the Musketeers [all for one, and one for all] is a good working rule of chivalry, but a less reliable working rule of market rivalry'.

[172] A Sofer, 'Joint Authorship: An Uncomfortable Fit with Tenancy in Common' (1998) 19 Loyola LA Entertainment LJ 1 makes the interesting argument (albeit in the US context, which has very different rules on joint ownership; see 8.6.2) that the particular vulnerability of joint owners, particularly joint authors, might be sufficient to establish the existence of a fiduciary duty due to the fact that their rights are so intertwined with each other.

[173] Vaver (n171) 16 argues that implied agreements can be used to modify the default ownership rules to more closely reflect the particular relationship between joint owners in dispute, thus usefully correcting the apparent inflexibility prescribed by co-ownership rules. See: *Brighton v Jones* [2004] EWHC 1157; *Godfrey v Lees* [1995] EMLR 307; *Beckingham v Hodgens* (n154); *Fisher v Brooker* [2009] UKHL 41. Implied licences are commonly relied upon in some creative industries: M Reed, 'Who Owns Ellen's Oscar Selfie? Deciphering Rights of Attribution Concerning User Generated Content on Social Media' (2015) 14 John Marshall Rev of Intellectual Property L 564.

An Inclusive, Contextual Approach to the Joint Authorship Test 261

of objective construction, this is a reasonable understanding of the parties' intent.[174] Where there is no formal contract, an implied licence might still be found on the basis of a trade custom or usage.[175] A licence might also be implied from conduct, e.g., based on the acceptance of royalties,[176] although it is also possible for implied licences to be gratuitous. In cases where one party commissioned another to provide a component of a composite work, courts have been willing to impose a trust implying an equitable assignment of copyright in that part to the commissioner, who intended to, and is capable of, exploiting the work as a whole.[177] It is not a far stretch from this for a court to determine that the conduct of contributing joint authors supports an implied, non-exclusive licence for any of them to exploit or use the work in appropriate cases where this accords with the common design envisaged in relation to the work.

Implied licences and implied contractual terms are not a panacea for hold-up issues. Implied licences must be no more than the minimum necessary to give effect to the parties' intentions.[178] Also, given their basis is the intent of the parties (as construed objectively by a court), the conduct of the parties may not support an implied licence.[179] There are

---

[174] *Ray v Classic FM* [1998] FSR 622, 641 approving the following overlapping conditions for implying a term into any agreement from *BP Refinery (Westernport) Pty Ltd v President, Councillors and Ratepayers of the Shire of Hastings* (1977) 52 ALJR 20 (PC) 26 (Lord Simon of Glaisdale): '(1) [the term] must be reasonable and equitable; (2) it must be necessary to give business efficacy to the contract, so that no term will be implied if the contract is effective without it; (3) it must be so obvious that "it goes without saying"; (4) it must be capable of clear expression; (5) it must not contradict any express term of the contract'.

[175] It will be necessary to show that the custom is invariable, certain and general (more than a 'mere' trade practice): Copinger et al. [5-224] and Chitty on Contracts, 32nd edn (access via Westlaw UK) [14-021]. See also: *Express Newspapers Plc v News (UK) Ltd* [1991] FSR 36, 45.

[176] *Redwood Music Ltd v Chappell & Co Ltd* [1982] RPC 109 (QB).

[177] Copinger et al. [22.78]. See: *Massine v de Basil* [1936-45] MCC 223 (CA); *Lucasfilm v Ainsworth* (n130) (CA) [196]-[208].

[178] A commissioner might, for example, have an implied licence to use a work for the purpose for which it was commissioned: *Ray v Classic FM* (n174). Usually only a non-exclusive licence is necessary, but an exclusive licence may be possible where warranted in the circumstances: *Coward v Phaestos Ltd* [2013] EWHC 1292 [248]-[249]. In exceptional circumstances, where necessary to ensure the business efficacy of a contract, a court may impose a constructive trust implying an equitable assignment of copyright to a commissioner: *Griggs v Evans* [2003] EWHC 2914 (Ch), [2004] FSR 31.

[179] There may be difficulty interpreting the parties' behaviour. O Fischmann Afori, 'Implied licence: An emerging new standard in Copyright law' (2009) 25 Santa Clara Computer & High Technology LJ 275, 325 makes the argument, in the US context, that the doctrine of implied licences should be freed from its contractual basis. In this way, he suggests it might be used as a tool for imposing terms on a case by case basis based on copyright policy considerations, thus, introducing a reasonableness standard which might help enable copyright law to adapt to the digital context. Nonetheless, he does not envisage this mechanism being used contrary to the express intentions of parties.

additional problems of uncertainty as it will not always be easy to predict when a court might imply a licence and what its terms will be.[180] Furthermore, a licence implied by conduct might be revoked where given gratuitously[181] (unless it is unconscionable to do so[182] or revocation is too late[183]). Implied licences also may not be particularly helpful in relation to opportunities to exploit the work which could not have been contemplated when the work was created. Faced with the limitations of implied licences and implied contractual terms, alternative ways of managing multiple ownership of a copyright interest should be considered.

8.6.2 A View from the United States

From a similar common law starting point, US courts have derived different rules on joint ownership.[184] Although one joint owner may not transfer or exclusively licence the copyright in a work independently,[185] any joint owner is permitted to use the work themselves or grant a non-exclusive licence to do so without the consent of the others (subject only to a duty to account).[186] US courts, thus, have less reason than UK courts to be concerned by hold-up issues. Yet, an even more restrictive approach to joint authorship has found favour for two main reasons.[187] First, there is the risk that competition between multiple owners, each willing to grant licences, will drive the price down and dissipate all profit.[188] Second, it is possible that creators fearing a loss of control over 'their' work might be discouraged from consulting with others.[189] Additionally, there are

---

[180] The burden will be on the person relying upon the licence as a defence to establish its existence and extent, see A Bell and G Parchomovsky, 'Copyright Trust' (2015) 100(5) Cornell LRev 1015, 1039 (discussed in the US context).
[181] *Godfrey v Lees* (n173). [182] *Brighton v Jones* (n173).
[183] For example, when the licence has become a contract: *Confetti Records v Warner Music UK Ltd* [2003] EWHC 1274 (Ch) [108].
[184] The common starting point being the common law property concept of a tenancy in common. United States courts, however, persuaded by a different view of the policy issues entailed, have adopted an approach to joint ownership which, in the view of commentators, is more closely aligned with the property law origin of this concept: T Kupferman, 'Copyright Co-Owners' (1945) 19(2) St John's LRev 95, 101–102; Spence, (n166) 11–12; H See, 'Copyright Ownership of Joint Works and Terminations of Transfers' (1982) 30 Kansas LRev 517, 518–521. Consider: *Carter v Bailey* 64 Me 458 (SC of Maine, 1874) 463 ' . . . if none be allowed to enjoy his legal interest without the consent of all, then one, by withholding his consent, might practically destroy the value of the whole use'.
[185] Copyright Act 1976 (US), s101 ('transfer of copyright ownership').
[186] On joint ownership in the US see: M LaFrance, 'Authorship, Dominance, and the Captive Collaborator: Preserving the Rights of Joint Authors' (2001) 50 Emory LJ 193; MB Nimmer and D Nimmer, *Nimmer on Copyright* (Matthew Bender 2016) §6.10.
[187] 2.5.3 and 6.2.5. [188] *Carter v Bailey* (n184) 463.
[189] *Aalmuhammed v Lee* 202 F3d 1227 (9th Cir, 2000) 1235.

An Inclusive, Contextual Approach to the Joint Authorship Test 263

doubts concerning whether it is fair to grant an ownership interest to a contributor who has made a relatively small contribution, particularly as a strong inference appears to apply that joint owners own equal shares of the copyright interest (absent an agreement to the contrary).[190] Although the US approach has the advantage of facilitating the distribution of works, it seems to undermine the status of copyright as property right because joint owners lose control of uses of the asset.[191] Internationally, this approach has not found much support, with most jurisdictions granting joint owners stronger rights as the UK has done. The US approach would seem a poor fit for the UK. In particular, allowing each contributor to licence the work independently with no regard to the shared common design does not seem to reflect the collaborative nature of a work of joint authorship, according to the UK definition, which yields something greater than the sum of individual contributions.[192]

If the UK approach appears too restrictive and the US approach too permissive, a mid-way position might present an ostensibly attractive option, e.g., consent from joint owners with interests representing a majority share sufficing for grant of a non-exclusive licence or the exercise of an exclusive right in relation to a work.[193] Such a provision might be accompanied by a duty to account to any non-consenting joint authors. On closer inspection, however, this hybrid solution presents its own problems. First, there is no principled basis for determining the appropriate quantum of copyright interest that should be required (e.g., a simple majority; a two thirds majority, etc.) – this would be a policy decision requiring a fairly arbitrary line-drawing exercise.[194] Second, in many cases it will difficult to establish the appropriate share allocation between joint owners based upon the significance of their contribution, which is likely to lead to complex

---

[190] *Carter v Bailey* (n184) 462. This position appears to be justified on the basis that determining the relative value of contributions would lead a decision-maker into the 'highly subjective area of aesthetic evaluation': 'Accountability Among Co-Owners of Statutory Copyright' (1958) 72 Harvard LRev 1550, 1564; Nimmer (n186) §6.08 argues that alternative interpretations of the US Copyright Act are possible and even desirable. Also: RR Kwall, 'Author-Stories: Narrative's Implications for Moral Rights and Copyright's Joint Authorship Doctrine' (2001) 75 Southern California LRev 1, 57.
[191] *Powell v Head* (n154).
[192] See 2.2. Indeed, the US definition of a 'joint work' is broader than in the UK, as it includes works made up of *interdependent* as well as inseparable contributions: Copyright Act 1976 (US), s101. This approach has been clearly rejected in the UK due to the concern that joint owners too willing to licence a work may ruin the value of the copyright (among other reasons): *Cescinsky v George Routledge* (n162) 330 (Rowblatt J).
[193] If this was not thought protective enough, a different proportion might be suggested, for example, a two thirds majority share.
[194] It is also unlikely that this line could be drawn in a way that is adapted to the variety of different creative contexts to which it would apply.

disputes.¹⁹⁵ Third, such a provision would undermine the value of authorship as a bargaining chip in negotiations, especially for those who have made smaller contributions. This, in turn, might skew the solutions reached by private ordering in favour of dominant contributors.¹⁹⁶ Finally, such a solution would not encourage teamwork and collective governance, instead it might incentivise some contributors to turn on others.

In the US context, Bell and Parchomovsky propose an ambitious solution: the copyright trust.¹⁹⁷ They argue that an inclusive approach to copyright ownership is necessary to ensure adequate incentives for collaborative creativity, but that this should not be at the expense of the streamlined, efficient exploitation of the work. In their view, both objectives might be achieved by concentrating the power of management in a single individual (the 'owner-trustee'¹⁹⁸), while diffusing the (financial) benefits of ownership among many contributors (the 'owner-beneficiaries').¹⁹⁹ The owner-trustee would owe a fiduciary duty to the owner-beneficiaries, being required to act in good faith to further their interests.

The copyright trust appears superficially attractive, since it permits all joint owners to share in the economic benefits of copyright, without impeding the exploitation of the work,²⁰⁰ but Bell and Parchomovsky's copyright trust scheme requires a number of supplementary rules inspired by property law and corporate law to ensure proper its governance.²⁰¹ Indeed, this reflects the experience in the UK concerning fragmentation of title to land owing to multiple ownership.²⁰² As a result of legislative

---

[195] The same problem presents itself in the current UK approach, but here the size of ownership share only affects the sharing of profits. If ownership share were to affect the right to control uses of a joint work, then one might expect greater proliferation of potentially complex disputes.

[196] Inequities risk undermining the creative community's collaborative spirit, see Kwall (n190) 58.

[197] They envisage the copyright trust operating as an additional legal tool that judges might avail themselves of where necessary, but also as a model parties might choose to adopt via contract. Their solution may seem attractive as a trust is a well-recognised instrument for simplifying the management of co-owned property and resolving disputes: RC Smith, *Plural Ownership* (OUP 2005) 209.

[198] Bell and Parchomovsky (n180) 1020, 1055–1056: This would be 'the individual or entity that has added the most value to the work and therefore has the highest economic stake in the success of the work'.

[199] Ibid.

[200] Ibid, 1059. Bell and Parchomovsky, however, appear to undermine the usefulness of their model by suggesting that it should only apply when the owner-trustee is easily identifiable and ownership of the parties can be cheaply determined. These are unlikely to be characteristic features of many joint ownership disputes involving large collaborations.

[201] Ibid, 1055.

[202] Law of Property Act 1925, s34(2) provides that there may be no more than four legal owners of land (additional right holders only enjoy a beneficial interest in land). See also:

intervention, now a statutory 'trust of land' arises whenever land is conveyed to more than four owners. The legal owners become trustees for themselves and any number of other beneficiaries. The legal title to the land is then co-owned by the four legal owners (as joint tenants),[203] with no limit to the number of beneficiaries who might hold their interests as tenants in common or joint tenants.[204] The operation of a trust of land requires a significant amount of supporting regulation and is accompanied by a broad discretion for courts to resolve disputes.[205] It would not be straightforward to introduce equivalent rules in the copyright context.

There are even more fundamental problems with this idea. As owner-beneficiaries lack any rights to control the use of a work, they are effectively treated as second-class owners which seems to undermine the proposal's equitable and egalitarian goals.[206] Casey and Sawicki argue that the likely disconnect between the copyright trust and social norms, which already operate very well to regulate collaborative creativity, would either mean that it has no impact at all (as the community will resist attempts to concentrate control) or would prove impossible to implement (contributors might become wary to involve a court for fear of exclusion from future projects in the industry).[207] Most significantly, there is no satisfactory way to determine who should be the owner-trustee, suggesting that this approach is likely to suffer from the same issues as the dominant author approach to joint authorship.[208] Thus, the copyright trust does not seem to be a desirable solution to this problem.

Trustee Act 1925, s34(2). MP Thompson, 'Beneficial Joint Tenancies: A Case for Abolition?' (1987) Conveyancer and Property Lawyer 29, 30.

[203] Law of Property Act 1925, s1(6).
[204] Note the over-reaching machinery contained in the Law of Property Act 1925, s2, which applies whenever property is bought or mortgaged via a contract with two or more title holders. In such a case a person's equitable property right is dissolved, detached from the property and reattached to moneys given by a third party for the property.
[205] E.g., Trustee Acts 1925 and 2000, Trusts of Land and Trustees Appointment Act 1997.
[206] It also assumes that the interests of authors can adequately be vindicated with a liability rule, rather than a property rule. This makes most sense under a strong economic incentive view of the rationale for copyright (as is dominant in the US, despite recent scholarship which has approached it with some scepticism, e.g., D Zimmerman, 'Copyright as Incentives: Did We Just Imagine That?' (2011) 12 Theoretical Inquiries in Law 29).
[207] A Casey and A Sawicki, 'The Problem of Creative Collaboration' (2017) 58 William and Mary LRev 1793, 1847–1848.
[208] See 2.5.3. Bell and Parchomovsky's own test favours investors, entrepreneurs and instigators. In most cases, the owner-trustee, in their view, is the person or entity that added the most *value* to the work (defined narrowly, as they seem to consider this to be the individual with the highest economic stake in the success of the work). They even suggest that in ' ... special cases, the court may assign the role of an owner-trustee to a smaller contributor if she has special managerial skills or is uniquely positioned to exploit the work commercially' (n180) 1056. Even if *value* were interpreted more broadly, this book demonstrates that the dynamics of creativity in the context of collective authorship often mean that it is impossible to identify a single person who might sensibly be held responsible for a work.

8.6.3 A Proposal for a Modest Legislative Amendment

Given the limits of the few 'off-the-shelf' legal tools best-suited to dealing with group ownership of rights, the current UK approach still appears to be the best option.[209] It encourages group rights to be self-managed by authorial groups according to their needs and in a way that can be more flexible and tailored to the relevant context. As a joint work, by very definition, is incapable of separation into its component parts, it makes most sense for joint author-owners to reach joint decisions concerning dealings with that work. Here, the CDPA's default rules facilitate self-management by placing all joint owners on an equal footing and thus giving them all a voice. The strong rights of each joint owner to control the work provides an incentive to adopt appropriate private ordering measures to allow for group governance of the exploitation of the work. Yet, disputes may still arise and the potential for hold-ups remains.

Here, a modest statutory amendment is proposed that would provide that one joint owner must not withhold their consent to licence or use a work *unreasonably*.[210] Similar provisions exist in other European countries, which like the UK, also adopt very protective rules of joint ownership. In Germany, for example, a joint owner may not unreasonably refuse to consent to the publication, exploitation or alteration of the joint work.[211] In Italy, should one or more joint authors refuse to authorise publication, modification, or a new use of work without due justification, the remaining joint authors may seek authorisation to do so from a judicial authority.[212] Copyright legislation in many other countries

---

[209] S Dusollier, 'Inclusivity in intellectual property' in GB Dinwoodie (ed) *Intellectual Property and General Legal Principles: Is IP a Lex Specialis?* (Edward Elgar 2015) 101. Dusollier is currently leading a promising project aiming to develop a tool better adapted to group rights founded on a principle of inclusivity; see: <www.sciencespo.fr/inclusive/content/project>.

[210] The absence of a solution to this issue is considered problematic by D Vaver *Intellectual Property Law* (Irwin Law 2011) 122. A similar suggestion was recommended to the US Copyright Office in a letter from Melville Nimmer dated 15 September 1958, 'Comments and Views Submitted to the Copyright Office on Joint Ownership of Copyrights' in *Joint Ownership of Copyrights* (US Copyright Office 1958) 5. He considered it necessary to couple such a measure with compulsory arbitration or another judicial mechanism for resolving disputes. Noting the difficulties determining 'reasonableness' in this area: 'Accountability Among Co-Owners of Statutory Copyright' (1958) 72 Harvard LRev 1550, 1558.

[211] German Copyright Act (Urheberrechtsgesetz, UrhG), Art 8(3), discussed in N Herrman and J Lehnhardt 'Germany' in B Allgrove (ed) *International Copyright Law: A Practical Global Guide* (Globe Business Publishing 2013) 203, 210.

[212] Italian Copyright Act (L. 22 April 1941, n633 Legge a protezione del diritto d'autore e di altri diritti connessi al suo esercizio), Art 10, '... in caso di ingiustificato rifiuto di uno o più coautori, la pubblicazione, la modificazione o la nuova utilizzazione dell'opera può essere autorizzata dall'autorità giudiziaria, alle condizioni e con le modalità da essa

likewise provides for court authorisation of the publication of a work in the situation where joint owners disagree.[213] Thus, the proposed statutory amendment should be accompanied by the grant of power to resolve licensing disputes among joint owners to the court or another appropriate forum.[214] It is also worth investigating the value of other supplementary amendments, such as a statutory limit on remedies where a joint owner has acted in good faith, or a statutory presumption of consent to use or licence a work in particular circumstances.

A range of factors might be relevant to the question of whether or not a joint owner has *unreasonably* withheld their consent to licence. A proposed use which would likely diminish the value of the copyright work might be reasonable grounds for withholding consent,[215] as might a use which is not accompanied by attribution[216] or one which risks subjecting the work to derogatory treatment.[217] Conversely, it might be unreasonable to deny a contributor permission to make a derivative work based upon that part of the work that they were largely responsible for. Thus, the special nature of

stabilite' discussed in M Perry and T Margoni, 'Ownership in Complex Authorship: A Comparative Study of Joint Works' (2012) 34(1) EIPR 22.
[213] P Kamina, *Film Copyright in the European Union* (2nd ed, CUP 2016) 369. See, for example, France (Intellectual Property Code, Law No 92-597 of 1 July 1992, Art L113-3(3)); Belgium (Economic Law Code, Laws of 10 and 19 April 2014, codifying the Law of 30 June 1994 on Copyright and Neighbouring Rights as amended, Art 4); Spain (Law on Intellectual Property, Royal Legislative Decree 1/1996 of 12 April 1996 as amended, Art 7); Japan (Copyright Act 1971, Arts 65 and 117); Korea (Copyright Act 1957, Art 48). In France, in addition, where the contributions of authors are of a different kind, each may, subject to an agreement to the contrary, separately exploit his or her own contribution as long as this does not prejudice the exploitation of the common work: Kamina, 173; N Bouche, *Intellectual Property in France* (2nd ed, Walters Kluwer 2014) 58. In addition, French law provides a category of 'collective work', which is a work created at the initiative of a natural or legal person who edits, publishes and discloses it under its direction and name (e.g., dictionaries, newspapers, computer programs, posters, elements of a car body). In such a work the contributions of the various authors are merged into the whole, so it is seen to be impossible to attribute to each of them a separate right over the whole work. The copyright in such a work is owned solely by the entrepreneur/initiator. For more see: Bouche 59–60.
[214] The Patents Act 1977, s37, for example, provides that the Comptroller might resolve similar disputes in the patent context on the basis that ' ... Parliament could not have intended it to be possible that exploitation of an invention could be frustrated by a deadlock situation. The whole point of the patent system was and is to encourage innovation and the exploitation of inventions': *Hughes v Paxman* [2007] RPC 2 (Jacob LJ) [13]. There is a similar justification to incentivise the creation and distribution of copyright works, although authorial control arguably has a greater role to play in copyright law.
[215] Conversely, it might be unreasonable to refuse permission for a use or licence which is likely to increase the value of, or demand for, the copyright work: see n163.
[216] This may be an important consideration in light of the considerable practical importance of credit in many creative contexts.
[217] Bearing in mind the relatively narrow scope of this right in the UK; see Bently et al. 296–302.

joint ownership arising from joint authorship is likely to be relevant. The fairness concerns already mentioned might be addressed by taking the relative value or significance of a joint author's contribution to the work into account. It would hardly seem 'reasonable' for a joint author-owner who has made a relatively small contribution to a work to block all subsequent exploitation on a whim. In some cases, the common design of contributors will shed light on the reasonableness of a joint owner's refusal. Many large collaborations have evolved models of collective decision-making to deal with these challenges (e.g., particle physics protocols). Judges should strive to uphold consensually developed strategies for managing collective authorship whenever reasonably possible.

It is hoped that such a 'reasonableness' requirement would encourage consultation and group governance of a jointly owned copyright interest whilst preventing hold-ups on the basis of capricious motives, grudges, etc. It would be desirable for the Intellectual Property Office to consult with creative communities and then provide guidance on good governance practices for collective activities, including indications of potentially reasonable/unreasonable grounds for withholding consent to a licence or proposed use of a joint work.[218]

In sum, therefore, there is a sliding scale of measures which might be adopted to manage joint ownership issues. In many situations, difficulties will be avoided by contract or other private ordering mechanisms, which are likely to provide the most appropriate solution. Where there is no prior agreement, or where the parties have not foreseen a particular scenario, the harshness of the joint ownership rules might be alleviated with a number of measures. In appropriate cases, implied licences or implied contractual terms might be relied upon to permit certain uses. Where it proves impossible to locate a joint owner, the orphan works licencing scheme provides an avenue to facilitate exploitation of the work.[219] Additionally, the proposed statutory amendments would provide valuable extra tools that might be relied upon to by a court[220] (or other appropriate forum[221]) to resolve intractable disagreements.

---

[218] The UKIPO already provides a number of business tools and guidance in relation to other aspects of intellectual property law (e.g., the licensing and use of orphan works): <www.gov.uk/government/collections/ip-for-business-events-guidance-tools-and-case-studies interactive-business-tools-and-training>.

[219] <www.gov.uk/guidance/copyright-orphan-works>.

[220] The Intellectual Property Enterprises Court will be a convenient forum for many disputes <www.gov.uk/courts-tribunals/intellectual-property-enterprise-court>.

[221] UK IPO might be tasked with this role, as it is already involved in settling terms in licence of right cases in respect of the UK design right: CDPA, s237. Another option might be the Copyright Tribunal (currently responsible for resolving disputes in relation to, inter alia, collective licensing schemes).

8.7 Final Note

Throughout popular culture, as well as in case law, and scholarship considered here, the concept of the 'author' as a singular creative genius is readily discerned. Although in the wider world, the romantic author has been pronounced 'dead',[222] some still see his ghost haunting copyright law today. The romantic author may have assumed a modern guise, living on in the tendency to concentrate authorship in the hands of a dominant author who takes charge of a creative project.[223] As the size of collaborations increase, the more likely it becomes that such a figure – if one exists – resembles an orchestrator, rather than a creator. Traditionally, it may have been expedient to hold one person responsible for collaborative work, but this is not (if it ever was), an accurate reflection of the way in which groups actually work together to create joint works. This fact has been appreciated in disciplines, such as science and film, where romantic author figures have been prominent in the past, but which now have moved towards more inclusive conceptions of authorship.

Although the rhetorical power of the romantic author trope may make the claims of dominant authors appear more plausible, I have suggested that a restrictive approach to joint authorship ultimately finds favour for primarily pragmatic, instrumental reasons (to simplify the exploitation of a work). The case studies show that this is likely to create side effects that are significantly worse than the ailment it seeks to cure. The pragmatic, instrumental approach is a distortion which distances the joint authorship test both from the reality of creativity and from copyright's notion of the author. Authorship is not defined in copyright law in terms of 'control',[224] but by the act of creation.[225] Even where a collective authorship group is hierarchically organised, responsibility for the protected expression will usually be shared as contributors, who use their own skills and judgement to make creative choices which shape their input to final product. I have argued that the current joint authorship test as worded in the CDPA conceives of collaborative work in broadly the same way that collective authorship groups do: as something *greater* than the sum of its parts. Yet,

---

[222] R Barthes, 'The Death of the Author' in S Heath (trans) *Image, Music, Text* (Fontana, 1977) 142; M Foucault, 'What is an author?' in D Bouchard (ed) *Language, Counter-Memory, Practice: Selected Essays and Interviews by Michel Foucault* (Cornell UP 1977).

[223] At its most extreme, in the US, the trend is towards recognising risk-takers such as investors and initiators as sole authors of collaborative work: 2.5.3. A Casey and A Sawicki, 'Copyright in Teams' (2013) 80 U of Chicago LRev 1683 use the theory of the firm to argue for the concentration of intellectual property rights with managers.

[224] Authorship is about more than merely signing a work: J Ginsburg, 'The Author's Name as a Trade Mark: A Perverse Perspective on the Moral Right of "Paternity"?' (2005) 23 Cardozo Arts and Entertainment LJ 379.

[225] s9. See 2.1.

this shared conception is obscured when courts adopt a restrictive approach when applying the test to the collaborations which come before them. This study of collective authorship reveals characteristics of collaboration that will often be present whatever the number of collaborators. Although it may be easier to identify a dominant author in a smaller collaboration, there still seems good reason to reject this approach as out of touch with copyright law's concept of authorship. This study has revealed few principled reasons to elevate one author to the exclusion of the others.

Based upon the experience of collective authorship in the case studies, when determining which efforts 'count' as authorship, ensuring that true creators gain access to the right of attribution should take priority over concerns of streamlining the economic exploitation of the work (and deliberately restricting authorship on this basis). This is further supported by the fact that ownership issues can be managed successfully with private ordering, even where large numbers of potential rights holders are involved. Private ordering allows for flexible, tailored solutions. For example, creators might separate out the economic and reputational incidents of authorship, allocating them to contributors in ways that best support their needs. Although the case studies demonstrate a natural interaction between private ordering and copyright law, they also suggest there is a need to regulate this relationship. By setting the default rules, copyright law should serve the role of a source of good authorship standards. This is enhanced by the interaction between legal and community standards in the application of the joint authorship test, which is partly a legal, and a partly a factual, question.

This book has argued for an inclusive, contextual approach to the joint authorship test that would demand better quality and more explicit reasoning. Decisions should be informed by creative realities and should not simply entrench power dynamics that already exist in creative communities. Authorship should be a flexible concept that can adapt to creative practices that differ over time, from place to place, and between creative communities.[226] By considering the social norms that apply to particular collective authorship groups, the joint authorship test can be applied in a flexible way that is sensitive to the creative context. This approach would allow the one-size-fits-all copyright regime to work in a more credible and socially-accepted way. It might also help to counteract the effect of cultural biases and elitist tendencies in the application of the

---

[226] The lack of international harmonisation of copyright on this point reflects the fact that the concept of authorship is partly contingent on local conditions. The very nature of authorship means that although a minimum threshold requirement might be harmonised, it is advisable to leave a margin of appreciation to Member States in relation to the contours of this concept as it applies in particular creative contexts.

authorship standard, by devolving the assessment of aesthetic values from judges to the perspectives of the creators themselves.

The proposal that judges ought to take social norms into account in applying the joint authorship test does not require a paradigm shift. Indeed, the case law suggests that judges already take some aesthetic criteria into consideration when applying the test, although they tend to do so covertly.[227] I have argued that there is value in a more overt, yet cautious, consideration of aesthetic criteria as reflected in the social norms that regulate collective authorship groups, in the application of the joint authorship test. As mass collaboration is becoming increasingly common in the digital age, if copyright law is to retain its credibility as the primary tool for regulating creativity, it must come to terms with the challenge of determining the authorship of works of collective authorship. It is hoped that the approach proposed in this book would bring the joint authorship test in line with the reality of collective authorship, while also providing a useful analytical framework to promote greater clarity in judicial decision-making. This solution draws upon the natural strengths of the UK's common law legal system and the flexible, incremental and problem-based approach to law-making that it allows.[228]

The current lack of good legal tools for regulating the rights of joint owners among one another is a matter that I have highlighted as meriting further investigation. I have suggested that the CDPA would be improved by providing courts power to resolve disputes when a joint owner is perceived as withholding their consent to a use of a joint work unreasonably. Yet, my argument in favour of an inclusive, contextual approach to joint authorship does not rely upon such an amendment. I argue that the optimal solution remains private ordering, which can provide a more nuanced approach in the governance of joint ownership. Private ordering allows for the flourishing of a greater diversity of creative models, some of which may be impeded by the ordinary operation of copyright law.[229] Strong ownership rights to control the use of collaborative work may incentivise creators to work together to adopt private ordering solutions to regulate uses of a collaborative work in a way that is more adapted to their needs. Such rights send a powerful message about the value authorship by supporting the claims of *all* authors for remuneration and recognition in respect of their contributions to collaborative work.

---

[227] 2.2, 2.3.3.
[228] The lack of explicit European harmonisation has left adequate space for courts to take an inclusive and contextual approach to the application joint authorship test, and such scope is even clearer post-Brexit.
[229] Wikipedia provides an example of a creative model that is impeded by current copyright law, hence the recourse to copyleft licences, see 3.3. These creative models might provide a valuable source of information for copyright policy makers about the merits of different approaches to the regulation of creativity.

This book reaffirms the importance of keeping the concepts of authorship and ownership in copyright law separate. The case studies demonstrate that the non-economic incidents of authorship are frequently either just as or even more important to creators than its economic incidents. The importance creators place on receiving authorship credit seems to suggest that the attribution right should enjoy broader application since currently, it must be asserted in very specific ways.[230] Thus, these case studies might provide additional support for the repeal of an assertion requirement which has already received scholarly criticism for seeming non-compliant with the Berne Convention.[231]

Equally, much of the current copyright debate, especially in common law jurisdictions, has failed to appreciate the role which non-economic incidents of authorship play in motivating creativity. The limitations of the economic incentive rationale for copyright protection are cast into sharp relief by the rise of sharing economies.[232] The fact that the case studies considered here concern artistic, literary and dramatic creations – works which fall squarely within the heartland of copyright law's authorial works – adds gravity to this critique. It suggests that the economic incentive story provides a weak basis for the copyright expansionism that has occurred in its name. There are important intrinsic and social dimensions to creativity, which require a more nuanced, contextual approach to the implementation of copyright law. An appreciation of the realities of creativity as glimpsed in these case studies points to an over-arching need to question the influence which instrumental, economic incentives-based reasoning should have in shaping future development of copyright law and policy.[233]

---

[230] s78.
[231] It is doubtful whether this requirement complies with the prohibition on conditioning the enjoyment and exercise of rights on any formality in Art 5(2), I Stamatoudi, 'Moral Rights of Authors in England: The Missing Emphasis on the Role of Creators' (1997) 4 IPQ 478, 503–504. The argument that the CDPA does comply is based on the English language version of Art 6bis, which provides the right of the author to 'claim' authorship of the work. Describing this argument as perverse: J Ginsburg, 'Moral Rights in the Common Law System' (1990) 1(4) Entertainment LRev 121, 128. A thorough analysis of moral rights implications of collective authorship is beyond the scope of this book, but is a worthy avenue for future research.
[232] Also sometimes referred to as gift or reputation economies.
[233] R Merges, *Justifying Intellectual Property* (Harvard UP, 2011) 3; M Lemley, 'Faith-based IP' (2015) 62 UCLA LRev 1328. An important resource in this debate is: J Silbey, *The Eureka Myth: Creators, Innovators, and Everyday Intellectual Property* (Stanford Press 2014). See also: JC Fromer, 'Expressive Incentives in Intellectual Property' (2012) 98 Virginia LRev 1745; O Bracha and T Syed 'Beyond Efficiency: Consequence-Sensitive Theories of Copyright' (2014) 29 Berkeley Tech LJ 229. The importance of the noneconomic incidents of authorship in motivating creators suggests a need to take a broader approach to implementing moral rights than the UK has been comfortable with to date: Stamatoudi (n231), Ginsburg (n231).

Bibliography

'Accountability Among Co-Owners of Statutory Copyright' (1958) 72 Harvard LRev 1550
'BECTU seeks screen credits for all VFX artists' (10 July 2017) <www.bectu.org.uk/news/2731>
'Creative Nation', Commonwealth Cultural Policy Statement, October 1994
Dracula (1992) (Film)
Halsbury's Laws of England (5th edn, LexisNexis 2012)
Jurassic Park (1993) (Film)
Pulp Fiction (1994) (Film)
'Report of the Board of Trade Copyright Committee' (Her Majesty's Stationery Company October 1952) Cmd 8662 ('Gregory Report')
'Report from the Commission to the Council, the European Parliament and the Economic and Social Committee on the question of authorship of cinematographic or audiovisual works in the Community of 6 December 2002' COM (2002) 691
'Report of the Royal Commission into Aboriginal Deaths in Custody', tabled in the Australian Federal Parliament on 9 May 1991
'The Collaborative Economy: Impact and Potential of Collaborative Internet and Additive Manufacturing' (Science and Technology Options Assessment Panel Study, European Parliament, PE 547.425, Dec 2015) <www.europarl.europa.eu/thinktank/fr/document.html?reference=EPRS_STU(2015) 547425>
The Nightmare Before Christmas (1993) (Film)
The Shining (1980) (Film)
Stopping the Rip-Offs: Intellectual Property Protection for Aboriginal and Torres Strait Islander Peoples, Australian Federal Government, October 1994 <www.ag.gov.au/Publications/Pages/StoppingtheripoffsOctober1994.aspx>
'The 7.30 Report', *ABC*, 19 August 2010 <www.abc.net.au/7.30/content/2010/s2988038.htm>
'The Collaborative Economy: Impact and Potential of Collaborative Internet and Additive Manufacturing' (Science and Technology Options Assessment Panel Study, European Parliament, PE 547.425, Dec 2015) <www.europarl.europa.eu/thinktank/fr/document.html?reference=EPRS_STU(2015)547425>
'Uniform Requirements for Manuscripts Submitted to Biomedical Journals' (1997) 277 JAMA 928

Adeney E, 'Unfixed Works, Performers' Protection, and Beyond: Does the Australian Copyright Act Always Require Material Form?' (2009) IPQ 77
— 'Authorship and Fixation in Copyright Law: A Comparative Comment' (2011) 35 Melbourne University LRev 677
Adler A, 'Against Moral Rights' (2009) 97 California LRev 263
Albertson Fineman M, *The Autonomy Myth: A Theory of Dependency* (The New Press 2004)
Allen RJ and Pardo MS, 'Facts of Law and Facts in Law' (2003) 7 International J of Evidence and Proof 135
Annas M, 'The Label of Authenticity: A Certification Trade Mark for Goods and Services of Indigenous Origin' (1997) 3(90) Aboriginal L Bulletin 4
Arnold R, 'Are Performers Authors?' (1999) EIPR 464
— 'Joy: A Reply' (2001) 1 IPQ 10
Arnold R, Bently L, Derclaye E, Dinwoodie G, 'IP Law Post-Brexit' (2017) 101 (2) Judicature 65
Astala M, 'Comment, Wronged by a Professor? Breach of Fiduciary Duty as a Remedy in Intellectual Property Infringement Case' (2003) 3 Houston Bus & Tax LJ 31
Astruc A, 'The Birth of the Avant Garde: Le Caméra Stylo', L'Écran français, 30 March 1948
Australian Senate Standing Committee on Environment, Communications, Information Technology and the Arts, *Indigenous Art – Securing the Future: Australia's Indigenous Visual Arts and Craft Sector*, (June 2007) ('Senate Report')
Ayres R, 'The Wandjina Case Illustrates the Lack of Protection for Indigenous Culture', *Art+Law*, Issue 3, September 2010
Bacharach S and Tollefsen D, 'We Did It Again: A Reply to Livingston' (2011) 69 (2) J of Aesthetics and Art Criticism 225
Bacharach S and Tollefsen D, 'We Did It: From Mere Contributors to Coauthors' (2010) 68(1) J of Aesthetics and Art Criticism 23
Balganesh S, 'Causing Copyright' (2017) 117 (1) Columbia LRev 1
Balganesh S, 'Unplanned Coauthorship' (2014) 100 Virginia LRev 1683
Barber B, 'Trust in Science' (1987) 25(1/2) Minerva 123
Barlow JP, 'The Economy of Ideas: Selling Wine Without Bottles on the Global Net' <www.eff.org/pages/selling-wine-without-bottles-economy-mind-glo bal-net>
Barnett J, 'Hollywood Deals: Soft Contracts for Hard Markets' (2015) 64 Duke Law Journal 605
Barron A, 'Copyright and the Claims of Art' (2002) 4 IPQ 368
— 'The Legal Properties of Film' (2004) 67 MLR 177
— 'Copyright Law and Musical Practice: Harmony or Dissonance?' (2006) 15 (1) Social and Legal Studies 25
Barthes R, 'The Death of the Author' in Heath S (trans) *Image, Music, Text* (Fontana, 1977) 142
Barzilai G, *Communities and Law: Politics and Cultures of Legal Identities* (U of Michigan Press 2003)

Bazerman C, 'Emerging Perspectives on the Many Dimensions of Scientific Discourse' in Martin JS and Veel R (eds), *Reading Science: Critical Functional Perspectives on discourses of Science* (Routledge 1988) 15

Beazley MJ, 'The Distinction between Questions of Fact and Law: A Question without an Answer?' (2013) 11 The Judicial Rev 279

Beebe B, 'Bleistein, the Problem of Aesthetic Progress, and the Making of American Copyright Law' (2017) 117 Columbia LRev 319

Behrendt L, Cunneen C, Libesman T, *Indigenous Legal Relations in Australia* (OUP 2009)

Bell A and Parchomovsky G, 'Copyright Trust' (2015) 100 Cornell LRev 1015

Bently L, 'Copyright and the Death of the Author in Literature and Law' (1994) 57 MLR 973

— 'R v Author: From Death Penalty to Community Service' (2008) 32(1) Columbia J of L & the Arts 1

— 'Authorship of Popular Music in UK Copyright Law' (2009) 12(2) Information Communication & Society 179

Bently L and Biron L, 'Discontinuities between legal conceptions of authorship and social practices: What, if anything, is to be done?' in van Eechoud M (ed) *The Work of Authorship* (Amsterdam UP 2014) 237

Bently L and Sherman B, *Intellectual Property Law* (OUP 2009)

Bently L, Sherman B, Gangjee D and Johnson P, *Intellectual Property Law* (OUP 2018)

Bhopal R et al., 'The Vexed Question of Authorship: Views of Researchers in a British Medical Faculty' (1997) 314 (7086) British Medical J 1009

Biagioli M and Galison P (eds), *Scientific Authorship: Credit and Intellectual Property in Science* (Routledge 2003)

Biagioli M, 'Rights or Rewards? Changing Frameworks of Scientific Authorship' in Biagioli M and Galison P (eds), *Scientific Authorship: Credit and Intellectual Property in Science* (Routledge 2003) 260

— 'Documents of Documents: Scientists' Names and Scientific Claims' in Riles A (ed) *Documents: Artifacts of Modern Knowledge* (U of Michigan Press 2006) 129

Bicchieri C and Muldoon R, 'Social Norms' in *Stanford Encyclopedia of Philosophy* <plato.stanford.edu/entries/social-norms>

Bicchieri C, *The Grammar of Society: The Nature and Dynamics of Social Norms* (CUP 2006)

Birnholtz J, 'When Authorship Isn't Enough: Lessons from CERN on the Implications of Formal and Informal Credit Attribution Mechanisms in Collaborative Research' (2008) 11(1) Journal of Electronic Publishing <dx.doi.org/10.3998/3336451.0011.105>

Biro MM, 'Smart Leaders and the Power of Collaboration', *Forbes* (3 March 2013), <www.forbes.com/sites/meghanbiro/2013/03/03/smart-leaders-and-the-power-ofcollaboration>.

Biron L and Cooper E, 'Authorship, Aesthetics and the Art World: Reforming Copyright's Joint Authorship Doctrine' (2016) 35 Law and Philosophy 55

Blackstone W, *Commentaries*, Volume 1

Bloomfield D, Collins K, Fry C and Munton R, 'Deliberation and Inclusion: Vehicles for Increasing Trust in UK Public Governance' (2001) 19 Environment and Planning C: Government and Policy 501

Bloore P, *The Screenplay Business: Managing Creativity and Script Development in the Film Industry* (Routledge 2012)
  Managing Creativity and Script Development in the Film Industry (Routledge 2013)
Bonadio E, 'Joint Ownership of Films in the Absence of Express Terms' (2012) 7 (7) JIPLP 493
Bodó B, 'Pirates in the Library – An Inquiry into the Guerrilla Open Access Movement' (8th Annual Workshop of the International Society for the History and Theory of Intellectual Property, CREATe, University of Glasgow, 6–8 July 2016) (available at SSRN: <ssrn.com/abstract=2816925>).
Bouche N, Intellectual Property in France (2nd ed, Walters Kluwer 2014)
Bowrey K, 'The Outer Limits of Copyright Law – Where Law Meets Philosophy and Culture' (2001) 12 L and Critique 75
  Law and Internet Cultures (CUP 2005)
  'Alternative IP?: Indigenous Protocols, Copyleft and New Juridifications of Customary Practices' (2006) 6 Macquarie LJ 65
  'Economic Rights, Culture Claims and a Culture of Piracy in the Indigenous Art Market: What Should We Expect from the Western Legal System?' (2009) 13(2) Australian Indigenous LRev 43–4
Bowrey K and Anderson J, 'The Politics of Global Information Sharing: Whose Cultural Agendas Are Being Advanced?' (2009) 18 Social and Legal Studies 479.
Boyle J, *Shamans, Software and Spleens: Law and the Construction of the Information Society* (Harvard UP 1996)
  'Second Enclosure Movement and the Construction of the Public Domain' (2003) 66 L and Contemporary Problems 33
Bracha O and Syed T 'Beyond Efficiency: Consequence-Sensitive Theories of Copyright' (2014) 29 Berkeley Tech LJ 229
Bracha O, 'The Ideology of Authorship Revisited: Authors, Markets, and Liberal Values in Early American copyright' (2008) 118 Yale LJ 186
  'How Did Film Become Property? Copyright and the Early American Film Industry' in B Sherman and L Wiseman, *Copyright and the Challenge of the New* (Wolters Kluwer 2012) 141
Breyer S, 'The Uneasy Case For Copyright: A Study of Books, Photocopies and Computer Programs' (1970) 84(2) Harvard LRev 281
Bruns A, *Blogs, Wikipedia, Second Life, and Beyond: From Production to Produsage* (Peter Lang 2008)
Buccafusco C, 'On the Legal Consequences of Sauces: Should Thomas Keller's Recipes Be Per Se Copyrightable?' (2007) 24 Cardozo Arts & Entertainment LJ 1121
  'Making Sense of Intellectual Property Law' (2012) 97 Cornell LRev 501
  'A Theory of Copyright Authorship' (2016) 102 Virginia LRev 1229
Burk D, 'Research Misconduct: Deviance, Due Process, and the Disestablishment of Science' (1995) 3 George Mason U Independent LRev 305
Burkitt D, 'Copyrighting Culture – The History and Cultural Specificity of the Western Model of Copyright' (2001) IPQ 146
Burleson K, 'Learning from Copyright's Failure to Build Its Future' (2014) 89(3) Indiana LJ 1299

Burns Coleman E, *Aboriginal Art, Identity and Appropriation* (Ashgate 2005)

Carter S, 'Custom, Adjudication and Petrushevsky's Watch: Some Notes from the Intellectual Property Front' (1992) 78 Virginia LRev 129

Casey A and Sawicki A, 'Copyright in Teams' (2013) 80 U of Chicago LRev 1683

Chander A and Sunder M, 'The Romance of the Public Domain' (2004) 92 California LRev 1331

Chemerinsky E, 'In Defense of Equality: A Reply to Professor Westen' (1983) 81 Michigan LRev 575

Chon M, 'New Wine Bursting From Old Bottles: Collaborative Internet Art, Joint Works, and Entrepreneurship' (1996) 75 Oregon LJ 257

Clark G and Davies I, 'Mediation – When Is It Not an Appropriate Dispute Resolution Process?' (1992) 3(2) Australian Dispute Resolution J 70

Claxton L, 'Scientific Authorship Part 2: History, Recurring Issues, Practices, and Guidelines' (2005) 589 Mutation Research 31

Cohen J, 'Creativity and Culture in Copyright Theory' (2007) 40 U of California Davis LRev 1151

Conley T, 'End Credits' in Biagioli M and Galison P (eds), *Scientific Authorship: Credit and Intellectual Property in Science* (Routledge 2003) 360

Coombe R, 'Contingent Articulations: A Critical Cultural Studies of Law' in Sarat A and Kearns T (eds), *Law in the Domains of Culture* (U of Michigan Press 1998)

The Cultural Life of Intellectual Properties: Authorship, Appropriation and the Law (Duke UP 1998)

'Fear, Hope and Longing for the Future of Authorship and a Revitalized Public Domain in Global Regimes of Intellectual Property' (2003) 52 DePaul LRev 1171

Cooper E, 'Joint Authorship in Comparative Perspective: *Levy v Rutley* and the divergence between the UK and USA' (2005) 62(2) Journal of the Copyright Society of the USA 245

Cooter R, 'Normative Failure Theory of Law' (1997) 82 Cornell LRev 947

Corbett S, 'Creative Commons Licences, the Copyright Regime and the Online Community: Is There a Fatal Disconnect?' (2011) 74(4) MLR 503

Cornish W, 'The Author as Risk-Sharer' (2002) 26 Columbia J of L & the Arts 1

Cornish W, Llewelyn D and Aplin T, *Intellectual Property: Patents, Copyright, Trade Marks and Allied Rights* (8th edn, Sweet & Maxwell 2013)

Craig C, *Administrative Law* (4th edn, Sweet & Maxwell 1999)

'Reconstructing the Author-Self: Some Feminist Lessons for Copyright Law' (2007) 15(2) J of Gender Social Policy and the Law 207

Copyright, Communication and Culture: Towards a Relational Theory of Copyright Law (Edward Elgar 2011)

Datta A, 'Collective Bargaining Agreements in the Film Industry: US Guild Agreements for Germany?' (2013) 2(1) Berkeley J of Entertainment and Sports L 200

Davenport R, 'Screen Credit in the Entertainment Industry' (1990) 10 Loyola Entertainment LJ 129

Davis P, 'An Authorship Accelerator' <scholarlykitchen.sspnet.org/2008/12/08/hep-authorship> dated 8 December 2008

Decherney P, *Hollywood's Copyright Wars: From Edison to the Internet* (Columbia UP 2012)

Department for Culture Media and Sport, 'A Future For British Film: It Begins with the Audience ... ' Film Policy Review, 2012

Derclaye E, 'Do Sections 3 and 3A of the CDPA Violate the Database Directive? A Closer Look at the Definition of a Database in the UK and Its Compatibility with European Law' (2002) 24(10) EIPR 466

'What is a Database? A Critical Analysis of the Definition of a Database in the European Database Directive and Suggestions for an International Definition' (2002) 5(6) JWIP 981

'Databases Sui Generis Right: Should We Adopt the Spin Off Theory?' (2004) 26(9) EIPR 402

'The Court of Justice Interprets the Database Sui Generis Right for the First Time' (2005) 30(3) Eur LR 420

'Database Sui Generis Right: What Is a Substantial Investment? A Tentative Definition' (2005) 36(1) Intl Rev of Intellectual Property and Competition L 2

'Case Comment: Infopaq International A/S v Danske Dagblades Forening (C-5/08): Wonderful or Worrisome? The Impact of the ECJ Ruling in Infopaq on UK Copyright Law' (2010) 32(5) EIPR 247

Dietz A, 'The Concept of Authorship Under the Berne Convention' (1993) 155 Revue Internationale du Droit d'Auteur 3

Dinwoodie G, 'Private Ordering and the Creation of International Copyright Norms: The Role of Public Structuring' (2004) 160 J of Institutional and Theoretical Economics 161

Dinwoodie G and Dreyfuss RC, 'Brexit and IP: The Great Unravelling?' (2017) 39 Cardozo L Rev 967

Diver A, '"A Just War": Protecting Indigenous Cultural Property' (2004) 6(4) Indigenous L Bulletin 7

Dodson M and Barr O, 'Breaking the Deadlock: Developing and Indigenous Response ecting Indigenous Traditional Knowledge' (2007) 11(2) Australian Indigenous LR 19

Dougherty J, 'Not A Spike Lee Joint? Issues in the Authorship of Motion Pictures Under US Copyright Law' (2001) 49 UCLA LRev 225

'The Misapplication of "Mastermind": A Mutant Species of Work for Hire and the Mystery of Disappearing Copyrights' (2016) 39 Columbia J L & Arts 463

Doyle G, *Understanding Media Economics* (2nd edn, Sage 2013)

Drahos P with Braithwaite J, *Information Feudalism: Who Owns the Knowledge Economy?* (Routledge 2002)

Drassinower A, 'From Distribution to Dialogue: Remarks on the Concept of Balance in Copyright Law' (2009) 34(4) J of Corporation L 991

Dreyfuss RC, 'Collaborative Research: Conflicts on Authorship, Ownership and Accountability' (2000) 53 Vanderbilt LRev 1161

Dusollier S, 'Open Source and Copyleft: Authorship Reconsidered?' (2003) 26 Columbia J of L and Arts 281

'The Master's Tools v the Master's House: Creative Commons v Copyright' (2005) 29 Columbia J of L and Arts 271

'Sharing Access to Intellectual Property through Private Ordering' (2007) 82 (3) Chicago-Kent LRev 1391

Dworkin G, 'Authorship of Films and the European Commission Proposal for Harmonising the Term of Copyright' (1993) EIPR 151

Dysart T, 'Author-Protective Rules and Alternative Licences: A Review of the Dutch Copyright Contract Act' (2015) 37(9) EIPR 601

Ebersbach A, Glaser M and Heigl R, *Wiki: Web Collaboration* (Springer 2006)

Eisenberg R, 'The Bargain Principle and its Limits' (1982) 95 Harvard LRev 741

'Proprietary Rights and the Norms of Science in Biotechnology Research' (1987) 97 Yale LJ 177

Eliades D, 'Power in Mediation – Some Reflections' (1999) 2(1) ADR Bulletin 4

Elkin-Koren N, 'What Contracts Cannot Do: The Limits of Private Ordering in Facilitating a Creative Commons' (2005) 74 Fordham LRev 375

'Tailoring Copyright to Social Production' (2011) 12(1) Theoretical Inquiries in L 309

Ellickson R, *Order without Law: How Neighbors Settle Disputes* (Harvard UP 1991)

Ellison D, 'Unauthorised Reproduction of Traditional Aboriginal Art' (1994) 17 UNSWLJ 327

Endicott T, 'Questions of Law' (1998) 114 LQR 292

Epstein R, 'Academic Fraud Today: Its Social Causes and Institutional Responses' (2010) 21 Stanford L & Policy Rev 135

European Copyright Society, 'Opinion on the pending reference before the CJEU in Case 310/17 (copyright protection of tastes)' (19 February 2018) available at: <europeancopyrightsocietydotorg.files.wordpress.com/2018/03/ecs-opinion-on-protection-for-tastes-final1.pdf>.

Everard D, 'Code of Conduct for Indigenous Art', *Art+Law*, June 2009, available at <www.artslaw.com.au/artlaw/archive/2009/09CodeOfConduct.asp>

Fauchart E and von Hippel EA, 'Norm-Based Intellectual Property Systems: The Case of French Chefs' (2008) 19(2) Organization Science 187

Field R, 'Mediation and the Art of Power (Im) balancing' (1996) 12 QUTLJ 264

Finbow K, 'Nicole Kidman: "I had no control over Grace of Monaco"', *Digital Spy*, 27 May 2014

Fischmann AO, 'Implied Licence: An Emerging New Standard in Copyright Law' (2009) 25 Santa Clara Computer & High Technology LJ 275

Fisher R and Ury W, *Getting to Yes: Negotiating Agreement without Giving in* (Houghton Mifflin 1981)

Fisher W, 'Property and Contract on the Internet' (1998) 73 U Chicago-Kent LRev 1203

'Theories of Intellectual Property' in S Munzer (ed) New Essays in the Legal and Political Theory of Property (2001) <www.tfisher.org/publications.htm>

Fisk C, 'Credit Where It's Due: The Law and Norms of Attribution' (2006) 95 Georgetown LJ 49

'The Jurisdiction of the Writers Guild to Determine the Authorship of Movies and Television Programs' (2010) English Language Notes 48(15), available at SSRN: <ssrn.com/abstract=1694043>

'The Role of Private Intellectual Property Rights in Markets for Labor and Ideas: Screen Credit and the Writers Guild of America, 1938–2000' (2012) 32 Berkeley J of Employment and Labour L 215

Foucault M, 'What Is an Author?' in D Bouchard (ed) *Language, Counter-Memory, Practice: Selected Essays and Interviews by Michel Foucault* (Cornell UP 1977)

Fox M, Ciro T and Duncan N, 'Creative Commons: An Alternative, Web-Based Copyright System' (2005) 16(6) Entertainment LR 111

Fox PS, 'Preserving the Collaborative Spirit of American Theatre: The Need for a 'Joint Authorship Default Rule' in Light of the Rent Decision's Unanswered Question' (2001) 19 Cardozo Arts & Entertainment LJ 497

Free D, 'Beckingham v Hodgens: The Session Musician's Claim to Music Copyright' (2005) 1(3) Entertainment and Sports LJ 93, available at <www.warwick.ac.uk/go/eslj/issues/volume1/number3>

Fromer JC, 'Expressive Incentives in Intellectual Property' (2012) 98 Virginia LRev 1745

Fugh-Berman AJ, 'The Haunting of Medical Journals: How Ghostwriting Sold "HRT"' (2010) 7(9) PLoS Med e1000335

Galison P, 'The Collective Author' in Biagioli M and Galison P (eds), *Scientific Authorship: Credit and Intellectual Property in Science* (Routledge 2003) 329

Gardner J, 'Some Types of Law' in Edlin D (ed) *Common Law Theory* (CUP 2007) 51

'The Many Faces of the Reasonable Person' (2015) 131 LQR 563

Garfield E, 'Giving Credit Only Where It Is Due: The Problem of Defining Authorship' (1995) 9(19) The Scientist 13

Garnett KM, Davies G, Harbottle G, Copinger WA and Skone James EP, *Copinger and Skone James on Copyright* (16th edn, Sweet & Maxwell 2011)

Garon J, 'Content, Control, and the Socially Networked Film' (2010) 48 U of Louisville LRev 771

Gaut B, 'Film Authorship and Collaboration' in Allen R and Smith M (eds), *Film Theory and Philosophy* (OUP 1997) 149

Geiger C, 'The Social Function of Intellectual Property Rights' in GB Dinwoodie (ed) *Intellectual Property Law: Methods and Perspectives* (Edward Elgar 2013) 153

Giblin R and Weatherall K (eds), *What If We Could Reimagine Copyright?* (ANU Press, 2017)

Gibson J, 'Justice of Precedent, Justice of Equity: Equitable Protection and Remedies for Indigenous Intellectual Property' (2001) 6(4) Australian Indigenous L Reporter 1

Ginsburg J, 'Moral Rights in the Common Law System' (1990) 1(4) Entertainment LRev 121

'Response to David Nimmer' (2001) 38 Houston LRev 231

'How Copyright Got a Bad Name For Itself' (2002) 26(1) Columbia J of L and the Arts 61

'The Concept of Authorship in Comparative Copyright Law' (2003) 52 De Paul L Rev 1063

'The Author's Name as a Trade Mark: A Perverse Perspective on the Moral Right of "Paternity"?' (2005) 23 Cardozo Arts and Entertainment LJ 379

'The Author's Place in the Future of Copyright' in R Okediji (ed) *Copyright in an Age of Exceptions and Limitations* (CUP, 2015) 60
Goldstein P, *Copyright: Principles, Law and Practice* (Little, Brown & Co 1989)
Golvan C, 'Aboriginal Art and Copyright: The Case for Johnny Bulun Bulun' (1989) 11(10) EIPR 346
'Aboriginal Art and the Protection of Indigenous Cultural Rights' (1992) 14(7) EIPR 227
'Aboriginal Art and Copyright: An Overview and Commentary Concerning Recent Developments' (1999) EIPR 549
Gomulkiewicz R, 'General Public License 3.0: Hacking the Free Software Movement's Constitution' (2006) 42(4) Houston LRev 1015
'Conditions and Covenants in License Contracts: Tales from a Test of the Artistic License' (2009) 17(3) Texas Intellectual Property LJ 335
'Open Source License Proliferation: Helpful Diversity or Hopeless Confusion?' (2009) 30 Washington UJ of L and Policy 261
Gonzalez AG, 'Viral Contracts or Unenforceable Documents? Contractual Validity of Copyleft Licences' (2004) 26(8) EIPR 331
Gøtzsche PC et al., 'Ghost Authorship in Industry-Initiated Randomised Trials' (2007) 4 PLoS Med e535
Gøtzsche PC et al., 'What Should Be Done to Tackle Ghostwriting in the Medical Literature?' (2009) 6(2) PLoS Med e1000023
Graber C, 'Aboriginal Self-determination vs the Proprietisation of Traditional Culture: The Case of Sacred Wanjina Sites' (2009) 13(2) Australian Indigenous L Report 18
Graber C and Taubner G, 'Art and Money: Constitutional Rights in the Private Sphere?' (1998) 18 OJLS 61
Grant BK, *Auteurs and Authorship: A Film Reader* (Blackwell 2008)
Gray D, *Setting up and Managing a Production Company* (Medialex Publications 2006)
Griffin J, 'The Changing Nature of Authorship: Why Copyright Law Must Focus on the Increased Role of Technology' (2005) IPQ 135
Guibault L, *Copyright Limitations and Contracts: An Analysis of the Contractual Overridability of Limitations on Copyright* (Kluwer Law International 2002)
'Wrapping Information in Contract: How Does it Affect the Public Domain?' in Guibault L and Hugenholtz PB (eds), *The Future of the Public Domain: Identifying the Commons in Information* (Kluwer Law International 2006) 87
Guibault L and Angelopoulos C, *Open Content Licensing: From Theory to Practice* (Amsterdam UP 2011)
Gusterson H, 'The Death of the Authors of Death: Prestige and Creativity among Nuclear Weapons Scientists' in Biagioli M and Galison P (eds), *Scientific Authorship: Credit and Intellectual Property in Science* (Routledge 2003) 281
Halbert DJ, *Intellectual Property in the Information Age: The Politics of Expanding Ownership Rights* (Quorum 1999)
Hamann K, 'Indigenous Australian Art Market Suffering Substantial Decline', 9 August 2013, transcript of ABC Radio report available at: <www.abc.net.au/pm/content/2013/s3822279.htm>
Handler M, 'Continuing Problems with Film Copyright' in Macmillan F (ed) *New Directions in Copyright Law: Volume 6* (Edward Elgar 2007) 173

Hargreaves I, 'Digital opportunity: A Review of Intellectual Property and Growth for HMG' (2011) available at: <webarchive.nationalarchives.gov.uk/20140606231343/http://www.ipo.gov.uk/ipreview>

Hawkins C, 'Stopping the Rip Offs: Protecting Aboriginal and Torres Strait Islander Cultural Expression' (1995) Aboriginal L Bulletin 3

Heile B, 'Who Wrote Duke Ellington's Music?' in A Rahmatian (ed) *Concepts of Music and Copyright: How Music Perceives Itself and How Copyright Perceives Music* (Edward Elgar 2015) 123

Henley M, 'Jacobsen v Katzer and Kamind Associates – An English Legal Perspective' (2009) 1(1) IFOSS L Rev 41

Herrman N and Lehnhardt J 'Germany' in Allgrove B (ed) *International Copyright Law: A Practical Global Guide* (Globe Business Publishing 2013) 203

Hick DH, 'Authorship, Co-Authorship, and Multiple Authorship' (2014) 72(2) J of Aesthetics and Art Criticism 147

Hobbs J, 'The $200m industry of cheap fakes ripping off Indigenous artists', *Brisbane Times*, 24 March 2018 <www.brisbanetimes.com.au/entertainment/art-and-design/the-200m-industry-of-cheap-fakes-ripping-off-indigenous-artists-20180324-p4z63m.html>

Hobson A, 'Imperial Stormtroopers, Art Works, and Copyright Defences' (2009) 4(1) JIPLP 16

Horton R, 'The Signature of Responsibility' (1997) 350 Lancet 5

Huang T, 'Gaiman v McFarlane: The Right Step in Determining Joint Authorship for Copyrighted Material' (2005) 20(1) Berkeley Technology LJ 673

Hunt E, 'Chanel's $2,000 boomerang criticised for "humiliating" Indigenous Australian culture', *The Guardian*, 16 May 2018, <www.theguardian.com/fashion/2017/may/16/chanels-2000-boomerang-criticised-for-humiliating-indigenous-australian-culture>

Iljadica M, *Copyright Beyond Law: Regulating Creativity in the Graffiti Subculture* (Hart Publishing 2016)

Jackson MW, 'Can Artisans Be Scientific Authors? The Unique Case of Fraunhofer's Artisanal Optics and the German Republic of Letters' in Biagioli M and Galison P (eds), *Scientific Authorship: Credit and Intellectual Property in Science* (Routledge 2003) 113

Janke T, 'The Carpet Case' (1995) 3(72) Aboriginal L Bulletin 36

—— *Our Culture: Our Future - Report on Australian Indigenous Cultural and Intellectual Property Rights* (Michael Frankel & Co and Terri Janke 1998)

—— *Minding Culture: Case Studies on Intellectual Property and Traditional Cultural Expressions* (WIPO 2003)

—— *Beyond Guarding Ground: A Vision for a National Indigenous Cultural Authority* (Terri Janke & Co 2009)

Jaszi P, 'Towards a Theory of Copyright: The Metamorphoses of Authorship' (1991) 2 Duke LJ 455

—— 'On The Author Effect: Recovering Collectivity' in Woodmansee M and Jaszi P (eds) *The Construction of Authorship: Textual Appropriation in Law and Literature* (Duke U Press 1999) 29

—— 'Is There Such a Thing as Postmodern Copyright?' (2009) 12 Tulane J of Technology & IP 105

T Janke and P Dawson, 'New Tracks: Indigenous Knowledge and Cultural Expression and the Australian Intellectual Property System' (Terri Janke and Company Pty Ltd, 2012) (<www.ipaustralia.gov.au/sites/g/files/ne t856/f/submission_-_terri_janke_and_company_ip_lawyers.pdf>)

Jensen C, 'The More Things Change, the More They Stay the Same: Copyright, Digital Technology, and Social Norms (2003) 56(2) Stanford LRev 531

Johnson P, '"Dedicating" Copyright to the Public Domain' (2008) 71(4) MLR 587

Jones AH, 'Can Authorship Policies Help Prevent Scientific Misconduct? What Role for Scientific Societies?' (2003) 9 Science and Engineering Ethics 243

Judge SK, 'Giving Credit Where Credit is Due: The Unusual Use of Arbitration in Determining Screenwriting Credits' (1997)13 Ohio State J on Dispute Resolution 221

Kahan D, 'Gentle Nudges vs. Hard Shoves: Solving the Sticky Norms Problem (2000) 97 U of Chicago LRev 607

Kamina P, *Film Copyright in the European Union* (CUP 2016)

Kaplan B, *Unhurried View of Copyright* (Columbia UP 1967)

Katz A, 'Taking Private Ordering Seriously' (1996) 144 U Pennsylvania LRev 1745

Kaufman R, 'After 5 Years, Heated Controversy Persists in Science Copyright Case' *The Scientist*, 14 September 1992 at: <www.the-scientist.com/?articles .view/articleNo/12483/title/After-5-Years-Heated-Controversy-Persists-In-Science-Copyright-Case>

Keen A, *The Cult of the Amateur: How Today's Internet Is Killing our Culture* (Doubleday/Currency 2007)

Kipen D, *The Schreiber Theory: A Radical Rewrite of American Film History* (Melville House 2006).

Kirgis P, 'Questions of Fact in the Practice of Law: A Response to Allen and Pardo's "Facts in Law and Facts of Law"' (2004) 8 International J of Evidence and Proof 47

Kleinart S and Neale M, *The Oxford Companion to Aboriginal Art and Culture* (OUP 2000)

Kupferman T, 'Copyright Co-Owners' (1945) 19(2) St John's LRev 95

Kwall RR, 'Author-Stories: Narrative's Implications For Moral Rights And Copyright's Joint Authorship Doctrine' (2001) 75 Southern California LRev 1

'The Author as Steward "for Limited Times": A Review of "The Idea of Authorship in Copyright"' (2008) 88 (3)Boston U LRev 685

The Soul of Creativity: Forging a Moral Rights Law for the US (Stanford UP 2009)

Lacey LJ, 'Of Bread and Roses and Copyright' (1989) Duke LJ 1532

Laddie H, Prescott P and Vitoria M, *The Modern Law of Copyright and Designs* (4th edn, LexisNexis 2011)

LaFrance M, 'Authorship, Dominance, and the Captive Collaborator: Preserving the Rights of Joint Authors' (2001) 50 Emory LJ 193

Lastowska G, 'The Trade Mark Function of Authorship' (2005) 85 Boston U LRev 1171

Lee YH, 'The Persistence of the Text: The Concept of the Work in Copyright Law' Part 1 (2018) 1 IPQ 22; Part 2 (2018) 2 IPQ 107

Lemley M, 'Intellectual Property and Shrinkwrap Licenses' (1995) 68 Southern California LRev 1239

'Romantic Authorship and the Rhetoric of Property' (1997) 75 Texas LRev 873

'Faith-Based IP' (2015) 62 UCLA LRev 1328

Lessig L, *Free Culture: How Big Media uses Technology and the Law to Lock Down Culture and Control Creativity* (Penguin Press 2004)

Remix: Making Art and Commerce Thrive in the Hybrid Economy (Penguin Press 2008)

Lessig L, 'The Regulation of Social Meaning' (1995) U Chicago LRev 943

The Future of Ideas: The Fate of the Commons in a Connected World (Vintage Books 2002)

Lipton J, 'Wikipedia and the European Union Database Directive' (2010) 26 Santa Clara Computer & Technology LJ 631

Litman J, 'Copyright Noncompliance (Or Why We Can't "Just Say Yes" to Licensing)' (1996) 29 NYU J of Intl L and Politics 237

'Real Copyright Reform' (2010) 96(1) Iowa LRev 1

Livingston P, 'Cinematic Authorship' in Allen R and Smith M (eds), *Film Theory and Philosophy* (OUP 1997) 132

Art and Intention (OUP 2005)

'On Authorship and Collaboration' (2011) 69(2) J of Aesthetics and Art Criticism 221

Lopez Romero T, 'Sui Generis Systems for the Protection of Traditional Knowledge' (2005) 6 International L: Revista Colombiana de Derecho Internacional 301

Loren LP, 'Building a Reliable Semicommons of Creative Works: Enforcement of Creative Commons Licenses and Limited Abandonment of Copyright' (2007) 14 George Mason LRev 271

Loshin J, 'Secrets Revealed: How Magicians Protect Intellectual Property without Law' in Corcos C (ed) *Law and Magic: A Collection of Essays* (Carolina Academic Press 2008) 123

Love J and Hubbard T, 'The Big Idea: Prizes to Stimulate R&D for New Medicines' (2007) 82 Chicago-Kent LRev 1519

Loux A, 'The Persistence of the Ancient Regime: Custom, Utility and the Common Law in the Nineteenth Century' (1993) 79 Cornell LRev 183

Macey J, 'Public and Private Ordering and the Production of Legitimate and Illegitimate rules' (1997) 82 Cornell L Rev 1123

Mackay E, 'Indigenous Traditional Knowledge, Copyright and Art – Shortcomings in Protection and an Alternative Approach' (2009) 32(1) UNSWLJ 1

MacMillan F, 'The Cruel C: Copyright and Film' (2002) EIPR 483

Macnab G, 'Johnny Depp's New Film Transcendence Is Yet Another Expensive Flop – So Has the Star Lost His Mojo?' *The Independent*, 30 April 2014

Madison M, 'Legal-ware: Contract and Copyright in the Digital Age' (1998) 67 Fordham LRev 1025

Mainous III AG, Bowen MA, Zoller JS, 'The Importance of Interpersonal Relationship Factors in Decisions Regarding Authorship' (2002) 34 Family Medicine 462

Mandel GN, 'The Public Perception of Intellectual Property' (2014) 66 Florida LRev 261

Maneker M, 'How the Australian Gov't Shattered Its Art Market', *Art Market Monitor*, 27 July 2016, available at: <www.artmarketmonitor.com/2016/06/27/how-the-australian-govt-shattered-its-art-market>

Manton B, 'Russian Ice Dancers Should Re-think their Routine' *Sydney Morning Herald*, 21 January 2010 <www.smh.com.au/opinion/politics/russian-ice-dancers-should-rethink-their-routine-20100121-mnwj.html>

Marrella F and Yoo CS, 'Is Open Source Software the New Lex Mercatoria?' (2006–7) 47 Virginia J of International L 807

Marchese D, 'Joint Ownership of Intellectual Property' (1999) 21(7) EIPR 364

Martin A, 'Possessory Credit' (2004) 45(1) Framework 95

Masiyakurima P, 'The Futility of the Idea/Expression Dichotomy in UK Copyright Law' (2007) 38 IIC 548

Matheson A, 'How Industry Uses the ICMJE Guidelines to Manipulate Authorship – And How They Should Be Revised' (2011) 8(8) PLoS Med. 1001072

McCausland S, 'Protecting Communal Interests in Indigenous Artworks after the Bulun Bulun Case' (1999) 4(22) Indigenous L Bulletin 4

McCutcheon J, 'The Vanishing Author in Computer-Generated Works: A Critical Analysis of Recent Australian Case Law' (2013) 36(3) Melbourne LRev 915

McDonagh L, 'Copyright, Contract and FOSS' in N Shemtov and I Walden (eds) *Free and Open Source Software* (OUP 2013) 69

McHenry L, 'Of Sophists and Spin-Doctors: Industry-Sponsored Ghostwriting and the Crisis of Academic Medicine' (2010) 8(1) Journalology 129

McFarlin T, 'An Idea of Authorship: Orson Welles, *The War of the Worlds* Copyright, and Why We Should Recognize Idea-Contributors as Joint Authors; (2016) 66(3) Case Western LRev 701

McLaughlin GM, 'Oral Contracts in the Entertainment Industry' (2001) 1(1) Virginia Sports and Entertainment LJ 101

McNary D, 'SAG-AFTRA Members Approve TV Animation Strike Authorization' *Variety* (18 July 2018) <variety.com/2018/tv/news/sag-aftra-tv-animation-strike-1202877662>

Merges R, 'The Concept of Property in the Digital Era' (2008) 45(4) Houston LRev 1239

'Locke for the Masses: Property Rights and the Products of Collective Creativity' (2008) 36(4) Hofstra LRev 1179

Justifying Intellectual Property (Harvard UP 2011)

'Foundations and Principles Redux: A Reply to Professor Blankfein-Tabachnick' (2013) 101 California LRev 1361

Merton RK, *The Sociology of Science: Theoretical and Empirical Investigations* (Chicago UP 1973)

Metzger A and Hennigs S, 'License Contracts, Free Software and Creative Commons' Commons' in M Schauer and B Verschraegen (eds) *General Reports of the XIXth Congress of the International Academy of Comparative Law, Ius Comparatum – Global Studies in Comparative Law* (Springer, 2017), Vol 24, 405

Mnookin R and Korhauser L, 'Bargaining in the Shadow of the Law: The Case of Divorce' (1979) 88 Yale LRev 950

Mnookin R, 'Divorce Bargaining: The Limits on Private Ordering' 18(4) J of L Reform 1015

Moglen E, 'Free Software Matters: Enforcing the GPL, I' <emoglen.law.columbia.edu/publications/lu-12.pdf>

Morgan R, 'How *Hamilton*'s Cast Got Broadway's Best Deal' *Bloomberg*, 28 September 2016 <www.bloomberg.com/features/2016-hamilton-broadway-profit>

Morphy H, *Ancestral Connections: Art and an Aboriginal System of Knowledge* (U of Chicago Press 1991)

Murphy R, 'Postscript: A Short History of British Cinema' in R Murphy (ed) *The British Cinema Book* (3rd edn, Palgrave Macmillan 2009) 417

Murray LJ, Piper S Tina and Robertson K, *Putting Intellectual Property in Its Place: Rights Discourses, Creative Labor, and the Everyday* (OUP 2014)

Myer R, Report of the Contemporary Visual Arts and Crafts Inquiry (2002) ('Myer Report')

Naremore J, 'Authorship' in Miller T and Stam R (eds) *A Companion to Film Theory* (Blackwell Publishing 2005) 9

Netanel NW, 'Copyright and Democratic Civil Society' (1996) 106 Yale LR 283

Nimmer D, 'Copyright in the Dead Sea Scrolls: Authorship and Originality' (2001) 38 Houston LRev 1

Nimmer MB and Nimmer D, *Nimmer on Copyright* (Matthew Bender 1998, 1976, 2011 and 2016 edns)

Notaro A, 'Technology in Search of an Artist: Questions of Auteurism/Authorship and the Contemporary Cinematic Experience' (2006) 57 The Velvet Light Trap 86

O'Reilly T, 'What is Web 2.0?' <www.oreillynet.com/pub/a/oreilly/tim/news/2005/09/30/what-is-web-20.html>

O'Sullivan M, 'The Pluralistic, Evolutionary, Quasi Legal Role of the GNU General Public Licence in Free/Libre/Open Source Software (FLOSS)' (2004) 26(8) EIPR 340

Obergfell EI, 'No Need for Harmonising Film Copyright in Europe?' (2003) 4 European Legal Forum 199

Oliar D and Sprigman C, 'There's No Free Laugh (Anymore): The Emergence of Intellectual Property Norms and the Transformation of Stand-up Comedy' (2008) 94 Virginia LRev 1787

Ong B, 'Originality from Copying: Fitting Recreative Works into the Copyright Universe' (2010) 2 IPQ 165

Oster J, 'Proposal for a Regulated Indigenous Art Industry' (2006) 6(18) Indigenous LBulletin 21

Parker RA and Bergman NA, 'Criteria for Authorship for Statisticians in Medical Papers' (1998) 17(20) Statistics in Medicine 2289

Perry M and Margoni T, 'Ownership in Complex Authorship: A Comparative Study of Joint Works' (2012) 34(1) EIPR 22

Pettie C, Seyd P, Whiteley P, *Citizenship in Britain: Values, Participation and Democracy* (CUP 2004)

Phillips J, 'Authorship, Ownership and Wikiship: Copyright in the Twenty-First Century' (2008) 3(12) JIPLP 788

Phillips R, 'Researchers' Objective Is to Get the Job Done' (1997) 315 British Medical J 747

Phillis M, 'Skepticism About an Analytical Distinction between Law and Fact' (Draft for 2011 ASLP PhD students' workshop, 1 August 2011) available at <ssrn.com/abstract=1956324>

Pila J, 'An Intentional View of the Copyright Work' (2008) 71(4) MLR 535

'Authorship and e-Science: Balancing Epistemological Trust and Skepticism in the Digital Environment' (2009) 23 Social Epistemology 1

'The "Star Wars" Copyright Claim: An Ambivalent View of the Empire' (2012) LQR 15

Poll G, 'Harmonization of Film Copyright in Europe' (2002) 50 J of the Copyright Society of the USA 519

Posner E (ed) *Social Norms, Nonlegal Sanctions, and the Law* (Edward Elgar 2007)

Posner E, 'Law, Economics and Inefficient Norms' (1996) 144 U Pennsylvania LRev 1697

'Norms, Formalities, and the Statute of Frauds: A Comment' (1996) 144 U Pennsylvania LRev 1971

'The Regulation of Groups: The Influence of Legal and Nonlegal Sanctions on Collective Action' (1996) 63 U of Chicago LRev 133

'Social Norms and Social Roles' (1996) 96 Columbia LRev 903

'Introduction' in Posner E (ed) *Social Norms, Nonlegal Sanctions, and the Law* (Edward Elgar 2007)

Law and Social Norms (Harvard UP 2009)

Posner R, *Law and Literature* (3rd edn, Harvard UP 2009)

Price M and Pollack M, 'The Author in Copyright: Notes for the Literary Critic' in Woodmansee M and Jaszi P (eds) *The Construction of Authorship: Textual Appropriation in Law and Literature* (Duke UP 1999) 439

Radin MJ and Wagner RP, 'The Myth of Private Ordering: Rediscovering Legal Realism in Cyberspace' (1998) 73 Chicago-Kent LRev 1295

Rafaeli S and Ariel Y, 'Online Motivational Factors: Incentives for Participation and Contribution in Wikipedia' in A Barak (ed) *Psychological Aspects of Cyberspace: Theory, Research, Applications* (CUP 2008)

Rahmatian A, *Copyright and Creativity: The Making of Property Rights in Creative Works* (Edward Elgar 2011)

Ramalho A and Gracia M, 'Copyright after Brexit' (2017) 12(8) JIPLP 669

Raustiala K and Sprigman C, 'The Piracy Paradox: Innovation and Intellectual Property in Fashion Design' (2006) 92 Virginia LRev 1687

Raymond E, 'The Cathedral and the Bazaar' <www.catb.org/~esr/writings/cathedral-bazaar/cathedral-bazaar>

Raz J, 'Rule of Law and Its Virtue' in *The Authority of Law: Essays on Law and Morality* (Clarendon Press 1979) 210

Reagle JM, *Good Faith Collaboration: The Culture of Wikipedia* (MIT 2010)

Reed M, 'Who Owns Ellen's Oscar Selfie? Deciphering Rights of Attribution Concerning User Generated Content on Social Media' (2015)14 John Marshall Rev of Intellectual Property L 564.

Reichman JH and Franklin JA, 'Privately Legislated Intellectual Property Rights: Reconciling Freedom of Contract with Public Good Uses of Information' (1999) 147(4) U of Pennsylvania LRev 875

Rennie D, Yank V and Emanuel L, 'When Authorship Fails: A Proposal to Make Contributors Accountable' (1997) 278 JAMA 579

Reynolds W and Moringello J, 'Survey of the Law of Cyberspace: Electronic Contracting Cases 2008–2009' (2009) 65 The Business Lawyer 317, available at <ssrn.com/abstract=1437162>

Rheinberger H, '"Discourses of Circumstance": A Note on the Author in Science' in Biagioli M and Galison P (eds), *Scientific Authorship: Credit and Intellectual Property in Science* (Routledge 2003)

Richardson W, *Blogs, Wikis, Podcasts, and Other Powerful Web Tools for Classrooms* (Corwin Press 2006)

Ricketson S, 'The Concept of Originality in Anglo-Australian Copyright Law' (1991) 9(2) Copyright Reporter 1

'People or Machines? The Berne Convention and the Changing Concept of Authorship' (1991) 16 Columbia J of L and the Arts 1

Ricketson S and Ginsburg J, *International Copyright and Neighbouring Rights: The Berne Convention and Beyond* (2nd edn, OUP 2006)

Rimmer M, 'Australian Icons: Authenticity Marks and Identity Politics' 2004 3 Indigenous LJ 139

'The Bangarra Dance Theatre: Copyright and Indigenous Culture' (2000) 9(2) Griffith LRev 274

'Heretic: Copyright Law and Dramatic Works' (2002) 2(1) QUT LRev 131

Ritter D, 'Trashing Heritage: Dilemmas of Rights and Power in the Operation of Western Australia's Heritage Legislation' (2003) 23 Studies in Western Australian History 195

Rivers T, 'Norowzian Revisited' (2000) EIPR 389

Rome E, 'Oscars: Visual Effects Artists Protest Outside Dolby Theatre' *Entertainment Weekly*, 25 February 2013 <insidemovies.ew.com/2013/02/25/oscars-visual-effects-protest-life-of-pi>

Rosati E, 'Originality in a Work, or a Work of Originality: The Effects of the Infopaq Decision' (2011) 33(12) EIPR 746

Rose M, 'The Author as Proprietor: Donaldson v Beckett and the Genealogy of Modern Authorship' (1988) 23 Representations 51

Authors and Owners: The Invention of Copyright (Harvard UP 1993)

'Copyright and Its Metaphors' (2002) 50 UCLA LRev 1

Rosen C, "Transcendence' is a Real Bad Flop for Johnny Depp', *The Huffington Post*, 21 April 2014 <www.huffingtonpost.com/2014/04/21/johnny-depp-transcendence-flops_n_5184999.html>

Rosenblatt E, 'A Theory of IP's Negative Space' (2011) 34(3) Columbia J of L and the Arts 317

Ross M, 'Authority and Authenticity: Scribbling Authors and the Genius of Print in Eighteenth Century England' (1992) 10 CAELJ 495

Rothman J, 'The Questionable Use of Custom in Intellectual Property' (2007) 93 Virginia LRev 1899

'Copyright, Custom and Lessons from the Common Law' in Balganesh S (ed) *Intellectual Property and the Common Law* (CUP 2013) 230

Sackville R (Justice), 'Legal Protection of Indigenous Culture in Australia' (2003) 11(2) Cardozo J of International and Comparative L 711

Sagy T, 'What's So Private About Private Ordering' (2011) 45(4) Law and Society Rev 923

Salokannel M, 'Film Authorship in the Changing Audio-Visual Environment' in B Sherman and A Strowel (eds), *Of Authors and Origins* (Clarendon Press 1994) 57

Sanger L, 'WHO SAYS WHAT WE KNOW: On the New Politics', *The Edge*, <www.edge.org/3rd_culture/sanger07/sanger07_index.html>

Sarris A, 'Notes on the Auteur Theory in 1962' in Grant BK (ed) *Auteurs and Authorship: A Film Reader* (Blackwell 2008) 35

Saunders D, *Authorship and Copyright* (Routledge 1992)

Sawyer K, *Group Genius: The Creative Power of Collaboration* (Basic Books 2007)

—— *Explaining Creativity: The Science of Human Innovation* (OUP 2nd edn 2012)

Schultz M, 'Fear and Norms and Rock & Roll: What Jambands Can Teach Us About Persuading People to Obey Copyright Law' (2006) 21 Berkeley Technology LJ 651

Schwab J, 'Audiovisual Works and the Work for Hire Doctrine in the Internet Age' (2011) 35 Columbia JL & Arts 141

Schwarcz S, 'Private Ordering' (2002) 97 Northwestern U LRev 319

Scott T, 'Changing Authorship System Might be Counterproductive' (1997) 315 British Medical J 744

See H, 'Copyright Ownership of Joint Works and Terminations of Transfers' (1982) 30 Kansas LRev 517

—— *Private Power, Public Law: The Globalisation of Intellectual Property Rights* (CUP 2003)

Sellors P, 'Collective Authorship in Film' (2007) 65 J of Aesthetics and Art Criticism 263

Seymore S, 'How Does My Work Become Our Work? Dilution of Authorship in Scientific Papers, and the Need for the Academy to Obey Copyright Law' (2006) 12 Richmond J of L & Tech 11

Shapin S and Schaffer S, *Leviathan and The Air-Pump: Hobbes, Boyle, and The Experimental Life* (Princeton UP 1985)

Shapin S, 'The Invisible Technician' (1989) 77 American Scientist 554

—— *A Social History of Truth: Civility and Science in Seventeenth-Century England* (Chicago UP 1994)

—— 'How to be Antiscientific' in Labinger JA and Collins H (eds), *The One Culture? A Conversation about Science* (Chicago UP 2001)

Sherman B, 'What Is a Copyright Work?' (2011) 12(1) Theoretical Inquiries in L 99

Schultz M, 'Fear and Norms and Rock & Roll: What Jambands Can Teach Us about Persuading People to Obey Copyright Law' (2009) Berkeley Technology LJ 651

Silbey J, *The Eureka Myth: Creators, Innovators, and Everyday Intellectual Property* (Stanford Press 2014)

Simone D, 'Recalibrating the Joint Authorship Test: Insights from Scientific Collaborations' (2013) 26(1) IPJ 111

'Copyright or Copyleft?: Wikipedia as a Turning Point for Authorship' (2014) 25(1) Kings LJ 102

Sismondo S, 'Ghosts in the Machine: Publication Planning in the Medical Sciences' (2009) 39 Social Studies of Science 171

Smith H, 'Community and Custom in Property' (2009) 10(1) Theoretical Inquiries in L 5

Smith RC, *Plural Ownership* (OUP 2005)

Smith J, 'Gift Authorship: A Poisoned Chalice?' (1994) 309 British Medical J 1456

Sofer A, 'Joint Authorship: An Uncomfortable Fit with Tenancy in Common' (1998) 19 Loyola LA Entertainment LJ 1

Spence M, *Intellectual Property* (OUP 2007)

Spence M and Endicott T, 'Vagueness in the Scope of Copyright') (2005) 121 LQR 657

Stamatoudi I, 'Moral Rights of Authors in England: The Missing Emphasis on the Role of Creators' (1997) 4 IPQ 478

'"Joy" for the Claimant: Can a Film Also Be Protected as a Dramatic Work' (2000) 1 IPQ 117

Steinberg NS, 'Regulation of Scientific Misconduct in Federally Funded Research' (2000) 10 South California Interdisciplinary LJ 39

Stern S and Lemmens T, 'Legal Remedies for Medical Ghostwriting: Imposing Fraud Liability on Guest Authors of Ghostwritten Articles' (2011) 8(8) PLoS Med e1001070

Stokes A, 'Authorship, Collaboration and Copyright: A View from the United Kingdom' (2002) Entertainment LRev 121

Strandburg K, 'User Innovator Community Norms: At the Boundary between Academic and Industry Research' (2009) 77 Fordham LRev 101

Sunstein C, 'Incompletely Theorized Agreements' (1995) 108 Harvard LRev 1733
Infotopia: How Many Minds Produce Knowledge (OUP 2006)

Swan A, 'Open Access and the Progress of Science' 95 American Scientist 198

Tankebe J, 'Viewing Things Differently: The Dimensions of Public Perceptions of Police Legitimacy' (2013) 51 Criminology 103

Tapscott D and Williams A, *Wikinomics: How Mass Collaboration Changes Everything* (Atlantic Books 2008)

Targosz T, 'Authorship by Deletion', *Kluwer Copyright Blog*, <kluwercopyright blog.com/2011/11/02/authorship-by-deletion-supreme-court-june-22-2010 -ii-csk-52710>

Tehranian J, 'Infringement Nation: Copyright Reform and the Law/Norm Gap' (2007) Utah LRev 537

'Sex, Drones & Videotape: Rethinking Copyright's Authorship-Fixation Conflation in the Age of Performance' (2017) 68 Hastings LJ 1319

'Copyright's Male Gaze: Authorship and Inequality in a Panoptic World' (2018) 41(2) Harvard J of L and Gender 343

Terrall M, 'The Uses of Anonymity in the Age of Reason' in Biagioli M and Galison P (eds), *Scientific Authorship: Credit and Intellectual Property in Science* (Routledge 2003)

Thompson MP, 'Beneficial Joint Tenancies: A Case for Abolition?' (1987) Jan/Feb Conveyancer and Property Lawyer 29
Todd A, 'Painting a Moving Train: Adding "Postmodern" to the Taxonomy of Law' (2008) 40(1) U of Toledo LRev 105.
Truffaut F, 'A Certain Tendency of the French Cinema' (1954) 31 *Cahiers du Cinéma* translated and reproduced in Grant BK, *Auteurs and Authorship: A Film Reader* (Blackwell 2008) 9
Tyler T, 'Compliance with Intellectual Property Law: A Psychological Perspective' (1996) 29 International L and Politics 219
Why People Obey the Law (Princeton UP 2006)
Tyler T and Jackson J, 'Popular Legitimacy and the Exercise of Legal Authority: Motivating Compliance, Cooperation and Engagement' (2014) 20(1) Psychology Public Policy and L 78
Vaidhyanathan S, *Copyrights and Copywrongs: The Rise of Intellectual Property and How It Threatens Creativity* (NYU Press 2001)
Valiela I, *Doing Science: Design, Analysis, and Communication of Scientific Research* (OUP 2001)
van Eechoud M, 'Along the Road to Uniformity – Diverse Readings of the Court of Justice's Judgments on Copyright Work' (2012) 1 JIPITEC 60
van Eechoud M (ed) *The Work of Authorship* (Amsterdam UP 2014)
Vaver D, *Copyright Law* (Irwin Law, 2000) 76
 Intellectual Property: Copyright, Patents and Trade-Marks (2nd edn, Irwin Law 2011)
 'Venturing into Intellectual Property Jointly and Confidentially' (2012) 25(1) IPJ 11,
Versteeg R, 'Defining "Author" for Purposes of Copyright' (1996) 45 American U LRev 1323
Vesterman W, 'The Death of the Scientific Author: Multiple Authorship in Scientific Papers' (2002) 8 Common Knowledge 439
Wacha J, 'Taking the Case: Is the GPL Enforceable?' (2005) 21 Santa Clara Computer & High-Technology LJ 451
Waelde C, 'What Is Beyond the Score?' in A Rahmatian (ed) *Concepts of Music and Copyright: How Music Perceives Itself and How Copyright Perceives Music* (Edward Elgar 2015) 23
Wager E, 'Authors, Ghosts, Damned Lies, and Statisticians' (2007) 4(1) PLoS Med e34
Walker RK and Depoorter B, 'Unavoidable Aesthetic Judgments in Copyright Law: A Community of Practice Standard' (2015) 109 (2) Northwestern U LRev 343.
Walshok M, *Knowledge without Boundaries: What America's Research Universities Can Do for the Economy, the Workplace, and the Community* (Jossey-Bass 1995)
Wartenberg T, 'Philosophy of Film' in Zalta EN (ed) *The Stanford Encyclopedia of Philosophy* (2014) <plato.stanford.edu/archives/fall2014/entries/film>
Warwick A, '"A Very Hard Nut to Crack" or Making Sense of Maxwell's Treatise on Electricity and Magnetism in Mid-Victorian Cambridge' in Biagioli M and Galison P (eds), *Scientific Authorship: Credit and Intellectual Property in Science* (Routledge 2003) 133

Watson P, 'Cinematic Authorship and the Film Auteur' in Nelmes J (ed) *Introduction to Film Studies* (5th edn, Routledge 2012) 142

Weatherall K, 'Culture, Autonomy and Djulibinyamurr: Individual and Community in the Construction of Rights to Traditional Designs' (2001) 64 MLR 215

Weinberg J, 'ICANN and the Problem of Legitimacy' (2000) 50 Duke LJ 187

Weinburg AM, 'Impact of Large-Scale Science on the United States' (1961) 134 (3473) Science 161

Wendland W, 'Intellectual Property, Traditional Knowledge and Folklore: WIPO's Exploratory Program – Part 1' (2002) International Review of Intellectual Property and Competition L 485

Wiseman L, 'The Protection of Indigenous Art and Culture in Australia: The Labels of Authenticity' (2001) EIPR 14

Woodmansee M, 'The Genius and the Copyright: Economic and Legal Conditions of the Emergence of the "Author"' (1983–1984) 17 Eighteenth Century Studies 425

'On the Author Effect: Recovering Collectivity' in Woodmansee M and Jaszi P (eds) *The Construction of Authorship: Textual Appropriate in Law and Literature* (Duke U Press 1999) 15

Woodmansee M and Jaszi P (eds) *The Construction of Authorship: Textual Appropriation in Law and Literature* (Duke UP 1999)

Zemer L, 'Contribution and Collaborations in Joint Authorship: Too Many Misconceptions' (2006) 1(4) JIPLP 283

'Is Intention to Co-author an Uncertain Realm of Policy?' (2007) 30(4) Columbia J of L and the Arts 611

The Idea of Authorship in Copyright (Ashgate 2007)

Ziman J, *Of One Mind: The Collectivisation of Science* (American Institute of Physics Press 1995)

Real Science: What It Is, and What It Means (CUP 2000)

Science in Civil Society (Imprint Academic 2007)

Zimmerman D, 'Copyright as Incentives: Did We Just Imagine That?' (2011) 12 (1) Theoretical Inquiries in L 29

Websites

(last accessed on 17 August 2018)

<en.wikipedia.org/wiki/Main_Page>
<en.wikipedia.org/wiki/Wikimania>
<en.wikipedia.org/wiki/Wikipedia:Barnstars>
<en.wikipedia.org/wiki/Wikipedia:Copyrights>
<en.wikipedia.org/wiki/Wikipedia:Dispute_resolution>
<en.wikipedia.org/wiki/Wikipedia:Editing_policy#Try_to_fix_problems>
<en.wikipedia.org/wiki/Wikipedia:Etiquette>
<en.wikipedia.org/wiki/Wikipedia:Five_pillars>
<en.wikipedia.org/wiki/Wikipedia:List_of_policies_and_guidelines>
<en.wikipedia.org/wiki/Wikipedia:Meetup>
<en.wikipedia.org/wiki/Wikipedia:Ownership_of_articles>

Bibliography

<en.wikipedia.org/wiki/Wikipedia:Text_of_Creative_Commons_Attribution-ShareAlike_3.0_Unported_License>
<en.wikipedia.org/wiki/Wikipedia:Text_of_the_GNU_Free_Documentation_License>
<en.wikipedia.org/wiki/Wikipedia:Welcoming_committee/Welcome_to_Wikipedia>
<en.wikipedia.org/wiki/Wikipedia:Wikipedians>
<fanfiction.wikia.com/wiki/A_Million_Penguins>
<stats.wikimedia.org/EN/TablesWikipediaEN.htm>
<public.web.cern.ch/public/en/About/Global-en.html>
<www.afc.gov.au/filminginaustralia/indigproto/fiapage9.aspx>
<www.alexa.com/siteinfo/wikipedia.org>
<www.arcbazar.com>
<www.artslaw.com.au/Indigenous/IndigenousArtistAndArtCentreAgreement.asp>
<www.australiacouncil.gov.au>
<www.bfi.org.uk/film-industry>
<www.creativecommons.org>
<www.culture.com.au/exhibition/niaaa/labelqa.htm>
<www.gooseberrypatch.com>
<www.gov.uk/government/collections/ip-for-business-events-guidance-tools-and-case-studies#interactive-business-tools-and-training>
<www.gov.uk/government/publications/digital-opportunity-review-of-intellectual-property-and-growth>
<www.gov.uk/guidance/copyright-orphan-works>
<www.indigenousartcode.org>
<www.mturk.com/mturk/welcome>
<www.melboume.vic.gov.au>
<www.oed.com>
<www.sciencespo.fr/inclusive/content/project>
<www.userfarm.com/en>
<www.victorsandspoils.com>
<www.wikipedia.org>

Index

Aboriginal Artists Agency, 110
aesthetic neutrality, 16, 42, 50–53, 60
aesthetic values, 118, 235, 242–243, 246–247, 271
Alvarez group, 146, 203
Arts Law Centre of Australia, 108, 125
ATLAS collaboration, 147
attribution practice, 91, 102–104, 137, 162, 163, 211
Australian Indigenous art (legal protection)
  authorship dynamics, 102–108
  Bulun Bulun v R & T Textiles, 101, 109, 112–122
  case law examples, 101, 109, 110–122
  certainty and social norms, 243
  collective/certification trademarks, 124–125
  contracts and, 125–126, 249
  copyright protection/subsistence in, 109–122
  creative realities of authorship, 102–104, 210
  cultural context, 105–108
  cultural identity, 102–104
  Dreamtime and, 103, 102–103
  insights for copyright law, 127–130
  introduction to, 100–101
  limited legacy of *Bulun Bulun v R & T Textiles*, 115–121
  meaning of authorship in, 205, 207, 208
  other (non-copyright) solutions for protection, 122–127
  private ordering and, 215, 220
  protocols and codes of conduct, 123–124
  sharing economy of, 210–211
  sui generis legislation, 123, 126–127
auteur theory, 167–168, 203
authorial credit (attribution), 49, 91, 102–104, 137, 162, 163, 211
authorial freedom, 74, 202
authorship
  authoritative pronouncement on, 225
  case law on, 9, 17–29
  characteristics of, 19
  coercion authorship, 140
  conceptual understanding of, 51–52, 59–63, 67–70
  copyright law *vs.*, 16, 212, 272
  copyright law's assumptions about, 11, 48, 54–55, 62–63, 68, 238
  cultural conceptions, 67–70
  defined, 17–29, 269
  determination in digital creations, 88
  different meanings of, 11, 68, 205–206, 229
  dynamics in Australian Indigenous art, 102–108
  dynamics in film collaborations, 161–169
  dynamics in science, 132–139
  dynamics in Wikipedia, 73–77
  fragmentation of, 137, 190
  ghost authorship, 140, 149, 216, 227
  gift authorship, 140, 150, 256
  guest authorship, 140, 150, 256
  of Indigenous art, 103–104
  individual authorship, 39–40, 60, 104
  introduction to, 15–16
  meaning in collective authorship, 203, 204–210
  normative dimension of, 20, 25–26, 53–58
  post-modern concept of, 61
  power relations in, 143, 245
  'romantic author' notion, 50, 59–62, 70–71, 118, 135, 155, 161, 168, 199, 203, 269–270
  social conceptions/norms of authorship, 67–70, 89, 205–206
  standard for joint *vs.* individual, 39–40, 60
  statutory presumptions on, 223
  summary of, 70–71
  theories on, 4–5, 58–70
authorship norms, 137, 204–210

Index

authorship standards, 224
autonomy
  of authors, 155, 161, 202
  in basic research, 136
  contract law and, 249
  film elements and, 171–172
  private ordering and, 216
  of Wikipedia contributors, 202

Bangarra Dance troupe, 125
bargaining power, 225, 241, 254
Barron, Anne, 231
Berne Convention, 18, 23, 181
Biagioli, Mario, 139
biomedical science collaborations, 139–145. *See also* scientific collaborations
Boyle, Robert, 135–136

case law on authorship, 9, 17–29
CERN collaborations, 136, 145–147
certainty of social norms, 243–244, 251
certification trademarks, 124–125
cinematographic works, 160
classic studio system in Hollywood, 192
codes of conduct, 123–124
coercion authorship, 140
collaboration. *See also* film collaborations; scientific collaborations
  ATLAS collaboration, 147
  biomedical collaborations, 237
  Collider Detector at Fermilab (CDF) Collaboration, 146
  in film, 182
  hydrogen bubble chamber collaboration, 146
  in joint authorship test, 31–34, 49, 57, 235, 251
  large-scale collaboration, 1, 2, 145
  NASA collaborations, 136
  particle physics collaborations, 145–147, 157–158
  requirement in film, 182
  social norms and, 253
  Wikipedia, 87–88
collaborative creativity, 2, 12, 44, 50, 67
collection of independent works, 84–85
collective action, 199, 215, 260
collective authorship
  copyright law and, 61, 201, 224–229
  creative process in, 201–204, 234, 246
  creative realities and, 210–212
  defined, 2, 201
  differing meanings of authorship, 205–206

  joint authorship and, 63–67
  joint authorship test and, 34, 250–256
  meaning of authorship in, 203, 204–210
  nature of, 10–11, 58, 201–204
  power dynamics of, 209–210
  private ordering and, 213–224
  responsibility for the work, 206–208
  social norms, 201, 204, 229
  status within particular communities, 208–209
  summary of, 229–230
collective bargaining, 196, 220
collective trademarks, 124–125
collectivisation of modern science, 132
Collider Detector at Fermilab (CDF) Collaboration, 146
colonialisation, 107
common design, 31–34, 47, 182, 251
common law, 119, 241
communal title, 116
communalism, 133
community norms of authorship, 153
community values and authorship, 205–206, 208–209
consensus-based processes, 74, 155
contextual approach to joint authorship, 12, 97, 232, 250–256, 270
contra proferentum rule in contract law, 220
contract law, 193, 220, 249
contracts
  Australian Indigenous art, 114, 125–126, 249
  film collaborations, 198, 249–250
  hard contracts, 195
  joint authorship test, 249–250
  objective construction, 261
  soft contracts, 195–196, 215
  time-limited option contracts, 196
contribution as 'not distinct,' 30, 69, 149, 183, 232
control in authorship, 66. *See also* creative control
Coombe, Rosemary, 69, 224
copyleft licences, 89, 90–95, 213–214, 217, 218, 222, 226
Copyright, Designs and Patents Act 1988 (CDPA)
  author/non-author approach to attribution, 223
  concept of authorship in, 17–29
  default authorship standard, 217, 218, 221, 266
  dramatic works, 160, 180–187
  entrepreneurial work, 27, 170–171, 176

Index

film collaborations, 159, 169, 170, 174–175, 186
introduction to, 9, 14
joint authorship test, 29–42, 247–248, 251
joint owner rights, 257–262
meaning of authorship, 17–29, 208
originality test, 21, 22–25, 60, 80, 83
presumptive employer ownership of copyright, 179
scientific journal article a literary work, 148
Copyright Act (1911), 100, 170, 185
Copyright Act (1956), 27, 30–31, 100, 170, 171, 180, 183
Copyright Act (1968) (Cth), 100, 111, 113, 117, 119
copyright infringement, 95–96
copyright law. *See also* Australian Indigenous art; Copyright, Designs and Patents Act 1988
assumptions about authorship, 11, 48, 54–55, 62–63, 68, 238
collective authorship and, 61, 201, 224–229
concept of authorship, 16, 17–29, 212, 272
concepts of subsistence, 59–60, 116, 120
creative reality and, 11
default entitlement under, 193–194
dramatic works, 160, 180–187
evidence-based policy making, 6–8
fairness of, 236–237, 268
film collaborations and, 165, 196–200, 209
internationalisation of, 3
introduction to, 1–6
non-compliance with, 3
normative goals, 8, 21, 23, 256–257
predominant justification for, 21
private ordering and, 216
role of, 11, 28, 52
scientific collaborations, 148–158
as a source of standards, 98, 217, 218, 221, 266
subsistence of copyright in film, 169–192
Wikipedia insights for, 95–99
copyright scholarship, 58–70
copyright subsistence, 59–60, 78–90, 109–122, 148–154, 169–192
copyright trust, 264–265
corporate authorship, 39–40, 60
cost-free incentives, 138
costumes and copyright, 173–174

Court of Justice of the European Union (CJEU), 8, 17, 19
create, defined, 19
Creative Commons Attribution-Sharealike 3.0 Unported Licence (CC-BY-SA), 91
creative commons licenses, 4, 91, 92, 214, 248
creative control, 56, 177, 188, 202, 206, 209, 234, 248
creative investment in films, 162
creative practices, 16, 26, 62, 212, 231, 251, 270
creative process
in collective authorship, 201–204, 234, 246
creative product *vs.*, 74, 206
iterative creative process, 79–80, 82
joint authorship test and, 229
meaning of authorship and, 206
private ordering and, 223
creative realities
biomedical collaborations, 237
collective authorship and, 210–212
film collaborations, 210, 240
joint authorship test and, 252
scientific collaborations, 210, 255
social norms and, 239
creative reality, 6, 11, 98, 210, 213–224
creator protection in films, 197–198
credibility of copyright law, 231, 235–236
credit in collective authorship, 211
credit value in scientific authorship, 138, 140
cultural conceptions of authorship, 67–70
cultural custodianship, 127
cultural identity in Australian Indigenous art, 102–104, 129
cultural self-determination, 129

database, defined, 84–85
default entitlement under copyright law, 193–194
digital environment, 72–73
directed commercial research, 136
director authorship credit, 163, 191
disinterestedness, 133, 151, 210, 222, 227
distinct contribution, 30, 69, 149, 183, 252
dominant author, 16, 64, 66, 131, 156, 191, 265, 269
dramatic significance and copyright, 185
dramatic works, 160, 180–187
Dreamtime in Australian Indigenous art, 102–103, 111

economic-incentive based view of copyright, 210, 211–212

Index

economic rights of authors, 21, 155, 158, 178
Edison, Thomas, 165
employer ownership of copyright, 179
Encyclopaedia Britannica, 73–74
End-User Licensing Agreements, 95
estoppel, 46
European Commission, 193
European harmonisation, 27, 256
express agreement of contractual nature, 114

factual dimensions of joint authorship test, 53–58
factual specificity, 43, 246
fairness of copyright law, 236–237, 268
false attribution of scientific authorship, 151
Federal Court of Australia, 109, 112, 228
fiduciary duty, 114–115, 128, 264–265
film collaborations
  authorship dynamics, 161–169
  contracts and, 192–196, 249–250
  copyright complexity within, 171–176
  copyright law and, 165, 196–200, 209
  costumes and copyright, 173–174
  creative realities of authorship, 210, 240
  editing of film and copyright, 186
  film as dramatic work, 180–187
  film as first fixation, 176–180
  historical note, 170–171
  introduction to, 159–160
  meaning of authorship, 206
  pragmatic reasoning and, 187–192
  principal director, 177
  private ordering and, 192–196, 199, 215, 220
  producer, 177
  props and copyright, 173–174
  subsistence of copyright, 169–192
film copyright term, 179–180
film credits, 161, 162, 194, 196–197
financial investment in films, 162
fragmentation of authorship, 137, 190
fraudulent authorship, 141
free culture of sharing, 93, 94
Free/Libre/Open Source Software movement, 90
Free Software Foundation's General Public Licence, 90–91
Free Software movement, 4
freelance documentaries, 178
French New Wave, 167

Ganalbingu people, 112–113
ghost authorship, 140, 149, 216, 227

gift authorship, 140, 150, 256
gift economy, 134–135, 210–211
Ginsburg, Jane, 4, 58, 62–63
GNU Free Documentation Licence (GFDL), 91
Goldstein, Paul, 63–67
Gregory Report, 170–171, 198
group management of jointly owned copyright, 257
guest authorship, 140, 150, 256

'hands-on' control over contributors, 202
hard contracts, 195
Hargreaves, Ian, 6
Hitchcock, Alfred, 166
hold-ups, 12, 45, 179, 183, 261–262, 268
Human Genome Project, 136
hydrogen bubble chamber collaboration, 146

idea/expression dichotomy, 41, 60, 97, 119, 148, 254
imaginative film components and copyright, 174–175
implied licenses, 183, 189, 261–262
incentive story of copyright protection, 13, 21, 211–212
inclusive approach to joint authorship, 11–12, 98, 150, 168–169, 232, 250–256, 270
independent legal standards, 239
Indigenous Australian Art Commercial Code of Conduct, 123–124
Indigenous cultural expressions. *See* Australian Indigenous art
Indigenous customary law, 102–104, 119
Indigenous Label of Authenticity, 124
individual authorship, 39–40, 60, 104
InfoSoc Directive, 22
innovator, 19–20
intellectual creation
  CDPA and, 28
  originality standard of, 29
  relevance to joint authorship test, 38
  test of, 17, 18, 22–25, 26–27
  Wikipedia as, 78
intellectual property rights
  certainty disputes, 244
  importance of, 2
  Indigenous cultural expressions *vs*., 106
  ownership by studios and production companies, 164
  standards, 227
  sui generis legislation, 123, 126–127

298   Index

International Committee of Medical
    Journal Editors (ICMJE), 141,
    142–143, 154, 155, 237
international copyright law, 18, 181
internationalisation of copyright law, 3
interpretation, 184–185
iterative nature of the creative process,
    79–80, 82

joint authorship
    concept of authorship, 17–29
    contextual approach to joint authorship,
        12, 97, 232, 270
    copyright case law on, 2, 3, 29–42
    defined, 29
    inclusive approach to joint authorship,
        11–12, 98, 150, 168–169, 232, 270
    introduction to, 15–16
    Nimmer v Goldstein approach, 63–67
joint authorship test
    aesthetic neutrality, 16, 42, 50–53, 60,
        246–247
    aesthetic values in, 118, 235, 242–243,
        246–247, 271
    analytical clarity and, 15, 42–53
    application characteristics, 118
    application to collective authorship, 201
    CDPA concept of, 29–42
    collaboration in, 31–34, 49, 57, 235
    common design in, 31–34, 49, 57
    contextual approach to, 250–256
    contribution as 'not distinct,' 30, 69, 149,
        183, 252
    court's failure to apply, 117
    critique of, 42–53, 246–250
    dangers of deferring to social norms,
        238–241
    factual and normative dimensions of,
        53–58
    factual specificity, 43, 246
    film collaborations, 160
    framework for considering social
        norms, 241
    inclusive approach to, 250–256
    introduction to, 9, 10, 231–233
    joint ownership and, 46, 256–268
    judicial characterisation of the contribu-
        tions, 156
    pragmatic instrumental approach, 9,
        43–50, 67, 70–71, 231, 247–250
    proof of intention, 33–34
    reasonableness requirement in, 268
    relevance of social norms, 232, 233–238
    revising critique of, 246–250
    right kind requirement, 13, 184

in scientific collaborations, 143–145, 158
significant contribution of the right kind,
    35–42, 184
social norms, 232, 233–238, 250–256,
    270–271
joint labouring in furtherance of a common
    design, 87–88
joint ownership, 46, 256–268
joint tenants, 258, 264–265
judicial reluctance to award protection, 60

laches, 46
large-scale collaboration, 1, 2, 145
Law Dictionary, 54
legal millefeuilles/scope of the work, 84,
    175–176
legal protection of Australian Indigenous
    art, background, 105–108
legislative reform, 6, 266–268
legitimacy of copyright law, 5–6, 237–238
liberty and private ordering, 216, 219
Litman, Jessica, 237

Malangi, David, 110
Malcolm X (film), 187–189
market economy, 134–135, 150,
    153
meaningful or significant contribution,
    56–57
mechanical copyright, 176
Merton, Robert, 132–133, 206
misappropriation, 25, 80
moral rights of authors, 18, 49, 60, 155,
    158, 179–180, 211
mutual support authorship, 140

NASA collaborations, 136
National Indigenous Arts Advocacy
    Association (NIAAA), 124
Neutral Point of View policy, Wikipedia,
    74, 75, 253
Nimmer, Melville, 63–67
non-compliance with copyright law, 3
non-dominant authors, 16
non-economic benefits of authorship, 154
non-economic consequences of authorship,
    154, 160, 272
non-exclusive licence, 44, 64, 262
non-profit community project, 73–77
normative dimension of authorship, 20,
    25–26
normative dimension of copyright law, 23,
    256–257
normative dimension of joint authorship
    test, 53–58

Index

objective construction of a contract, 261
objective determination of a question of fact, 54, 57, 88, 118, 252
Ong, Burton, 117
organised scepticism, 133
originality test, 21, 22–25, 60, 80, 83
originator/source and authorship, 19–20
Our Culture: Our Future report, 124

particle physics collaborations, 145–147, 157–158. *See also* scientific collaborations
performance, 184–185
pharmaceutical industry authors, 141, 142–143, 144
policy implications of social norms, 245–246, 251
Posner, Eric, 222
possessory credits, 163, 197
post-modern concept of authorship, 61
power dynamics of collective authorship, 209–210
power relations in authorship, 143, 245
pragmatic instrumental approach
  dominant author, 9, 156
  film copyright, 187–192, 199
  joint authorship test, 9, 43–50, 67, 70–71, 231, 247–250
pre-existing clan-owned designs, 110–111
presumptive employer ownership of copyright, 179
principal director, 177
private ordering
  benefits and limitations of, 216–224
  collective authorship and, 213–224, 229
  copyright law and, 98
  film collaborations, 192–196, 199
  joint ownership and, 260
  less successful examples of, 215–216
  scientific authorship, 139–147
  successful examples of, 213–215
producer in film collaborations, 177
proof of intention, joint authorship, 33–34
proof-reading and copyright authorship, 185
property law, 257–258, 264–265
props and copyright, 173–174
protocols for dealing with Australian Indigenous cultural expressions, 123–124

raw footage in film making, 191
reasonableness requirement in joint authorship test, 268

representativeness consideration of social norms, 244–245, 251
Reserve Bank of Australia, 110
responsibility in scientific authorship, 138
restrictions of number of authors, 46
revenue-sharing, 45
romantic author, 50, 59–62, 70–71, 118, 135, 155, 161, 168, 199, 203, 269–270
Rothman, Jennifer, 240

Sarris, Andrew, 168
science values and openness, 227
scientific collaborations
  application of copyright law, 148–154
  authorial responsibility and credit, 138
  biomedical science, 139–145
  creative realities of authorship, 210, 255
  dynamics of authorship in, 132–139
  insights for copyright law, 154–158
  introduction to, 131–132
  joint authorship test, 143–145, 148–154, 158
  meaning of authorship, 205–206, 207–208
  particle physics, 145–147
  private ordering and, 214, 216, 217, 218, 222
  regulating with private ordering, 139–147
  sharing economy of, 210–211
screen credits. *See* film credits
Screen Writers Guild, 167
self-determination, 216, 219, 249
self-government of credit, 195
self-management rules, 266
self-regulated creativity on Wikipedia, 97
sense of community on Wikipedia, 76, 77
Seymore, Sean, 139, 143–145, 227
share-alike provisions, 93
sharing of responsibility in collective authorship, 201
significant contribution of the right kind, 35–42, 46–47, 56, 69, 87, 184
social conceptions/norms of authorship, 67–70, 89
social norms
  certainty consideration, 243–244, 251
  in collective authorship, 201, 204, 229
  dangers of deferring to, 238–241
  framework for considering, 246
  joint authorship test, 232, 233–238, 250–256, 270–271
  policy implications, 245–246, 251
  private ordering and, 219, 224
  representativeness consideration, 244–245, 251

soft contracts, 195–196, 215
Standard Author List, 146
Stanford Linear Detector (SLD)
    Collaboration, 146–147
star power in films, 166
statutory presumptions on authorship, 223
statutory 'trust of land', 264–265
studio structure, 163
subsistence in copyright law, 17–29, 95
sui generis legislation, 123, 126–127
suitable, defined, 8
Sunstein, Cass, 76
sweat of the brow, 22–25

tenants in common, 44, 90, 178, 257–258
three-dimensional objects and copyright, 175
time-limited option contracts, 196
top-down norms, 234, 245
traditional cultural expressions. *See*
    Australian Indigenous art
trivial contributions, 35, 98, 148
Truffaut, François, 167
Trust of Land, 264–265

ultimate arbiter factor, 40, 48
under-inclusive approach to joint authorship, 150
unfair competition, 22, 25

universalism, 133
unsigned deals, 196
US Copyright Act (1976), 33–34
US joint ownership, 262–265

valuable contribution, 56
'Village Pump' section of Wikipedia, 75

Web 2.0 technology, 72–73
Wikipedia
    authorship dynamics in, 73–77
    autonomy of contributors, 202
    content on, 1
    contributors as copyright authors, 86–90
    copyleft licences, 89, 90–95, 214, 218, 222, 226
    copyright subsistence on, 78–90
    creative commons licenses, 90–95, 248
    creative realities of authorship, 210
    as database, 84–85
    division of labor, 202
    insights for copyright law, 95–99
    introduction to, 72–73
    meaning of authorship in, 205, 206–207
    Neutral Point of View policy, 74, 75, 253
    originality test, 78–86
    sharing economy of, 210–211
Writers Guild of America (WGA), 194, 197

Cambridge Intellectual Property and Information Law

Titles in the Series (formerly known as Cambridge Studies in Intellectual Property Rights)

Brad Sherman and Lionel Bently
The Making of Modern Intellectual Property Law

Irini A. Stamatoudi
Copyright and Multimedia Products: A Comparative Analysis

Pascal Kamina
Film Copyright in the European Union

Huw Beverly-Smith
The Commercial Appropriation of Personality

Mark J. Davison
The Legal Protection of Databases

Robert Burrell and Allison Coleman
Copyright Exceptions: The Digital Impact

Huw Beverly-Smith, Ansgar Ohly and Agnès Lucas-Schloetter
Privacy, Property and Personality: Civil Law Perspectives on Commercial Appropriation

Catherine Seville
The Internationalisation of Copyright Law: Books, Buccaneers and the Black Flag in the Nineteenth Century

Philip Leith
Software and Patents in Europe

Geertrui van Overwalle
Gene Patents and Clearing Models

Lionel Bently, Jennifer Davis and Jane C. Ginsburg
Trade Marks and Brands: An Interdisciplinary Critique

Jonathan Curci
The Protection of Biodiversity and Traditional Knowledge in International Law of Intellectual Property

Lionel Bently, Jennifer Davis and Jane C. Ginsburg
Copyright and Piracy: An Interdisciplinary Critique

Megan Richardson and Julian Thomas
Framing Intellectual Property: Legal Constructions of Creativity and Appropriation 1840–1940

Dev Gangjee
Relocating the Law of Geographical Indications

Andrew Kenyon, Megan Richardson and Ng-Loy Wee-Loon
The Law of Reputation and Brands in the Asia Pacific Region

Edson Beas Rodrigues, Jr
The General Exception Clauses of the TRIPS Agreement: Promoting Sustainable Development

Annabelle Lever
New Frontiers in the Philosophy of Intellectual Property

Sigrid Sterckx and Julian Cockbain
Exclusions from Patentability: How the European Patent Office Is Eroding Boundaries

Sebastian Haunss
Conflicts in the Knowledge Society: The Contentious Politics of Intellectual Property

Helena R. Howe and Jonathan Griffiths
Concepts of Property in Intellectual Property Law

Rochelle Cooper Dreyfuss and Jane C. Ginsburg
Intellectual Property at the Edge: The Contested Contours of IP

Normann Witzleb, David Lindsay, Moira Paterson and Sharon Rodrick
Emerging Challenges in Privacy Law: Comparative Perspectives

Paul Bernal
Internet Privacy Rights: Rights to Protect Autonomy

Peter Drahos
Intellectual Property, Indigenous People and Their Knowledge

Susy Frankel and Daniel Gervais
The Evolution and Equilibrium of Copyright in the Digital Age

Edited by Kathy Bowrey and Michael Handler
Law and Creativity in the Age of the Entertainment Franchise

Sean Bottomley
The British Patent System and the Industrial Revolution 1700–1852: From Privileges to Property

Susy Frankel
Test Tubes for Global Intellectual Property Issues: Small Market Economies

Jan Oster
Media Freedom As a Fundamental Right

Sara Bannerman
International Copyright and Access to Knowledge

Andrew T. Kenyon
Comparative Defamation and Privacy Law

Pascal Kamina
Film Copyright in the European Union (second edition)

Tim W. Dornis
Trademark and Unfair Competition Conflicts

Ge Chen
Copyright and International Negotiations: An Engine of Free Expression in China?

David Tan
The Commercial Appropriation of Fame: A Cultural Critique of the Right of Publicity and Passing Off

Jay Sanderson
Plants, People and Practices: The Nature and History of the UPOV Convention

Daniel Benoliel
Patent Intensity and Economic Growth

Jeffrey A. Maine and Xuan-Thao Nguyen
The Intellectual Property Holding Company: Tax Use and Abuse from Victoria's Secret to Apple

Megan Richardson
The Right to Privacy: Origins and Influence of a Nineteenth-Century Idea

Martin Husovec
Injunctions against Intermediaries in the European Union: Accountable but Not Liable?

Estelle Derclaye
The Copyright/Design Interface: Past, Present and Future

Magdalena Kolasa
Trade Secrets and Employee Mobility: In Search of an Equilibrium

Péter Mezei
Copyright Exhaustion: Law and Policy in the United States and the European Union

Graham Greenleaf and David Lindsay
Public Rights: Copyright's Public Domains

Ole-Andreas Rognstad
Property Aspects of Intellectual Property

Elena Cooper
Art and Modern Copyright: The Contested Image

Paul Bernal
The Internet, Warts and All: Free Speech, Privacy and Truth

Sebastian Felix Schwemer
Licensing and Access to Content in the European Union: Regulation between Copyright and Competition Law

Daniela Simone
Copyright and Collective Authorship: Locating the Authors of Collaborative Work